EARTH AT RISK

EARTH AT RISK

An Environmental Dialogue
between Religion and Science

*edited by Donald B. Conroy and
Rodney L. Petersen*

Humanity
Books

an imprint of Prometheus Books
59 John Glenn Drive, Amherst, New York 14228-2197

Published 2000 by Humanity Books, an imprint of Prometheus Books

04 03 02 01 00   5 4 3 2 1

Library of Congress Cataloging-in-Publication Data

Earth at Risk: advancing the environmental dialogue between religion and science / edited by Donald B. Conroy and Rodney L. Petersen.
     p.   cm.
Includes bibliographical references.
ISBN 1–57392–817–8 (pbk.)
    1. Human ecology—Religious aspects—Christianity. 2. Religion and science. I. Conroy, Donald B. II. Petersen, Rodney Lawrence.
BT695.5 .E255 1999
261.8'362—dc21   99-057948

Printed in the United States of America on acid-free paper

CONTENTS

5

SECTION FIVE: STRATEGIES FOR EDUCATION, MINISTRY, AND BUILDING SUSTAINABLE COMMUNITIES

PREFACE

The impetus for this book originally came out of the "life and work" section of the Church and Society stream of international Christian ecumenical effort associated with the World Council of Churches (WCC). At its Sixth Assembly held in Vancouver (1983) its third overarching framework for ecumenical ethical reflection in the history of the WCC was embarked upon and defined as "a conciliar process of mutual commitment (covenant) for justice, peace and the *integrity of creation*" (JPIC).[1] The WCC's world convocation in Seoul, Korea (1990) agreed on ten short Affirmations in the areas of justice, peace, and the integrity of creation.[2] Under the auspices of its Theology of Life Programme (Unit III) these Affirmations were taken up for reflection by Case Study groups throughout the world.[3] The purpose of these study groups was to deepen theological reflection, to draw upon wide scholarly input, and to promote dialogue in the churches and in society.

An effort was made both to draw upon traditional "experts" and to find new areas of expertise among people whose human anguish in the struggle for justice and peace in creation qualified them to speak.

The articles collected in this volume come in part from the study process on Seoul Affirmation 7, "the creation as beloved of God." Faculty in the schools of The Boston Theological Institute (BTI), research scientists and engineers, area activists, church and community leaders, and others participated.[4] Related to this study was a North American Native Workshop on Environmental Justice which took place on the campus of Iliff School of Theology 16–19 March 1995 which, in this separate context, drew upon the expertise of indigenous peoples of the North American continent.[5] A major participating organization in this work was the North American Coalition on Religion and Ecology (NACRE). Several other organizations and scholars were also represented. This wider perspective is here seen in the breadth of authors contributing to this volume and the range of their institutional affiliations. The present study is part of an increasing number of works focused on rethinking Christian and other faith-based traditions in relation to a just and sustainable society that is in harmony with the natural environment.[6]

Although this work is based within a Christian context, efforts were made to include representative voices and viewpoints from the Jewish, Muslim, and other religious and secular communities. In addition to these people represented here, others involved are related to the Union of Concerned Scientists (UCS), the National Religious Partnership for the Environment (NRPE),[7] the Center for Respect of Life and Environment, and its related project Theological Education to Meet the Environmental Challenge (TEMEC).

Although the study process on "Creation as Beloved of God" came to a culmination at Earth Day XXV (1995), it also eventuated in a larger conference and series of dialogues in the Boston area on the topic of "Consumption, Population, and the Environment" (1995–96), funded by The Pew Charitable Trusts.[8] Likewise, a parallel process undertaken by the North American Coalition on Religion and Ecology focused on the complementary theme of "Caring for Creation." This originated with the 1990 Intercontinental Conference on Caring for Creation and the Scholarly Seminar, held at the College of Preachers of the National Cathedral in Washington,

NOTES

1. Ans van der Bent, *Commitment to God's World: A Concise Critical Survey of Ecumenical Social Thought* (Geneva: WCC, 1995), pp. 58–77. The previous two include the concept of a "responsible society," articulated at Amsterdam (1948), and of a "just, participatory and sustainable society," a paradigm which prevailed from the early 1970s to the Vancouver Assembly (1983).

2. The convocation in Seoul brought to a head controversy about the relationship between ecclesiology and ethics, theological reflection and wide academic input, and about the nature of how "expertise" in related fields is defined. See articles in *The Ecumenical Review* 43, no. 3 (July 1991).

3. The ten Affirmations are the following: (1) All exercise of power is accountable to God. (2) God's option for the poor. (3) The equal value of all races and peoples. (4) That male and female are created in the image of God. (5) That truth is at the foundation of a community of free people. (6) We affirm the peace of Jesus Christ. (7) The creation as beloved of God. (8) That the earth is the Lord's. (9) The dignity and commitment of the younger generation. (10) That human rights are given by God. See *Affirming Life: Theology of Life: An Invitation to Participate* (Geneva: World Council of Churches, 1995).

4. The Boston Theological Institute is a consortium of university divinity schools, schools of theology, and seminaries of which five are historically Protestant, three are Roman Catholic, and one is Greek Orthodox. Added to the unique theological nature of the BTI is its relationship and proximity to major research and engineering universities and laboratories in the United States. See *Christianity and Civil Society: Theological Education for Public Life*, ed. Rodney Petersen (Maryknoll: Orbis Books, 1993).

5. This event was reported on separately by Jace Weaver, ed., *Defending Mother Earth: Native American Perspectives on Environmental Justice* (Maryknoll: Orbis Books, 1996), and by George Tinker in April, 1995, at the conference in Boston as reflected in his article in this volume.

6. Special note should be made of the volume edited by Dieter Hessel, *Theology for Earth Community: A Field Guide* (Maryknoll: Orbis Books, 1996), and to the earlier volume by Wesley Granberg-Michaelson, *Redeeming the Creation: The Rio Earth Summit: Challenges for the Churches* (Geneva: WCC. 1992).

7. The NRPE was brought together in 1992 in response to an "Open Letter to the Religious Community" (January 1990), written by thirty-four prominent scientists, and the subsequent "Joint Appeal" (1991) by persons

representing the religious, scientific and public policy communities. It represents constituencies defined by the U.S. Catholic Conference, the National Council of Churches of Christ, the Coalition on the Environment and Jewish Life, and the Evangelical Environmental Network.

8. This work led to the production of the video "Living in Nature" and the volume, *Envisioning Equity in Consumption, Population, and the Environment* (forthcoming, 1997). Both video and book distributed through Sheed and Ward Publishers.

9. A major conference was held in Washington, D.C., June 16–18, 1997, to bring this research together and clarify the relationship between religious/ethical thinking and community/economic development around the theme of ethics and sustainability. This gathering, called the Interfaith Consultation on Environmental Values, Sustainable Community, and Public Policy, was convened by NACRE/ICORE during the week preceding the United Nations General Assembly Special Session on the occasion of the Fifth Anniversary of the 1992 Earth Summit. Some thirty-five international scholars and leaders met at the World Bank and the Catholic University of America; they forged new bridges for dialogue and produced *The Washington Declaration of Interdependence*. Cf. *EcoLetter* (fall 1997): 12–16.

10. The field of environmental studies and the relationship of communities of faith is so rich and growing, readers are encouraged to access the website made available by Timothy Weiskel at the Center for the Study of Values in Public Life, Harvard Divinity School, and the one being developed by Audrey Chapman, Program of Dialogue Between Science and Religion, American Association for the Advancement of Science.

11. Richard J. Neuhaus, *In Defense of People: Ecology and the Seduction of Radicalism* (New York: Macmillan Co., 1971), pp. 151–61. See in relation to lifeboat (Hardin) and triage (Ehrlich) ethics and as critically assessed by K. S. Schrader-Frechette, ed., *Environmental Ethics* (Pacific Grove, Calif.: Boxwood Press, 1981); Garrett Hardin, "Living on a Lifeboat," *Bioscience* 24, no. 10 (1974); Paul Ehrlich, *The Population Bomb* (New York: Ballantine Books, 1968) and Brennan Hill, "An Environmental Ethic," *Christian Faith and the Environment* (New York: Orbis Books, 1998).

ACKNOWLEDGMENTS

With thanks to Adam Kissel, BTI Operations Manager, and Ryan Howell and Michael Newton, NACRE staff assistants, for their editorial help in bringing this volume together. Additional assistance for various phases of this program was given by numerous students, staff, and faculty in the schools of the Boston Theological Institute. Special thanks to Rev. Barbara Smith-Moran. Director, The Faith and Science Exchange, a program affiliate of the BTI, and to Brian Boisen, Charlotte Caldwell, Jessica Adande Davis, William B. Jones, Amy Langston, Donna LaRue, and Rebecca Petersen, who helped to facilitate different events which contributed to this study process.

EDITORS' NOTES

The chapter by Larry Rasmussen is adapted with permission from *Earth Community, Earth Ethics: Theology for the Third Millennium* (Maryknoll: Orbis Books, 1996).

The chapter by George Tinker has been edited from an article in *Defending Mother Earth: Native American Perspectives on Environmental Justice,* ed. Jace Weaver (Maryknoll: Orbis Books, 1996), pp. 153–76.

1. INTRODUCTION

The twenty-first century opens with both the religious and scientific communities increasingly concerned about an earth at risk. By raising this issue for the Christian community, Ian Barbour, a physicist and theologian, opens this book with the concern being raised by all peoples: How do we live in and understand the world of which we are a part? Barbour's own work and methodology bridges the fields of science and religion.[1] It is illustrative of the concerns of this book. His introduction begins with a summary of Lynn White's classic accusation that Christian theology fostered environmental degradation through its double alienation of God from nature and of human from nonhuman life forms.[2] However, Barbour suggests the "more friendly" perspectives that Christians have had toward nature while lamenting a third alienation, that of redemption from creation. Barbour's contention, that theology more carefully considered draws us to concern for social justice and long-term sustainability, concludes with specific suggestions for church-based and other community organizations as they seek to sow seeds for cooperation in dealing with ecological degradation and environmentally induced conflict.[3]

The contemporary devaluation of theology and its separation from general philosophical reflection is a crisis that impedes our ability to deal

17

with an earth at risk.[4] Barbour suggests that scientific and religious approaches make use of conceptual models as they endeavor to deal with mystery. Both are tested in community. They are overlapping domains that need to be reformulated in light of each other.[5] The failure to understand each other's language and orientation, their fracture, constitutes a grave social threat. Barbour proceeds to underscore the oneness of humanity and nature and draws us to issues of ecojustice set in the context of long-term sustainable practices which churches, synagogues, and other faith communities and voluntary associations should foster.

What we mean by "nature" shapes the direction of our discussion.[6] Other terms that might be and are used with reference to ecological concern are "earth," "environment," "world," "cosmos," "universe," "matter," or even "things." Whatever it is we mean, it is not something that we can easily objectify. We ourselves are made of the very stuff about which we are discussing. As the theologian Jürgen Moltmann reminds us, "What we call the environmental crisis is not merely a crisis in the natural environment of human beings. It is nothing less than a crisis in human beings themselves."[7] To call that stuff about which we are talking "matter" or, to imply more, "creation," is to say something about ourselves as much as about our world.[8] This suggests not a blind alley of obscurantism or prejudice, but a deeper mystery within our environment. The twentieth century has shown us that this mystery is as open to manipulation as it is inviting of religious wonder and scientific speculation. In fact, without a common understanding or unified epistemology about nature, the symbols of our worship life become eviscerated and science devolves into mere technique.

The phrase "the integrity of creation," which stands behind the framing of the Affirmation that began this volume, was added to two existing concerns (justice and peace) of the member churches of the World Council of Churches at Vancouver in 1983.[9] The emerging conceptual framework for ecumenical ethics, "Justice, Peace, and the Integrity of Creation," might be seen as more a statement of mission than as demonstrable fact or accepted doctrine.[10] The historical and linguistic implications of the term are drawn out by D. Preman Niles, who writes that the term "tries to bring together the issues of justice, peace and the environment by stressing the fact that there is an integrity or unity that is given in God's creation."[11]

This discussion is grounded in thinking that extends back to the Conference on Church and Society (Geneva, 1966), which had the theme "Christians in the Technical and Social Revolutions of our Time."[12] The

Fourth Assembly of the WCC (Uppsala, Sweden, 1968) and the WCC's Central Committee (1969) urged further work in this area at a time when many physical and social scientists were beginning to alert the human community of the danger of resource depletion and environmental collapse. A series of Working Committees on Church and Society in the early 1970s began to link concern for social justice with an awareness of growing ecological problems. The conference "Science and Technology for Human Development: An Ambiguous Future—and Christian Hope," held in Bucharest, Romania (1974), was a result of this thinking.[13] The Fifth Assembly of the WCC (Nairobi, Kenya, 1975) received this work and, stimulated by the able thinking of the Australian biologist Charles Birch, adopted through its Central Committee in the following year, the program area "The Struggle for the Just, Participatory, and Sustainable Society." The Committee authorized work for a conference in 1979 which was eventually held at the Massachusetts Institute of Technology (MIT) on "The Contribution of Faith, Science, and Technology in the Struggle for a Just, Participatory, and Sustainable Society" (July 1979).[14]

In his remarks at the MIT conference "Nature, Humanity, and God in Ecological Perspective," Charles Birch contended that we have created a mechanistic cosmology of science out of what was once perhaps a useful tool in severing the cord for science and religion from a worldview suffused with superstition and magic, but that this cosmology is now threatening to redefine who we are.[15] Birch argues for a more integrative approach, suffused with subjectivity, in our relations with nature as informed by process theology. Similar concerns are taken up by Gerhard Liedke from the perspective of continental Protestant theology and by Vitaly Borovoy reflecting Russian Orthodox thinking, but without recourse to a new ontology to address the breach between the human and non-human creation.

The Section Report, "Humanity, Nature, and God," is of special interest because of the way it grounds "a just, participatory and sustainable society" in "the relation between God, humanity and nature."[16] The Report is structured around five points: (1) The relation between God, humanity, and nature in contemporary Western thought is said to be marked by opposition and epistemological dualism. In this context God vanishes and humanity emerges as a substitute god over against nature. (2) The relation of this triad in biblical thought is seen to be characterized not by opposition but by the drawing together of creation and salvation in Christ. Society and ecosystems are intimately interconnected. Justice and sustainability cannot be separated. (3) In the context of our technological world, what needs to be emphasized is not our separateness but rather the relatedness between God and God's creation. Concepts such as humanity as "the maker" (*homo faber*) and as having dominion (*dominium*) need to be integrated with that of the biblical *imago dei*.[17] (4) The Christian understanding of God, humanity, and nature calls us to express solidarity with those of other living religious traditions. (5) A number of recommendations are given in order: (i) renewed science and religion dialogue, (ii) fresh inter-religious dialogue, (iii) deepened reflection on the nature of Christian hope with respect to society and the future, (iv) a sense of church life which expresses respect for all creation, and (v) continued dialogue on the issues of the Report at the local level.[18]

The work of the NET conference continues to stand as a watershed in contemporary ethical environmental thinking on such areas as ecology and worldview, mind/soul-body dualism, epistemology and the nature of reality, and personal and nonhuman identity.[19] The preparations for the Seoul convocation (1990),[20] context for the ten Affirmations that constitute the agenda for the Theology of Life Programme,[21] and subsequent events have done little to alter the questions raised at MIT. The issues themselves have deepened in complexity in the context of conflicting post-Cold War cultural sensitivities and interests.[22]

Perhaps the most important insight raised at MIT had to do with the relationship between ecology and worldview, as this one issue helps to shape the conception of so many others.[23] We can credit people like Thomas Berry and Brian Swimme for helping us awaken to the importance of understanding the contributions of the spiritual and historical stories of all peoples, as partners at a table set by contemporary mechanistic science and the older Western Jewish and Christian theologies.[24] What is new since MIT is the way in which the debate over "the integrity of creation" has been drawn into that over Gospel and culture, a debate that can be as threatening to believing communities as it is enriching of faith and theology.[25]

By pursuing the theme "Creation as Beloved of God" in the context of an earth at risk, this study began where MIT left off, "humanity and nature in the context of the work of God as Creator and his goal for his creation."[26] It was left up to the participants, however, to work with this phrase as they saw fit. Certainly in the history of Christian theological reflection the meanings embedded in our Affirmation have meant the God as understood in the Hebrew Scriptures, or the Christian Old Testament, and the

New Testament. This God has been understood as Creator of a creation defined theologically, with the aid of Greek philosophy, in such creeds as the Niceno-Constantinopolitan creed of the early and undivided Church (fourth century). That creed articulates a worldview, shared in some ways with Judaism and Islam, which understands God to be separate from this creation, not by way of dualism but so as to affirm its essential goodness. A continual pattern of interaction is implied in God's covenantal relationship with humanity and all living things, giving substance to the term "beloved." Christians understand this relationship to culminate in Jesus Christ as Messiah and final prophet, a person of two natures (fully divine and fully human) as defined at the Fourth Ecumenical Council of Chalcedon in 451.

This worldview, grounded more fully for Christian theology in Christ's death and resurrection, opened debate in the second century over the question of dualism, a second point raised at the MIT conference. As part of his critique of the doctrine of reincarnation in the fourth century, Jerome, among others, affirmed the unity of the mind, or soul, with the body, finding salvation or the human transcendence of death in resurrection.[27] This implied a unified spiritual/material reality for personal identity. A third point raised at MIT, that of epistemology in relation to the nature of reality, has divided Western philosophy into Realists, Semi-Realists, and Nominalists. The latter philosophy has opened the way to modem empiricism and our contemporary crisis over personhood in relation to mechanism, a fourth point discerned at the MIT conference.

Whether nature (from *natura* in Latin or *physis* in Greek) is best understood in mechanistic terms or is symbolic of a deeper mystery is a question once again arrived at by our culture at the onset of the twenty-first century. And whether we use words like "nature," "creation," or "earth," it is important to note that there can be agreed upon language, but it is clear that there is no neutral terminology.[28] This is not said so as to imply a moral relativism behind language. Indeed no less a sociobiologist than E. O. Wilson reminds us of the stakes involved in how we answer this question when he writes, "The great philosophical divide in moral reasoning about the remainder of life is whether or not other species have an innate right to exist. The decision rests in turn on the most fundamental question of all, whether moral values exist apart from humanity, in the same manner as mathematical laws, or whether they are idiosyncratic constructs that evolved in the human mind through natural selection, and thus of the spirit."[29] Among the world's leaders few have been clearer about how the nature of our answer to Wilson's question must shape our pattern of behavior in the world of nature than Pope John Paul II or Orthodox Ecumenical Patriarch Dimitrios of Constantinople.[30]

What makes contemporary debate over the environment, as encapsulated in the Affirmation "Creation as Beloved of God," of such interest for an earth at risk is the way in which it takes the most mundane and turns it to the apparently abstract. Congregations of faith, asked to discuss the use of Styrofoam cups in church functions, are led to inquire about their most fundamental life assumptions. Debate over the spotted owl leads to reflection with other Christians, Jews, and Muslims. Decisions which need to be made concerning pollution in local drinking water or toxic waste drive communities to reflect on issues of ecological justice and the premises from which they are derived. The environmental crisis is not just about ecology. It mirrors the understanding and attitudes that we have about ourselves. It reminds us that our "inner ecology" helps to define and give shape to the "outer ecology."[31]

Rodney L. Petersen

NOTES

1. See Ian Barbour, *Religion in an Age of Science and Ethics in an Age of Technology*, vols. 1 and 2 of *The Gifford Lectures, 1989–90, 1990–91* (San Francisco: HarperCollins, 1990, 1993).

2. Lynn White Jr., "The Historical Roots of our Ecological Crisis," *Science* 155 (1967): 1203–1207. White scores Christian theology's arrogance toward nature. He argues that Christianity bears a huge burden of the guilt for the contemporary ecological crisis despite a few positive moments as with Francis of Assisi. White's argument has been criticized by, among others, Thomas Sieger Derr, "Religion's Responsibility for the Ecological Crisis: An Argument Run Amok," *Worldview* 18, no. 1 (January 1975): 39–45.

3. See suggestions made by Katrina S. Rogers, "Sowing the Seed of Cooperation in Environmentally Induced Conflicts," in Mohamed Suliman, ed., *Ecology, Politics, and Violent Conflict* (London: ZED Books, 1999), pp. 259–72.

4. Such devaluation might be seen in the quite different positions represented by the philosopher Max Oelschlaeger (cited by Barbour), which

seems to foster a separation of linguistic from ontological reality, or the physicist Carl Sagan, cited as finding emotional energy in faith communities but not the rational resources to deal with the environmental crisis. Oelschlaeger's book argues that only the churches as repositories of moral values outside of the common economic paradigm can provide the leadership and energy to deal with the environmental crisis, *Caring for Creation: An Ecumenical Approach to the Environmental Crisis* (New Haven: Yale University Press, 1994).

5. The importance of drawing together the two cultures is outlined by C. P. Snow, *The Two Cultures: And a Second Look—An Expanded Version of the Two Cultures and the Scientific Revolution* (Mentor MP 557, 1964).

6. See article "Nature," by Paulos Mar Gregorios and John Habgood, *Dictionary of the Ecumenical Movement*, ed. Nicholas Lossky et al. (Geneva: WCC Publications, 1991), pp. 715–20. The distinction between nature in its manifold forms of conception and a doctrine of creation is made with implications for social policy.

7. Jürgen Moltmann, *God in Creation: A New Theology of Creation and the Spirit of God*, trans. Margaret Kohl, *Gifford Lectures, 1984–1985* (San Francisco: Harper and Row, 1985), p. xi.

8. George H. Williams, "Christian Attitudes Toward Nature," *Christian Scholar's Review* 2, no. 1, 2 (fall 1971): 3–35; 112–26. This essay remains a helpful survey of seven views, or scriptural antinomies, of nature which have been held throughout the history of the Christian church: (1) the involvement or noninvolvement of nature in the fall of man; (2) nature as decaying or constant; (3) nature as a distinctive creation for its own sake and for the praise of the creator, or nature as the realm of man's stewardship or exploitation; (4) nature as benignant or nature as malign; (5) the book of nature and the book of scripture as mutually exclusive or complementary; (6) the significance of the cultivated landscape as mediating God's grace or salvation, found to be totally segregated from nature; (7) mankind only or the whole creation subject to salvation. Compare Ian L. McHarg, "The Place of Nature in the City of Man," in *Western Man and Environmental Ethics: Attitudes Toward Nature and Technology*, ed. Ian G. Barbour (Reading, Mass.: Addison-Wesley, 1973), p. 175.

9. A discussion of the phrase and its biblical and theological connotations is found in *Reintegrating God's Creation: A Paper for Discussion* (Geneva: WCC, Church and Society Documents, no. 3, September 1987).

10. Douglas John Hall, "JPIC: The Message and the Mission," *The Ecumenical Review* 41, no. 4 (October 1989): 492–500; and D. Preman Niles,

Between the Flood and the Rainbow: Interpreting the Conciliar Process of Mutual Commitment (Covenant) to Justice, Peace, and the Integrity of Creation (Geneva: WCC, 1992). See also Ronald Preston, "Humanity, Nature, and the Integrity of Creation," pp. 552–563. Preston's point concerning the neglect of previous studies in ongoing WCC work is important in order to chart developing but heretofore unnoticed tendencies in thinking. When taking up the theme "Creation as Beloved of God," consideration should be given to the MIT conference on "Faith, Science, and the Future" (12–24 July 1979).

11. The citation is from *A Conversation with D. Preman Niles: Answers to Questions that are often asked about the JPIC process of the Conciliar Process of Mutual Commitment (Covenant) to Justice, Peace, and the Integrity of Creation* (Geneva: WCC, n.d.) as found in Douglas John Hall, *The Steward* (Grand Rapids: Eerdmans, 1990), p. 186. See also Charles Birch, "Peace, Justice, and the Integrity of Creation: Some Central Issues for the Churches," in *Report and Background Papers of the Meeting of the Working Group*, Potsdam, GDR, July 1986 (Geneva: WCC, Church and Society, n.d.). See Niles, *Between the Flood and the Rainbow*, pp. 1–7.

12. Philip Potter, "Why Are the Churches Concerned," in *Faith and Science in an Unjust World*, vol. 1 (Geneva: WCC, 1980), pp. 21–29.

13. "Science and Technology for Human Development: The Ambiguous Future and the Christian Hope," Report of the 1974 World Conference in Bucharest, Romania, in *Anticipation*, no. 19. The idea of a sustainable society is conceived and defined in such a way as to permit equity in consumption and ethical reflection about the introduction of new technologies (p. 12).

14. See the Conference *Plenary Presentations* (vol. 1), ed. Roger L. Shinn, and *Reports and Recommendations* (vol. 2), ed. Paul Albrecht, published as *Faith and Science in an Unjust World* (Geneva: WCC, 1980). Of particular interest are papers by Charles Birch, "Nature, Humanity, and God in Ecological Perspective" (vol. 1, pp. 62–73) and his remarks at Nairobi (1975); Gerhard Liedke, "Solidarity in Conflict" (1, pp. 73–80); and Vitaly Borovoy, "Christian Perspectives on Creation in a Time of Ecological Unsustainability" (1, pp. 80–86).

15. Birch writes that "Mechanism as a worldview has let us down. The critical social context for science and religion today is not the world as a machine but the world in ecological crisis" (ibid., vol. 1, p. 65).

16. Albrecht, *Faith and Science in an Unjust World*, vol. 2, pp. 28–38.

17. The Report goes on to make a point rich in connotations about the nature of this integration and balance: "The need to protect and pre-

serve nature should not make us forget that according to the biblical witness, nature must be reshaped by humanity and adapted to human needs. In this respect, the situation of the rich countries of the earth is completely different from that of the poor countries. In the rich countries nature has been so thoroughly reshaped that humanity lives in an artificial world, whereas in the poor countries it has not yet been sufficiently adapted to human need and there is still much work to be done (although not necessarily in the pattern of the rich countries" (ibid., vol. 2, pp. 33–34).

18. Further issues as they would pertain to the work of the MIT conference are found in *Faith, Science, and the Future*, ed. Paul Albrecht (Philadelphia: Fortress Press, 1978); and *Science and Our Future*, ed. Paulos Mar Gregorios (Madras: Christian Literature Society, 1978).

19. Charles C. West analyzes the shortcomings of later ecumenical social thought in relation to the MIT conference in "Ecumenical Social Thought in the Post-Cold-War Period," *The Ecumenical Review*, 43, no. 3 (July 1991): 305–76.

20. The international consultation on "The Integrity of Creation" at Granvollen, Norway (1988), should be cited for a listing of mistaken approaches and attitudes to creation theology, e.g., reductionism in theology, scientific-technological hybris, a romantic response, a neo-apocalyptic response, and a utopian response. See the report, *Integrity of Creation: An Ecumenical Discussion*, Granvollen, Norway, 25 February–3 March 1988 (Geneva, WCC, 1988).

21. See the preface for information on the nature of this Program of the World Council of Churches.

22. Samuel P. Huntington's article in *Foreign Affairs* (1993) and subsequent book *The Clash of Civilizations and the Remaking of World Order* (New York: Simon and Schuster, 1996) summarizes the difficult global cultural debate before us and shows the way in which environmental factors will be dealt with by contemporary societies.

23. On this note the important work encapsulated in *Worldviews and Ecology: Religion, Philosophy, and the Environment*, ed. Mary Evelyn Tucker and John A. Grim (Maryknoll: Orbis Books, 1994). The continuing work of the Center for the Study of World Religions, Harvard University, should be cited for its growing programming in this area.

24. Thomas Berry and Brian Swimme, *The Universe Story: From the Primordial Flaring Forth to the Ecozoic Era* (San Francisco: Harper and Row, 1992).

25. On this see the "Tentative Conclusions" of Ans van der Bent, *Com-*

mitment to God's World: A Concise Critical Survey of Ecumenical Social Thought (Geneva: WCC, 1995), pp. 177–216. Van der Bent writes, "Certain other religions can shed light on how Christian theology has indeed withdrawn from the field of cosmology by concentrating too intensively on human history" (p. 201).

26. Albrecht, *Faith and Science in an Unjust World*, vol. 2, p. 32.

27. Writing on the quality of Christ's identity following the resurrection, the linguist and biblical commentator Jerome outlines an anthropology that will shape Christian thinking in successive centuries on the nature of resurrection in distinction from reincarnation. See *Epistula* LIX 3, pp. 543–44.14 in *Corpus scriptorum ecclesiasticorum Latinorum, Epistolae,* ed. Isidorus Hilberg, vol. 54.

28. Everett Mendelsohn, "The Social Construction of Scientific Knowledge," *Society and the Sciences,* 1, no. 3–26 (1977). On the literary use of the term "nature" see Jaroslav Pelikan, "An Introduction to Ralph Waldo Emerson's Nature of 1836," in *Nature: A Facsimile of the First Edition* (Boston: Beacon Press, 1985), pp. 1–66.

29. Edward O. Wilson, *In Search of Nature* (Washington, D.C.: Island Press, 1996), p. 175.

30. This was affirmed in John Paul II's address at Yankee Stadium, New York (1979), and has been repeated since then in the encyclicals, *Centesimus Annus* (1981) and *Sollicitudo Rei Socialis* (1988), and even more clearly in his "World Day of Peace" message (1990). In 1989 His Holiness Ecumenical Patriarch Dimitrios of Constantinople declared 1 September, the first day of the Byzantine Ecclesiastical Year, as Environmental Protection Day.

31. Vera Shaw develops this theme in a helpful way for churches and study groups in *Thorns in the Garden Planet: Meditations on the Creator's Care* (Nashville: Thomas Nelson Publishers, 1993); and see Philip Sherrard, *Human Image: World Image: The Death and Resurrection of Sacred Cosmology* (Ipswich, England: Golgonooza Press, 1996).

1
RELIGION IN AN ENVIRONMENTAL AGE

Ian G. Barbour

AN INTRODUCTORY PERSPECTIVE

During the 1970s we began to be aware of local environmental problems, especially the pollution of air, water, and land. Laws enacted by national and state governments have slowed the growth of many of the pollutants whose effects were immediately evident, and some steps were taken to preserve wildlife and natural environments. But in the 1990s scientists have told us about environmental impacts that are global, long-term, and cumulative. Topsoil is being rapidly eroded by intensive agriculture, overgrazing, and deforestation. Every year we are losing an area of tropical rainforest larger than the whole state of Pennsylvania. Each year we lose perhaps fifty thousand endangered species, and with them we lose forever whole libraries of genetic information. Changes in the global climate caused by carbon dioxide from the burning of fossil fuels cannot be accurately predicted, but they are likely to be large enough to disrupt patterns of rainfall and agriculture. The world population is growing by eighty million each year, which is like adding the entire population of Mexico to the globe every year.

Industrial growth and the depletion of global resources by affluent nations raise additional questions of long-term sustainability which we have hardly begun to address.[1]

Since I am both a believer and a theologian coming from the Christian community, my goal is to consider how the Christian churches might respond to these environmental threats. With our common Earth at risk similar questions are being asked by members of Jewish, Islamic, Buddhist, and other religious traditions, but in this discussion I will focus on the Christian community and leave it to others to answer from their own traditions. After this introduction, I will explore views of God and human nature and their implications for a Christian environmentalism. Then I will look at questions of social justice and long-term sustainability. Finally, I will offer some practical suggestions concerning the life of faith communities.

An Indictment of Christianity

The discussion of theology and ecology in the 1970s was evoked by Lynn White's thesis that Christianity carries a heavy burden of responsibility for environmentally destructive attitudes in Western culture. White traced these attitudes back to two aspects of biblical thought. First, biblical thought separated God from nature. Reacting to the nature-religions of the surrounding cultures, the Israelites held that God was revealed primarily in history rather than in nature. Nature was desacralized and God's transcendence was emphasized over God's immanence. Second, the Bible separated humanity from nonhuman nature. According to Genesis, human beings were given dominion over all other creatures. Humanity alone was said to be made "in the image of God" and set apart from all other creatures.[2]

When environmentalists repeated White's charges, some biblical scholars replied that human dominion is not absolute in Genesis because humanity is always under God; we are called to responsible stewardship. Moreover, many biblical passages celebrated the beauty of nature and its value to God, quite apart from its usefulness to us.

Other scholars acknowledged the alienation of humanity from nature in classical Christianity but attributed it to the dualism of body and soul which came into early Christianity from Hellenistic rather than from biblical sources. A different kind of reply to White came from historians who said that economic forces were more important than religious beliefs in the growth of environmentally destructive practices. They pointed to the rise of capitalism in which nature was viewed as a resource for human use and private profit, and the rise of technology and industry through which human ability to harm nature increased dramatically. Other critics said that non-Christian cultures at various periods of history have perpetrated environmental damage just as severe as that in Christian cultures.

Feminist authors claimed that patriarchal views were a major contributor to environmental destruction. They saw the oppression of women by men and the oppression of nature by human beings through technology as rooted in a common set of hierarchical, dualistic, patriarchal assumptions. Men and technology were identified with the first term in each of the polarities of reason/emotion, mind/body, objectivity/subjectivity, and control/nurture. Women and nature were associated with the second term in each case. These feminists proposed more holistic and ecological models of the relation of both God and humanity to nature.[3]

My own conclusion is that many factors entered into Western attitudes toward nature and that Lynn White oversimplified a complex historical phenomenon. But the two problems that he emphasized, the separation of God and nature and the separation of humanity and nature, were indeed characteristic of medieval and subsequent Christian thought. To these I would add a third problem: the increasing separation of redemption from creation. Theology, preaching, liturgy, and ritual focused on the doctrine of personal redemption rather than on the doctrine of creation. In the Middle Ages the goal of life was the salvation of one's eternal soul. Redemption was an escape from creation rather than the fulfillment of creation. In much of later Christian thought, including many conservative and evangelical authors in our own day, nature is the stage or backdrop for the drama of salvation, but not an essential part of the drama. White's historical account may be questioned, but he was surely right that the environmental crisis calls to the church for theological reflection.

An Ecumenical Approach

An interesting analysis of the potential contribution of the churches to environmental policy is given by Max Oelschlaeger in *Caring for Creation: An Ecumenical Approach to the Environmental Crisis*. He argues that fundamental environmental issues have not been addressed because short-term economic criteria have dominated policy choices. Citizens vote according to their individual economic interests. Politicians run on platforms of economic growth and lower taxes. Economists measure progress by the GNP, which omits environmental costs and discounts future costs and benefits. Corporations seek immediate profits and have enormous power over elected representatives through their campaign contributions. As a nation we are dedicated to a high-consumption lifestyle, and we assume that new technologies or technical fixes will overcome any problems created by industrial growth.[4]

Oelschlaeger's thesis is that the church is the only institution that can effectively challenge this dominance of short-term economic criteria in public policy. The church has been a strong voice in political life in the past, not least in the abolition of slavery, in women's suffrage, in the civil rights movement, and in opposition to the Vietnam War. Today it is one of the few institutions in which individualism can be challenged and the public good discussed. Oelschlaeger grants that many churches focus exclusively on personal salvation, or have been co-opted by the prevailing consumerism, or restrict themselves to a narrow range of public issues. But he claims that the church has an enormous potential to influence environmental politics because it can ask basic questions about the goals of life. It can support nonmarket values such as social justice, environmental preservation, and the welfare of future generations. He notes that the Catholic church and all the major Protestant denominations have issued strong environmental statements.

Oelschlaeger says that creation stories in any culture are particularly important because they place individual life in a wider context of meaning. Creation stories are emotionally evocative and they support shared values and patterns of behavior. As 95 percent of Americans say they believe in God, they would have a strong voice for the environment if they united around the common theme of "caring for creation." Oelschlaeger gives examples of environmental writings from across the theological spectrum: conservatives such as Francis Schaeffer and Calvin DeWitt; moderates such as Susan Bratton, James Nash, and the U.S. Catholic Bishops; liberals including John Cobb, Jay McDaniel, Teilhard de Chardin, and Rosemary Ruether; and radicals like Thomas Berry and Matthew Fox. His fifth category, which he calls "alternative creation stories," includes goddess feminism and Native American traditions. He says that instead of arguing about differing truth claims among these diverse theologies we should take a pragmatic approach, seeking consensus at the level of political action. We should not get involved in debates with biblical literalists about whether to accept or reject evolution. Instead, we should seek common ground in "caring for creation" in order to save our endangered planet.

I agree with Oelschlaeger that we must cooperate ecumenically, drawing from our varied traditions in a common effort to promote the care of the earth. However, I disagree with his assertions that theological differences are unimportant and that science and religion are totally unrelated. He holds that neither science nor religion provides true statements about reality; they are both sociolinguistic cultural constructions that are useful in human life. Drawing from pragmatist and linguistic philosophers, he argues that science and religion are independent language systems which can only be judged by their usefulness. Science is "another among many language games that humans play" and it should not be accorded a privileged position. By contrast, I would argue that in both science and religion we try to understand reality, but in neither do we find unchanging or complete certainty.

GOD AND NATURE

Let us look at the first issue raised by Lynn White: God's relation to nature. I will summarize five themes that support a Christian environmentalism.

Stewardship of Nature

Many recent theological writings, especially by conservative and evangelical authors, give prominence to the biblical injunction of stewardship. According to Deuteronomy, "The earth is the Lord's." The land belongs ultimately to the God who created it; we are only trustees or stewards, responsible for its welfare and accountable for our treatment of it. Several biblical passages call for humane treatment of domestic animals. The Sabbath is a day of rest for the earth and other living things as well as for people. Every seventh year the fields are to lie fallow; the land deserves respect and it will cry out if mistreated (Lev. 25:1). In many rural churches today, Land Stewardship Sunday is celebrated in June, and the conservation of soil and other natural resources is encouraged. This stewardship concept can be extended to all natural resources and all forms of life.[5]

Stewardship is not human-centered since it includes responsibility to God and concern for the welfare of other creatures. But unless it is coupled with other biblical themes, it readily can be distorted to assign a purely utilitarian value to nature. Taken alone, it seems to objectify nature and distance humans from it as a sphere for us to manage. But when taken with other themes, stewardship can contribute to an ethic of care and responsibility for the natural world.

Celebration of Nature

Genesis 1 ends with an affirmation of the goodness of the created order. The idea of creation is a great unifying framework, encompassing all forms of life. The covenant after the flood includes all creatures (Gen. 6:19). Many of the Psalms refer to the value of nature apart from its usefulness to us (e.g., Ps. 148:9–10). Psalm 104 celebrates the rich diversity of nature and concludes: "O Lord, how manifold are thy works. In wisdom Thou hast made them all; the earth is full of thy creatures" (Ps. 104:24). At the end of his dialogue with God, Job is overwhelmed by the majesty of natural phenomena, including strange creatures that are of no use to humanity (Job 40–41). Jesus spoke of God's care for the lilies of the field and the sparrows of the air, and several of his parables use images from the natural world. Among recent authors, James Nash has argued that God's love extends to include all creatures. We in turn respond by loving what God loves, and by caring for God's beloved creatures.[6]

Celebration goes beyond stewardship because it sees nature as valuable in itself. On this theme the churches have made considerable progress. Liturgies and prayers expressing gratitude for the created order are more common than they were twenty-five years ago. Some excellent new hymns have been written and appear in new denominational hymnbooks. In addition to Thanksgiving harvest festivals, congregational services built around creation are sometimes offered at other times of the year, though they are obviously far outweighed by the number of services built around redemption or the historical events celebrated in the church year. Only rarely is celebration accompanied by repentance for our attitudes and actions which have been harmful to the natural world.

The Holy Spirit in Nature

The biblical idea of Spirit seems to me particularly helpful in thinking about God's relation to nature. In the opening verses of Genesis, "the Spirit of God was moving over the face of the waters." The Hebrew word for spirit, *ruach*, also means breath; God breathes the breath of life into the creation. Several of the Psalms speak of the presence of the Spirit in nature. In Psalm 104, the Spirit is the agent of continuing creation in the present: "Thou dost cause the grass to grow for cattle and the plants for man to cultivate. . . . When thou sendest forth thy Spirit, they are created." The same root is found in the word "inspiration"; the Spirit inspires the prophets and the worshiping community. Jesus received the Spirit at his baptism, and according to Luke he was full of the Holy Spirit as he started his ministry. The activity of the Spirit marked the birth of the church at Pentecost. Within the Bible, reference to the Spirit thus ties together God's work as Creator and as Redeemer. The Spirit is also free of the male imagery associated with Father and Son.[7]

However, the early church tended to identify the work of the Spirit almost exclusively with redemption. As the doctrine of the Trinity was developed in the Western church, the Holy Spirit was subordinate to the Eternal Son and was said to come from the Son. In the Middle Ages the sacraments and the institutional church were taken to be the main channels for the operation of the Spirit. Protestantism saw the work of the Spirit in the life of individual believers. The Spirit was said to witness within us to the truth of scripture, or to bring us to conversion to Christ. Pentecostal and charismatic groups held that the work of the Spirit is manifest in prophecy, speaking in tongues, and other unusual powers. In all of these cases, the biblical understanding of God's indwelling presence in nature as the life-giving Spirit was ignored. Greater attention to the Spirit can help us find a better balance between transcendence and immanence in thinking about God's relation to nature today. The motif of the seventh assembly of the World Council of Churches in 1991 was "Come, Holy Spirit: Renew the Whole Creation."

The Redemption of Nature

The prophetic vision of future harmony and wholeness, or *shalom*, includes the whole of creation and not humanity alone. Hosea says that human actions harm nature. "Therefore the land mourns and all who dwell in it languish, and also the beasts of the field, and the birds of the air, and even the fish of the sea are taken away" (4:1–3). Hosea envisions God making a new covenant that includes all creatures: "And I will make for you a covenant on that day with the beasts of the field, the birds of the air, and creeping things on the ground" (2:18). Paul writes that "the whole creation has been groaning in travail together until now," but he is confident that it all will take part in the final fulfillment (Rom. 8:2). The eschatological vision of the healing and renewal of creation looks to a future event but also casts light on the present and the goals of our own actions.[8]

Other biblical passages affirm that Christ as the Eternal Son had a role in creation as well as redemption. Paul writes that "all things were created through him and for him. He is before all things, and in him all things hold together" (Col. 1:16). In the early church, Irenaeus maintained that in Christ God had entered the world to transform the whole creation and bring it into the divine life. Drawing on the Eastern Orthodox tradition, Paulos Gregarios has recently developed the image of the Cosmic Christ and the inclusion of all of nature in the domain of redemption.[9] The Greek Orthodox Metropolitan John of Pergamon holds that as priests of creation we can offer not just the bread and wine but all of nature to God. We can lift the material world with us into the realm of salvation and eternal life. Both Christ and humanity, he says, are essential links between God and the world to bring the redemption of all creation.

I see here an affirmation of the value of the natural world because it is included in the realm of redemption. On the other hand I see a danger in overemphasizing the idea that nature needs redemption. Some theologians have asserted that nature is fallen because of human sin. In particular, the idea that death and suffering entered nature because of human sin is surely incompatible with our understanding of evolutionary history, though we can acknowledge that sinful human actions have harmed other creatures whose lives are intimately bound with ours. We can act as priests of creation in celebrating it and holding it up to God, but we cannot claim to be the only mediators between God and creation if we affirm God's presence and activity in the world.

The Sacred in Nature

A further step in asserting the value of nature is the belief that the sacred is present in and under it. Eastern Orthodoxy celebrates the goodness and beauty of creation and finds God's presence in it, holding that the infinite is manifest in the finite. Celtic Christianity, influenced by pre-Christian nature-worship in Britain and Ireland, expresses a deep love of the natural world and a conviction that God is immanent in it. Several Anglican authors suggest that all of nature, and not just the bread, wine, and water of the sacraments, can be a vehicle of God's grace. These traditions have a strong sense of the community of life and they seek to heal the divisions within it.[10] To Teilhard de Chardin, matter is permeated by creative power and by spirit, and all nature is sacred. In *The Divine Milieu* he acknowledges the presence of the divine throughout the created order as well as in human life.

Some of the great Christian mystics have affirmed the presence of the sacred in nature. Meister Eckhart, Hildegarde of Bingen, and Julian of Norwich expressed a world-affirming rather than a world-denying mysticism. They held that in meditation and in a response of all-inclusive love we can realize the divinity within us and within nature. Matthew Fox has advocated a creation-centered spirituality that responds in awe and wonder to the cosmos as understood by modern science. He says that by stressing original sin classical Christianity failed to appreciate creation as "original blessing." He urges us to celebrate the sacredness of nature in song, dance, ritual, and art. Fox sees himself as remaining within the Christian tradition and reinterpreting it, though the person of Christ is not as central in his writings as in those discussed above.[11]

One of course can go even further and seek the sacred in nature quite apart from Christianity. Many people have reported an experience of the holy in a natural setting. Nature poets such as William Wordsworth and Alfred Tennyson and essayists such as Ralph Waldo Emerson and John Muir testify to a spiritual aspect of nature. Rachael Carson, Loren Eisley, and other scientists have spoken of their awe, humility, and gratitude in confronting the natural world. This more experiential dimension of encounter with nature can greatly enrich our lives and motivate our action, whether we interpret it within a theistic, a pantheistic, or a naturalistic framework.

Within a Christian context, the sacredness of nature is qualified by some of the other themes above. Transcendence is a spatial metaphor but it need not be understood literally as referring to God's distance from the world in a way that excludes immanence. There is, to be sure, some tension between the sacramental sense of the sacredness of what is and the prophetic awareness of the imperfection of the present and the sacredness of what might be. There are dangers in a romanticism that neglects struggle and cruelty among creatures and sinfulness in human life. Some of the nature poets and mystics have lacked the prophetic recognition of the social structures of power and injustice that do violence to people and to the natural world. I believe that these five themes (stewardship, celebration, the Holy Spirit, the redemption of nature, and the sacred in nature) must be taken together and combined with a concern for social justice, which I will consider later.

HUMANITY AND NATURE

We have been looking at God's relation to nature. Let us turn to the second issue raised by Lynn White: the relationship of humanity to the rest of nature.

Human Nature: Beyond Dualism

Genesis states that we are made in the image of God. The *imago Dei* has usually been interpreted as a human ability such as rationality, spirituality, or responsibility. It has often been taken to set us apart totally from all other creatures and to justify our dominion over them. But other authors have suggested that the image refers to our relation to God, and our capacity to reflect God's purposes—which include respect for all creatures. The story of Adam's fall cannot, of course, be taken literally in the light of evolutionary history, but it can be taken as a powerful symbolic expression of human sinfulness, where sin is understood as self-centeredness and estrangement from God and other people—and also from the world of nature.

In the Bible, body, mind, and spirit are looked on as aspects of a single personal unity. The self is a unified bodily agent who thinks, feels, wills, and acts. The body is not considered the source of evil or something to be denigrated or escaped. People in their wholeness are the object of God's saving purposes. In the biblical view, selfhood is always social, for we are constituted by our relationships and the covenants we enter. We are always persons-in-community, not isolated individuals.

Under the influence of late Greek thought, the early Church increasingly viewed a human being as a separate soul temporarily inhabiting a body, a dualism continued in the modern period in Descartes' distinction between mind and matter. An absolute line was drawn between humanity and all other creatures, for only humans were said to have souls or the capacity for rational thought. In the eighteenth and nineteenth centuries, many authors found such a dualism untenable and kept only one half of it, the material side. For them, human beings as well as the rest of nature were to be explained in materialistic and reductionistic terms.

Today we can reject reductionistic materialism and acknowledge human beings as responsible people, without reverting to dualism. As in the biblical view, we can accept the holistic character of people as integrated centers of thinking, feeling, willing, and acting. We can accept the social and bodily character of selfhood. Taking science into account, we can think of ourselves as many-leveled psychosomatic beings. Most biologists acknowledge the distinctiveness of human self-consciousness, language, and culture. Human beings are capable of intellectual and artistic creativity and personal relationships far beyond anything found among other creatures. We are indeed set apart from the rest of nature, but not in the absolute way which classical Christianity maintained.[12]

Kinship with All Creatures

Human kinship with other forms of life is stated or implied in a number of biblical passages. The story of Noah is myth rather than history, but in its own way it acknowledges the value of biodiversity. The Psalms refer to our companionship with other creatures. For St. Francis, a spiritual bond connects us with all creatures, and St.

Benedict promoted agricultural and resource practices that treated nature with respect. In Celtic Christianity, other creatures are our companions in the fellowship of creation.

We must learn also from contemporary science about our kinship with all forms of life. We are united in a common cosmic story that goes back to the early stars in which were formed the atoms in our brains and in all plants and animals. Evolutionary history shows our descent from common ancestors. The same genetic code is found in all life forms. We share with the higher primates 99 percent of our DNA, and we share many DNA sequences with lower life forms. Diverse species evolved together and influenced each other's evolution. Ecology has shown our interdependence today, and we know that diversity is essential to the health of an ecosystem. Our welfare depends on the welfare of the web of life of which we are a part.

We can also learn from indigenous religious traditions that have had a strong sense of kinship among all creatures. Native Americans conceive of nature as an extended family, a community of beings with reciprocal responsibilities. All forms of life are members of a natural social order, whose harmony and balance should be maintained. Humans are linked to other creatures and dependent on them, as portrayed in tribal stories and acknowledged in tribal rituals. Human beings may have to kill buffalo and other animals for food and clothing, but all creatures should be treated with respect because they, too, participate in a spiritual world whose power is experienced in dreams and visions. Native Americans also feel a strong identification with the land and with particular mountains and rivers that have been important in their history.[13]

Process Theology

The process philosophy of Alfred North Whitehead and his followers is ecological in holding that every entity is constituted by its relationships. It is evolutionary in accepting a long history of continuous change in which no absolute lines can be drawn between successive forms of life. Process thought tries to develop a set of philosophical categories applicable to all levels of reality. Every unified entity is thought of as a moment of experience. The character of that experience varies widely between an amoeba with rudimentary responsiveness, an animal with conscious purposes, and a self-conscious human being reflecting on future goals. Process philosophy offers an alternative to a mind/body dualism, without adopting materialism on the one hand or idealism on the other. It holds that all integrated entities have an objective, external aspect and an experiential, internal aspect. Interiority or experience is present in lower forms, but only at higher levels of complexity does mind or consciousness emerge.[14]

According to process thought, all creatures have value to God and to each other, and all have intrinsic value as centers of experience. But creatures vary widely in their richness of experience and in their contribution to the experience of other beings, so they are not equally valuable. This view would lead us to work for the welfare of all forms of life, but it also suggests priorities when the needs of human and nonhuman life conflict. Process thought differs from a biocentric ethics, which says that we should choose whatever actions further the welfare of the ecosystem as a whole, regardless of the interests of individuals. It shares with advocates of animal rights a concern for the suffering of individual animals, but it extends that concern to all forms of life in varying degrees. A human being is more valuable than a mosquito to itself, to other beings, and to God. Because process thought holds that individuals are constituted by their relationships, process thought stands between the holism of biocentric ethics and the idea of rights possessed by animals as individuals.

Process theologians also have a distinctive answer to the question of God's relation to nature. We saw that traditional theology emphasized divine transcendence and the gap between God and nature. At the opposite extreme, Romanticism, pantheism, nature mysticism, and some of the New Age movements today have emphasized immanence, which usually leads to an impersonal God or identifies God with nature. According to process thought, God transcends nature but is also immanent in the temporal process, for

God is present in the unfolding of every event. This implies that nature is not to be exploited, on the one hand, or worshiped, on the other, but is to be respected and appreciated, for it is the scene of God's continuing activity. Process theologians share with many feminist authors the conviction that God acts by empowerment from within rather than by coercive power from without.[15]

ECOJUSTICE

Let us consider next the relation between environmental preservation and social justice, first within industrial nations and then globally among nations.

Environmental Justice in Industrial Nations

The effects of environmental damage fall very unevenly on different groups in society. The urban poor are exposed to higher levels of air pollution, water pollution, noise, and lead poisoning than citizens with higher incomes, and they have little economic or political power to defend themselves from such risks. Environmental injustice is a product not only of economic differences but also of residential and social inequalities. For example, black children from middle-income families are three times as likely to have lead poisoning as children from white families of identical income, and 60 percent of all African Americans live in communities with toxic waste sites. Companies looking for a site for a new waste facility are likely to choose an already polluted area in which they expect to encounter little opposition. There is evidence of discrimination in government decisions as to which sites will be cleaned up first, which has led to legislation seeking to enforce equal environmental protection. Another example of unequal risks is the high exposure to pesticides among migrant farm workers, who are predominantly Hispanic.[16]

Questions of social justice also arise when environmental regulations seem to jeopardize the jobs of workers. Companies often

have threatened to close plants if pollution standards were tight-
ened. A few such plants, especially those with heavily polluting or
inefficient technologies, have actually closed, but most plants stayed
open and the costs of pollution control were passed on to consumers. Overall, technologies for controlling pollution and im-
proving efficiency have added more jobs to the economy than were
lost by environmental regulations. When restrictions on the logging
of old growth trees on public lands in Oregon were proposed in
order to preserve the spotted owl and other endangered species,
the timber industry claimed that massive unemployment would
result. Indeed, some mills have closed, but others are still in business using smaller trees from private tree farms. Among displaced
millworkers, nine out of ten who entered a federally financed
retraining program have found new jobs. In one year the state
added 100,000 jobs and had the lowest unemployment rate in a generation.[17]

While the demands of justice and of environmental preservation
do sometimes conflict, they often can be combined. The exploitation
of nature and of workers are typically products of the same economic
and political forces. In Appalachia, both the landscape and the
miners suffered because of the power of coal companies in state leg-
islatures. The marketplace neglects indirect costs, whether borne by
nature or by people. Labor unions and environmentalists often have
been on opposite sides of local and national issues, but now we see
them cooperating on occupational health and safety and in
demanding greater accountability by corporations and government
bureaucracies. A political strategy dedicated to both justice and the
environment will require a broad alliance that includes labor, environmental groups, community organizations, urban and civil rights
advocates, the women's movement—and the churches.[18]

Environmentalists often have neglected social justice, while
social reformers often have neglected the environment. The religious community can bring these values together in a distinctive way
because it believes God cares about both nature and people. The
National Council of Churches combined these concerns when it
started its program on ecojustice. The World Council of Churches

at its sixth assembly in 1983 adopted the theme "Justice, Peace, and the Integrity of Creation." Virtually all Protestant and Catholic statements on the environment have taken up issues of social justice.

Global Justice and the Environment

Inequalities between nations are far greater than those within nations. Consumption by industrial countries is responsible for a grossly disproportionate share of global pollution and resource use. On average, a U.S. citizen consumes as much of the world's resources as forty citizens of India. Clearly the whole world could not possibly live at the level of U.S. affluence. More grain is consumed by livestock in the United States and the former Soviet Union than by the entire human population of the Third World. Our dogs and cats are better fed than most of the children in Africa. Each week 250,000 children die from malnutrition and the diseases associated with it, while the United States pays farmers to reduce production of grains and dairy products. We import one billion dollars in agricultural products each year from Central America, where a quarter of the children are malnourished.[19]

In many developing nations the best land is used for nonfood or luxury food crops for export rather than staple crops for local consumption. Enough food is produced globally to meet everyone's dietary requirements, but the rich can outbid the poor in the global supermarket. Vast areas of forest in Brazil have been cleared for export timber or to produce beef for American fast-food restaurants. In most of the Third World, land is concentrated in the hands of a few wealthy landowners, except for a few countries in which land reform has been achieved either peacefully or by revolutionary governments. Third World countries make larger payments in interest on debts than they receive in new loans and investments, resulting in a net flow of fifty billion dollars each year from South to North, paid for largely by the export of crops, timber, and natural resources.

The Bible expresses the conviction that God is on the side of the poor and works for the liberation of the oppressed. The conviction goes back to the time of Moses and the liberation of the Hebrew slaves from Egypt. The ancient prophets spoke of God's judgment on their nation for allowing the rich to exploit the poor. Jesus opened his ministry by quoting Isaiah: "The spirit of the Lord is upon me because he has anointed me to preach good news to the poor. He has sent me to proclaim release to the captives . . . to set at liberty those who are oppressed" (Luke 4:18). Today we hear the cry of the earth as well as the cry of the people who are victims of unjust institutions. Our continued addiction to power and affluence are called into question.

SUSTAINABILITY

I said at the outset that the question of long-term sustainability is raised in a new way by the environmental problems of which we have recently become aware, such as global climate, resource depletion, and population and consumption trends. Let me suggest four ways in which the churches might respond.

A Long-Term View

Degraded land, eroded soil, and decimated fisheries and forests will take many decades to recover. We are living off biological capital, not biological income. Many of the impacts of our technologies will be felt by future generations. Radioactive wastes from today's nuclear power plants will endanger anyone exposed to them 10,000 years from now. The world of politics, however, takes a very short-term view. Political leaders find it difficult to look beyond the next election. The main concern of business and industry is this year's bottom line. Economic calculations give little weight to long-term consequences because a time discount is applied to future costs and benefits.

The biblical tradition, by contrast, takes a long-term view. Stewardship requires consideration of the future because God's purposes include the future. The Bible speaks of a covenant from generation to generation "to you and your descendants forever." The land, in particular, is to be held as a trust for future generations. This long-term perspective derives from a sense of history and ongoing family and social life, as well as accountability to a God who spans the generations. So it is not surprising that sustainability has been a major theme in statements of the World Council of Churches, several Protestant denominations, and the U.S. Conference of Catholic Bishops.[20] A long-term view is also common among scientists, especially those who are familiar with the long sweep of cosmic and evolutionary history.

Consumption and Visions of the Good Life

Conservation policies in industrial nations would contribute substantially to a more just and sustainable world. Greater efficiency, waste recovery, and cleaner technologies can cut down on both pollution and resource use. But I believe we must go beyond efficiency and look at our patterns of consumption. Our society presses powerfully toward the escalation of consumption. By the age of twenty, the average American has already seen 350,000 television commercials. The mass media hold before us the images of a high-consumption lifestyle. Self-worth and happiness are identified with consumer products. Our culture encourages us to try to fill all our psychological needs through consumption. Consumerism is addictive, and like all addictions it involves the denial of its consequences. Yet several studies have shown that there is very little correlation between happiness and income or wealth, whereas happiness does have a high correlation with marriage relationships, family life, work satisfaction, friendship, and community involvement.[21]

The Christian tradition offers a vision of the good life that is less resource-consumptive than prevailing practices. It holds that, once basic needs are met, true fulfillment is found in spiritual growth, personal relationships, and community life. This path is life-affirming, not life-denying. Religious faith speaks to the crisis of meaning that underlies compulsive consumerism. We should seek a level of sufficiency that includes neither ever-growing consumption nor joyless asceticism. A vision of positive possibilities and an alternative image of the good life are likely to be more effective than moral exhortation in helping people to turn in new directions. For most people in our nation, restraint in consumption is indeed compatible with personal fulfillment. We can try to recover the Puritan virtues of frugality and simplicity, both in individual lifestyles and in national policies.[22] For the Third World, of course, and for low-income families in industrial nations, levels of consumption must rise substantially if basic needs are to be met.

Population Growth

Population growth is outpacing agricultural production and is increasing pressure on erodible soils, grazing lands, water, and fuel-wood supplies. The average number of children per couple has been slowly falling in most of the Third World, but the total population is growing faster than ever because of the large number of young people entering childbearing years. Indonesia saw a 42 percent drop in fertility rates from 1970 to 1985, mainly through village health and family planning centers. In other cases, such as Thailand, Sri Lanka, and the state of Kerala in India, family planning was part of a broad program of improvement in education, women's literacy, health care, and economic development.

At the U.N. Population Conference in Cairo in 1994, women were for the first time strongly represented in both governmental and nongovernmental delegations. The Program of Action adopted by the conference gave major emphasis to the empowerment of women through access to education, health care, and political and economic equality. The document recognized that birth rates fall when women have more control over their lives. It also called for access to "safe, effective, affordable and acceptable methods of family planning of their choice." Moreover, it pointed to the importance of economic development both as a goal in itself and as a way of encouraging population stability. But the funds pledged to further these goals were quite incommensurate with the magnitude and urgency of the program recommended.

Many church groups were active participants among the nongovernmental organizations at the meetings preparing for Cairo, though the Vatican alone had official standing because of its status as a state. At Cairo the Vatican stood virtually alone in totally opposing contraception as well as abortion, and it dominated much of the agenda in the first days of the conference. On this issue the Vatican does not even have the support of most Roman Catholics; nine out of ten Catholics in both the United States and Mexico reject the church's teaching, and they practice contraception in almost exactly the same proportion as non-Catholics. Conservative Protestants do not object to contraception, but they have been concerned that the U.N. would promote abortion as a means of controlling family size, and on those grounds they persuaded the Reagan and Bush administrations to withdraw support for U.N. population programs.

Mainstream Protestant groups have tried to separate the questions of contraception and abortion. They also have insisted that family planning must be included in the wider context of socioeconomic development in the South and disproportionate consumption and pollution by the North. Most Protestant leaders hold that human sexuality serves not only the goal of procreation but also that of expressing love and unity in marriage, so contraception is an acceptable means of responsible family planning. There is little recognition, however, that beyond the welfare of individual families, global justice and the integrity of creation are at stake in personal and social decisions about family planning.[23]

Sustainable Development

During the 1970s, leaders in the Third World and in the U.N. and the World Bank promoted economic development but seldom gave attention to its environmental impacts. In 1987, however, the Brundtland Report to the U.N. showed in detail how poverty accelerates environmental deterioration (especially in overuse of marginal lands and sources of water and fuelwood), which in turn perpetuates poverty. The report advocated sustainable agriculture, including conservation of soil and water, diversification and rotation of crops, and reduced use of chemicals. It said that industrial growth must be based on technologies that are less polluting and resource-intensive and more energy-efficient and decentralized than the large-scale heavy industries promoted by national leaders and international agencies in the past.

The U.N. Conference on Environment and Development at Rio in 1992 brought these two topics together for the first time. Largely because of pressure from the Bush administration, the agreements reached on forests, endangered species, and global climate were very modest, and almost nothing was done to provide additional financial resources or to facilitate the transfer of environmentally sound technologies to the Third World. There was little discussion of refinancing the debt load or altering the tariffs and terms of trade that perpetuate the role of developing nations as suppliers of raw materials. The churches were well represented in the preparatory conferences for Rio and in the Forum which ran in parallel with the official sessions. Many church groups continue to urge increased U.S. agricultural and technical assistance and more equitable terms of trade, in the interest of justice and peace as well as sustainability.

Sustainable global development will require a reordering of national priorities in the United States and in other countries. With the end of the Cold War, the center of our foreign policy must shift from the containment of communism to human well-being and the preservation of our planet. If a third of the seven hundred billion dollars the world spends on arms each year were spent on sustainable agriculture, reforestation, energy conservation, renewable energy sources, and family planning, the prospects for the whole planet would be dramatically altered.[24]

THE ROLE OF THE CHURCH

How can these concerns be expressed in the life of the church?

1. *Worship:* We can give greater attention to the natural world in sermons, hymns, liturgy, and prayers. In the balance between creation and redemption, the central focus must of course be on redemption, for it is in the person of Christ that we have experi-

enced God's love and forgiveness. In encounter with God we can find the healing of our brokenness and the renewal of our lives. But this renewal can empower us to seek reconciliation with other people and with the created order.

2. *Religious Education*: Respect for nature, concern for social justice, a vision of the good life, and a global perspective can be presented in the Sunday School, in youth programs, and in adult study groups. Environmental awareness and stewardship should be part of Christian education—starting in nursery school. Nature experiences and environmental education can be tied to the Christian faith in weekend outings, wilderness trips, and summer camps. We can also seek more opportunities to learn from the scientists, doctors, engineers, and technical experts in our congregations. Each church must also examine its own practices in energy conservation, recycling, and the uses of any land it owns.

3. *Social Action*: The primary social task of the church is to motivate its members to act. We can work with other citizens in environmental and public interest groups whose goals we share. But at times the church is called to take a stand on significant issues in public debate and to support specific legislation aimed at social justice and the protection of the environment. To make wise decisions it must be aware of scientific data as well as ethical goals. Our concern about the endangered planet and its oppressed people must find expression both in our individual lives and in public policy decisions. The Christian vision of the good life in a just and sustainable society is relevant to personal choices and also to politics at local, state, and national levels.

4. *Seminaries and Higher Education*: Courses on the theology of nature and on environmental ethics are needed in colleges and seminaries if future laity and clergy are to be prepared to deal with these questions. The articulation of a theology of nature and the reformulation of doctrines of God, creation, and human nature are primarily a task for theologians, but we all can contribute to it. University campuses and church-related colleges are promising contexts for greater dialogue and interaction between the scientific and religious communities.

5. *Denominational Support*: State and national denominational offices can encourage these efforts, even at a time when they are under financial pressure. Educational resources to assist ministers and laity in sermons, worship, and programs for youth and adults can relate environmental and technological issues to Christian theology and ethics. They can help us learn to think globally and act locally. Denominations could more actively promote a broadly envisioned Environmental Sabbath on the first Sunday in June, and distribute materials for it.

6. *Ecumenical Cooperation*: Here I come back to Oelschlaeger's thesis that we must join other religious groups in a common effort to promote the care of the earth. We can support the Ecojustice Program of the National Council of Churches and the activities of the World Council of Churches on "Justice, Peace, and the Integrity of Creation." There are also interfaith groups such as the North American Coalition on Religion and Ecology and the National Religious Partnership for the Environment. The Worldwide Fund for Nature brought leaders of all the major religious traditions together at Assisi, Italy in 1986 and has continued to encourage the development of a global environmental ethic. An even greater diversity was represented in Chicago in 1993 at the Parliament of World Religions, in which care of the earth was a prominent theme.

7. *Educational and Professional Implications*: Ethical issues arise frequently in applied science, as was evident above in the discussion of ecojustice. Teachers can help students analyze ethical issues in terms of social justice and other values. Some universities have programs in Technology and Public Policy, or in Science, Technology, and Society, which examine policy decisions requiring value judgments in balancing diverse social and environmental consequences. Such policy questions also arise in courses in energy, agriculture, resources, transportation, communications, and other technological fields. Values inevitably enter any discussion of priorities in scientific research and development. Moreover, practicing scientists and engineers encounter questions of professional ethics and social responsibility in their work. Religious faith does not provide simple

answers to these personal decisions on the job, but it does offer a wider context in which to consider them.

Let me leave you with a final image, the familiar view of the earth as seen by astronauts on the moon. The spinning globe is a blue and white gem in the vastness of space. The Christian tradition affirms that our Earth is indeed "Beloved of God," a gift to be cherished and preserved, but it is also "At Risk" due to our human failure to be good stewards and responsible caretakers. Now the decision is ours. Earth has adequate resources for all humankind and other forms of life, if we learn to use its resources wisely and share them equitably. Our task is to work for the preservation of the planet and the flourishing of the community of life.

NOTES

1. See Lester Brown et al., *State of the World 1999* (New York: W. W. Norton, 1999); *World Resources Institute, World Resources, 1998–99* (New York and Oxford: Oxford University Press, 1998); World Council of Churches Study Project, *Climate Change and the Quest for Sustainable Societies* (Geneva: WCC, 1998).

2. Lynn White, "The Historical Roots of our Ecologic Crisis," reprinted in *Western Man and Environmental Ethics,* ed. Ian G. Barbour (Reading, Mass.: Addison-Wesley, 1973).

3. For example, Rosemary Radford Ruether, *Gaia and God: An Ecofeminist Theology of Earth Healing* (San Francisco: HarperSanFrancisco, 1992); Carol Adams, ed., *Ecofeminism and the Sacred* (New York: Continuum, 1993); Mary Heather MacKinnon and Moni McIntyre, eds., *Readings in Ecology and Feminist Theology* (Kansas City: Sheed and Ward, 1995).

4. Max Oelschlaeger, *Caring for Creation: An Ecumenical Approach to the Environmental Crisis* (New Haven: Yale University Press, 1994).

5. Douglas John Hall, *Imaging God: Dominion as Stewardship* (Grand Rapids: William B. Eerdman, 1986); Peter DeVos, ed., *Earthkeeping in the Nineties* (Grand Rapids: William B. Eerdman, 1991).

6. James Nash, *Loving Nature: Ecological Integrity and Christian Responsibility* (Nashville: Abingdon Press, 1991). See also Larry Rasmussen, *Earth Community, Earth Ethics* (Maryknoll, N.Y.: Orbis, 1996).

7. G. W. H. Lampe, *God as Spirit* (Oxford: Clarendon Press, 1977); Alasdair Heron, *The Holy Spirit* (Philadelphia: Westminister Press, 1987); Mark I. Wallace, *Fragments of the Spirit: Nature, Violence, and the Renewal of Creation* (New York: Continuum, 1996).

8. George Kehm, "The New Story: Redemption as Fulfillment of Creation," in *After Nature's Revolt: Eco-Justice and Theology*, ed. Dieter Hessel (Minneapolis: Fortress Press, 1992).

9. Paulos Gregarios, "New Testament Foundations for Understanding the Creation," in *Tending the Garden*, ed. Wesley Granberg-Michaelson (Grand Rapids: William B. Eerdman, 1987).

10. John Habgood, "A Sacramental Approach to Environmental Issues," in *Liberating Life: Contemporary Approaches to Ecological Theology*, ed. Charles Birch, William Eakin, and Jay McDaniel (Maryknoll, N.Y.: Orbis, 1990).

11. Matthew Fox, *The Coming of the Cosmic Christ: The Healing of Mother Earth and the Birth of a Global Renaissance* (San Francisco: Harper & Row, 1988); see also Brian Swimme and Thomas Berry, *Universe Story* (San Francisco: HarperSanFrancisco, 1992).

12. See Ian G. Barbour, *Religion and Science: Historical and Contemporay Issues* (San Francisco: HarperSanFrancisco, 1997), chapter 10.

13. George Tinker, "Creation as Kin: An American Indian View," in *After Nature's Revolt*, ed. Dieter Hessel; John A. Grim, "Native American Worldviews and Ecology," in *Worldviews and Ecology*, ed. Mary Evelyn Tucker and John A. Grim (Maryknoll, N.Y.: Orbis Press, 1994).

14. John B. Cobb Jr. and David Ray Griffin, *Process Theology: An Introduction* (Philadelphia: Westminster Press, 1976); see also I. G. Barbour, *Religion and Science: Historical and Contemporary Issues*, chapter 11.

15. Jay McDaniel, *Of God and Pelicans: A Theology of Reverence for Life* (Louisville: Westminster/John Knox, 1989).

16. Robert Bullard, ed., *Confronting Environmental Racism* (Boston: South End Press, 1993); Laura Westra and Peter Wenz, eds., *Faces of Environmental Racism: Confronting Issues of Global Justice* (Lanham, Md.: Rowman and Littlefield, 1995).

17. Robert Stivers, "The Ancient Forests of the Pacific Northwest: The Moral Debate," *Theology and Public Policy* 52, no. 2 (1993): 27–48.

18. Ian G. Barbour, *Ethics in an Age of Technology* (San Francisco: HarperSanFransciso, 1993), chapters 2, 3.

19. Lester Brown, Christopher Flavin, and Sandra Postel, *Saving the Planet* (New York: W. W. Norton, 1991).

20. Presbyterian Eco-Justice Task Force, *Keeping and Healing the Creation* (Louisville: Presbyterian Church USA, 1989); Environmental Task Force, Evangelical Lutheran Church in America, *Caring for Creation* (Minneapolis: ELCA, 1991); U.S. Conference of Catholic Bishops, "Renewing the Earth," *Origins* 21 (1991): 425–32.

21. Alan During, *How Much is Enough: The Consumer Society and the Future of the Earth* (New York: W. W. Norton, 1992); Paul Wachtel, *The Poverty of Affluence* (Philadelphia: Free Press, 1983); Michael Argyle, *The Psychology of Happiness* (New York: Methuen, 1987).

22. James Nash, "Toward the Revival and Reform of the Subversive Virtue: Frugality," *Annual of the Society of Christian Ethics* (1995): 137–60; David Shi, *The Simple Life: Plain Living and High Thinking in American Culture* (New York: Oxford University Press, 1985).

23. Susan Power Bratton, *Six Billion and More: Human Population Regulation and Christian Ethics* (Louisville: John Knox, 1992); James B. Martin-Schramm, *Population Perils and the Churches' Response* (Geneva: World Council of Churches, 1997).

24. United Nations Development Programme, *Human Development Report* (New York: Oxford University Press, 1998).

QUESTIONS FOR DISCUSSION

1. In what ways does the practice of your faith or beliefs affect the way in which you use material resources? Are there particular texts or individuals in your tradition that guide your thinking and practice? How are your practices the same or different from others who may hold similar or different beliefs?

2. What images in your mind do you have of God? Why are these ideas important to you? Are there ways in which your conception of God shapes your attitude to the environment? What about your understanding of population issues or your pattern of consumption?

3. What aspects of your current pattern of worship are most challenged by the environmental movement? Which environmental issues do you find most troubling when you think of them in relation to your faith? Are they such tangible issues as questions of resource scarcity, population growth, and patterns of consumption or are they the more intangible issues such as the apparent religious syncretism or pantheism held by some environmentalists?

2. SCIENCE IN DIALOGUE WITH RELIGION

The opening article in this section by scientist Charles Puccia sketches a picture of a planet at risk: global climate change; ozone depletion; withering ecosystems, habitats, and species; the degradation of water; and toxic pollution. He concludes that the environmental battleground is really about its effects upon humanity in relation to the web of life. This conclusion is further confirmed by a growing number of studies on the relationship between ecological degradation and regional violence.[1] That the scientific enterprise and a life of faith have much in common, clear in Puccia, is the operating premise for Ian Hutchinson. While science and faith may differ in method and substance, each requires the other.

Science without religion loses its ethical guide. Religion without science lacks the substance and contextual resources with which to understand the world. This synthetic approach to the environment especially draws us to a discussion of Earth's carrying capacity and the over-consumption of its resources.[2] Theology is challenged as never before by the concept of a "full Earth" and the question of global sustainability. The inability to find a technological "fix" for these and other factors draws science into dialogue with economics, politics, and the religious attitudes which shape our conception of the world and the legitimacy of its institutions and social arrangements.[3]

Concern about how little has been done to change our course toward ecological disaster[4] leads Timothy Weiskel to ask troubling questions at just the time when there is renewed interest in the study of macrohistorical processes. A part of the interest in general historical trends and the ability to study these with new accuracy is an understanding of human cultures in the full context of their socioecological evolution. Weiskel cites five of these: climate history and human affairs, the origins and ecological impact of urbanization, paleopathology and the natural history of disease, the historical ecology of colonialism, and the decline of ancient civilizations. After surveying the data that each of these fields produces, he concludes that our system of public belief is in need of radical revision if we are to survive as a species.

Each of the authors in this section begins with an array of factual data and ends with questions of value. Puccia notes troubling issues of ecojustice embedded in the environmental debate. Hutchinson points to different concerns relating to patterns of population ethics and overconsumption. Weiskel asks why, if we are aware of the crisis, are we unable to act more consistently and forthrightly? The ecological predicament draws attention to a division between facts and values in our culture as no other single issue does because of its holistic nature.[5]

Yet the divide between the descriptive language of religion and of science is not quite so clear cut as it once was. Like the polar caps which we fear are diminishing, a thaw is occurring between the practitioners of these languages. Some years ago chemist and philosopher Michael Polayni began to show us one way to begin to bring the sciences into conversation with religion.[6] Despite their own skepticism in different directions, both astrophysicist Stephen Hawking[7] and astronomer Robert Jastrow[8] have pointed to another through recent developments in astrophysics. Such discoveries as the Big Bang and contemporary debate over the nature of evolution have driven physicist Freeman Dyson to ask whether the universe knew we were coming.[9] Another physicist, Paul Davies, writes that science has advanced to the point where formerly religious questions now can be seriously tackled by scientists.[10]

While a thaw may be occurring in the face of the pressing ecological issues, the question still remains about how these two languages are to relate to each other.[11] Ian Barbour suggests categories of conflict and independence which give way to dialogue and, perhaps, integration.[12] Preferring "contact" and "confirmation" to Barbour's latter two modes of interaction, theologian John F. Haught helpfully develops his typology in relation to a number of different scientific disciplines and issues.[13] Arguing for "consonance," in a strong or weak sense whereby science and theology, if not in harmony, at least mark out a common domain of questions, Ted Peters argues that this perspective alone allows both science and theology to carry out a crossdisciplinary conversation within a common world of meaning.[14] Seeking a consonant voice in ecology is a pressing issue today. The typologies of such people as Barbour, Haught, or Peters help to map out the terrain.[15]

It is often clear enough today why science is important to religion. In fact, for some like physicist James Gleick, "God's turf" now belongs "not to the theologian, but to the scientist."[16] A scientific explanation for events is so plausible that religion fails to provide the coherence which was once thought to be its function. For scientists like Carl Sagan, the effort to get the religious community involved with ecology has been to marshall only its moral energy—but even here questions emerge for many about whether religion can provide an adequate basis for an ecological ethics.[17] Like a diffident lover, religious communities have been of two minds with respect to such wooing. For some it is the world of dualistic (Cartesian) science, already wed to technology and market-expansion, that is the problem. This scientism has foisted upon the world a domineering anthropomorphism often blind to issues of ecojustice. The recovery of a nondualistic religious vision is what is required. Others have come to the table but are unsure how their religious identity engages ecology, whether as signs of transcendence (symbolic instrumentalism) or as symbols embedded in religious forms of life (linguistic pragmatism).[18]

Although there were always voices questioning the relationship between science and a narrowing mechanistic positivism, European and Anglo-American societies grew to accept its division of facts from values, increasingly practiced from the Enlightenment into the modern period. Writing with David Hume's epistemological skepticism in mind, Immanuel Kant's work and legacy was to put empirical knowledge on a firmer footing—but to the detriment of religious understanding, which was never satisfactory to Kant.[19] Although the "real" God escapes knowledge, as Kant defines God in his *Critique of Pure Reason* (1781),[20] the *idea* of God is valuable for speculative thought in at least three ways: (1) the concept of God helps to distinguish between appearances and things-in-themselves, (2) it helps explain the mystery of intuition, and (3) it promotes scientific inquiry in that confidence in the intelligibility and unity of the world is assumed. While each of these three areas now has fallen subject to hermeneutical and cultural debate,[21] the criticism of those faulting science for fostering a spirit of detachment contributing to a collapse of European values appears tame today.[22]

The wall of separation that once stood between the world of facts and that of values is being chipped away. Ethical questions are being framed by such new sciences as sociobiology, genetics, and the discoveries of astrophysics. The need to draw science more fully into the ethical and conceptual work of theology was underscored by the General Secretary of the World Council of Churches, Philip Potter, in a keynote address at the Conference on Faith, Science, and the Future in 1979 at MIT.[23] The emergence of fields like "science studies," grounding the "language" of the sciences in a discipline like anthropology, has focused the attention of science on its embeddedness in larger cultural questions which involve religious understanding and practice.[24]

The language of facticity needs values, and a coherent ethic for the environment requires all the information that the sciences can muster. That such a dialogue is possible is the result of many startling discoveries about the nature of our world in the twentieth century and comes out of a different intellectual climate in the philosophy of science and the sociology of knowledge since the Second World War.[25] Wolfhart Pannenberg is one of a number of theologians who draws these issues together in the search for hypothetical consonance in the description of reality.[26] His theology is an example of how additional perspectives on the Seoul WCC Assembly's affirmation "Creation as Beloved of God" are opened up through a dialogue between science and religion.[27]

Pannenberg finds the sciences drawn into a larger framework of intelligibility through the reflective discipline of theology.[28] He writes that increasing attention needs to be given to the relationship between natural laws and the contingency of individual events. Arguing in a way that parallels Polanyi's idea of tacit knowledge, Pannenberg finds that scientific formulas, in whichever discipline they may be developed, ignore their contexts. This leads to the mistaken conclusion that the actual course of events is determined by the laws of nature whereas contingency gets ignored. Nature, Pannenberg argues, ought to be understood as historical and natural laws as the uniformities abstracted from contingent events.[29]

History rather than determinacy provides the "gate" for increased traffic between science and religion, notes theologian Ted Peters, adding that this is a space in which both theologians and practitioners of the new sciences are at home.[30] The very existence of the world, its conservation and its governance, are all aspects of this history. To talk about the contingent existence of the world is to raise the question of a creation in time, an idea which resonates with Christian theology (*creatio ex nihilo*). The word "creation" implies derivation and attendant issues of value: Is purpose given or embedded in nature? Debate over the environment begins here.[31]

Uniform laws, as discerned in the flow of contingent events, raise the question of conservation, continuing signs of a creator maintaining regularity and predictability. Here Pannenberg's theology might stress the *beloved* aspect of our Seoul Affirmation. Whether this is warranted or not draws theology into dialogue with the philosophy of science, concerning the extent to which reality can be personified. As theology pushes the question of a personal God, physicists like Freeman Dyson and Paul Davies find themselves driven to speculate about the implications of an anthropic principle given the evolution of the universe as we know it. Such "personalism," a conclusion consonant with the two languages of science and theology, might offer renewed energy for scientific discovery and the stewardship of earth's resources.[32]

Care for creation involves governance. It evokes the question of how the Creator, and perhaps humanity as well, participate in the management of nature. Pannenberg implies by the providential activity wherein God aims to accomplish God's tasks, not a *telos* or entelechy, but that nature itself is to find its own fulfillment.[33] This idea relates to the point raised in the introduction by the Australian biologist Charles Birch who, drawing from Alfred North Whitehead, finds in process theology the conceptual tools for a theology of nature. However, governance may also imply resistance. This reminds us that in Christian theology creation is not an extension or emanation of God. It is an object of God's love, free to depart from or participate in God's purposes.[34] The arena for this drama is history. If history is the "gate" through which science and religion meet, we are drawn into an evolving drama which includes conversation with all peoples of living faith.

Rodney L. Petersen

NOTES

1. Mohamed Suliman, "The Rationality and Irrationality of Violence in Sub-Saharan Africa," in Mohamed Suliman, ed., *Ecology, Politics, and Violent Conflict* (London: Zed Books, 1999), pp. 25–44.

2. A number of valuable studies have been funded in the areas consumption, population, and the environment by such foundations as The Pew Charitable Trusts and its Global Stewardship Initiative, and the John D. and Catherine T. MacArthur Foundation. Among studies available, see "The Ethics of Consumption," Report from the Institute for Philosophy and Public Policy (School of Public Health, University of Maryland, College Park, Maryland). Occasional papers and bulletins from other groups have proliferated in recent years, the range of which includes The Union of Concerned Scientists, American Association for the Advancement of Science, Committee on Women, Population and the Environment, the Office of

Policy Planning and Education, U.S. Environmental Protection Agency, and various agencies attached to the United Nations family of organizations. For an example of interfaith discussion on pertinent issues, see Azizah al-Hibri, Daniel Maguire, and James B. Martin-Schramm, *Religious and Ethical Perspectives on Population Issues* (Washington, D.C.: The Religious Consultation on Population, Reproductive Health, and Ethics, 1993).

3. Ian Barbour, "Technology and Theology," *Bulletin of Science, Technology, and Society* 16, nos. 1–2 (1996): 4–7. See additional issues of this journal which draws in relation to each other issues of technology and justice. Among the increasing number of theorists drawing attention to this relationship is John B. Cobb Jr., *Sustaining the Common Good: A Christian Perspective on the Global Economy* (Cleveland, Ohio: The Pilgrim Press, 1994).

4. Bruce Babbitt, Secretary of the Interior of the United States of America, and the atmospheric scientist Michael McElroy, Harvard University, both offered sustained appeals for a deeper conversation between science and religion toward a deepened sense of ecological responsibility at the conference, "Consumption, Population, and the Environment: Religion and Science Envision Equity for an Altered Creation," sponsored by The Boston Theological Institute with the American Association for the Advancement of Science (AAAS), 9–11 November 1995.

5. C. P. Snow argued that one of the salient problems of our age is noncommunication between the "literary" culture and the "scientific" culture, that their fracture constitutes a grave social threat. See *The Two Cultures: And a Second Look—An Expanded Version of the Two Cultures and the Scientific Revolution* (Mentor MP 557, 1964).

6. Michael Polanyi argues for a holistic approach to knowledge, understood tacitly, and unknown by looking simply at component parts, in *Personal Knowledge* (New York: Harper Torchbooks, 1964), and *The Tacit Dimension* (Garden City: Doubleday Anchor, 1967). Parallel and additional perspective on the construction of reality is seen in Michael A. Arbib and Mary B. Hesse, *The Construction of Reality* (Cambridge: Cambridge University Press, 1986).

7. Theorizing on the basis of the big bang Stephen Hawking argues that while the universe might not be eternal, so also it might not have had a clear temporal beginning, in *A Brief History of Time: From the Big Bang to Black Holes* (New York: Bantam Books, 1988), pp. 140–41.

8. Robert Jastrow writes that although many astronomers would have preferred it otherwise, the big bang theory appears to support the biblical doctrine of creation, in *God and the Astronomers*, 2d. ed. (New York: W. W.

Norton and Co., 1992), p. 116. On theories of consonance, see Gerald L. Schroeder, *Genesis and the Big Bang* (New York: Bantam Books, 1990).

9. Freeman Dyson, *Infinite in All Directions* (New York: Harper and Row, 1988), p. 298.

10. Paul Davies, *God and the New Physics* (New York: Simon & Schuster, 1983); and *The Mind of God: The Scientific Basis for a Rational World* (New York: Simon & Schuster, 1992).

11. For example, a new openness is seen in Roman Catholicism since the Second Vatican Council declared the natural sciences to be free from ecclesiastical authority, calling them autonomous disciplines. See the message of His Holiness Pope John Paul II, in *Physics, Philosophy, and Theology: A Common Quest for Understanding*, ed. John Russell, William Stoeger, and George V. Coyne (Vatican Observatory, Vatican City State, 1988), p. M1.

12. Ian Barbour, *Religion in an Age of Science*, vol. 1 of *The Gifford Lectures, 1989–1991* (San Francisco: HarperCollins, 1990), pp. 3–30.

13. John F. Haught, *Science and Religion: From Conflict to Conversation* (New York: Paulist Press, 1995).

14. Peters sees four "dead ends" in the science and religion dialogue: (1) scientism (sometimes called secular humanism) which argues that science provides all the knowledge we need to know, (2) ecclesiastical authoritarianism, (3) scientific creationism, and (4) a "two-language" theory whereby it is argued that science speaks with an objective and public language while religion speaks with an existential and personal language. He offers helpful criticism on each of these positions in Peters, ed., *Cosmos As Creation* (Nashville: Abingdon Press, 1989), pp. 13–19. In his opinion, the dialogue between science and theology requires a deepening understanding of the theological implications of scientific knowledge around four themes: (1) a recognition that the world of nature is dynamic and changing, (2) the need for a doctrine of continuing creation (*creatio continua*) to complement the traditional idea of creation out of nothing (*creatio ex nihilo*), (3) the interpretation of scripture in light of current scientific knowledge, and (4) a sense of wonder and speculation about the place of humanity in the cosmos or God's creation.

15. For further examples, see the work dedicated to the Society of Ordained Scientists by biochemist Arthur Peacocke, *Theology for a Scientific Age: Being and Becoming—Natural and Divine* (Oxford: Basil Blackwell, 1990); also helpful is Holmes Rolston III, *Science and Religion: A Critical Survey* (New York: Random House, 1987), chaps. 4–5.

16. James Gleick, writing in the January 4, 1987, issue of the *New York*

Times Magazine as cited in Ted Peters, ed., *Cosmos as Creation* (Nashville: Abingdon, 1989), p. 12.

17. John Passmore, *Man's Responsibility for Nature* (New York: Scribner's, 1974), p. 184. Passmore argues that we will fail to deal adequately with our ecology so long as we believe we will be delivered from the effects of environmental degradation.

18. See the distinction made by Robert C. Neville between these traditions, pragmatism itself divided between those who take their cue from Charles Peirce and those directed variously by Ludwig Wittgenstein, in *The Truth of Broken Symbols* (Albany: State University of New York Press, 1996), preface and chaps. 2–3.

19. Following the writing of *Critique of Pure Reason* (1781), Kant wrote his *Critique of Practical Reason* (1788) in which he discerned a "felt" need for religion which results from a moral law. This moral functionalism became the basis for a moral theology of use in the world of values if not in that of facts. In *Religion Within the Limits of Reason Alone* (1793), Kant admits no supernatural revelation but equates Christian theology with the religion of practical reason. A modern restatement of this might be seen in the systematic theology of Gordon Kaufman, *God the Problem* (Cambridge: Harvard University Press, 1972), criticized for its "residual Cartesianism." More recently Kaufman has drawn his attention to constructive reflection around the area of ecotheology.

20. On the basis of knowledge, defined by Kant in the *a priori* categories of understanding (reason) together with empirical data (experience), metaphysics is shown not to be a genuine science and arguments for God's existence speculative.

21. Concern for the rationality of science in light of its current detractors can be seen in the Conference "The Flight from Science and Reason," sponsored by The New York Academy of Sciences, 31 May–2 June 1995. See n. 20 above.

22. The three points are raised by Nels F. S. Ferré in the context of his article, "The Immorality of Science," *Religion in Life* 10, no. 1 (Winter 1941): 31–40. This critique is applied specifically to the emergence not only of scientific positivism. Similar concerns with respect to technology are developed by the sociologist Jacques Ellul: "Technique is the translation into action of man's concern to master things by means of reason, to account for what is subconscious, make quantitative what is qualitative, make clear and precise the outlines of nature, take hold of chaos and put order into it" (p. 43). This mentality has become, for Ellul, the reigning

mythology of our epoch. See his study, *The Technological Society* (New York: Alfred A. Knopf, 1964).

23. Drawing upon ecumenical reflection back to the origins of Life and Work Movement (Stockholm, 1925), Potter stresses the importance of the right use of technology in "Science and Technology: Why Are the Churches Concerned?" in *Faith and Science in an Unjust World*. Report of the World Council of Churches' Conference on *Faith, Science, and the Future*, vol. 1, ed. Roger L. Shinn (Geneva: World Council of Churches, 1980), pp. 21–29. An earlier expression of this concern can be seen in C. F. von Weizsäcker, *The Relevance of Science: Creation and Cosmogony, Gifford Lectures, 1959–1960* (London: Collins, 1964). Von Weizsäcker writes, "Anyone neglecting to further his theoretical understanding of our complex world as much as he can, will in the long run do more harm than good in his practical efforts" (p. 9).

24. John Horgan, *The End of Science: Facing the Limits of Knowledge in the Twilight of the Scientific Age* (Helix Books/Addison-Wesley, 1996); and compare Gerald Holton, *Science and Anti-Science* (Cambridge, Mass.: Harvard University Press, 1993). See also Antonio R. Damasio, *Descartes' Error: Emotion, Reason, and the Human Brain* (New York: Avon Books, 1994).

25. Philosophers of meaning such as Wilhelm Dilthey, Hans-Georg Gadamer, and Jürgen Habermas have underscored the notion that all experience of meaning participates in with widest context of meaning. Pannenberg develops this point by arguing that God is the all determining reality and is the hypothesis which explains most adequately the whole experience of reality.

26. Wolfhart Pannenberg, *Toward a Theology of Nature: Essays on Science and Faith*, ed. Ted Peters (Louisville: Westminster/John Knox Press, 1993). For further examples, see the work dedicated to the Society of Ordained Scientists by biochemist Arthur Peacocke, *Theology for a Scientific Age.*

27. Stephen Toulmin describes different paradigms through which Christian theology has worked in history in its effort to understand nature and its larger cosmology, in "Religion and the Idea of Nature," *Religion, Science, and Public Policy*, ed. Frank T. Birtel (New York: Crossroad, 1987), pp. 67–78. In North America the following centers and Foundation are among those helping to deepen the science-religion dialogue: The Templeton Foundation, The Center for Theology and the Natural Sciences (Berkeley), The Chicago Center for Religion and Science, The Center for Theological Inquiry, The Faith and Science Exchange (Boston Theological Institute), and The Institute for Religion in an Age of Science.

28. In making his case for theology as a science in dialogue with the natural sciences, Pannenberg offers a careful analysis of the terms *naturwissenschaften* and *geisteswissenschaften* in *Theology and the Philosophy of Science,* trans. F. McDonagh (Philadelphia: Westminster Press, 1976), p. 72; more fully in his *Systematic Theology* (Grand Rapids: Eerdmans, 1991). See also the early work of David Tracy, *Blessed Rage for Order* (New York: Seabury, 1975); and Bernard Lonergan, *Insight: A Study of Human Understanding* (New York: Philosophical Society, 1958).

29. See Pannenberg, "God and Nature," trans. Wilhelm C. Linss, in *Toward a Theology of Nature,* ed. Peters, pp. 50–71.

30. Peters wrties, "To the theologian, the enduring forms of nature right along with single events appear as the contingent product of the activity of a free God." See his introductory essay in *Toward of Theology of Nature,* p. 10.

31. Lesslie Newbigin, *Foolishness to the Greeks: The Gospel and Western Culture* (Geneva: World Council of Churches, 1986), pp. 65–94. An understanding of critical realism as a place where a philosophy of science and theology might meet is given by W. van Huysteen in *Theology and the Justification of Faith* (Grand Rapids: Eerdmans, 1989), chap. 9; and in Michael Banner, *The Justification of Science and the Rationality of Religious Belief* (Oxford: Clarendon Press, 1990).

32. Davies writes that the success of mathematics in describing nature points to a deep link between the human mind and the organization of the world, in *The Mind of God,* pp. 140–60. Haught, *Science and Religion,* pp. 27–46. What is meant by "God" see Alister Hardy, *The Spiritual Nature of Man* (Oxford: Clarendon Press, 1979), p. 1. See John Barrow and Frank Tipler, *The Anthropic Cosmological Principle* (Oxford: Clarendon Press, 1986) and compare John Polkinghorne, *Science and Creation* (London: SPCK, 1988).

33 Ted Peters, whom I am following here, contrasts this with the medieval (Thomas Aquinas) purpose of the *visio Dei* whereby God in God's self is goal or scholastic Protestantism which finds praise of God as the chief end of creation. Both ideas proximate concepts of divine narcissism in Peters' view, in *Toward a Theology of Nature,* p. 11.

34. Many different ways have been developed to express this. Perhaps the most graphic is the idea of "the Omega Point," as developed by Teilhard de Chardin, *Hymn of the Universe* (New York: Harper & Row, 1965). Other models of God's interaction with the world are presented in Peacocke, *Theology for a Scientific Age,* pp. 135–83; for preaching, see Thomas F. Torrance, *Preaching Christ Today. The Gospel and Scientific Thinking* (Grand Rapids: Eerdmans, 1994), pp. 41–71.

2
THE EARTH AT RISK
Encountering Environmental Limits
Charles J. Puccia

INTRODUCTION

Over a quarter century ago the term *ecology* entered the popular lexicon and soon became synonymous with the term *environment.* The mass media, politicians, and the general public did not distinguish between ecological science and a newly defined term called *the environment,* which came to connote ecological science mixed with politics and economics within the context of the natural (biological) world. Remarkably few scientific moral issues within society beget stronger public reaction. Medicine and social health care come to mind, as well as the military applications of physics and chemistry. Ecological science, or its value-laden stepchild environmentalism, has become another.

Parallels and paradoxes abound in these duality debates between the demands of science and the needs of society. Every duality results in conflict and paradox. For example, societies can use physics to create nuclear bombs, high-tech missiles, or sophisticated landmines to take away lives, ostensibly in order to save lives. Whose lives get taken and whose get saved becomes an important question for society to answer. Similarly, an "environmental crisis" results when uncontrolled exploitation of natural resources creates jobs and financial wealth, but also destroys that which sustains human life and undermines biological and geological wealth of natural resources.

Within the environmental debate is the cynical view that portrays scientists as suspect, questions their motivation, and doubts the "facts" of science. This view sees scientists as a group pursuing their own political agenda. Critics of the ecological crisis have a constant refrain: the facts, if presented to reasonable people, should be above suspicion. Hence if some reasonable people can find fault with an environmental "issue," then surely the facts themselves become doubtful and the science biased. The conclusions might be, however, that if knowledge were infinite, absolute, and indisputable, then there would be no controversy—and, we should hasten to add, no further need for science. When facts are generally widely accepted, such as that the earth circles the sun or that daylight and temperature trigger perennial plants either to grow or to go dormant, they mute critics and make science believable. When facts are inconclusive or not fully overwhelming, like the triggering mechanism of phytotoxic algal blooms, "red tides," in which pollution seems to be a major factor, then scientists have work to do, while critics of environmental science often use the inconclusive nature of the facts to point at the environmental scientists and cry, "Charlatans!" In cases where scientific inquiries require more study, like into the causes of red tide, or whether the spotted owl will go extinct if forests are cut in order to save logging jobs or prevent the decline of industry through "overregulation of industrial effluent," neither the facts nor scientists are at fault. At issue is not ecological science but environmental science; in other words, not facts but social justice.

What follows is a discourse on the scientific facts in five cases representative of major issues in ecology/environment and the environmental debate: global climate change, atmospheric ozone depletion, loss of ecosystems and habitats, clean water, and toxic pollution. The last section reviews the position of scientists and people in the religious community within the environmental debate. The conclusion goes far beyond a call for more research, more data, and more information in an attempt to gain facts. It stands for a moral resolution to the environmental conflict arising from injustice. Furthermore, this chapter suggests that scientists have an obligation and a right to behave with moral standards, like everyone, whether in the religious community or not. An appeal that scientists work with the religious community to look at the moral issues behind the science-and-society conflict deepens the moral discussion.

THE NECESSITY OF SCIENCE

Ecological and environmental sciences describe, explain, and extrapolate the condition of the world; religion does the same. Scientists share with religious communities ethics and morals, so this is not a difference between them either. Science struggles to understand the world and the transformations made in it, and religion considers what the condition of the world ought to be. Science intends to describe and explain the world, to help us know where we are heading. Religion uses beliefs and tradition to help us decide where we ought to be going. Yet for religious communities to consider the "ought," they need to know "where are we now." In other words, scientific information makes it possible to discuss values, while discussing values requires having knowledge.

Among the great paradoxes of modern times must be that we know more about the world now than in all previous human history, yet that this knowledge does not prevent us from destroying the world or transforming it beyond moderate modification. We may also disbelieve that the current course leads to a less desirable world. Such dismal news surely resonates poorly, while predictions of a better future are well received. Modern science and technology have shown great promise to benefit people and society, but so, too, did the unleashing of mechanization in the nineteenth century. Is there any wonder that people, at least in the United States, give credence to voices that proclaim the environmental crisis is being solved? Clearly the religious community needs what good science thinks of the environmental crisis. Since religion needs to know the

facts, then it seems worthwhile to give a quick review of five important areas of concern. These are not the only problems of the ecological crisis, but they form a broad-brush portrait of what is hap-
pening.

GLOBAL CLIMATE CHANGE

By now most people have heard of global warming or climate
change via television, newspapers, magazines, and even film. Most
people would be surprised to learn that the point of the discussion
is not just about temperature. Further, most would doubt that a 2°F
to 6°F (0.5°C to 1.5°C) temperature rise is really important (see
appendix, figure 1). Indeed the change rests not on just a single
temperature in a single day, but on the average temperature over a
year, and it does matter. People know not to plant their gardens
before a certain date, even though the temperature might only
change by a few degrees—the difference between no frost and frost
makes a big difference to the small seedling. Yet everyone also
knows about increased intensity of floods, hurricanes, and periods
of drought—and thus global warming becomes climate change with
these effects. The evidence strongly points to an alteration in climate because we have changed the atmosphere above us.

Among the truly international efforts to understand climate
change is the Intergovernmental Panel on Climate Change (IPCC),
composed of recognized and well-respected scientists from countries around the world and sponsored by the World Meteorological
Society and the UN Environment Programme. After the first report
of the IPCC was issued, Dr. John Houghton, head of the British
Meteorological Service, remarked that less than ten of the two hundred scientists of the IPCC dissented from the report, something he
called a "remarkable consensus." At the second World Climate Conference of the IPCC in 1995, the international community of scientists issued compelling arguments for taking global warming and climate change seriously.

In October 1995 the IPCC issued the three-volume *Climate*

Change 1995: The IPCC Second Assessment. Hundreds of scientific and technical experts from academia, from private and national research laboratories, and from nongovernmental organizations helped to prepare the 1995 report. Thousands more conducted objective peer reviews. The resulting views came from analyses of more than 20,000 articles. Thus, the *Second Assessment* reached as well as anywhere in scientific studies a massive, policy-neutral review of the current state of understanding of climate change science, reaching conclusions that include:

1. Greenhouse gases in the atmosphere have increased significantly in the last three decades. That this can lead to global warming has been known since the last century.
2. Computer models indicate that a doubling of greenhouse gas concentrations would significantly warm the Earth.
3. Conditions for other planetary systems, in particular Venus, support the predictions of computer simulations.
4. A warming trend has clearly occurred over the last two decades.

Having arrived at a framework agreement on climate change and emissions regarding the highly industrialized countries in the 1997 Kyoto Conference, significant work is still to be done on implementation schedules and practical strategies for cutting back emissions and for new approaches to deal with developing countries' responsibility for curtailing future emissions, especially as they strive to meet expanding energy needs under greater consumer demands.

Another way to understand recent causes for alarm is that today carbon dioxide concentrations seem to be 20 percent higher than they had been over the past 160,000 years. Each year some twenty-two billion tons of carbon dioxide are added to the atmosphere from the burning of fossil fuels.

We know which countries emit the most greenhouse gases (see appendix, figure 2). It might be expected that the bigger the country, the greater the emissions, but, as we know, consumption patterns are not equal. The United States leads all countries in both total carbon emissions and per capita emissions. As expected, industrialization leads to greater per capita carbon emissions, yet at least two industrialized countries, France and Japan, show per capita carbon emissions almost as low as those of developing countries like China, Mexico, and Poland.

Two conclusions can be drawn. First, issues of north/south equity cannot be ignored. A strong backlash against global climate predictions from within developed countries is justifiably expected. Developing countries will find it difficult to believe that the advanced industrial countries truly support environmental safeguards, rather than economic self-interest, when emitting the greatest amount of greenhouse gases.

Second, carbon emissions are closely tied to fossil fuel burning, primarily for transportation and electricity generation. The disproportionate per capita emissions, even between the United States and other developed countries, does not increase confidence in the sincerity of Americans who express a desire to safeguard the planet. Nearly two-thirds of the greenhouse gas emissions comes from the industrialized nations. Of course, as the developing nations with large populations turn to industrialized technology, this ratio may change. Recently, for example, the Chinese government announced a plan to begin manufacturing and selling cars that burn fossil fuel. Therefore, regardless of the future ratio of emissions, one can conclude that there is a high probability that more greenhouse gases will be emitted into the atmosphere rather than less (see appendix, figures 3, 4).

On the encouraging side, atmospheric data in recent computer models for CO_2 emission rates appear to show a decline.[1] Furthermore, Edmonds and his colleagues Gardner and Brenkert suggest, in their model of fossil fuel emissions worldwide between 1975 and 2075, that energy efficiency by the consumer, labor productivity, and the elasticity of demand for energy in the developing world are probably the most important determinants of CO_2 emission variation. In other words, less CO_2 goes into the atmosphere with increasing efficiency. Workplace efficiency means increasing worker productivity or increasing demands on workers; consumer efficiency simply means that the worker goes home and changes lifestyle or home conditions to decrease energy use. Also, people at higher income levels seem to use less energy per dollar as their income rises. Of course, the wealth of an individual does not change the distance to travel from Chicago to New York—energy demand appears to be elastic. Regardless of the explanation for a slowing of CO_2 emission rates, it still remains that CO_2 emissions are at the highest level ever in recent history, but the opportunity for abatement does suggest that a rising trend need not be inevitable, provided action is taken.

Ozone Below And Above: Too Much And Too Little

How much ozone is there in this world—and what is ozone, anyway? Not so long ago, most people had never heard of ozone. In fact, in the not too distant past, terms like ecology, habitats, pollution, biodegradable, and a host of such terms never entered a normal conversation. They just weren't part of the lexicon necessary for most people to cope with life or to earn a living.

Ozone is a simple molecule with three oxygen atoms that stick together. Normally, two oxygen atoms form the ubiquitous oxygen molecule that lets us breathe, permits fire, and upon meeting hydrogen forms water. But three together is "strange." Ozone even has an odor, the pungent smell after a severe thunderstorm. Ozone can be formed by high combustion, as from gasoline engines in automobiles.

As in real estate, ozone location is everything. Ozone high up in the stratospheric atmosphere, roughly between ten to fifty kilometers (seven to thirty miles), protects life. On the other hand, ozone just over the earth's surface in the troposphere, from the ground to about ten kilometers (seven miles), is a pollutant. Humans, other animals, and plants don't do well "breathing" ozone. Federal standards consider 120 parts per billion the maximum allowable. Ozone is an irritant to the lungs, just like cigarette smoke. Bronchial tubes become constricted, reducing lung capacity and leading to emphysema and respiratory infections. But in the stratosphere, ozone reduces the sun's ultraviolet light from reaching the surface—ozone molecules are cosmic sunglasses.

Ozone scarcely exists in the upper atmosphere. If all the ozone were captured from the upper atmosphere and brought down to Earth it would be about three millimeters thick; about as thick as a computer floppy disk or a pizza. All of this ozone is stacked up over our heads, in a column, and not equally distributed. The earth has a mantle of air composed of several molecules including ozone. About 90 percent of the ozone resides in a small portion of the stratosphere, between fifteen and forty kilometers (ten to twenty miles). The rest of the ozone floats in the other parts of the atmosphere (i.e., troposphere, mesosphere). Consequently, the ozone forms a column over any part of the earth's surface.

Ozone depletion has both a seasonal and latitudinal component. Both hemispheres have experienced a reduction in total-column ozone, with the greatest reduction at the middle and high latitudes. Dramatic losses recorded at the southern latitudes around the Antarctic continent have produced the vivid description of an "ozone hole." That hole represents a thinning that is also occurring at other latitudes, but not as much. Recently, however, there have also been reports of total-column ozone loss at tropical latitudes. The trend within the lower stratosphere recently has been about a 10 percent loss per decade.[2] During periods of intense ozone depletion, ultraviolet light radiation has increased.

The worry over ozone loss extends beyond humane or sentimental concern for penguins. Ozone protects all people, animals, and plants from harmful ultraviolet radiation. Ultraviolet radiation is a form of light that has short wavelengths; light itself is a portion of the electromagnetic spectrum. Trisecting further the ultraviolet spectrum into UV-A, UV-B, and UV-C wavelengths leads to the following classification: UV-C, at 200–290 nanometers (nm), is the most dangerous to humans, penetrating cell walls to be absorbed by DNA and disrupt protein metabolic processes. UV-B, at broader wavelengths of 290–320 nm, also enter the cell wall and are absorbed to a significant degree, but not as much as UV-C. There is only minimal absorption of UV-A in the ultraviolet range of 320–400 nm.[3]

Luckily, UV-C is blocked effectively by the atmosphere, while UV-B depends on ozone as a filter. The effects of UV-B radiation, like all radiation, does not depend solely on the rate of exposure, because the effects accumulate. Unlike, say, for aspirins, where taking two a day for ten days is not the same as taking twenty aspirins in one day, for UV-B, the amount of exposure over ten days or one day has nearly the same effect. UV-B produces both melanoma and nonmelanoma skin cancers. Melanoma skin cancer, which effects a 25 percent mortality rate each year in Americans who contract it, rose 83 percent from 1982 to 1989. An increase in UV-B radiation will also produce increases in cataracts and suppression of the immune system.[4] In plants, increases in UV-B radiation retard growth and can produce smaller leaves. Food quality may also be affected, as the UV-B alters the chemical composition of plants and their uptake of minerals. The evidence that UV-B harms productivity in phytoplankton and zooplankton, the food source for fish, suggests a threat to fisheries.

WITHERING ECOSYSTEMS, HABITATS, AND SPECIES

Estimates on the number of species that become extinct each day vary among scientists, ranging between twenty-five and seventy species per day (Dobson, 1996—but some estimates are even higher). Extinction rates are determined by examining the fossil record, the historical record, and the known number of species in a particular group. The fossil record, for example, suggests that normally from two to five species become extinct per year. In the historical record of two specific groups, birds and mammals, a different picture emerges. Since 1600 the incidences of extinction in mammals have numbered 60, or approximately 0.15 per year. However, the extinction rate in the last century for mammals has been about one per year, over six times higher. The current rate per century is about 1 percent of all mammals, which is a jump even from the extinction rate of the 1600s. Unfortunately, the extinction rates for both mammals and birds may be low estimates, because undiscovered bird and mammal species in tropical forests have not been countable.

Geographical extinction patterns also have shifted. Typically in the seventeenth to mid-nineteenth century, extinctions on islands outpaced mainland extinctions, often at double, triple, or quadruple rates. While there were many reasons for this trend, certainly among them was the arrival of humans to these islands. Humans brought tools for hunting the larger mammals, destroyed habitats, and brought with them small animals, like dogs, cats, and goats (and, inadvertently, predatory rodents). These new predators, including the humans, often were too ruthless for an endemic species to survive.

Habitat loss may seem to creep along in small increments, but on a time scale of even fifty or one hundred years, much is lost. For example, between 900 and 1900 C.E., the natural habitats in Europe were converted to agricultural land at about 0.1 to 0.3 percent per year; at this rate, in less than one thousand years more than 50 percent of the original natural habitat has been lost. In the United States, the rate of loss from 1600 until 1900 is higher at about 0.7 to 1.0 percent per year. In comparison, the modern rate of natural habitat loss in the tropical rainforest equals the highest rate seen in the United States, or 1.0 percent per year. In some places it is even worse: Brazil, at 2.2 percent, and India, at 3.3 percent.

If species are to be protected, then we need to know the current status of particular species as well as the general status of habitats. One method has been to use a classification scheme that uses terms like *endangered* or *threatened*. Unfortunately, the definition of terms is not as simple as it might appear. The World Conservation Union—known as the IUCN—provides one widely recognized standard for definitions in their *Red Data Books*. But even the IUCN definitions are not uniform, sporting variation among the *Red Book on Threatened Birds of the Americas* and the books on mammals. A proposal for a new classification of a species as threatened is based on five population traits, including observed decline, geographical

range, total population, projected decline, and extinction probability. While the merits of a new standard are valuable, the practical
implementation universally among all *taxa* is daunting.

Examining the ten countries with the greatest number of threatened vertebrates reveals that in three categories the United States
ranks first: reptiles, amphibians, and fishes. The United States ranks
ninth for birds. Only for mammals is the United States absent from
the top ten.[5]

Threats to vertebrates come primarily from a variety of human
impacts, including:

1. Changes to natural habitats, including destruction, alteration, or subdivision into small fragments. Activities like
   farming, pastoral grazing, forestry, fire, pollution, and development contribute to habitat destruction.
2. The exploitation of species for commercial purposes. Examples include hunting and fishing, taking of animals for fur
   and hides, and pet and botanical trade.
3. The introduction of species from other geographical loca-
   tions, either accidentally or intentionally, which can disrupt
   the local, natural ecology, including displacing predators and
   introducing new species without local predators or without
   competing species.
4. Inadvertent destruction of species through other activities.
   This may include the capture of marine mammals in fishing
   nets, the entrainment of fish in intake valves of coastal power
   plants, and the discharge of effluent into air and water from
   commercial enterprise.
5. Diseases introduced into wild populations from domesticated animals and livestock, or from plant species. A well-
   known example in the United States is the chestnut blight in
   American varieties from the introduction of European
   species.

Species with highly local populations or limited range are particularly susceptible to threats from these impacts.

For most threatened mammal species more than one of the above factors are causes. The single most important factor is the destruction of habitat. One particular habitat loss documented in the United States is the wetlands. In 1980, the loss since 1780 across the United States ranged from 91 percent in California to 87 percent in Missouri, 52 percent in Texas, 49 percent in Louisiana, 45 percent in Florida, and 42 percent in Minnesota. Concern for the loss of wetlands has continued to the present day.

LIFE DEPENDS ON CLEAN WATER

Sometimes the simplest, most basic facts get ignored. Above all else, we should remember the importance of clean water to human life and to life in general on the Earth. In recent news, the possible presence of a few small ice crystals on the moon was by itself astounding.

Extensive work has been done to protect the water environment. Criteria and standards were developed long before the U.S. Environmental Protection Agency (EPA); Boards of Health across the United States and various ministries and agencies worldwide have pursued clean water supplies. The pioneering work of John Snow in England, for example, recognized the spread of cholera as a result of the communal water well. Parenthetically, it explained why more women than men got cholera.

From a public standpoint, the numbers that generally attract the most attention are labeled MCL (maximum contaminant level) and MCLG (maximum contaminant level guideline). MCL and MCLG levels are different for different chemicals. MCL and MCLG for specific compounds are often cited and debated. One compound of major concern in public water supplies is lead. The MCL for lead is zero at the EPA, and a level of 0.015 mg/L (milligrams of substance per liter of water) requires action to safeguard health. Nitrate and nitrite MCL levels are set at 10 mg/L and 1 mg/L, respectively. In the farm belt, these inorganic substances enter drinking water through fertilizers and are of major concern to citizens.

It should be noted that the EPA regulations under the Safe Drinking Water Act only cover public water systems. Moreover, the microbial content of water is covered under the Total Coliform Rule (54 FR 27544-27568) and the Surface Water Treatment Requirements (54 FR 27486-27541), which means that they apply only to public systems using surface water or groundwater directly influenced by surface water.

With all this official care, the question arises of why the public should remain attentive. We can seek the answer by looking at a few specific issues, related to human health and recreation, and to wildlife.

Waterborne Diseases

A 1993 "Morbidity and Mortality Weekly Report of the Center for Disease Control" gives a summary, developed from surveillance in 1991–92, of waterborne disease outbreaks.[6] Most striking in the report is that disease outbreak varies considerably, and not always occurs at large catastrophic levels. Hence local events tend not to gain national or worldwide attention—yet this pattern was broken in Milwaukee.

Milwaukee defines the moment that *Cryptosporidium* reached public consciousness. In March and April, the protozoa parasite affected an estimated 403,000 people, causing watery diarrhea. However, *Cryptosporidium* outbreaks preceded Milwaukee. In August of 1991 about 551 people in Pennsylvania suffered from infection with *Cryptosporidium,* and then in two separate outbreaks in Oregon in February and May of 1992, another 3,000 or more individuals ingested the parasite. Probably one of the most disturbing aspects of this news is that it has been estimated that 27 percent of raw water sources in both pristine and polluted water samples across the United States contain *Cryptosporidium* oocysts, or the dormant stage of the protozoa. It should be noted that the Centers for Disease Control (CDC) does not give much credence to oocyst estimates because of the difficulty of getting the data. Moreover, neither the viability nor the attack rate of oocysts on the general public is known. In the February outbreak in Oregon, oocyst levels were low and the attack rate less than 5 percent, far lower than places with oocyst levels ten times greater.

The other well-known protozoan parasite is *Giardia lamblia.* In 1912, there were 123 cases of giardiasis in California, Idaho, Nebraska, and Pennsylvania. The CDC believes that waterborne disease outbreaks are probably under-reported and under-recognized, but the extent is not known. The states with the most outbreak reports may not necessarily be the states with the most outbreaks. In addition, community water systems are more likely to be recognized as sources of outbreaks than private or individual systems. Acute disease is more likely to be reported than chronic, low-level exposure to a pathogen or chemical.

Cryptosporidium is resistant to chlorine disinfection and Giardia requires consistent and adequate levels of disinfection to be effective. Ozone treatment proves effective against *Cryptosporidium* but is too costly for large municipal systems. The only really effective treatment comes from good filtration and protecting the water supply at the source. At least one study cited by the CDC suggests that appreciable numbers of people, between occasions of larger outbreaks, get diarrheal illness with the consumption of water that meets current water quality standards.

TOXIC POLLUTION

In the 1950s a television commercial promoted the idea that "living better through chemistry" made America great. Since that time, advances in chemistry have produced marvelous space-age products, new synthetic materials, semiconductors, and a plethora of other products. Roughly 60,000 kinds of chemicals are manufactured yearly. Each chemical eventually enters the environment and may remain as the same compound for hundreds of years, or degrade into other compounds, which themselves can further degrade or remain in the environment. The residence time before a chemical compound finally degrades to natural compounds or elements will vary greatly. During this time, the chemicals enter human, animal, and plant life either intentionally or through indirect paths. Tracking chemical products through their cyclic flux in biotic and abiotic processes primarily comes from the concerns for human health, alterations to nature, and effects that alter the earth's ability to support life.

Harmful chemicals conjure up for most people toxic waste from industrial processes. Indeed, toxic waste released during manufacturing should be of concern. But toxic materials are also intentionally produced: they are emitted as a product. In addition, some of the toxic materials are not products of modern, advanced chemistry, but have been with us for a long time, such as lead or arsenic or asbestos. The intentional use of chemicals for household and commercial use that end in municipal landfills or industrial landfills can be as significant a problem as industrial waste. Surprisingly, some municipal landfills may be as toxic as industrial landfills.

Texas A&M University scientists examined leachate and groundwater from published data between 1979 and 1988,[7] covering nineteen municipal solid-waste landfills and thirty-nine industrial- and mixed-waste landfills. While identification, classification, and comparison of waste and chemicals has many procedural problems, the researchers nevertheless found some results surprising. In particular, of thirty-nine chemicals detected at both municipal and industrial landfills, nineteen were found at a higher concentration in the municipal landfills than in the industrial landfills. One reason is that some chemicals, like isophorone, an EPA-classified carcinogen, is used in lacquers, coatings, inks, pesticides, and photographic supplies. This product is widely used in both industrial and commercial products. Consequently, the leachate levels at some municipal landfills sometimes exceed those at commercial landfills.

Perhaps the most widespread exposure to chemicals of people, animals, and plants comes from pesticide application. In 1990, about 2.5 million tons of pesticides were applied worldwide. In the United States, 600 types of pesticides amounting to 500,000 tons are applied annually.[8] Pesticides have a single purpose: to kill unwanted organisms. In achieving this goal, chemical pesticides also harm, intentionally or indirectly, other living creatures, including humans.

Many harms to humans from certain pesticides are well known, including the following:

- phenoxyherbicides cause soft-tissue sarcoma, stomach and colon cancer, and teratogenesis;
- herbicides in the family of triazines and arsencials lead to ovarian cancer;
- carbonates produce chromosome defects and sperm abnormalities;
- organochlorines like DDT and chlordane lead to brain and liver cancer, chromosome defects, high cholesterol and triglyceride levels, and disruption of nerve function leading to tremors and muscular weakness.

Less well known is that pesticides not only can lead to cancer or disruption of the nervous system, but increasing evidence suggests that pesticides can suppress the immune system. Scientifically controlled experiments suggest that organochlorine, organophosphate, carbamate, and metallic pesticides induce immunotoxicity. Yet other recent studies appear to contradict this conclusion. Until more research has been completed with a full evaluation of all the studies, doubt remains over the exact relationship between pesticides and immunotoxicity.

Pesticides harm life by design. Yet most pesticides do not kill the intended target, be it an insecticide against insects or a herbicide against weeds, partly because the pesticide never reaches its target. Another reason is that pests build up resistance to chemicals: in 1955 about thirty or forty species were resistant to pesticides, but by 1988 the number of resistant species totaled over five hundred. Worse, pesticides often harm useful species, such as predators of the pests. Even when a pesticide is "guaranteed harmless" to helpful insects and plants, indirect effects still can cause more harm to the "good" species than to the "bad." Finally, pesticides harm humans—current debate is simply over the kind and the magnitude of the harm. The ubiquitous and diverse array of chemicals released into the environment and to which humans are exposed, coupled with the difficulty in conducting epidemiological studies, makes it very hard to be specific and give scientifically infallible proof.

SCIENCE, RELIGION, AND ENVIRONMENT: A SCIENTIST'S REFLECTION

Environmental facts have become a familiar staple in our common knowledge about the world. The previous sections reviewed the loss of species, the emissions from fossil fuel, water that is unclean, and the depletion of global resources. The current debate about what is real and what is exaggeration tends to overlook the acquisition of those facts in two ways.

First, scientists are often denigrated because of uncertainties in knowledge and the debates within the science regarding the sometimes conflicting data (as in the pesticide/immunotoxicity relation described previously). Rather than denigrate, we should exalt the human challenge to construct knowledge, a task that will never be complete. What we know has come at a human cost: ecologists toil to get the best information they can. Scientists use ingenuity, dedication, and plain sweat and tears to get the data that can be put aside so easily by politicians and profit seekers. Like everyone, scientists make mistakes. Yet it is the struggle, the hardship, the wish to get it right that gives us the best information available.

Second, another issue has emerged about environmental sciences recently concerning environmental organizations. We have been told that environmentalists and ecologists do not extol the success of the last quarter century or so. Perhaps this is true. The Clean Air Act, the Clean Water Act, and the Endangered Species Act have worked. Yet some would use this against us. They would claim that all the problems are solved. If environmental groups counter that we have not gotten far enough, that we need the reauthorization of these acts, then a cry often comes that this is simply a "New Age" agenda.

Our response should be that we are still learning about the environment. What if we told the real message, the message that may be just too hard to bear? We will never cease to require resolve and vigilance, for we will always have environmental problems. The reason is simple: when it comes to problems embedded in nature and complex social systems, we will never have a final solution. This is not because nature is capricious but because our solutions today tend to become the problems of tomorrow. That is why we always need science.

I fear that we do not understand the real meaning of the environmental battleground. This battle is not just about wildlife, species survival, and greenhouse gases. Beyond impacts to nature, there are effects on people. Environmental degradation causes poverty, hunger, disease, social unrest, and violence. Harm to our environment is unequally and liberally distributed upon the low-income and poor, the disenfranchised, members of minorities, and the powerless; it is history repeated in a new form. Do not imagine we will all feel global warming equally. Do not think that the loss of biodiversity and the concomitant loss in medical treatment will be equal for all. Toxic waste will reach some children more than others, depending on which side of the tracks we live on and the color of our neighborhood. And when the harm goes too far, when too many get hurt, do not imagine that these same people who deny it now will not look for a scapegoat in all the old and horrible ways.

Sometimes we misunderstand our own folklore and in so doing miss the essence for the long-view. Take the case of sustainable development. In all the recent documents and words written about it, we struggle to search for examples of what this means. Modern industrialized society forfeits any claim to such notion, so we see examples from indigenous populations, or in some far-away and long-ago ancestors, and in a small number of religious communities such as the Amish. Without a proper view, we receive the wrong message. The Amish, for example, show great effort to sustain their farms, use "gentle" farming methods, and strive to preserve the land for future generations. They consume only what they need and share both natural and human resources. We would say they follow sustainable living. But is this cause or is this consequence? Might we not say that their mission or purpose is to pursue their religious beliefs as a religious community, and that doing so results in sustainable practice?

The environmental concerns of the next decade will start with a recognition of the connections between environmental justice and equitible community development. We begin within ourselves and our own communities, however ill formed and ill defined they may be. Scientists should begin to renew their commitment and responsibility to people. Religious communities that so often extol the common good must make that a priority. Science calls on the community of shared knowledge, but has increasingly hidden behind specialization and made research funds available to more selective, mainstream, highly placed, and well-connected individuals and institutions, with but tokens cast around to others, which gives substance to the deceit of the scientific community.

If we make this call to environmental groups, let us demand more of those who make profits from people and the environment, addressing isseus of salaries, employment, equitable practices, and creating room for nurturing rather than exploitive practices in society. From the government, too, we should demand policies that do not impoverish communities or diminish health care for this or successive generations. People with pens should attend international meetings. This is a prescription for the environment that takes the long view.

NOTES

1. J. A. Edmonds, J. M. Reilly, R. H. Gardiner, and A. Brenkert, *Uncertainty in Future Global Energy Use and Fossil Fuel CO_2-Emissions 1975 to 2075* (Oak Ridge, Tenn.: Carbon Dioxide Information Analysis Center, Oak Ridge National Labratory, 1996).

2. M. Tolba et al. Also, cf. Lester R. Brown et al., "Charting a New Course for Oceans," in *State of the World 1999* (New York and London: W. W. Norton, 1999), p. 87.

3. Alexander Leaf, "Loss of Stratospheric Ozone and Health Effects of Increased Ultraviolet Radiation," in *Critical Condition*, ed. E. Chivian, M. McCally, H. Hu, and A. Haines (Cambridge, Mass.: MIT Press, 1993).

4. UCS, ed., "Fact Sheet: Stratospheric Ozone Depletion," *World Scientists' Briefing Book* (Cambridge, Mass.: Union of Concerned Scientists Press, 1993).

5. World Conservation Monitoring Center, *Global Diversity: Status of the Earth's Living Resources*, ed. Brian Groombridge (London: Chapman & Hall, 1992).

6. V. 42:SS-5, Nov. 1993 (Atlanta: Centers for Disease Control).

7. K. W. Brown and K. C. Donnelly, "An Estimation of the Risk Associated With the Organic Constituents of Hazardous and Municipal Waste Landfill Leachates," in *Hazardous Waste and Hazardous Materials*, vol. 2 of *Conservation and Biodiversity*, ed. Andrew Dobson (Scientific American Library, 1996), pp. 70–71.

8. D. Pimentel, A. Acquay, M. Biltonen, P. Rice, M. Silva, J. Nelson, V. Lipner, S. Giordano, A. Horowitz, and M. D'Amore, "Assessment of Environmental and Economic Impacts of Pesticide Use," in *Environment, Economics, and Ethics*, ed. D. Pimentel and H. Lehman (n.p., 1993), pp. 47–84.

QUESTIONS FOR DISCUSSION

1. Recent studies show that people among different countries are more satisfied with life in relation to their relative level of income rather than on the basis of absolute wealth. Greed begets dissatisfaction, and equity a greater sense that the quality of life is generally good. Does this seem consistent with your own observations? If so, would you suggest that people in a more equitable society are more likely or less likely to seek reduction in energy consumption or other products to reduce global climate change? Can you think of examles to support your case? Any counterexamples?

2. Basic needs for everyone are food, clothing, and shelter; in modern, developed countries, we also would include jobs and health care. What could be added to this list? Does the list differ for people in developing countries? by quantity? by quality? by item? If so, does the difference in the list depend on wealth, distribution of wealth, or other factors? Why might this be important to understand the perception of the environmental crisis?

3. Throughout human history thousands of plants and animals have become extinct. This fact might be unrelated to humans, a simple artifact of the data, or a direct result of human social structure and activities. One part of the argument for protection of species and biodiveristy today rests not on the fact that extinction occurs, but that the rates of extinction have accelerated in the last century. Recent and current human activity does affect the outcome of species survival; that the rates of extinction are increasing cannot be explained as an artifact. Within the most recent human history (the past 1,000 to 5,000 years) and modern times (the past 500 years) a difference in social structure has occurred in a qualitative way, not just technologically. Is this important? For example, what difference would it make to species preservation if agriculture had no commercial value? Would it make sense to develop programs for sustainable development or to preserve biodiversity if it meant con-

tinued exploitation of people? the suppression of women? the violation of human rights? Explain what these connections might mean, and why it is relevant to a discussion of biodiversity and the protection of species.

3

INTERPRETING THE WORLD
The Relationship of Science, Technology, and Belief
Ian Hutchinson

EYES OF SCIENCE, EYES OF FAITH

For at least half a century, and some would say for much longer than that, there has been a popular prejudice that religious faith in general, and the Christian faith in particular,[1] is incompatible with rationality. Although I do not accept this prejudice, there might be some superficial justification for this view. The Bible does seem full of incidents whose claims are easily (not necessarily correctly) attributable to the gullibility of an earlier, unscientific age. It might seem natural that scientists, trained to insist on rational explanation and consistent observation, would be less likely to accept the claims of faith than those in the humanities. However, the opposite is often true, confirmed by recent sociological studies.[2]

A commitment to rationality and religious faith is often found among the giants of science. For example, Johannes Kepler, Isaac Newton, Michael Faraday, and James Clerk Maxwell, to name just a sample from physics, were deeply committed Christians. The well-publicized disputes about origins are hardly sufficient to overshadow the obvious fact that scientists have historically had less difficulty accommodating the intellectual challenges of faith than have, say, humanistic philosophers. There are, perhaps, many reasons for this. What may be broadly termed "postmodernism" has, in recent years, become a predominant philosophy in much of the humanities. One of the tenets of thoroughgoing postmodernism is that all knowledge is political. There is, postmodernists claim, no such thing as objective truth; instead there are competing agendas that determine what will qualify as knowledge. Science is viewed similarly.

Scientists overwhelmingly disagree. This is not because scientists are necessarily all naive realists (or even realists at all), but predominantly because scientists think that there is an objective world "out there." When we do science we feel that, far from being free to construct what will count as knowledge how we like, we are faced with a stubborn, hard, self-existing world—a world that is what it is, not necessarily what we would want it to be. Scientific understanding, and I mean here the natural sciences, is mined from the hard rock of a world probed by careful measurement and disciplined, mathematical thought. Scientists think that what they and their predecessors have discovered is true knowledge about the way things are. We admit that the knowledge is not perfect, and may be refined as more is discovered, but it is not a mere social construct.

I find here a striking parallel with my Christian faith. God is a reality "out there," God who is what he is, not necessarily what we would want him to be. Christians do not think that they have all the truth, but we also don't think that our faith is a mere social construct. This is not to deny that there are differences between scientific and religious knowledge both in methods and substance. Science is by choice and method an impersonal description of the world, with purpose ruled out from consideration *ab initio*. By contrast, religious faith focuses on the personal and purposeful questions of life. What counts as evidence and demonstration in these two spheres is often very different. Despite all these differences, I find that in the modern academy my science and my faith seem to have more in common with each other than they do with the many swirling intellectual fashions. I suspect that this is part of the explanation for an apparently greater affinity for religious faith to be found among scientists than among nonscientist intellectuals.

There is also much that science and Christianity have in common concerning creation—and a cogent case can be made that sees Christianity as the mental ground from which modern science grew.[3] Johannes Kepler, for example, discovered in 1605 that the planetary orbits follow ellipses, not circles as had been held for millennia on the basis of philosophical dogma. This insight opened the way for Newton and modern physics. It has been said that Kepler's deductions were "the first natural laws in the modern sense: precise, verifiable statements about universal phenomena . . . expressed in mathematical terms."[4] The same Kepler exclaimed, "O God, I am thinking your thoughts after you." He wrote of his intense desire to know, "can I find God, whom I almost touch with my hands when I contemplate the universe, also in my own self?"[5] The awe before the grandeur of creation, which finds expression throughout the Bible, is much the same as the wonder that is evoked by our scientific discoveries of the inexpressibly complex and magnificent universe. The bestsellers of modern cosmology evoke the psalmist's cry, "When I look at thy heavens, the work of thy fingers, the moon and the stars which thou hast established; what is man that thou art mindful of him?" (Ps. 8:3, 4).

Yet, there are endless examples of scientists who subscribe to the view that religious faith has been debunked by science. Their outlook remains a powerful force. Even scientists who acknowledge the importance of faith, and call for religious leaders to join in seeking to solve the global environmental challenges, often fail to give due respect to the authority of religious doctrine and tradition. While it may be true that preachers and pastors exert influence and authority over congregations (and hence over society), what authority they do exert is a consequence of their faithfulness and not some self-sustaining, blank-check authority that can be expended. Therefore, a religious response to threats to creation must be grounded in the teachings of faith. Congregations will not follow a lead that is contrary to, or even disconnected from, their faith.

A corresponding lack of appreciation by Christians of science and its methodology is also a cause for concern. There is, of course, the extreme fundamentalism that rejects a scientific understanding of natural history in favor of a story that is more amenable to a literalistic interpretation of the Bible. This position is well known, powerful, yet often adopted with inconsistency. Its practitioners often embrace all too readily the technological fruits of scientific knowledge, while at the same time rejecting the knowledge itself. Despite the undoubted concern and goodwill of many such fundamentalists, their approach debilitates any serious attempt to grapple with the global environmental crisis because it reflects a refusal to accept the world as it really is.

The different perspectives of science and faith are crucial and complementary when we go beyond thinking about what creation is, to thinking about what to do with it. It is here that we need both the critical, down-to-earth, factual perspective that science brings and the spiritual, personal, moral perspective of our faith. Either perspective, on its own, finds a lack of resources that prevents it from providing a balanced judgment on which to base human action.

POPULATION AND CONSUMPTION: SCIENCE'S VIEW AND SCIENCE'S ROLE

It is easy to be overwhelmed by the complexity of current ecological and environmental challenges—pollution, its origins in irresponsibility or neglect, ozone depletion, global climate change, acid rain, the ecological stress in northern forests, and human impact on the rainforest habitats. Our hearts sink at the impossible task of documenting and perhaps preserving even a small fraction of the biodiversity at risk. The complexity of the problems is very great, as great as creation itself. Yet it seems that we tend to focus, rather perversely, on this complexity rather than on the very simple underlying causes of environmental degradation: human population and human consumption. No dispassionate assessment of the situation from a scientific point of view could fail to recognize this as the basic driving factor behind most of the steady environmental damage.[6]

First we need to recognize religion's responsibility in the frequent obfuscation of this point. Lynn White's charge that Christianity bears responsibility for the abuse of creation, because of its teaching that nature is separate from God and that mankind is separate from the rest of nature and rightly master of it, is not my main concern. Indeed, all too frequently religious people are reticent to acknowledge the population problem because they think that to do so would undermine fundamental ethical principles: the sanctity of human life and many derivative moral teachings. This is a justified concern, but it seems folly to avoid the main issue because of discomfort with its possible implications, and focus on peripheral questions. Christianity and other religions need to tackle one of the most urgent theological challenges of the day: how to value human life and activity within the context of a "full earth."[7] Only in that context can we become comfortable with addressing the underlying problems of our impact on creation.

The environmental impact per person is diverse and hard to quantify. One critical measurement of impact is the energy consumption per capita. There is historically a very strong correlation between the overall material consumption of a society and its energy consumption. Roughly speaking, the world average energy consumption per person is one kilowatt. This total is made up of a whole variety of different types of consumption: transportation, lighting, manufacturing, agriculture, heating, and so on. A way to get a feel for its magnitude is to say that it is equivalent to the energy that would be used if each person in the world kept a domestic electric space heater operating round the clock. In North America, by contrast, the per capita energy consumption is nearly ten times the world average and in the other major industrialized nations, five times the average. While in the poorest nations average consumption is about one-tenth of a kilowatt. Following this model, it is inconceivable that the whole present world population would be sustainable if all had the level of consumption typical of the industrialized nations. The impact per capita would be roughly five times what it is now.

Although conservation and other efficiencies could lower consumption in the industrial countries, it is important to realize that the potential for conservation is limited. A persuasive case can therefore be made that we are already past the sustainable world population, living on environmental capital, and avoiding even more drastic consequences only because most of the world's population lives in more or less abject poverty. Of course, energy consumption is not the whole story. It is probably the case that the environmental impact per person does not grow as fast as energy consumption in moving toward technological development. However, this fact cuts both ways: it allows improvement in the developing world without as much increase in the environmental stress, but it means that any reduction in energy usage by the industrialized nations may not yield as much reduction in environmental damage as we might have hoped. Meanwhile the population will have doubled again to ten billion by 2050. Even if by a tremendous effort of technological innovation and social change we manage to reduce our environmental impact by then, we will have done no better than stand still in our total impact on the earth's resources.

Science and technology are, in a certain sense, implicated as a cause of the problems we now face. When the media discuss the role of science and technology in its impact on creation, most commonly they focus on problems such as the toxic wastes left by technological processes. This focus tends to be on the *failures* of science and its technological applications, or else on the obviously deleterious side effects. In the present context, however, it becomes clear that it is the *successes* of technology that are the really serious problem for the earth. The human population has grown dramatically precisely because of science's successes. Improvements in health care and sanitation, made possible by our scientific understanding of the causes of disease, are the most important factor underlying the reduction in mortality and consequent population growth. Our development of engineering and agricultural productivity based on the physical and biological sciences has enabled us to maintain that growth far beyond what would once have led to mass starvation. Ironically, the advances that seem most unequivocally beneficial to humankind are those most responsible for the unchecked population growth and resulting environmental impact. Add to that the ability that technology places in our hands to shape our world, and we realize that the disillusionment with science and technology that characterizes much of present academic debate is quite understandable. Understandable—but, if taken to extremes, potentially misguided—to this point we will return.

THE END OF THE BIG FIX

One respect in which present disillusionment with science and technology is not misguided is the abandonment of the "endless frontier" mentality. For much of this century, an underlying vision has been of constant improvement in material welfare driven by technological innovation. There was an implicit belief, dominating society's expectation, that all material wants could and would eventually be met by the continuous expansion of scientific knowledge into an endless frontier, and by the resulting technological expansion. Even when the environmental impact of our expanding technological capabilities began to become significant, the Pavlovian reaction was automatic: to look for a technological fix for each problem as it arose. Are we short of energy resources? Invent another energy technology. Is food scarce? Improve the productivity of agriculture through fertilizers. Are we making too much waste? Find a way to recycle the waste. Does the new technology have problems of its own? Bring in a fix for that problem. The reaction to each problem, whether caused by human want or by the consequences of earlier technological developments, was to look for the technological fix. Finally, the late twentieth century seems set to reject this faith in the technological fix, and not a moment too soon.

It is not initially obvious that the endless frontier mentality is doomed to failure. What determines whether a strategy of one technological fix chasing the problems of the previous one will work is a question of convergence or divergence. One could imagine a situation in which each succeeding technological fix raised fewer problems than its predecessor. If so, then the sequence might rapidly converge on a stable situation where things were "fixed" and the endless frontier mentality would have worked. Alternatively, it might happen that each succeeding fix introduces even bigger problems than the previous one. In that case the sequence of problems "diverges" and we are sooner or later overwhelmed by the result. It looks as if, globally, we are slightly in the second situation: diverging.

A similar consideration was brought to our attention during the consultation by Harvard astronomer and historian of science Owen Gingerich. He referred to a simple mathematical model that was published in 1960[8] to describe the dynamics of a population in a situation where cooperation between its members enables a species to improve its rate of survival as its population increases. Such is plausibly the case for the human population. Elementary considerations lead to a mathematical equation governing the population size. The equation has the property that at a particular finite time its solution becomes infinite. The meaning of this mathematical divergence is that within a limited time, any population governed by this equation will become so large that a catastrophe will occur that causes the underlying assumptions of the model to break down. In the context of human population, this catastrophe was predicted, by fitting the model to the historic population data, to occur in the year 2026. The authors whimsically referred to this moment at which the solution becomes infinite as "Doomsday." Of course, many debatable assumptions go into applying this model to human population. However, the sobering fact is that even today, thirty-five years later, and more than halfway to the predicted doomsday, the equation derived is tracking the actual growth of the population to within two years.

Regardless of the details of specific models, even if the technological solutions are not diverging, even if the doomsday equation is not an accurate model of the population, it is clear that technology cannot keep pace with the present human expectations for continual increase in material possessions. It is this nonscientific factor that we ought, on the basis of our religious teaching, have been able to anticipate. There ought never to have been any doubt to a Christian that the potential for human greed would outstrip the ability of technology to provide for it. Let us determine to adopt once and for all the maxim that there is no technological fix for the environment. This does not mean that we should abandon efforts to mitigate environmental problems by technological means. On the contrary, it seems likely that by deliberate choice of technology we can determine whether we are on a converging or diverging sequence. Efforts to develop and adopt more benign technologies in the whole spectrum of human activities are vital and should be supported, although with an emphasis on long-term consequential considerations. These will not, by themselves, overcome the underlying problems of too many people wanting too many things. Technological efforts should not distract us, therefore, from addressing the main problems of population and consumption.

Recognizing that there is no technological fix for the environment does not automatically lead to a repudiation of the truth claims of science. We do need to counterbalance the excessive expectations of technological progress. We need to recognize that technological progress, based on science, cannot solve the majority of our problems because those problems are human, not technical. This realization does not reflect the failure of science in describing the natural world. Rather, it reflects our flawed hopes for the application of science, and perhaps the overoptimism of scientists in arguing the case for society's support of their research. It does not change the trustworthiness of our well-established scientific understanding of nature, an area in which there is potential for a disconnect between what scientists think and postmodernism. There is among many scientists an openness to reconsider the merits of technology versus humanity and to refocus technological expectations into an altogether more sustainable path. This is reflected at my own institution, MIT, in a recent emphasis on educating students concerning the context of engineering and science within large complex societal systems and concerning the human factors of engineering applications.

A SCIENTIST'S VIEW ON THE
HUMANITIES AND ARTS

When scientists like me emphasize the inability of science and technology to fix the problems of creation, because those problems are primarily human, we naturally are concerned with what the other key disciplines will do with the challenge. We want to work with those in these other arenas to see a holistic response. A large part of the value of the conversation from which this book arises is the chance to hear others discuss their expertise and comment on our own disciplines. If we accept the assessment that the underlying cause of much of the environmental danger we now face is a combination of population and consumption, then it seems that some obvious issues arise for various disciplines.

Economics and politics, for example, seem to be dominated by the notion that growth is inherently good. "Expansion" of the economy *is*, almost by definition, good; "contraction" or "recession" is bad. Yet movement towards a sustainable economy, if our diagnosis is correct, absolutely requires a contraction in the total consumption. This may happen by reduction in per capita consumption or by reduction in the number of people; either way, we are asking for the exact opposite of what most economists seem to honor. I am usually filled with foreboding when I listen to the economists pursue their normal course, because it seems so counter to the long-term good of creation and of humanity. It was refreshing to hear, during these conversations, economist Neva Goodwin's advocacy of a development toward a globally "middle class" lifestyle. Her point was that perhaps 1.1 billion of the world's population are the global poor, about 1.1 billion (the industrialized nations) are the global rich, and the rest are the middle class. Expressed in terms of lifestyle, take travel for example: the poor walk; the middle classes cycle or bus; the rich take a car or airplane. She says both poor and rich should be developing toward that middle-class lifestyle, arguably a more healthy, happy, and fulfilling standard. Goodwin cites a survey indicating that the peak of Americans' satisfaction with their life was in 1957, when we had far less in the way of material prosperity than today.

Refreshing as that is, it still seems far away from the world of most economists. It sounds contrary to the guiding principle of maximizing wealth by which most economists think that people and nations by nature decide their actions. It stands in direct challenge to the competitive capitalism that for many is a more cherished faith than any religion. It does so at a time when capitalism has vanquished its communist challenge, making its adoptive parent, America, the undisputed superpower and international competition seems to push inexorably toward greater consumption and growth. Our consumptive Western lifestyle leads us to dependency on foreign oil and hence to increasing weakness in relationship with oil-producing nations. Our response is mostly not to moderate our lifestyle's demands. Instead, it is to seek economic and military power to ensure that the channels of supply stay open.

Military consumption itself is one of the worst polluters of our environment. Military conflicts may lead directly to obvious environmental calamities, such as the oil fires of Kuwait. More insidiously, the consumption at home that supports military power has been characterized by the most flagrant disregard for the consequent environmental pollution. The chemical spills at military bases by armed forces bent on meeting their own mission at all costs, the chemical and radioactive contamination at the arms factories— these are just beginning to be obvious to everybody. Still, we don't seem to have the political will to stop the damage that they are doing and to clean up the contamination we already have. More often than not in the press of political decisions, external threats are considered justification for the plants and bases continuing their damaging activities. In the face of such pressures, calls for a development toward lower-impact technology as a lifestyle choice are liable to sound like utopian dreams more than practical strategies. A transformation is required if we are to move in an orderly way toward the less consumptive future we know is inevitable for a global politics of peace and stability.

Neva Goodwin brought us another thought concerning nonscientific disciplines, and especially the arts, which struck a deep chord. The way she put it is this. We have two education systems in this country and each of them spends about 150 billion dollars per year. One is the system of formal education: schools, colleges, and so on. The other is advertising. Our formal education system has many objectives and many messages. Advertising has one message: "Consume." We have given advertising more than just the license to drum out this message ten minutes of every TV hour. We have given it the largest single influence over the artistic and literary content of our programming in virtually all of broadcasting. Sponsors can shape what we see and hear with their underlying theme. They show us, and hence validate in our minds, the happy consumers they want us all to be. Scientists often have been criticized for being too captive to the military-industrial complex. But the cultural leaders are often captive, too, in their own way, to the forces of consumerism that maintain the media and mold their message.

SCIENCE AND FAITH FACE THE FUTURE

That the natural creation suffers because of human sin is a conclusion central to Christian theology. Paul the Apostle writes, "the creation was subject to futility" and "the creation waits with eager longing for the revealing of the sons of God"(Rom. 8:19–22). While many people have thought of this "suffering creation" as a quaint or poetic fancy, a hard-nosed scientific analysis of the state of nature leads us to the same conclusion but through a different meatphor. Creation is suffering in all sorts of ecologically damaging ways due to the activities of humankind. This suffering of creation is not something that can be fixed by technology. Although technology has given us the ability to influence creation with unprecedented power, it also extends damaging influences that come from human desires within individuals and society. That the creation suffers because of sin illustrates a remarkable convergence of religious and scientific viewpoints on the state of creation that is sobering for scientists and for people of faith. Scientists are starting to take more seriously biblical teaching on this point. Christians need to reconsider the extent to which they have discounted some of their faith's teachings which need to be re-emphasized for creation's sake.

Consider, for example, our first issue of consumption. The Bible is full of instruction that could become a key resource for a new outlook.[9] Even something so elementary as the ten commandments discourage current levels of consumerism in industrialized society. Covetousness, universally condemned, is the basis of modern advertising and consumerism. Many religious traditions, not least of which are the Jewish and Christian, reject the vision of an ever expanding economy, substituing an ethic that often sees refraining from economic activity as the compelling moral dynamic. The teachings about Sabbath and Jubilee that are found in Leviticus (25:1–24) are untapped resources for this purpose. If anything, American society continues to devalue and de-emphasize sabbath observance, a symbolic trend that must be reversed. A sabbath rest for the benefit of creation is as vital for the recovery of people as for that of our planet. These observations illustrate the many theological and religious resources available to address the question of consumption. These resources can and must become a spiritual basis for a change in lifestyle and material expectations in the industrialized countries, leading to a more benign human impact on the planet. The spiritual commitments that Christians as well as people in other faith communities already acknowledge call us to a more thoughtful lifestyle.

Consider, for example, our second issue, that of population. Since having too many people is the underlying problem, what are the religious resources to address the question of a "full" earth, remembering the Genesis command (1:28) to fill it? Christians have a lot to reconsider in this area. On the face of it, biblical teachings tend to be in the direction of encouraging procreation, viewing population growth as a good, which it undoubtedly was when the Bible was written. Moreover, some Christian traditions have overlaid additional doctrines such as a prohibition of artificial birth control on top of biblical instructions. Some commentators and theologians seek to redefine biblical teachings concerning procreation and sexuality as purely contingent based on the pragmatic needs of the society: In earlier societies a high rate of procreation was necessary to maximize the number of children born. Others, including this author, find such an argument simplistic. Sexuality, not merely a matter of procreation and pleasure, is integral to what it means to be human. Sexual moral teaching is expressed in terms that leave no doubt that it is to be taken not merely as pragmatism but as a reflection of reality and of God's will, whether dealing with gender identity and sexual practice, adultery, fornication, and so on. Population issues today demand that Christians as well as all people reconsider what is truly fundamental and what is a matter of interpretation in their traditions.

The need exists for a more constructive and proactive theological position concerning population, one that Christians can recognize clearly as true to the fundamentals of their faith. Perhaps the idea that sins are often a perversion of the good gifts and commands of God provides a way forward. Gluttony, for example, is an excess of something that is inherently a good gift. Is it possible, I wonder, that we shall come to see excessive procreation as an imbalanced perversion of the command to "fill the earth"?

Does hope that we can reverse consumptive economic desire, or control world population through deliberate decisions about our procreation seem fansical? Perhaps. I find it hard to conceive how the entrenched opinions and attitudes that have brought us to the present situation can be reversed in the manner it seems that they must be if we are to avoid a catastrophe. Still, this is not a counsel of despair. Both faith and science see a future. An analysis which reveals the poverty of human ability to solve the problems we face also sends me back to my theological foundations: Salvation, whether spiritual or ecological, is not within human power, but with God all things are possible (Matt. 19:26).

There is some comfort from science, small though it may be. It is to recall the remarkable adaptability of life to its circumstances, and the resilience of life, as a whole, to the vicissitudes of this planet's experiences. Life on earth will continue despite what humans may do to the environment. What is not so clear is whether, and in what manner, human life will continue. If we humans exhaust the resources on which we depend for our food and sustenance, there will be a reckoning for our species that will parallel the decimation we have wrought on other animals. If we fill our world with the wastes of our exorbitant consumption, we will have to live in those wastes and suffer the disease and degradation they will bring. But there will arise a new balance within the biosphere, one way or the other, as life on earth adjusts to the result. The natural creation, though precious, is not a static or precarious creature to be destroyed outright by our profligacy. Life will continue, with or without us. And perhaps, just perhaps, our own adaptability will enable us to be a part of that new balance.

Neither of these perspectives promote passive acceptance of whatever will come. It is a Christian heresy to adopt a fatalistic attitude, and merely wait in the hope of the Second Coming. This is the error of the early Thessalonian believers who waited idly for the Lord, whom Paul admonished to work (2 Thess. 3:6–13). Christian hope looks for Christ's coming, but in the meantime counsels work for the benefit of all. And for a scientist, recognizing life's resilience does not deny the real loss of so much beauty and abundance in the creation, which will occur if we fail to respond to the present challenge.

We must work, believer and scientist, respecting our different sources of authority, to promote policies that will save creation from the worst that may befall—recognizing, though, that we may already be past the point where major dislocation of society is eventually unavoidable. If that is so, then the urgency is also to develop theology and technology that will enable us to deal with the over-full earth and its consequences. What will human ethics look like in a situation in which it is obvious that the existence of too many people has brought about the downfall of all our hopes? How then will we interpret the sanctity of human life? And what will be the point of ever more technologically advanced methods to prolong human life, in a situation where much of the human population is dying for lack of the barest natural resources? Perhaps these are the questions that will be faced by our children and grandchildren. Perhaps we need to start now to give answers to them that will work practically.

NOTES

1. I am a Christian and can speak with any serious understanding only about the Christian faith. So when what I write emphasizes Christianity, it is not intended as a snub to other religions, but a recognition that they deserve a more knowledgeable spokesman than I am.

2. Robert Wuthnow, *The Struggle for America's Soul* (Grand Rapids: Eerdmans, 1989), p. 146.

3. E.g., Stanley L. Laki, *The Road of Science and the Ways to God* (Chicago: University of Chicago Press, 1978).

4. Arthur Koestler, *The Sleepwalkers* (Harmondsworth, England: Pelican, 1968), p. 318.

5. Johannes Kepler, *Gesammelte Werke*, eds. W. v. Dyke and Max Caspar, vol. 27, p. 79, cited by Koestler, in *The Sleepwalkers*.

6. There was a rather remarkable unanimity among the scientists at the consultation that excessive population is the underlying cause of the present global environmental problems.

7. Ian H. Hutchinson, "Faith's Failure of Nerve," *Crosscurrents* 40 (1990): 213.

8. H. von Foerster, P. M. Mora, and L. W. Amiot, *Science* 132 (1960): 1291.

9. See, for example, Ronald J. Sider, *Rich Christians in an Age of Hunger* (Illinois: Intervarsity Press, 1977).

QUESTIONS FOR DISCUSSION

1. Is it possible for science and religious faith to be full partners in the enterprise of environmentalism without compromising their internal authority?

2. Are we convinced that human population is already at the point of exceeding the sustainable capacity of the ecosystem and, if so, what religious resources are there to address this problem?

3. Is there any realistic hope that an environmental catastrophe that transforms human life on earth can be avoided?

4

DENYING THE EVIDENCE
Science and the Human Prospect
Timothy C. Weiskel

THE EVIDENCE FROM THE NATURAL SCIENCES

T he evidence from the natural sciences is by now pretty clear. Humankind is facing major adjustments and perhaps dramatic reversals in the coming decades as the cumulative affects of resource constraints, population growth, and global environmental change begin to register in our daily lives.

What used to be an occasional warning from a lonely prophetic figure like Harrison Brown, Paul Ehrlich, Garrett Hardin, Lester Brown, or Herman Daly has now become a veritable chorus of voices repeating largely the same basic theme: if human societies do not change their patterns of energy use, material consumption, and reproductive behavior, life for many humans and other species as well in the twenty-first century is likely to be nasty, brutish, and short.[1] In 1992 a group of over one hundred Nobel Laureates reiterated this message in a document called "World Scientists' Warning to Humanity," declaring quite plainly that

> human beings and the natural world are on a collision course. Human activities inflict harsh and often irreversible damage on

both the environment and on our critical resources. If not checked, many of our current practices put at serious risk the future that we wish for human society and the plant and animal kingdoms, and may so alter the living world that it will be unable to sustain life in the manner that we know. Fundamental changes are urgent if we are to avoid the collision our present course will bring about.[2]

The Nobel Laureates were not alone in the scientific community to voice concern. In February 1992 the Royal Society of Great Britain and the National Academy of Sciences issued a common statement reflecting their anxiety about present trends of human development and environmental transformation.[3] Addressing themselves specifically to those who think that "thanks to science" humankind can overcome the constraints of the natural systems in which our societies are imbedded, these sober scientists issued a sober reminder that technological optimism may be misplaced.

Scientific and technological innovations, such as in agriculture, have been able to overcome many pessimistic predictions about resource constraints affecting human welfare. Nevertheless, the present patterns of human activity accentuated by population growth should make even those most optimistic about future scientific progress pause and reconsider the wisdom of ignoring these threats to our planet. Unrestrained resource consumption for energy production and other uses, especially if the developing world strives to achieve living standards based on the same levels of consumption as the developed world, could lead to catastrophic outcomes for the global environment.[4]

It is hard to imagine a more stark presentation of the crisis. Terms like "irreversible damage" and "catastrophic" are not normally employed in the staid vocabulary of professional scientists. One can only assume that they have been moved to such extreme expression by the gravity of the situation at hand. However, despite these repeated warnings it does not appear that the public at large is gripped by a sense of crisis or convinced that radically different forms of behavior are required of them in the immediate future.

While the United Nations Conference on Environment and Development (UNCED), known as the "Earth Summit," succeeded in 1992 in drawing up an impressive list of concerns and ambitious proposals for action on a number of important environmental issues, it appears that little has been done since then to reverse worrisome global trends of deforestation, desertification, soil loss, carbon consumption, and human population growth. Industrial countries are openly conceding that they are not likely to meet the agreed targets of reducing carbon consumption to 1990 levels by the year 2000, and without substantial progress in that realm it seems unrealistic to expect developing countries to bear the brunt of global carbon constraints while all parties seem to agree it would be a good idea. Nearly five years after the UNCED gathering in Rio de Janeiro, a sense of discouragement was palpable among global environmental leaders. A Reuters reporter captured the mood at the conclusion of a the recent World Conservation Conference in a brief report in October 1996:

> Maurice Strong, . . . Secretary-General of the United Nations Conference on Environment and Development four years ago, told reporters that despite lofty promises made in Rio de Janeiro, the developed world was reneging on its commitments. During a news conference after a panel discussion at the World Conservation Congress, a ten-day gathering of 2,000 environmental specialists, Strong said the global environment was still deteriorating. "We have not made the fundamental change of course that the Rio [Conference] indicated was absolutely essential if we are going to have a sustainable future in the twenty-first century," Strong said.[5]

TROUBLING QUESTIONS FOR THE SOCIAL SCIENCES

This state of affairs presents social scientists with major problems of explanation. The basic question is simply this: What accounts for this massive and pervasive social somnolence?

Other questions cascade forward from this basic puzzle. How

can modern society have become so systematically ignorant of or indifferent toward the catastrophic fate that surely awaits it? How could we have been so thoroughly anesthetized to our objective condition? Have any other societies ever faced parallel circumstances? What was their history of perception and reaction to similar crises? How can we have drifted into such a state of collective amnesia and denial? Can contemporary societies hope to learn anything from the ecological dynamics surrounding the growth and subsequent collapse of former civilizations in time to avert similar forms of catastrophe?

These are, admittedly, big questions, ones rarely asked by professional social scientists in these days of controlled microresearch and heightened academic specialization. Yet unless these "macro" questions are focused upon and answered with clear analysis, widespread debate, and collective understanding, social scientists will have little to contribute to preserving the human prospect in the years and decades to come.

Perhaps the first question to pose ourselves is this: How is it that professional social scientists could lose sight of these big issues? There is no doubt that for several decades in the twentieth century—until perhaps the seminal work of Fernand Braudel—doing research on questions of large-scale social change and writing "Grand History" to account for society-wide delusions was considered bad form for a professional social scientist.[6]

This had not always been so. A century ago Grand History was still a flourishing pastime. It seemed especially popular among the elite classes of the reigning imperial powers of nineteenth-century Europe. Indeed, much of modern social science traces its foundation to the early attempts at grand sociohistorical synthesis that sought to discover the origins of social forms and customs from kinship, to marriage, to religion or the state. In accord with the overarching metaphor of evolution which dominated nineteenth-century thought, nineteenth-century scholars of social form sought to account for human history in one or another unilinear scheme of progressive transformation. Fustel de Coulanges, Lewis Henry Morgan, Karl Marx, Frederick Engels, Henry Sumner Maine, and

Johann Jakob Bachofen all elaborated histories predicated on a succession of putative "stages" through which they thought humankind had developed to its present state.[7]

The trouble with these early, ingenious, and intricate schemes was that they were largely conjectural. Apart form the allusions to classical texts and the odd reference to travelers' accounts, evidence for the grand assertions of these armchair theorists was scanty. They had, in effect, engaged in the writing of "pseudohistories," the specifics of which had far more to do with the particular social theories that each thinker was seeking to forward than they did with any verifiable circumstances in the remote or recent past.

Early twentieth-century social science abandoned the historical mode of explanation precisely in order to distance itself from the embarrassing excesses of conjectural pseudohistory. A few masterful European intellects continued to pen broad historical narratives, working feverishly to write what might be called "total" or "totalizing" histories of the world. Oswald Spengler's *The Decline of the West* (1926–28) and Arnold J. Toynbee's magisterial twelve-volume *A Study of History* (1934–61) were perhaps the two most famous attempts to try to integrate the newly available historical evidence of the twentieth century within an overarching scheme of historical interpretation. The scope and grandeur were on the scale of the work of Edward Gibbon (1737–74) a century and a half earlier in *The History of the Decline and Fall of the Roman Empire,* and their sweep of historical generalization was every bit as grand even if their data was understandably more massive and complex.[8]

While these works and other big surveys—like that of the history of philosophic thought by Will and Ariel Durant[9]—were fascinating reading for the general public, professional historians and social scientists generally avoided them. Professionals preferred instead to undertake more precise and delimited research monographs on subjects where the historical documentation or social data could be more adequately "controlled." Grand History—if engaged in at all—was something to be done in private, on one's own time, or perhaps at the end of a career when one's colleagues might forgive a dottering mind a wistful glance over the shoulder at the big picture.

Indeed, in the feverish specialization that characterized American academe during the postwar boom of economic and educational expansion, big questions were studiously avoided. Interdisciplinary work was regarded with suspicion, as if it might detract from both the growing budget and the disciplinary loyalty that was expected within each academic department. As one scholar observed, it was commonly acknowledged that an academic discipline was simply "a group of scholars who had agreed not to ask certain embarrassing questions about key assumptions."[10] In this manner, the big questions were shunned. Instead, individuals advanced their academic careers through hyperspecialization and honed more and more narrow forms of expertise on particular subjects, "keeping-all-other-things-equal."

THE REFOCUS UPON MACRO-HISTORICAL PROCESS

Although this hyperspecialization of social science has proved dysfunctional for our understanding of our current global circumstance, it still persists. Much of the institutional momentum that drove hyperspecialization and the reward structure that produced disciplinary myopia from the 1950s through the 1980s is still very much with us in the universities of the 1990s. Those who established their careers in this earlier period are now in the process of selecting their professional successors, so it is hardly surprising that powerful forces still persist in working to perpetuate this narrowness of vision.

Nevertheless, countertendencies are emerging as well. For purely intellectual reasons, if not for structural ones, it is now becoming more and more apparent that disciplinary boundaries and the departments that enshrine them often function as a threat to necessary inquiry and productive synthesis. Hence, despite institutional pressures that discourage it, there is growing evidence that social scientists are beginning once again to ask the large questions about macrohistorical and metahistorical processes: How do societies, cultures and civilizations emerge? What enabled past civilizations to flourish? Why did they prove to be so ephemeral—lasting, at most, a few hundred years? Can anything be learned from the sadly repetitive syndromes of growth, expansion, and collapse that have characterized one civilization after another?

Perhaps the urge to answer these questions stems from a mounting sense of precariousness and impending resource decline in our own culture. Or perhaps it is simply that the cumulative evidence, gleaned from decades of painfully detailed archaeological and textual analysis, seems to cry out for an effort to synthesize the newly found material. Whatever the origins for the impulse, it is clear that social scientists are now turning once again with renewed interest and refined methodology to examine processes of metahistorical social transformation.

Two major developments have encouraged the renewed focus on metahistorical processes in recent years: first, the elaboration of laboratory techniques that can be applied to archaeological and historical artifacts; second, the adoption of computer technology for record keeping and data analysis, which has revolutionized the conduct of historically focused social science. These technologies have allowed archaeologists, culture historians, and anthropologists to reexamine a whole range of questions that had for a long time fallen out of intellectual favor.

In particular, new and scientifically meaningful statements now can be made about the circumstances surrounding the emergence, efflorescence, and subsequent collapse of ancient civilizations. As the investigation proceeds the ratio between available data and interpretive generalization shifts, and tentative hypotheses become more and more robust with the tests of more comprehensive sets of data. Macrohistorical questions—those dealing with transformations over long periods—now can be meaningfully addressed. Similarly, metahistorical questions—those dealing with the controlled comparison between civilizations—can be posed with new rigor.

NATURAL SCIENCE, SOCIAL SCIENCE, AND HISTORICAL ECOLOGY

Emerging from this process is a new level of understanding about historical ecology and human affairs. In effect, the stark distinction between what is "natural science" and what is "social science" has begun to fade as insights from each field are used to further the understanding of the other. What is emerging might be referred to as the natural history of human cultures or the historical ecology of social formations, or, more broadly, an understanding of human cultures in the full context of their socioecological evolution.

It is useful to highlight some of the major ways in which a combined natural and social science study of the past can enlarge our understanding of our current circumstance. In particular, historical ecology has emerged as a powerful new field of research synthesis, yielding insights in the realms of (1) climate change and its impact in human history; (2) the origins and ecological impact of urbanization; (3) paleopathology and historical epidemiology; (4) the ecology of colonialism; and (5) the complex circumstances accompanying the collapse of ancient civilizations. Each of these subject areas of historical ecology deserves brief mention.

1. *Climate History and Human Affairs*: The availability of new techniques, including deep-sea sediment core sampling, dendochronology, limnology, glaciology, and palynology have enabled scientists to reconstruct regional and localized climate sequences, in some cases with a considerable degree of precision, for periods stretching back as far as tens of thousands of years. Because of the complexity of weather phenomena, modeling the global shifts in past climates is considerably more difficult, but as more and more dispersed data is being acquired and correlated, the broad shape of previous climate regimes is being clarified.

The results of climate research suggest several middle-level empirical generalizations that seem both simple and profound. They are simple in the sense that in light of the evidence they seem like straightforward commonsense conclusions. The observations prove profound, however, when juxtaposed with our contemporary circumstances and the evident folly of common practice and current assumptions in many areas of public policy formulation and popular belief.

Most generally, and perhaps most sobering, is the observation from scientific research that local and regional climates have in the past changed dramatically in relatively short periods of time. These radical shifts have resulted at times in massive, costly, and sometimes traumatic disruption to the infrastructure and patterns of livelihood of cities, regions, and entire civilizations. Just how local alterations in weather have been related to an overall pattern of global climate change is the subject of considerable debate, but periods of rapid climatic shift in particular regions are now beginning to be understood in greater detail.

Because humans and their domesticated plants and animals need a continuous supply of water, shifts in rainfall volume, its periodicity, and its spacial distribution have proved to be some of the most powerful parameters affecting the limits of human social organization. It may not be of much significance that average global climate measures have not varied a great deal in the last 10,000 years because the determinative questions in human affairs have been not so much the mean annual parameters of the system as a whole, but rather the particular performance of localized weather regimes. Reid Bryson and Thomas Murray and have demonstrated in a short volume entitled *Climates of Hunger* that some climates—particularly those in the Mediterranean region and the Middle East—have experienced climate fluctuations with major social consequences. More disconcerting still is the realization that large portions of humankind may well have become *even more*—not less—vulnerable to regional climatic perturbation over the course of human history.[11]

This observation may at first seem counterintuitive because of many popular myths about the nature of social evolution in human groups. For a long time in academic circles and popular understanding, the whole combination of changes known as the "agricultural revolution" was thought to have *liberated* humankind from direct dependence upon nature and its seemingly random fluctuations. We now know that this was not so. The whole package of socioecological changes associated with the agricultural revolution may have changed the scale and scope of human dependence on nature, but it did not *liberate* humankind from nature in any meaningful sense. Scientific research increasingly confirms what common sense and the logic of ecosystems suggest in this instance, and that is simply this: by domesticating selected plants and animals and basing subsistence production on this radically narrowed range of species, humans effectively narrowed their ecological "niche-width." Henceforth humans were all the *more* subject to the localized perturbations of nature since relatively minor fluctuations could be devastating for the radically narrowed range of tolerance that characterized the domesticates themselves when compared to the wild species.

In effect, human groups became tied to an econiche defined by the tolerance properties of their own domesticates. By mastering plant and animal reproduction humans had become slaves to agricultural production and victims of crop vulnerability. Shortage or excess of rain or merely relatively slight variations in its periodicity and distribution could have devastating impacts upon particular regions. In coming to depend upon domesticates for their food supply, humans had put "all their eggs into one basket"—or, at any rate, a very few baskets. While paleopathological evidence of prehistoric foraging populations suggests that they, too, suffered occasionally from periodic severe nutritional stress, due most probably to drought, the incidence of severe or chronic malnutrition *increases* in absolute terms with the emergence of urban-based agriculture. As archaeologist Mark Cohen has recently concluded, "evidence from both ethnographic descriptions of contemporary hunters and the archaeological record suggests that the major trend in the quality and quantity of human diets has been downward."[12]

2. *Urbanization: New Patterns of Dependence on Nature:* One highly adaptive short-term response to the fluxes of production caused by variable weather conditions in the agricultural econiche was for human groups to hyperproduce storable agricultural commodities

during favorable periods to be able to ride through times of climatic duress. Dessicatable grains including barley, wheat, rice, and sorghum proved most amenable to this kind of accumulation. But once again, by concentrating a high proportion of their activity on the production of these select few domestic species, human groups were not liberated from nature but rather became, in a collective sense, all the more subject to its cycles and variations.[13]

It is probable that one of the reasons why this increased *collective* vulnerability to variations in natural processes has not been widely recognized or commonly understood is that the social adaptations accompanying the agricultural revolution masked the collective costs of the transformation. In effect, new social hierarchies made it possible to distribute nutritional stress in a highly differential manner. Elite groups, upon whom we have depended for accounts of the past and whose skeletal remains have been most carefully preserved, were not among those to have been most severely affected by the new patterns of vulnerability. It was peasants and commoners who probably suffered most severely when natural perturbations diminished food supplies. Until recent paleopathological techniques made it possible to examine their collective plight, our archaeological sample has been skewed in favor of the experience of societal elites. It is hardly surprising that for those classes that benefited most from the new social arrangements, conditions of life improved. For these groups there may well have been a sensation of being "freed" from dependence upon nature, but it would be a major conceptual error to mistake their experience for that of the social collectivity as a whole.

Considered in intervals of decades and centuries, the social groups that proved most successful under this new structure of dependence upon nature were those that could (1) mobilize the labor necessary to overproduce foodstuffs in favorable times; (2) devise effective mechanisms of storage and distribution for deferred consumption; (3) defend and protect *both* their arable land and their accumulated food stocks; and (4) organize labor to construct and maintain artificial environments that served to buffer or regulate fluctuations in water supply so as to deliver it to the simplified range of domesticates at optimum times for plant growth. Each one of these selective pressures and their mutual interaction over time combined to create a powerful positive feedback loop that favored the rapid growth of hierarchically organized urban societies.

Henceforth cities constituted a major new chapter in the ecological experience of humankind. The intricate dynamics of urban-rural relationships have restructured natural landscapes for millennia ever since the advent of the first urban centers in the ancient world. The urban-rural dynamic is predicated upon an asymmetrical exchange between cities and their supporting countryside. In terms of the flow of matter and energy, cities can be said to be parasitic upon their surrounding countryside. Urban-based elites with no direct experience of agricultural production repeatedly gain inordinate influence over the disposition and control of production decisions in rural areas. These urbanized elites came to exercise this power for a series of strategic reasons relating to their functional role in exchanging, storing, or distributing produce, their managerial role in mobilizing periodic labor corvées, their adjudicative role in settling disputes, their ceremonial role in presiding over religious activities, or their military role in defending strategic territory or possessions. The particular combination of roles played by various urban elites in different cultures varied considerably, but their overall relation to rural populations was strikingly similar.

As long as these powerful urban elites recognized and respected the natural limits of the ecosystems of the rural populations upon which they ultimately depended, periods of stable production could endure. Sadly, however, urban-based decisions concerning the rate and nature of resource extraction in rural areas were frequently made with little knowledge or understanding of the limits of rural production systems. The long-term results could be repeatedly catastrophic, engendering cycles of urban growth and collapse, which in turn left whole ecological regions permanently transformed.

3. *Paleopathology and the Natural History of Disease.* There has been another major and enduring ecological consequence of the urban revolution. The evolution of cities afforded new opportunities for the growth, transmission, and chronic persistence of pathogens that

came to use humans and their domesticated species as hosts. In effect, by congregating in cities and engaging in intense local interaction combined with periodic long-distance exchanges with other cities, humans created the ideal conditions for the evolution and expansion of various kinds of bacteria, viruses, parasites, and pests.

As with common myths about agriculture "freeing" humankind from the domination of nature, so, too, it is in the study of disease. It should not be blithely assumed that the health of human populations has simply improved in some sort of uniform or progressive manner since the emergence of sedentary agriculture, the evolution of social complexity, and the elaboration of systematic scientific theories about natural process. To be sure, the development of the microbial theory of disease in this past century has transformed the ecology of human existence in our time, but this change is quite recent in human history and may well prove to be ephemeral in the long run.

In any case, new evidence from archaeologists seems to support the conclusion that many forms of degenerative and lethal diseases were not reduced over the course of culture history but actually emerged along with the growth of civilization. Europeans in this regard may have been until recent times some of the most diseased populations in history. Archaeologist Mark Cohen concludes his work on *Health and the Rise of Civilization* by emphasizing that "we must substantially revise our traditional sense that civilization represents progress in human well-being—or at least that it did so for most people for most of history prior to the twentieth century. The comparative data simply do not support that image."[14] He goes on to point out that our misunderstandings have followed largely, as in the case of nutrition, from the problem of over-representing the case of the privileged classes and from simply projecting our expectations backwards on the basis of an assumed continuum of human improvement.[15] It is, thus, clearly a mistake to portray the history of the world in general as simply an anterior projection of unfortunate European circumstance.

4. *Historical Ecology of Colonialism*: With a new sensitivity to historical epidemiology, colonial historians have begun to focus upon

the ecology of colonialism in considerable detail. The progression of human colonial enterprises—especially those that emerged from the expansion of Europe since the Renaissance—is often well documented from a sociopolitical point of view. After all, groups set out with explicit intentions that often had to be justified to royal sponsors, state treasuries, or joint-stock companies. Nevertheless, the effort to give an ecological account of colonial phenomena is relatively recent.

In biological terms, of course, the notion of colonization has long been understood as a particular type of biological process having to do with the arrival of exogenous species in new environments or the radical simplification of existing environments and the subsequent restoration of plant and animal communities over time. Forest fires, volcanoes, and receding ice sheets all create circumstances that allow for the colonization of newly created or radically altered environments by invading life forms. Biologists have studied the processes of plant and animal colonization quite independently of human involvement or intentionality for decades.

At this point, social scientists are beginning to examine the insights of these biological studies to analyze colonizing episodes in human history. The results of this new approach to human history are often quite disturbing. Although humans many be very powerful agents in the biological processes that constitute colonialism, they rarely understand the scope or magnitude of their complex role as they proceed to act. It is only years, decades, or centuries later that the underlying patterns of biological and ecological interaction become strikingly apparent.[16]

In broad terms it now seems clear that although colonial episodes frequently can be quite profitable in economic terms, they equally often are likely to be ruinous to localized environments in ecological terms. The nature of the colonial enterprise determines the character of the devastation involved. Some colonial endeavors are based on straightforward resource extraction like mining, timbering, rubber tree tapping or Brazil nut collection. Others involve the explicit attempt to expand the agricultural production of a selected foodstuff or cash crop species. In these instances, massive soil erosion and the subsequent siltation of rivers and sedimentation of estuaries can frequently create an enduring and devastating ecological signature of colonialism. In still other instances, the importation of exogenous crops and their expanded production—either on newly created plantations or as part of widely dispersed peasant communities—can also substantially transform agricultural land-use practices in very short order.[17]

One of the most alarming phenomena associated with the ecology of colonialism is the syndrome known as "plant genetic collapse"—a patterned sequence of biological transformations that leads to the radical simplification or total extinction of indigenous animals and plant genetic material. Rarely is it the explicit intention of human groups in charge of colonial efforts to destroy or render extinct local species, yet it is equally rare for them to avoid doing so in practice. The process often involves the agronomic displacement of local varieties of foodstuffs in favor of exogenous or putatively "improved" crop varieties which show exceptional economic promise. Local agricultural plant varieties—many of which represent specific adaptive advantages for pest resistance or extreme weather tolerance—can become extinct simply through the neglect of the peasant communities that have found the newly introduced varieties more desirable or immediately profitable under new market conditions.

In the context of the current forms of international aid this kind of progressive biological impoverishment can be the net result of even the most noble assistance program, if careful attention is not given to the socioecological impact of the aid program. In some instances, aid programs seek to extend the cultivation of plant varieties that have been selected specifically to grow best in petro-intensive environments with artificial fertilizer subsidies and the concomitant application of herbicides and pesticides.

In the short run, provided that all the required petroleum inputs are continuously available, the crop in question may do quite well for several years. In the longer run, however, local varieties may have passed completely out of cultivation through neglect, thus impoverishing the range of agricultural variety in the region. In addition, the topsoil and groundwater regimes may have been significantly altered and sometimes poisoned with the petrochemicals and fertilizers. Moreover, even when the new petro-intensive cultivars prove entirely successful with minimal off-farm impact, the local populations that grow them are henceforth committed to purchasing petroleum inputs. As petroleum becomes more expensive, their operating costs are bound to increase, sometimes beyond the level that they can afford in order to stay in farming.

Finally, with such highly specialized systems installed for the newly "improved" varieties, farmers lose the flexibility necessary to respond to changing weather and climate conditions. Irrigated rice can only be sustained if irrigation systems have water to run through them. If the rivers or rains fail, farmers are often forced off the land altogether, either into famine centers and refugee camps or off to the urban centers in search of other employment. Once peasants in this circumstance have left the rural regions for the cities, there is a high probability that their farming skills and their expertise concerning local crops and cropping techniques will be lost forever. Third World urban centers are growing at rates that outstrip their already high population growth rates, and many of these cities in Africa and elsewhere can only be sustained with constant food subsidies from western agricultural surpluses.

The cumulative effect of the innumerable local transformations resulting from the ecology of colonialism has been to mold the world's agricultural production systems in several distinctive ways. Increasingly, Third World agricultures have come to focus on producing cash crops for export while these same countries have become dependent upon higher and higher levels of foodstuff imports. The industrialized countries for their part are correspondingly addicted to a pattern of foodstuff overproduction and export to earn foreign exchange, while they continue to import cash crops from tropical countries. The impact of this global food web on the soils, forests, water quality, and water supply has been in many cases devastating to local ecosystems in *both* the Third World and in the rural areas of the industrialized world. Roy Rappaport summarizes the linked and asymmetrical character of the global situation from his observations as a field anthropologist and suggests that the future biological stability of such a radically simplified and hyper-coherent global food system is by no means assured: "The anthro-pocentric trend I have described [e.g., redesigning all local ecosys-tems primarily to meet *human* needs] may have ethical implications, but the issue is ultimately not a matter of morality or even of *Realpolitik.* It is one of biological viability."[18]

5. *The Decline of Ancient Civilizations:* The accelerated deteriora-tion of colonial ecosystems in the contemporary world has encour-aged some historians to reexamine long abandoned questions about the decline and fall of ancient civilizations. The seeming ubiquity of the syndromes of decline in the Third World suggests that similar syndromes of deterioration may well have been opera-tive in other periods of history. While "decline and fall" speculations in the past were heavily grounded in ideological and philosophic argumentation, now historians come armed with new scientific data and computer models to interpret that data. General climate models have been used to clarify the agro-climatological conditions of past civilizations as they enter collapse phases. In one instance, scholars have applied analytical techniques similar to those used by Jay Forrester, Donella Meadows and others in their early presenta-tions to the Club of Rome concerning *The Limits to Growth* in order to model the parameters of the collapse of Classical Mayan civiliza-tion.[19]

The results of these modeling attempts and other comparative studies in decline are mixed, as one might expect from early stages of any investigation.[20] Nevertheless, two suggestive insights emerge from the whole range of recent studies on the collapse of ancient civilizations. First, civilizational decline and collapse seem to involve syndromes of accelerated deterioration caused by multiple feed-back processes; second, in times of crisis the "intelligentsia" in ancient cultures (taken here to mean all those included in the urban-based elites) may well have failed to perceive the crisis at hand and may have actually contributed to systemwide collapse by blindly pursuing fallacious and quite partial remedies to systemwide problems or simply by projecting their own special interests as those of the general public.

Material circumstances and ecological constraints played a fundamental role in the circumstances leading up to the decline of civilizations, but also important as syndromes of collapse got underway were two further factors that might be considered "ideological" in nature. On the one hand the accelerating nature of the complexity in the system as a whole exceeded the perceptual apparatus of the elites that were supposed to act as regulators or governors of systemic process. In general systems terms, the information mechanisms necessary to trigger the negative feedback processes that would stabilize the system failed to function properly. In a sense their "science"—that is, their ability to observe, integrate, synthesize, and explain events—lagged behind the quickening pace of the events themselves.

Beyond this, the social capacity for cooperation that would have been required in any attempt to reverse the syndromes of decline was itself strained beyond its level of tolerance. Anthropologists have pointed out that initially a crisis situation can engender improved social cooperation in small-scale groups, but after certain thresholds of heightened or prolonged stress social groups tend to fragment, as each special interest tries to make the best of a declining circumstance for itself and its immediate allies.[21] The intelligentsia and the religious elites are no exception to this pattern. Indeed, their self-interested arguments are often the most thoroughly dysfunctional for the crisis at hand, yet they are proposed in the heightened rhetoric of systemwide necessity and absolute virtue. Lowe summarizes a salient case of this kind of behavior, drawing upon the Classical Mayan material. Briefly, according to his understanding of the archaeological data, it is clear that the Mayan ritual priesthood actually functioned to accelerate the Classical Mayan collapse by reacting inappropriately to a circumstance of declining agricultural production. The priests were thought to mediate between humans and the gods to assure agricultural productivity. When the agricultural system began to decline, however, the priests sought to extract greater and greater taxes from the peasantries in order to undertake heightened sacrificial activity.[22]

CONCLUSION

These observations from the study of historical ecology resulting from a combined synthesis of natural and social science research suggest some very sobering insights about our current ecological predicament. To begin with, it is clear that several major tenets of our modern public belief system now require substantial revision. Contrary to popular belief, for example, from an ecological point of view the development of agriculture in human history did not "free" humankind from its dependence on nature. On the contrary, the development of the agricultural econiche has restricted the range of plant species upon which humans came to depend and made them collectively more vulnerable to the variations of nature, perturbations of climate, and new forms of crop blights and pestilence.

Moreover, since the benefits of agricultural production were not uniformly distributed, poorer classes were often the first to suffer constraints in time of scarcity. Prolonged urban settlement also led to the emergence of endemic and epidemic diseases, often striking those classes that were under most nutritional stress.

Furthermore, it is clear that the urban elites that came to dominate the sociopolitical structures of these agricultural societies did not always clearly understand the ecological limits or precariousness of their circumstance. In ecological terms cities have always proved to be parasitic upon their supporting rural peasantries. As biologists have emphasized, however, parasitism is a delicate position to maintain over time. While there is by definition an asymmetrical flow of goods and services in parasitic relationships, there nonetheless has to be enough vitality remaining in the supporting population for the system to remain viable. If parasitism deteriorates into a predator-prey relationship, the entire structure can collapse quickly.

In other words, if urban elites failed to impose some restrains on their growing power over the lives of rural populations, it was frequently the case that they preyed upon these populations beyond the point of sustainability. Either they attempted to extract more surplus than the land itself would generate or they sought to squeeze peasants beyond the point that they would endure. In either case, when urban-rural relationships shifted from parasitism to predator-prey relations, the entire social system frequently experienced upheaval.

The combination and interaction of all of these factors has meant that human history since the advent of urban organized agriculture has been a turbulent affair, marked by recurrent famine, disease, pestilence, and open warfare. Humans have, in effect, fashioned for themselves what ecologists would call a "hypercoherent" ecosystem—that is to say, a system which is so tightly interwoven that any shift in its external parameters or internal components can have rapid, disequilibrating and potentially destructive consequences for the system as a whole.

The human population is no more secure than its food supply. In spite of its technological capacities and marvelous industrial achievements, our contemporary society remains in a very important sense an agricultural society. We may think we are a postindustrial society with a postmodern culture, but there is simply no such thing as a postagricultural society. Despite our dazzling technological achievements, we have not transcended the natural world in any significant sense. Indeed, we have made our societies ever more vulnerable to any systemwide shifts in its parameters—some of which, like the climate, we may already be altering by our patterns of unsustainable consumption.

If the social sciences have anything enduring to contribute to understanding our current predicament, it is that our system of public belief is in radical need of revision if we are to survive as a species. The myth that continuous growth is both good and possible is ubiquitous in the public sphere in our day. It is a blind and worshipful obedience to this article of public faith that misdirects our public policy and makes us incapable of formulating the kind of measured policies of self restraint that are called for by scientists and environmental leaders alike.

NOTES

1. Occasional warnings about localized population growth and resource constraints have been made ever since the seminal work of Thomas Malthus in the late eighteenth century. In the modern era, a small number of social and natural scientists began to focus on the global nature of these problems in the 1950s and 1960s. See particularly: Harrison Brown, *The Challenge of Man's Future: An Inquiry Concerning the Condition of Man during the Years That Lie Ahead* (New York: Viking Press, 1954), and his book *The Next Hundred Years: Man's Natural and Technological Resources* (New York: Viking Press, 1957); Paul Ehrlich, *The Population Bomb* (New York: Ballantine Books, 1968); Garret Hardin, *Nature and Man's Fate* (New York: The New American Library, 1959), and his *Biology: Its Principles And Implications* (San Francisco: W. H. Freeman, 1966); and Lester R. Brown, *Man, Land, and Food: Looking Ahead at World Food Needs* (Washington, D.C.: U.S. Department of Agriculture, Economic Research Service, Regional Analysis Division, 1963).

By the 1970s the number of warnings increased, particularly in conjunction with the United Nations' first environment conference in Nairobi, Kenya in 1972. See Paul R. and Anne H. Ehrlich, *The End of Affluence: A Blueprint for Your Future* (New York: Ballantine Books, 1974); Herman Daly, *Steady-State Economics* (San Francisco: W. H. Freeman, 1972); and his edited volume *Toward a Steady-State Economy* (San Francisco: W. H. Freeman, 1973); see also Donella H. Meadows et al., *The Limits to Growth: A Report for the Club of Rome's Project on the Predicament of Mankind* (New York: Universe Books, 1972); and Lester Brown, *Population and Affluence: Growing Pressures on World Food Resources* (Washington, D.C.: Overseas Development Council, 1973), *In the Human Interest: A Strategy to Stabilize World Population* (New York: Norton, 1974), and *The Global Politics of Resource Scarcity* (Washington, D.C.: Overseas Development Council, 1974).

The recent scientific statements of alarm of the 1990s are largely extending, refining, and amplifying the warnings that have been made by these early prophetic voices since the 1950s.

2. Union of Concerned Scientists, introduction to *Scientists' Warning to Humanity* (Cambridge: UCS, 1992).

3. The Royal Society and the United States National Academy of Sciences, *Population Growth, Resource Consumption, and a Sustainable World* (issued February 1992), from the preface by Sir Michael Atiyah, President,

The Royal Society of London and Dr. Frank Press, President, The U.S. National Academy of Sciences. This report was issued by these scientific bodies in preparation for and anticipation of the United Nations Conference on Environment and Development (UNCED), held in June 1992 in Rio de Janeiro.

4. Royal Society and the National Academy of Sciences, "The Reality of the Problem," section of the *Population Growth* report.

5. "Earth Summit Pledges Abandoned, Official Says," *Reuters*, October 1996, published in *ENN Daily News*, 21 October 1996.

6. The French social historian Fernand Braudel is the exception to the trend toward microspecialization. He drew upon and extended the *Annales* school of social research in France and focused his attention upon what he termed *l'histoire de la longue durée*—"long-term" or "large-scale" history. This corresponds to what we refer to here as "Grand History." More than any other single historian he has drawn the attention of social scientists back to the "big questions" of the persistence and transformation of cultural forms in the face of constraint throughout history. For example, much of the research by the American sociologist Immanuel Wallerstein and his associates and students on "world-systems theory" has been undertaken at the Fernand Braudel Center for the Study of Economies, Historical Systems and Civilizations, established at the State University of New York at Binghamton in tribute to Braudel's lifelong work. Braudel's numerous works include *The Mediterranean and the Mediterranean World in the Age of Philip II* (New York: Harper & Row, 1972–74); *Capitalism and Material Life, 1400–1800* (New York: Harper & Row, 1973); *Méthodologie de l'histoire et des sciences humaines* (Toulouse: Privat, 1973); and *The Structures of Everyday Life: the Limits of the Possible* (New York: Harper & Row, 1981).

7. Most notable of these grand theories of the stages of human progression were those of Lewis Henry Morgan, *Ancient Society* (Tucson: University of Arizona Press, 1985); Fustel de Coulanges, *La cité antique* (Paris: L. Hachette et cie, 1870); Henry Sumner Maine, *Ancient Law: Its Connection with the Early History of Society, and Its Relation to Modern Ideas* (London: J. Murray, 1866); and Karl Marx himself. See particularly Karl Marx and David McLellan, *Marx's Grundrisse* (London/New York: Macmillan, 1980).

8. Oswald Spengler, *The Decline of the West*, trans. Charles Francis Atkinson (New York: A. A. Knopf, 1926–28); Arnold Joseph Toynbee, *A Study of History* (London: Oxford University Press, 1934); Edward Gibbon, *The History of the Decline and Fall of the Roman Empire* (London: Printed for W. Strahan and T. Cadell in *The Strand*, 1776).

9. Will and Ariel Durant, *The Story of Civilization*, 11 vols. (New York: Simon and Schuster, 1935).

10. Mark Nathan Cohen, *Health and the Rise of Civilization* (New Haven: Yale University Press, 1989), p. viii.

11. Reid A. Bryson and Thomas J. Murray, *Climates of Hunger: Mankind And the World's Changing Weather* (Madison: University of Wisconsin Press, 1977).

12. Cohen, *Health and the Rise of Civilization*, p. 132.

13. Ibid., p. 134.

14. Ibid., p. 141.

15. Ibid.

16. See in particular Alfred W. Crosby Jr., *The Columbian Exchange: Biological Consequences of 1492* (Westport, Conn.: Greenwood Press, 1972); and his *Ecological Imperialism: The Biological Expansion of Europe, 900–1900* (New York: Cambridge University Press, 1986).

17. For more detailed discussions of these rapid transformations, see Timothy C. Weiskel, "Agents of Empire: Steps Toward an Ecology of Imperialism," *Environmental Review* 11, no. 4 (1987): 275–88; "Toward an Archaeology of Colonialism: Elements in the Ecological Transformation of the Ivory Coast," in Donald Worster, ed., *The Ends of the Earth: Perspectives on Modern Environmental History* (New York: Cambridge University Press, 1988), pp. 141–71; and "The Ecological Lessons of the Past: An Anthropology of Environmental Decline," *The Ecologist* 19, no. 3 (May/June 1989): 98–103. In addition, see Timothy C. Weiskel, *Environmental Decline and Public Policy: Pattern, Trend, and Prospect* (Ann Arbor: Pierian Press, 1992), chaps. 2–4.

18. Ibid.

19. D. Hosler, J. A. Sabloff, and D. Runge, "Simulation Model Development: A Case Study of the Classic Maya Collapse," in *Social Process in Mayan Prehistory*, ed. N. Hammond (London: Academic Press, 1977), pp. 553–84. See Donella Meadows, *Limits to Growth*, for elaboration of the dynamic systems model used as a basis for this study.

20. See John W. G. Lowe, *The Dynamics of Apocalypse: A Systems Simulation of the Classic Maya Collapse* (Albuquerque: University of New Mexico Press, 1985); Joseph A. Tainter, *The Collapse of Complex Societies* (New York: Cambridge University Press, 1988); and Norman Yoffee and George L. Cowgill, eds., *The Collapse of Ancient States and Civilizations* (Tucson: University of Arizona Press, 1988).

21. For a more extended discussion of both the tendencies toward a

decline in objective perception and the collapse of social cooperation, see *Environmental Decline and Public Policy,* chapter 5; and Charles D. Laughlin Jr. and Ivan A. Brady, "Introduction: Diaphasis and Change in Human Populations," in *Extinction and Survival in Human Populations,* ed. Charles D. Laughlin Jr. and Ivan A. Brady (New York: Columbia University Press, 1978), pp. 1–48.

22. Lowe, *The Dynamics of Apocalypse,* p. 98. Lowe's work is based upon that of D. Hosler, J. A. Sabloff, and D. Runge, "Simulation Model Development," and their work draws in turn upon that of G. R. Willey and D. B. Shimkin, "The Maya Collapse: A Summary View," in *The Classic Maya Collapse,* ed. T. P. Culbert (Albuquerque: University of New Mexico Press, 1973), pp. 63–115.

QUESTIONS FOR DISCUSSION

1. In what ways has the agricultural revolution "freed" us from nature? Are there ways in which we are more dependent upon nature than ever before?

2. Summarize in your own words the ways by which a given region's ecology shapes human patterns of settlement and civilization.

3. Weiskel suggests that our system of public belief is in radical need of revision if we are to survive as a species. How would you define the nature of that public belief? What aspects of this public belief must be changed if we are to live in light of the information which Weiskel presents?

3. **RELIGION CARING FOR CREATION**

The previous section ended with the author arguing from the perspective of the social sciences that our system of public belief is in
need of radical revision if we are to survive as a species. Such an argument, coming from the social or natural sciences, draws us to reflect on
religion in relation to values.[1] Richard J. Clifford begins this section by
noting that while Christianity and Judaism are religions centered in a
Book, each has developed an interpretive tradition for reading Scripture. Augustine of Hippo (354–430 C.E.) helped to shape the dominant
tradition for Roman Catholics and Protestants. This tradition tended
toward anthropomorphism, finding redemption in Jesus Christ. It was
characterized by a moderate dualism, giving priority to questions of
spirituality. Without challenging this tradition, Clifford writes that the
biblical idea of the process of creation does not imply a dichotomy
between nature and human beings. Rather, the world that emerges
reveals a human race that is embedded in emergent materiality.

Early in this drama the *locus classicus* (Genesis 1) for "dominion"
theories of human oversight or stewardship of nature appears. The
literary structure of the text presents humans as fully a part of the
web of creation, while only they directly encounter God. Their rule

images God's rule: it is to foster the continuity and fruitfulness of all life according to God's order. Any latent anthropomorphism is subject to a withering critique in the book of Job. The ancient world depicted by Genesis 2–11 shows an earth that shares in the consequences of humanity's sin. Death, the ultimate effect of this alienation, is mitigated by a foreshadowing of restoration, first through Eve and then, in the post-diluvian world, in the covenantal blessing given to all sentient and vegetative life.[2] Clifford concludes: there is a relative, not absolute, anthropomorphism in the Jewish and Christian Bibles; God is the power behind fertility and infertility in the natural world; the cosmogony found in the Bible connects patterns in human society and the natural environment. God's work—creation out of chaos, and new creation out of sinful human history—is inextricably intertwined with the state of the earth.[3]

Michal Smart begins with the phrase, "God created the earth," implying a purposeful creation shaping environmental concern. The care for creation shapes Jewish ritual whereas its destruction is tantamount to blasphemy. The weekly cycle of time with its focus on the Sabbath acknowledges the goodness of creation. This divine stamp on space and time shapes the Jewish view of social justice and eco-justice in the acknowledgment of the Sabbath or Jubilee Year. Such "macro" events replicate the concern found in everyday life seen in the blessing required every time something is taken from the earth. God's compassion extends to all species, and their ordering in creation is expressive of God's will as further articulated in the covenant between creator and creation. This covenant tempers individualism and establishes an intergenerational responsibility.

The question of religion's partnership with environmental concern receives added attention through deepening aspects of mysticism in our developing global culture.[4] However, just as religion can become characterized by manipulative practices, self-deception, and escapism, so also its apparent opposites, contemporary postmodernism and philosophies of deconstruction, as well as forms of environmental spirituality. For example, the mysticism of Deep Ecology seeks to emphasize our capacity to love beings across space and time. It scores the limits of a purely instrumental use of nature.[5] Deep

Ecology asks us to see ourselves as a part of the web of life, for example as a part of the rainforest trying to save itself. Herein lie the advantages and liabilities of Deep Ecology. Like other forms of mysticism, it can slide into an attempt to escape society. If we really love nature, Gottlieb adds, we are called to love people and to seek justice. Together with Smart and Clifford, Gottlieb challenges us not to abandon nature, but to see it as part of a larger vision, to view nature through the lens of history. It is in this context that we find ethics and transcendence, the twin axes along which an authentic social self develops.

Gottlieb continues a theme we have seen in each of our authors: Environmentalism needs to embrace environmental justice. As such, a chastened Deep Ecology can serve to deepen our spiritual temperament as we work for a just social transformation. It can also remind us that Christian theology has been so focused on the second article of the creed, redemption through Jesus Christ, that the first and third articles, dealing with God and creation as well as the Holy Spirit and sanctification, have often been overlooked. An inter-religious dialogue that draws upon the faith perspectives and world views of others can help to shape a more inclusive and nuanced perspective for an earth at risk.[6]

Each of the articles in this section alerts us to the fact that we read our holy scriptures in whichever tradition they stand through certain lenses. This enables us to see some things and to overlook others.[7] The fact that there are different ways of reading and "seeing" has been important in contemporary discussions of shifting paradigms for understanding.[8] For example, Orthodoxy has remained less dualistic than some Western spiritualities, more centered on pre-Scholastic schools of mysticism. The Orthodox Christian approaches God's creation with thanks (eucharist) and is characterized by asceticism in spiritual life.[9] The variety of perspectives among Roman Catholics includes but is wider than Augustine's "spiritualizing" of the Bible.[10] Among Protestants the interpretive spread is also wide, with Evangelicals, for example, found in the array of positions from the "Wise Use" Movement on the extreme right to quite activist and communitarian views among postconservative Evangelicals.[11]

A critique of inherited patterns of interpretation can only be done schematically and in the most cursory fashion in this section introduction. Already mentioned is the influence of process theology as a way of discerning the evolving pattern of life and cocreative work of humanity.[12] The moderate dualism found in Augustine has been criticized by theologies of embodiment which have tended to emphasize more immanental conceptions of God, as in the work of Sallie McFague, who finds the universe or world as God's body to be an organic model from which to consider every major theological topic.[13] Feminist and Womanist perspectives might also be cited.[14] Speaking out with one voice against an older theology conceived of in terms of the metaphor of male dominance,[15] feminist theologies form an array of positions from reference to "Mother Earth" and *Gaia* as poetic metaphors to new forms of dualism that find in *Gaia* a parallel to Isis, Astarte, and all of the "Great Mothers" of Antiquity.[16]

Indigenous and Native American spiritualities should be singled out for special attention.[17] Vine Deloria Jr. describes the appeal of such spirituality in a time of collapsing values in Euro-American culture, the disillusionment with Civil Rights and power movements and, earlier, over Vietnam, of an escape into drugs and return to Mother Earth. Sadly, he and other Native writers score negatively a romantic and often fraudulent turn to Native American spirituality as part of this search for authenticity.[18] Indians have been typed as exemplary "stewards" of the land[19] but also as pillagers of nature,[20] ecoterrorists out to exterminate animal life for the sake of the fur trade.[21] In the lens of contemporary ecological concern, Native peoples have been viewed as the first American "bioregionalists,"[22] as sensitive to the web of life through reciprocity,[23] and as reflecting environmental ethics in ritual and mythology.[24] In assessing such ideas, Jace Weaver writes that Native peoples are "neither saints nor sinners in environmental matters. They are human beings."[25] Valuable characteristics are exhibited despite wide Native diversity: (1) the practice of reciprocity and natural conservation so that ample resources exist for themselves and their progeny, (2) an emphasis upon community for purposes of collective survival, and (3) a sense of nature as an organic whole. The belief that indigenous peoples have a special contribution to make to environmental consciousness transcends native experience in North America and includes, for example, the Celtic and Sammi peoples of Europe, the Maori of the South Pacific, tribal groups in Africa or South Asia, and indigenous peoples of Central and South America.[26]

A diffuse New Age spirituality runs through environmental concern. As defined in relation to Deep Ecology, a pattern of deepening commitment might run as follows: (1) a "shallow" perspective which favors land conservation, stewardship, and the preservation of endangered species;[27] (2) an intermediate collection of approaches, including the land ethic of "ecosaint" Aldo Leopold[28] and the animal-liberation movement of Peter Singer,[29] denying exclusive supremacy to human interests but acknowledging human responsibility for the ecosphere; (3) Deep Ecology, formulated by Arne Naess, William Devall, and George Sessions,[30] calling for a non-human ethic which would provide ecospheric equalitarianism and biodiversity; and (4) Deep Green Ecology, a deepening of Deep Ecology to a more critical and inductive style.[31]

Reflection on Scripture and alternative theologies has inevitably led to discussion about other worldviews or living religious traditions in relation to ecology, a topic of increasing study.[32] As a part of contemporary postmodernism, a deepening interest has developed into what wisdom other religions have to offer about how to live in harmony with nature.[33] There is a growing consensus that our environmental crisis is so complex that no one religious tradition or philosophical perspective has the solution to it.[34] Tu Wei-ming argues for a post-Enlightenment mentality that mobilizes the spiritual resources of the ethico-religious traditions (Greek philosophy, Judaism, Christianity), non-Western axial-age civilizations (Hinduism, Jainism, Buddhism, Confucianism, Taoism, Islam), and the spiritual resources of primal traditions.[35] There is a wide field for discussion here that includes how we live together in one world holding different worldviews.[36]

But the question is even more profound. To put it in Christian terms, the environmental crisis presents us with the question of a "green grace," nature as mediator of God's goodness and salvation, or a "red grace," the sacrifice of Jesus Christ as revelation of God's goodness and agent of salvation—the extent to which religion itself is a product of culture or of nature.[37] The universality of religion in historical time and geographical space seems evident today from anthropology. But is religion a subset of culture[38] or of nature?[39] Or does religion stand in tension between the two, a natural impulse made manifest in culture?[40] If the answer to the first question is on the side of culture, then positing the existence of religion is to affirm a dualism such that the phenomenon of religion cannot be treated as an aspect of nature. This opens up a set of questions with respect to environmental issues and how they are approached. If the answer to the second question is in the affirmative, however, then epistemology is more foundational and culture less subject to reification. When dealing with environmental issues the phenomenon of religion is more embedded and areas for discussion clearly crosscultural. A breach has been made for such debate as revolves around the place of natural and revealed theology.[41] However, it is not the purpose of this book to answer this question. It is sufficient here to have raised the issue of nature and nurture as it applies to religion.

We might conclude with three points that relate to the Seoul Affirmation, "Creation as Beloved of God." First, it appears that the environmental crisis is causing us to reflect more deeply upon relationships, how we interpret our relationship to God and to community in the widest sense as inclusive of all sentient life. Douglas John Hall asks us to consider whether we are above nature, in nature, or with nature; Hall himself opts for the third.[42] Christian theology will hold this interconnectedness in tension with the distinction that God is the "Ground" of Being (Tillich) but yet distinct.[43] Second, how we live out these relationships becomes a matter of ecojustice. "Religion caring for creation" cannot mean an environmentalism simply defined as wilderness preservation or the maintenance of biodiversity. People are natural. We are a part of nature. The concern for social and human health is as important as the general health of the planet.[44] This interrelationship is taken up by Leonardo Boff as an extension of Liberation Theology.[45] Finally, we do come back to the nature or nurture question: Certainly for the Christian, and also for adherents of many other faiths, the issue of salvation in light of the environmental crisis is neither red grace nor green grace alone. Indeed, it is to learn to live "between the flood and the rainbow."[46]

Rodney L. Petersen

NOTES

1. E. O. Wilson, *Sociobiology: The New Synthesis* (Cambridge, Mass: Harvard University Press, 1975); cf. G. E. Pugh, *The Biological Origins of Human Values* (New York: Basic Books, 1977), and with R. Trigg, *The Shaping of Man* (Oxford: Blackwell, 1982). Walter Burkert writes of a religious sense and practice proceeding from biological imperatives in *Creation of the Sacred: Tracks of Biology in Early Religions* (Cambridge, Mass: Harvard University Press, 1996).

2. Calvin DeWitt, ed., *The Environment and the Christian: What Can We Learn from the New Testament?* (Grand Rapids: Baker Books, 1991).

3. The biblical book of Leviticus is a rich source for reflection on the interrelationship between spirituality and materiality for both the Hebraic and Christian traditions. See Walter Brueggemann, *The Land* (Philadelphia: Fortress Press, 1977); and Chris Wright, "Biblical Reflections on Land," in *Evangelicals and the Environment: Theological Foundations for Christian Environmental Stewardship*, guest ed. J. Mark Thomas, *Evangelical Review of Theology* 17, no. 2 (April 1993): 153–75.

4. See his study, *Forcing the Spring. The Transformation of the American Environment Movement* (Washington, D.C.: Island Press, 1993).

5. See the discussion of mysticism in Joseph Dalby, *Christian Mysticism and the Natural World* (Greenwood, S.C.: Attic Press, 1949).

6. David Burrell and Elena Malits, *Original Peace: Restoring God's Creation* (New York: Paulist Press, 1997), pp. 3–4. Note the reference to Nicholas Lash, *Believing Three Ways in One God* (Notre Dame: University of Notre Dame, 1993) and John McDade, "Creation and Salvation: Green Faith and Christian Themes," *The Month* 23 (1990): 433–41.1.

7. H. Paul Santmire, *The Travail of Nature: The Ambiguous Ecological*

Promise of Christian Theology (Minneapolis: Fortress, 1985). Santmire distinguishes two thrusts in the history of Christianity out of its Hebraic and Hellenistic contexts, a spiritual and an ecological motif in continuing tension with one another. See also Robert Booth Fowler, *The Greening of Protestant Thought* (Chapel Hill: University of North Carolina, 1995). In broad strokes the author traces the increasing influence of environmentalism on American Protestantism since the first Earth Day (1970).

8. Crawford Knox, *Changing Christian Paradigms and their Implications for Modern Thought* (New York: E. J. Brill, 1993). The author focuses his work on the contributions of Augustine in shaping a particular way of reading the Bible in the West, arguing that pre-Augustinian and Biblical understandings cohere more closely with the conceptions of modern science.

9. The ascetic nature of Orthodoxy suggests the need for a God-centered prayerful self-discipline to curb our appetitive desires, particularly significant in light of population and consumptive patterns as they bear upon the carrying capacity of the earth. That Orthodoxy is awakening to its global ecological role was seen pointedly in 1989 when His Holiness Ecumenical Patriarch Dimitrios of Constantinople declared September 1, the first day of the Byzantine Ecclesiastical Year, as Environmental Protection Day, Gennadios Limouris, ed., *Justice, Peace, and the Integrity of Creation: Insights from Orthodoxy* (Geneva: WCC Publications, 1990).

10. "The JPIC Process: A Catholic Contribution," *The Ecumenical Review* 41, no. 4 (October 1989): 591–602. The concept of the integrity of creation is found in Pope John Paul II's encyclical "Sollicitudo Rei Socialis" (1987), par. 26.

11. An early Evangelical voice on behalf of ecological responsibility is that of Francis S. Schaeffer, *Pollution and the Death of Man: The Christian View of Ecology* (Wheaton: Tyndale House Publishers, 1970); cf. more recently, J. Mark Thomas, ed., *Evangelicals and the Environment: Theological Foundations for Christian Environmental Stewardship*, a dedicated edition of the *Evangelical Review of Theology* 17, no. 2 (April 1993). See here for leading Evangelical voices on environmental stewardship and ecological concern. The Evangelical concern to link issues of personal Christian discipleship with environmental ethics is seen in Vera C. Shaw, *Thorns in the Garden Planet: Meditations on the Creator's Care* (Nashville: Thomas Nelson, 1993). See Wesley Granberg-Michaelson, *A Worldly Spirituality: The Call to Take Care of the Earth* (San Francisco: Harper & Row, 1984).

12. The philosophy of Alfred North Whitehead has been of particular

value in shaping the thinking of such process theologians as John Cobb or of biologist and philosopher Charles Birch.

13. Sallie McFague, *The Body of God: An Ecological Theology* (London: SCM, 1993).

14. Jane Cary Peck and Jeanne Gallo, "JPIC: A Critique from a Feminist Perspective," *The Ecumenical Review* 41, no. 4 (October 1989): 573–81; Rosemary Radford Reuther, *Liberation Theology: Human Hope Confronts Christian History and American Power* (New York: Paulist Press, 1972), p. 115; and *Gaia and God: An Ecofeminist Theology of Earth Healing* (San Francisco: HarperCollins, 1992).

15. Contrary to the cautious attitude toward nature as a realm of immense mystery in medieval Europe, the seventeenth-century English philosopher Thomas Hobbes regarded nature as existing solely for human usage: "She is no mystery, for she worketh by motion and geometry. . . . [We] can chart these motions. Feel then as if you lived in a world which can be measured, weighed and mastered and confront it with audacity." Quoted in Basil Wiley, *The Seventeenth Century Background* (Garden City, N.Y.: Doubleday-Anchor, 1950), pp. 95–96.

16. Judith Plaskow and Carol P. Christ present helpful essays (in section 2) in understanding the nature of and motivation for goddess spirituality, in *Weaving the Visions: New Patterns in Feminist Spirituality* (San Francisco: Harper & Row, 1989). An Alternative view is expressed by Loren Wilkinson, "Gaia Spirituality: A Christian Critique," in *Evangelicals and the Environment: Theological Foundations for Christian Environmental Stewardship*, ed. J. Mark Thomas, *Evangelical Review of Theology* 17, no. 2 (April 1993): 176–89.

17. Vine Deloria Jr., *God is Red* (New York: Grosset and Dunlap, 1973). In Deloria's opinion Christianity has forsaken nature and an ecological era requires the spiritual resources of Native American religions for spiritual guidance. The recovery of Native spirituality is set more clearly in the context of the collapse of values in contemporary society in the 2d ed. (Golden, Colo.: Fulcrum, 1992), pp. 52–53.

18. This romantic search is sometimes symbolized in the fraudulent version of speech by Chief Seattle (Duwamish) in 1854. See Rudolf Kaiser, "Chief Seattle's Speech(es): American Origins and European Reception," in Brian Swann and Arnold Krupat, eds., *Recovering the Word: Essays on Native American Literature* (Berkeley: University of California Press, 1987), pp. 497–536. See Andy Smith, "For All Those Who Were Indian in a Former Life," in Carol Adams, ed., *Ecofeminism and the Sacred* (New York: Continuum, 1993), pp. 168–71.

19. Donald A. Grinde Jr. and Bruce E. Johansen, *Ecocide of Native America: Environmental Destruction of Indian Lands and Peoples* (Santa Fe: Clear Light Publishers, 1995); and Djelal Kadir, *Columbus and the End of the Earth: Europe's Prophetic Rhetoric as Conquering Ideology* (Berkeley: University of California Press, 1992).

20. George Weurthner of Earth First! blames Native peoples for the extinction of the woolly mammoth and desertification of the Sonora, and Dave Foreman sees them as a threat to the habitat. See in Ward Churchill, *Fantasies of the Master Race: Literature, Cinema, and the Colonization of American Indians*, ed. M. Annette Jaimes (Monroe, ME: Common Courage Press, 1992), pp. 195–96.

21. Calvin Martin, *Keepers of the Game: Indian-Animal Relationships and the Fur Trade* (Berkeley: University of California Press, 1978), pp. 105–108. Modern society has little to learn from Native American peoples, pp. 187–88.

22. Jay B. McDaniel, *With Roots and Wings: Christianity in an Age of Ecology and Dialogue* (Maryknoll: Orbis Books, 1995), p. 68. Sensitive to Native American objections over the appropriation of their religious traditions, McDaniel nevertheless has been criticized for inappropriately importing Native "spiritual lessons" into his own concerns.

23. Dennis McPherson and J. Douglas Rabb, *Indians from the Inside: A Study in Ethno-Metaphysics* (Thunder Bay, Ontario: Lakewood University Centre for Northern Studies, 1993), p. 90.

24. Donald A. Grinde Jr. and Bruce E. Johansen, *Ecocide of Native America: Environmental Destruction of Indian Lands and Peoples* (Santa Fe: Clear Light Publishers, 1995); and Djelal Kadir, *Columbus and the End of the Earth: Europe's Prophetic Rhetoric as Conquering Ideology* (Berkeley: University of California Press, 1992), p. 30.

25. See the helpful introductory chapter by Jace Weaver, ed., *Defending Mother Earth: Native American Perspectives on Environmental Justice* (Maryknoll: Orbis Books, 1996).

26. Thomas Berry with Thomas Clarke, *Befriending the Earth: A Theology of Reconciliation Between Humans and the Earth* (Mystic, Conn.: Twenty-Third Publications, 1991); Jay B. McDaniel, *Earth, Sky, Gods, and Mortals: Developing an Ecological Spirituality* (Mystic, Conn.: Twenty-Third Publications, 1990). This interest in the contribution of indigenous peoples is particularly evident in programming at the World Council of Churches and in its study Theology of Life (Unit III).

27. John Passmore, *Man's Responsibility for Nature* (London: Duck-

worth, 1974). The book was criticized for an anthropocentric framework and instrumentalist perspective on the natural world.

28. For example, see the land ethic of Aldo Leopold (*Sand County Almanac*, 1949) or the work of historian Lynn White (1967). Leopold claims that a biblically inspired Abrahamic ethic underlies our misuse of the land, and claims that John Muir took Judeo-Christianity to task before · the turn of the century, arguing that narrow-minded religionists could not conceive of the idea that God cared for the rest of creation as well as humankind.

29. Peter Singer, *Animal Liberation: A New Ethics for Our Treatment of Animals* (New York: Avon, 1975).

30. Arne Naess, *Ecology, Community, and Life-Style* (1976, 1989) and William Devall and George Sessions, *Deep Ecology: Living as if Nature Mattered* (1985). Naess stresses life-forms' self-realization, developed from Spinoza into a cosmology of biotic *Bildung*.

31. On forms of Deep Ecology and metaphysical naturalism, see George Sessions, "Shallow and Deep Ecology: A Review of the Philosophical Literature," in *Ecological Consciousness: Essays from the Earthday X Colloquium*, University of Denver, 21–24 April 1980, ed. Robert C. Schultz Jr. and Donald Hughes (Washington, D.C.: University Press of America, 1981), chap. 19.

32. See the series on Religions of the World and Ecology facilitated by The Center for the Study of World Religions at Harvard University, Cambridge, Mass., and edited by Mary Evelyn Tucker, Bucknell University.

33. Harold Coward, ed., *Population, Consumption, and the Environment* (Albany: State University of New York, 1995). See for the different ways in which the major world religions view issues of population and resource consumption.

34. This is the premise of the book edited by Mary Evelyn Tucker and John A. Grim, *Worldviews and Ecology: Religion, Philosophy, and the Environment* (Maryknoll: Orbis Books, 1994).

35. Tu Wei-ming, "Beyond the Enlightenment Mentality," in ibid., pp. 19–29.

36. Huntington, *Clash of Civilizations*, pp. 64–66, 47–48. George H. Williams explores the term "mercy" and its linguistic roots in a number of different cultures with the view of finding a cross-cultural basis for environmental ethics, "Mercy in the Grounding of a Non-Elitist Ecological Ethic," in *Festschrift in Honor of Charles Speel*, ed. J. Sienkiwicz and James Betts (Monmouth, Ill.: Monmouth College, 1996). The works of John

Hick, Paul Knitter, and Gavin D'Costa mark out different positions in the debate about the unique nature of Christian salvation. Special attention should be given to the ongoing discussion on Gospel and culture facilitated by the World Council of Churches. See S. Wesley Ariarajah, *Gospel and Culture: An Ongoing Discussion within the Ecumenical Movement* (Geneva: WCC, 1994).

37. Burkert, *Creation of the Sacred: Tracks of Biology in Early Religions*, pp. 1–33.

38. Clifford Geertz, *The Interpretation of Cultures* (New York, 1973). The perspective largely follows from the work of sociologist Emile Durkheim, *The Elementary Forms of Religious Life* (1918) and his idea of "collective representations." The continuing impact of the primacy given culture is seen in contemporary semiotics, structuralism, and poststructuralism.

39. See Burkert's discussion and general characteristics of religion, *Creation of the Sacred*, pp. 5–8.

40. Unresolved here is whether religious symbols are instrumental, with the implication of transcendence, or pragmatic with respect to divinity (Charles Peirce) or to religious forms of life (Ludwig Wittgenstein and Derrida). See Robert Cummings Neville, *The Truth of Broken Symbols* (Albany: State University of New York Press, 1996), chaps. 2–3.

41. In the Christian theological tradition, this question touches on the debate over natural theology between Emil Brunner and Karl Barth. See Romans 1.

42. Douglas John Hall, *The Steward: A Biblical Symbol Come of Age* (Grand Rapids: Eerdmans, 1990), pp. 191–214. Sensitivity to the interconnectedness of things has been an attractive feature of some religions, e.g., see the Buddhist scholar Masao Abe, *Zen and Western Thought*, ed. William R. LaFleur (Honolulu: University of Hawaii Press, 1985).

43. Joseph Sittler, "Ecological Commitment as Theological Responsibility," *Zygon: Journal of Religion and Science* 5 (1970): 558. See Hall's discussion, "The Ontology of Communion," in Hall, *Imaging God: Dominion As Stewardship* (Grand Rapids: Eerdmans, 1986), pp. 113ff.

44. A. J. McMichael, *Planetary Overload: Global Environmental Change and the Health of the Human Species* (Cambridge: Cambridge University Press, 1993).

45. Leonardo Boff, *Ecology and Liberation: A New Paradigm* (Maryknoll: Orbis Books, 1995). He writes, "The dominant trend of Christian reflection has not taken . . . creation to any profound level of consideration. For historical and institutional reasons, there has been much more considera-

tion of redemption" (pp. 45, 47). See Roger Gottlieb, *Forcing the Spring: The Transformation of the American Environmental Movement* (Washington, D.C.: Island Press, 1993).

46. This is the title of the book compiled by D. Preman Niles, *Between the Flood and the Rainbow: Interpreting the Conciliar Process of Mutual Commitment (Covenant) to Justice, Peace, and the Integrity of Creation* (Geneva: WCC, 1992). See also James A. Nash, *Loving Nature: Ecological Integrity and Christian Responsibility* (Nashville: Abingdon, 1991).

5
BIBLICAL SOURCES
Witness to the Interpretive Value of the Earth
Richard J. Clifford

At the center of both Judaism and Christianity is a Book—the Bible. Though the Christian Bible with the New Testament is larger than the Jewish Bible, one can still say that the Bible has formed the hearts, minds, and imaginations of Jews and Christians for millennia. Both religions owe to the Bible much of their understanding of God, the human person and human community, and, relevant to this discussion, the relation of the human community to nature.

It is important to the approach of this chapter to note that neither Judaism nor Christianity takes its Bible "straight" or unmediated. Both religions read it within recognized traditions of interpretation developed over the centuries. For Jews the tradition is partly the Mishnah (a law code brought to closure about 200 C.E.) and the Babylonian and Jewish Talmuds (systematic commentaries on the Mishnah composed between 400–600 C.E.). Even the traditional Jewish name for the Bible, Tanakh, is interpretative, suggesting an order to the various biblical books: a core (the Pentateuch) and successive elaborations (the prophets and other writings). Tanakh is an acronym for Torah (Pentateuch), Nebiim

(Prophets, divided info former [Joshua to Kings] and latter [the major and minor prophets]), Ketubim (writings, books not included under the previous two headings). Christians also have their interpretative tradition, which is discussed below under "New Testament."

Traditions of interpretation are not unvarying but change and develop in the course of history according to the needs and interests of the believing community. Approaches to the Bible have waxed and waned. One generation or epoch may read the Bible in a way that yields little significance for a later age. The allegorical reading of the Old Testament, for example, so congenial to the Church Fathers (authors of classical texts up to the seventh and eighth centuries C.E.), was vehemently rejected by many readers in the Renaissance and the sixteenth-century Reformation. Today, another shift is taking place in the way many people read the Bible. This shift reflects concerns of contemporary Western culture—heightened awareness of the connectedness of the human race and nature, of the complexity and fragility of the environment, and of the need for global justice. These concerns are beginning to constitute a veritable interpretative tradition. This new tradition calls into question the hitherto dominant tradition, which may be called Augustinian and is common among Protestant and Roman Catholic Christians. The Augustinian tradition, to characterize it broadly, concentrates on human beings and their need for redemption by Christ; it tends to distinguish the material and the spiritual, giving priority to the latter.[1] Nature and the environment therefore are not at the forefront of that consciousness. The new consciousness described above will not and should not replace the dominant tradition but will bring a fresh perspective, enabling us, like the householder in Matthew's Gospel, to bring forth from the storeroom both the new and the old (Matt. 13:52). This paper will attend to an issue neglected by previous readings—the natural environment. We will first discuss the Hebrew Scriptures, called Tanakh in Judaism and the Old Testament in Christian tradition. We will then discuss the New Testament.

HEBREW SCRIPTURES/OLD TESTAMENT

The Bible does not have a specific word for "nature" or "environment," but the theme of creation, or cosmogony, includes it. At creation God determined the way human beings relate to "the world." The concept of creation in the Bible differs from our conceptions of creation. To understand aright the biblical notion of nature it is important to note the differences. There are three important differences: the process of creation, the world that emerges, and the manner of reporting.[2]

1. *The process of creation*: Ancient Near Easterners generally imagined creation on the model of human making or of natural activity, e.g., the gods formed the world as an artisan works clay, or commanded it to exist as a king's word makes things happen, or as a warrior defeats an enemy. Ancients did not make the modern dichotomous distinction between "nature" and human beings, and sometimes used psychic and social analogies to explain nonhuman phenomena. Today we do not usually use human activity as a model for understanding impersonal forces. Influenced by scientific and evolutionary thinking, we generally understand creation as the impersonal interaction of physical forces extending over aeons.

2. *The product or world that emerges*: To the ancients, a *populated* world emerged from God's hand. Human society is prominent, and it is usually imagined concretely, with a culture that includes kingship, tools, and physical environment (marshes, rivers, animals). Today we usually imagine creation issuing in the order of planets and stars, *prior to* the emergence of life. Human society and culture are not in our mind when we speak of creation. The human race is imbedded in the material world, a point that will be especially important in the covenant and in the prophets' historical narratives.

3. *Manner of reporting and criteria of truth*: Ancients often described creation as a drama, whereas we write scientific reports. Each type of recording corresponds to the conceptualization of creation: evolutionary, according to "impersonal" laws of nature, or

dramatic, modeled on human activity or the activity of nature. To explain new data scientists offer new hypotheses, whereas ancient poets devised new stories or introduced variations on existing tales. We sometimes find it difficult to take ancient creation stories seriously, for among us stories serve the purpose of entertainment or illustration. We do not customarily use stories as a route to philosophical or theological truth.

Genesis 1

With these differences in mind, we look first at the most influential creation text in the Bible, Gen. 1:1–2:3, creation in seven days.[3] Parallelism is a biblical standard for developing ideas. The parallel structure of the six days in Genesis 1 shows the relation of the human race to the environment.[4]

"Began": Chaos

1.	Light (Day)/Darkness (Night)	= 4.	sun/moon
2.	*raqià* between waters	= 5.	fish & birds from waters
3.a)	dry land	= 6.a)	animals
b)	vegetation		b) man: male/female

Day 7: "finished" fulfills "began" of v. 1

As the outline shows, the universe that arises in Genesis 1 is a *system*, a network in which the elements of the world are related to each other. Ancient cosmogonies were systems, at least implicitly. In comparison with the systems in the cosmogonies of ancient Mesopotamia (modern Iraq), Genesis 1 stands out for its complexity and coherence, and for not being totally oriented to the care and feeding of the deity. The above parallel scheme displays some of the interconnections: days 1–3 correspond to days 4–6, whereas day 7 (God's rest) stands outside the series as a climax. Though penultimate in relation to the whole week, the man and woman on day six are the center of a web stretching backward and forward through all seven days. The fifth-day divine blessing of the birds and fishes (1:22) is repeated in expanded form to the human couple (1:28). The phrase describing the reproduction of each species, how it will continue in existence, "plants yielding seed, and fruit trees bearing fruit in which is their seed, each according to its kind" (1:11, 21, 24), is specially formulated for the human race: "male and female he created them." Sexuality, "male and female," is the human version of the reproductive capacity inherent in life forms, a means for sustaining the universe.[5] Further, the human race is linked to each of the three constituent tiers of the world by dominion over sea, heaven, and earth (1:26). The human race rules (1:26) the animal life of each of the three domains as the sun and moon govern day and night. And only the human race by its climactic day-six position (and by its freedom to respond to the divine word) directly encounters God. Only the human race can articulate a verbal response to the Creator. Genesis depicts human beings in royal terms, which is suggested by the words "image" and "likeness" (found in Mesopotamian royal inscriptions) and by the verbs "rule" and "subdue."[6]

In the Genesis system the human race is the linchpin of a harmonious universe, spanning, uniting, and bringing it before God. In the course of the week of creation the world is increasingly made fit for *human* habitation; darkness is made into night that is restful for people and enveloping waters into seas that provide food and transportation.

The divine commands to the couple in verses 26–28 seem to belie the picture of the human race as a constituent part of the world. We must, therefore, look closely at their meaning. The command in Gen. 1:26, 28 "to have dominion over" the fish, birds, cattle, and creeping things and "to fill the earth and subdue it" at first glance seems to give permission to the human race to manipulate and exploit the world. And so it has been understood by many readers. A close look at the narrative context, however, shows that the verbs do not intend such an instrumental view of the nonhuman world. As noted, human dominion is to be exercised in a royal way, since "image" and "likeness" and the verbs of ruling are used of kings in comparable extra-biblical accounts. The king was believed to be an image of his divine patron, acting for his god, and so resembled the god *dynamically*, through his care for his god's domain. Genesis applies to the human race what other texts apply to the king. The human race exercises dominion over the three realms of sea, heavens, and earth. How this dominion works in practice is illustrated in the actions of the just Noah prior to the flood: he brings two (male and female) of every kind of animal into the ark to keep them alive with him (6:19). God's command to the first human being in 1:28 to be fruitful and multiply, i.e., to continue in existence, evidently implies that the human race is to see to the existence of other forms of life. It is important to note that Noah's saving the animals was not out of sheer self-interest (to ensure a supply of food), for in the pre-Flood period humans were not permitted to kill them for meat (1:29–30). Only as a concession to the sorry inclination of people to violence did God permit them to kill animals for food (9:1–5).

Another troublesome phrase for an environmental reading of Genesis is the phrase in verse 28, "subdue the earth," for the Hebrew verb *kābāš*, "to subdue," implies forceful military domination. Here again the narrative context shows that this verb, too, does not give blanket permission to exploit the earth. Syntactically, the verb expands and completes the preceding phrase "fill the earth" ("fill the earth and subdue it") rather than the following phrase "have dominion over." The fish and birds were told in verse 22 "increase and multiply and fill the waters of the sea" but not "subdue it." The addition of the verb "subdue" addressed to the human race in verse 28 seems to presume that they will encounter obstructions as each nation takes its proper habitat. The underlying idea seems the same as in Genesis 10: God gives to each people its own land. So also Deut. 32:8–9: "[God] set up the boundaries of the peoples after the number of the sons of God; while the Lord's own portion was Jacob, his hereditary share was Israel." Each nation must take its divinely apportioned land; Israel is given Canaan but must wrest it from its inhabitants. "Earth," then, is not land in general but the particular land given to each nation, "territory." "Subdue" is probably an anticipatory reference to Israel's conquest of Canaan (Josh. 18:1 and Num. 32:22, 29 use the same verb), which is regarded as typical for all nations.[7] The forcefulness implicit in the verb is associated with each nation's first-time seizure of their God-given land. In short, "subdue the earth" means "Subdue your territory!" rather than "Manipulate the environment!"

In summary, the opening chapter of the Bible shows us the human race delegated to exercise on earth God's sovereign rule. There rule does not, however, put them *above* the world, for they are *within* its dense system. That rule, handed down to Noah, is exercised in chapters 6–9 by enabling the species of the world to survive the Flood.

We conclude our discussion of Genesis 1 by noting its orientation to the future, its "eschatology." Seven times God declares that creation is good. The statement is not an empirical deduction but a divine word that will prevail over all contrary forces. The world *God* made will prevail in the end. God intends the world to be a system oriented to him (theocentric) rather than to the human race (anthropocentric). Distortions of that original order will not endure. The end (*Endzeit*) will be like the beginning (*Urzeit*). The last book of the Christian Bible ends with a reference back to Genesis 1: creation is renewed (Rev. 21:1–22:5), chaos having been forever vanquished (Rev. 19:11–20:15).[8] Many biblical texts speak of the original order and harmony that will appear in the new age, e.g., Isa. 11:1–9; 65:25; Ezek. 47:1–12; and Rev. 21:1–22:5.

Having examined in detail a text that has been seen as the fountainhead of biblical anthropocentrism, we turn to the topic of anthropocentrism. Lynn White remarks, "Especially in its Western form, Christianity is the most anthropocentric religion the world has ever seen." He cites the place of human beings in the creation stories as the source of this perspective.[9] The picture is not quite so simple as White portrays it. For one thing, biblical creation accounts (when correctly understood) are theocentric. The place of human beings is circumscribed on the one hand by the sovereign God and on the other by the world of which human beings are a constituent part.

Moreover, one book in the Bible subjects anthropocentrism itself to critique—the Book of Job. Provoked by his losses and suffering and by the three "friends," Job complains bitterly in lengthy speeches of God's treatment of him and the universe. He demands a response. God's answer to Job in the climactic chapters 38–41 is simply a description of the world in two parallel speeches. The speeches contain a shock: human beings are not the goal or purpose of creation and their knowledge is decidedly limited (chapter 28). Moshe Greenberg explains: "How different this survey of creation is from that of Genesis 1 or the hymn to nature of Psalm 104. Here man is incidental—mainly an impotent foil to God. In Genesis 1 (and its echo, Psalm 8), teleology pervades a process of creation whose goal and crown is man. All is directed to his benefit; the earth and its creatures are his to rule. . . . Job, representing mankind, stands outside the picture, displaced from its center to a remote periphery."[10] It should be said, however, that Job is important in the book. God directs a long speech exclusively to him and pays him the supreme compliment of listening to his every word and answering him in detail. The book, however, reinterprets biblical anthropocentrism and subordinates it to an irreducible theocentrism.

Genesis 2–11

Another creation account, Genesis 2–11, also shows that the human race is part of a system. The length and sophistication of the story illustrates the historical, cultural, and ecological dimensions of the system. The story falls within the genre of creation-flood epic, which through narrative explores human culture.[11] The following plot can be abstracted from the extant examples: the gods create the world and the human race; human disturbance of the gods provokes them to send an annihilating flood; after the flood the gods restore their creation but adjust the design of the human race so that the human population will never again get out of hand.

In Genesis 2–11 the human race (represented by typical figures) acts within a history driven by cause and effect, is thoroughly rooted in its environment, and is subject to a just and powerful God. The man(*'adam*) is created from earth (*'adamâ*, in 2:7; the wordplay underlines the close link) and becomes a living being when God breathes into his nostrils the breath of life.[12] In Gen. 2:8, the man is created to be a gardener, whose work is required for the earth to bloom (2:6). God brings all animals and birds to the man so he can name them: "and whatever the man called every living creature, that was its name" (2:19). Naming in the account does not mean simply possessing power over another, since the man in 2:23 names his wife whom God gives him as a "compatible helper" (traditional "helpmeet," corrupted to "helpmate") in contrast to the subordinate and "incompatible" animals previously brought to him. From the context, naming connotes appropriate authority, affinity, and care.[13]

The primordial bond between human beings and the earth appears also in the series of alienations suffered by Adam and Eve because of their sin. According to chapter 3, Eve's future childbearing will occur in pain and Adam's gardening will be achieved by the sweat of his face upon a resistant soil ("cursed is the ground because of you"). In chapter 6, several generations after Adam and Eve, the earth is again affected by human disobedience. "Now the earth was corrupt in God's sight, and the earth was filled with violence. And God looked on the earth and it was corrupt; for all flesh had corrupted its ways upon the earth. And God said to Noah, 'I have determined to make an end of all flesh, for the earth is filled with violence because of them; I am about to destroy them along with the earth' " (6:11–13). "Earth" occurs six times and the verb "to corrupt" is used both of human beings and of the environment. Earth shares in the frightful consequences of human sin.

After the flood God restores the system; the human race is again its responsible center (chapter 9). To Noah and his household God reaffirms the original command of Gen. 1:28: "Be fruitful and multiply, and fill the earth" (9:1). In contrast with comparable postflood restorations where the gods put limits on human population (childbirth demons, celibate women, mortality), God does not alter the original blessing; the original design was perfect. But there is one change: "The fear and dread of you shall rest on every animal of the earth," as well as on birds, creeping things, and fish (9:2). All animals are given to the human race for food. There is a proviso, however: the blood of a slain animal must be poured on the ground, for the blood is the life (9:4–6). The life shared by humans and animals is not under human authority; it is sacred, directly under God. As if in compensation for the new vulnerability of the animals, God makes a single covenant with both humans and animals that witnesses to the bond between all sentient beings: "I am now establishing my covenant with you and your descendants after you, and with every living creature that is with you, the birds, the cattle, and every beast of the earth with you, all who came out of the ark . . . that never again shall all flesh be destroyed by the waters of a flood" (Gen 9:9–11). The rainbow is the covenant's sign, signaling that all future rainstorms will end short of deluge.

The Prophets

In the historical and prophetic books, Israel's relation to the Lord was conceived as a covenant, originally made when the people escaped from the *land* of Egypt to live henceforth in the *land* of Israel. Land therefore figures prominently in the curses and blessings contingent upon obedience or disobedience to the covenant. The curses were often couched in military and agricultural terms: invasion or protection of the land; abundance or famine. Both Leviticus 26 and Deuteronomy 28 put the covenant curses and blessings within a frame of natural abundance and deprivation.

The eighth-century prophets Amos and Hosea were the first to preach that the covenant as Israel had known it was ended. They promulgated the curses but they also raised the hope that after the judgment the blessings of the covenant would be renewed. Hosea announced a time when Yahweh would take back "my grain in its time, and my wine in its season; and I will take away my wool and my flax" (Hos. 2:9 [Hebrew 2:11]). In Hosea's postpunishment restoration, God will "make for you a covenant on that day with the wild animals, the birds of the air, and the creeping things of the ground; and bow, sword, and war I will abolish from the land; and I will make you lie down in safety" (Hos. 2:18 [Hebrew 2:20]). In Amos 4:4–11, God uses five natural afflictions—famine, drought, blight and mildew, plague, and a Sodom-and-Gomorrah-like "overturning"—to punish and warn Israel. The post-judgment restoration of Israel (Amos 9:11–15) likewise means both political and environmental shalom: the rebuilding of the davidic kingship, the defeat of enemies, and abundant fertility: "The mountains shall drip sweet wine, and all the hills shall flow with it." Another prophetic book, Isaiah, develops two relevant themes: salvation as the healing of nature and salvation as the purification and restoration of the holy city of Zion. Isaiah 35 is memorable: "The wilderness and the dry land shall be glad, the desert shall rejoice and blossom. . . . Then the eyes of the blind shall be opened, and the ears of the deaf unstopped."

NEW TESTAMENT[14]

Early Christianity, it is now recognized, was originally one among several different "Judaisms" in Palestine of the first century C.E. Early Christians accepted the Jewish Scriptures as their own, finding within its pages evidence that Jesus was the messiah. To Christians, Jesus ushered in the New Age predicted by the Scriptures, especially the prophets: God was now "judging" the world, that is, intervening to establish a new order, the "kingdom of God." According to Mark 1:15, Jesus proclaimed, "This is the time of fulfillment. The kingdom of God is at hand. Repent, and believe in the gospel." The ancient promises were fulfilled in Jesus' words and deeds, including covenant blessing and restoration of the harmony that prevailed at the moment of creation.

The New Testament understanding of human beings in their natural environment is essentially that of the Old Testament: human beings are an integral component of the good world created by God. Damaged by sinful human behavior, the world in its human and nonhuman aspects is to be redeemed, recreated by Christ. And human beings, irreducibly corporal and in their earthly habitat, are to be saved, healed in "body and soul."

What did Jesus himself think and teach about the natural environment? One shorthand way of getting to the thinking of Jesus is through the parables, generally an indicator of Jesus' creativity. In his parables Jesus frequently uses analogies from nature. The parables presume God is revealed in nature in such a way as to illuminate the Kingdom: "Hear this! A sower went out to sow" (Mark 4:3); "To what shall we compare the kingdom of God, or what parable can we use for it? It is like a mustard seed that, when it is sown in the ground, is the smallest of the seeds on the earth. But once it is sown, it springs up and becomes the largest of plants and puts forth large branches, so that the birds of the sky can dwell in its shade" (Mark 4:30–32). Against anxiety and unnecessary striving, Jesus advises, "Look at the birds of the sky. . . . Learn from the way the wild flowers grow" (Matt. 6:26, 27). Jesus' language should not be considered merely "poetic," a concrete and memorable way of putting a truth. His metaphors reveal something profound about the structure of being; there is an underlying unity between the world of everyday experience and the reign of God.

Relatively few New Testament passages deal explicitly with creation or the environment, but the basic New Testament proclamation—Jesus Christ has been raised from the dead—is a major statement about human beings' relation to the natural world. The resurrection is interpreted as a new creation because Christ, the representative human being, has defeated death, *the* enemy of the race and hence of the world. Christ's act is like the defeat of darkness and waters (the primordial human enemy) in the first creation. His resurrection, as representative human being, raises up the world as a system because the human race is an integral part of that system.

A particularly clear statement of Christ's act as new creation is the hymn in Col. 1:15–20: "He is the image of the invisible God, *the first born of all creation.* For in him were created all things in heaven and on earth, the visible and the invisible, whether thrones or dominions or principalities or powers; all things were created through him and for him. He is the head of the body, the church. He is the beginning, *the firstborn from the dead.*" Creation and reconciliation are described in parallel stanzas, verses 15–17 and 18–20.

In creation Christ was the image (*eikōn* as in Gen. 1:27–28) of the invisible God, the firstborn of creation in the sense that the created world is modeled on him, oriented to him, subordinate to him, coheres in him. The phraseology is largely derived from Genesis 1 and texts of personified wisdom such as Proverbs 3:19–20 and 8:1–36. In Genesis darkness and chaos were overcome so that the human community can be formed. Proverbs urges people to shun the path of death for the path of life.

Though the whole universe is created anew, creation begins at a particular point—the chosen people. New life radiates out from the risen Christ upon those closest to him. New Testament writings express the idea of life in a variety of ways, e.g., "remaining in Christ," obeying Christ, the bread of life and the wine in the Gospel of John, but occasionally they employ the word *creation* for the emergence of the new people, as in 2 Cor. 5:17: "So whoever is in Christ is a new creation; the old things have passed away; behold new things have come. And all this is from God, who has reconciled [Col. 1:20] us to himself through Christ and given us this ministry of reconciliation." The text alludes to Isa. 43:18–21, where the new act of God is described in the language of both creation and redemption. Gal. 6:15 uses "new creation" similarly.

The hymn in John (originally perhaps verses 1–5, 10–11, 14) resembles Col. 1:15–20 in blending Genesis 1 and wisdom texts to describe the work of Christ: "In the beginning was the Word, and the Word was with God, and the Word was God" (v. 1). The hymn employs metaphors which are further developed in the body of the Gospel: Jesus is the true light illuminating humankind and is Wisdom addressing words of life to his followers. John transposes the light and divine word of creation in Genesis 1 to the ethical plane. The darkness and disorder resulting from unbelief are overcome by God's word and light in Christ. Christ is legitimated by the Scriptures as the Word and the Wisdom who brings the world to completion.

The Synoptic gospels are less grandly reflective than the Fourth Gospel on Christ as the creator, but even here Christ's salvation means the healing of the people and their environment, as is clear in the healing miracles. In Matt. 11:5–6 Jesus fulfills Isa. 61:1 and 35:5–6 ("the blind receive their sight, the lame walk, the lepers are cleansed, the deaf hear, the dead are raised, and the poor have the good news preached to them"), even though there is no explicit reference to the Isaian healing of the wilderness.

CONCLUSIONS

The anthropocentrism of the Bible is relative, not absolute. It is bounded on the one side by a pervasive theocentrism and, on the other, by the created world of which the human race is a constituent part, albeit the crowning part. The human race rules as God's representative, or image, over the world as a system, not over the world as discrete manipulatable elements. Human beings are the *responsible* center of the world, in the root sense of ability to respond. Their dominion maintains the will of the creator regarding the world. The Book of Job adds its own radical qualification to biblical anthropocentrism. Chapters 38–41 insist that God created the world for his own inscrutable purpose and not for the human race; human beings will never fathom the divine purpose of the world (ch. 28). But paradoxically human beings are important in the book and in the created world.

Though not identified with nature, God is the power behind the fertility and infertility of the natural world. Depending on the quality of its relation to God, Israel experiences that world as nurturing or destructive. God is particularly present in the land of Israel; the people live from its riches and define themselves as a nation by its soil. The formulation of the covenant blessings and curses presumes Israel's rootedness in the land—security or invasion, fertility or blight.

Biblical cosmogonies connect human society and natural environment. Human sin blights the earth and divine salvation restores the people *and* their environment. In visions of the future the Bible sometimes does not distinguish sharply between the human and nonhuman world. For example, in Isaiah 65 and its New Testament fulfillment in Rev. 21:1–22:5, recreated Zion has its buildings restored, its faithful poor vindicated, and nature appears again in its original harmony.

The New Testament interprets the resurrection of Jesus as a new creation; Christ's rising from the dead defeats the primordial enemy of human community in a manner analogous to the first creation when chaos was defeated and the human race began to live. The analogy was easy for ancient Near Eastern people to draw, for they understood creation primarily as the emergence of a people. New creation is not, however, identical to first creation, for first creation creates out of chaos or nothingness whereas new creation creates out of sinful or ambiguous human history.

NOTES

1. It is this interpretative tradition that Lynn White seems to have in mind when he severely criticizes the Bible and the way in which it was read in the West for encouraging antinature views. See "The Historical Roots of Our Ecological Crisis," *Science* 155 (1967): 1203–1207, reprinted in *The Environmental Handbook,* ed. Garrett De Bell (New York: Ballantine, 1970), pp. 12–26; idem *Science* 156 (1967): 737–38. For a Roman Catholic critique of the "Augustinian" reading, see Gabriel Daly, *Creation and Redemption* (Wilmington: Glazier, 1989) and "Creation," in *Commentary on the Catechism of the Catholic Church,* ed. M. Walsh (London: Geoffrey Chapman, 1994), pp. 82–11.

2. These remarks are drawn from R. Clifford, "The Hebrew Scriptures and the Theology of Creation," *Theological Studies* 46 (1985): 507–523.

3. An excellent orientation to the topic of creation in the Bible with ample bibliography is the collection of essays in *Creation in the Old Testament,* ed. B. W. Anderson; *Issues in Religion and Theology,* vol. 6 (Philadelphia: Fortress, 1984), especially the essay by Anderson, "Creation and Ecology," pp. 152–71. See also R. A. Simkins, *Creator and Creation: Nature in the World view of Ancient Israel* (Peabody, Mass.: Hendrickson, 1994) and T. Hiebert, *The Yahwist's Landscape: Nature and Religion in Early Israel* (New York: Oxford, 1996).

4. See B. W. Anderson, "A Stylistic Study of the Priestly Creation Story," in *Canon and Authority*, ed. G. W. Coats and B. O. Long (Philadelphia: Fortress, 1977), pp. 148–62.

5. Phyllis Bird, " 'Male and Female He Created Them' Gen 1:27b in the Context of the Priestly Account of Creation," *Harvard Theological Review* 74 (1981): 146–47.

6. "Male and Female," pp. 140–44.

7. Lohfink, "The Priestly Document and the Limits of Growth," in *Great Themes from the Old Testament* (Edinburgh: T. & T. Clark, 1982), pp. 167–82, and R. J. Clifford, "Genesis 1–3: Permission to Exploit Nature?" *The Bible Today* 26 (1988): 133–37.

8. Westermann, *Beginning and End in the Bible*, vol. 31 of *Facet Books Biblical Series* (Philadelphia: Fortress, 1972).

9. "The Historical Roots of Our Ecological Crisis," p. 20.

10. "Job," in *The Literary Guide to the Bible*, ed. R. Alter and F. Kermode (Cambridge: Harvard University Press, 1987), p. 298.

11. David Damrosch proposes the genre label in *The Narrative Covenant: Transformations of Genre in the Growth of the Biblical Tradition* (San Francisco: Harper, 1987), chaps. 1–3. The genre includes Mesopotamian compositions such as the Sumerian Flood Story (Thorkild Jacobsen's "Eridu Genesis"), "The Rulers of Lagash," tablet XI of Gilgamesh, and Atrahasis. See further R. Clifford, *Creation Accounts in the Ancient Near East and in the Bible* (Washington, D.C.: Catholic Biblical Association, 1994), pp. 42–49, 74–82.

12. Biblical anthropology does not presuppose a spirit-body dualism; the human person is an enfleshed spirit. The occasional contrast in the Bible between "flesh" and "spirit" is not internal (body-soul) but external; "flesh" is the human person relying on personal strength whereas "spirit" is God's power.

13. Indispensable on chaps. 2–3 is Phyllis Trible, "A Love Story Gone Awry," in *God and the Rhetoric of Sexuality* (Philadelphia: Fortress, 1978), pp. 72–143.

14. The following pages owe much to my article, "The Bible and the Environment," in *Preserving the Creation: Environmental Theology and Ethics*, ed. K. W. Irwin and E. D. Pellegrino (Washington, D.C.: Georgetown University Press), pp. 19–24.

QUESTIONS FOR DISCUSSION

1. Is it legitimate to come to the Bible with one's own and other contemporary questions? What do you think are some *new* questions of today, not asked in previous times?

2. Do you think that certain emphases of the Bible, e.g., anthropocentrism, patriarchy, and neglect of nature, have contributed to Christian disinterest in the environment? Does the Bible itself subject the above emphases to critique? Where?

3. How does one's understanding of creation—its motive, its role in the story of the world and of the holy community, its purpose—affect our understanding of the environment?

4. Do you think that the concept of new creation in the New Testament is a helpful way to understand the resurrection?

6

THE EARTH MATTERS
Foundations for an
Environmental Ethic
Michal Fox Smart

IN THE BEGINNING

"In the beginning," the Torah tells us, "God created heaven and earth" (Gen. 1:1). There are whole worlds within every word of this sentence. "In the beginning, God created heaven and earth." In a sense, all the sophisticated reflection and detailed argumentation in which we have begun to engage as a community ultimately boils down to this one utterance, this most fundamental tenet: the world is God's creation. Seen through the lens of religious tradition, life is not a cosmic accident devoid of ultimate meaning. Somehow, who we are, what we are, that we are at all, matters. It matters very much, to the God who made us.

The perception that the world is a purposive creation of God adds a uniquely religious dimension to issues of environmental concern. Upon witnessing the extinction of a species, for instance, the biologist mourns the loss of millions of years of genetic development and adaptation. As Jews, many of us, too, mourn the loss of such a rich inheritance. Yet, we might also ask: Does it matter to God? For an increasing number of religious people, our tradition's

165

proclamation that the world is God's creation implies that ecological destruction must matter to the Creator, and consequently, that engaging with environmental concerns is a central part of what it means to be faithful in our generation. In our society's wanton behavior and disregard for other creatures' existence, there is something more than callousness and greed, something more than blissful ignorance. There is a shirking of religious responsibility. There is a gesture of blasphemy. If we are to bear witness to God, we must decry the destruction of God's Creation.

THE PURPOSIVENESS OF EVERYTHING IN CREATION

The Bible's portrayal of the world as God's creation implies that there is divine intention for the existence of all plant and animal species. Midrash Rabbah states this explicitly: "Even things which you see in the world as superfluous, such as flies, fleas, and mosquitoes, even they are part of the wholeness of Creation, and the Holy One, Blessed be He, carries out His purpose through everything, as it is written: 'And God saw all that He had made, and behold, it was very good' " (Gen. Rabbah 10:7).[1] This attribution of divine intention to the "natural" lends a degree of inherent value to every part of the created world, and should foster an attitude of humility when human ambitions and the needs of other creatures come into conflict.

Understanding the world as God's creation also provides a basis for valuing the material world in general, and therefore disdaining waste. For this reason, the rabbis said that "one who tears his clothes in anger, or one who breaks his tools in anger, or one who wastes his money in anger you should regard as an idolater" (B. Shabbat 105b).

THE GOODNESS OF CREATION

In deciding whether to preserve other species or wilderness areas, and at what cost to people, environmental ethicists struggle to articulate a value for other species and natural elements beyond their utility. On this subject, the Torah reinforces religious intuition with an explicit and powerful claim: that God's Creation is good. The land and the seas, the trees and grass, the sun, moon, and stars and the passing seasons which they proclaim, the world's fish and birds, the creeping things and beasts of the earth—each of these is recognized by God, in the Torah's opening passages, to be good. In fact the phrase "and God saw that it was good" is repeated in mantra-like fashion throughout the first tale of creation, appearing in Gen. 1:4, 10, 12, 18, 21, and 25. Goodness appears to be the defining characteristic of the created world.

Significantly, God observes that these initial creations, both flora and fauna, energy and inert matter, are good independent of humanity, which does not come into existence until Gen. 1:26. As such, the first tale of Creation provides an important balance to our usual way of thinking, which is expressed in the second Creation story.[2] The earth provides resources which sustain and enhance human life, and that is good. Yet in the biblical world view, the value of creation is not expressed only in terms of economic value or utility to people. Creation is of value because every creature, even the earth itself, stands before God and is beheld to be good in the eyes of its Creator.

The judgment "very good" appears on the sixth day (a day whose creations include insects and land animals, as well as humans), and refers explicitly to all which God had created thus far: "And God saw everything that He had made, and behold, it was very good" (Gen. 1:31). This is, in fact, the seventh pronouncement of goodness within the seven days of creation, thereby conveying a sense of goodness to the whole of the created world. This material world—a world of humans, plants, animals, and inert creation together—"Behold," Scripture tells us, "it is very good."

And on the seventh day, Creation is made holy: "And God blessed the seventh day, and sanctified it; because on it He rested from all his work which God created to do" (Gen. 2:2–3). Unlike months or days or years, the weekly cycle has no corollary in the physical universe. It is distinctly unnatural. As such, the place of the Sabbath within the scheme of Creation should not be underestimated. For the sanctification of the seventh day weaves an element of the supra-natural into the very fabric of the natural world.[3]

The essential goodness of Creation is reflected elsewhere in the Bible, as well. Throughout the Torah, the bestowal of life is identified with God's blessing, while God's curse is the destruction of life and the processes which sustain it.[4] In the Book of Job, two entire chapters proclaim the achievements of a Creator who delights in all beings (Job 38–39).[5] There, as well, the Bible recounts that Creation sang for joy upon its own coming into being, as did the Heavenly host. "Where were you when I laid the foundations of the earth?" God asks Job, ". . . when the morning stars sang together, and all the sons of God shouted for joy?" (Job 38:4, 7)

THE EARTH IS THE LORD'S: DIVINE OWNERSHIP OF ALL THAT EXISTS

> And the land shall not be sold forever: For the land is Mine, and you are strangers and sojourners with me. (Lev. 25:23)

Mainstream Jewish tradition infers from the Torah's portrayal of God as Creator that the world still and always belongs to its Creator. In the words of Ps. 24:1, "the earth is the Lord's and all which fills it, the world and all its inhabitants." Because the world is God's property, it is not available to human beings to exploit at will. Indeed, Jewish tradition as a whole rests upon the premise that we do not have unrestricted use of Creation, including our own bodies. Countless laws serve to mediate Jews' interaction with the world, detailing when and which actions and parts of God's world are allowable to us, and which are forbidden.[6] Indeed, it is precisely Jewish law's restriction of one's autonomous will that runs so counter to modern sensibilities. Thus, although the Torah grants human beings a status distinct from plants and other animals, it simultaneously imposes absolute limits on human behavior and use of God's world.[7]

God's perceived ownership of the world is further manifested in

Judaism's bold vision of social justice. *Zedaqah,* the Hebrew word for giving to those in need, does not mean charity. It means justice. For all we possess is ultimately a gift of God. The wealthy are no more deserving of wealth than the poor, nor do they own their wealth in an ultimate sense. It is not generosity of spirit, therefore, but right-eousness which demands that resources be redistributed such that the basic needs of all people be met.

Moreover, traditional Jewish practices stemming from God's ownership of the world urge us to consider not only social justice (meaning just relations between people) but also ecological jus-tice—meaning just relations between human beings and other crea-tures. Time and again, specific religious observances address both of these realms of concern, interwoven and grounded in the same philosophy. For example, Shemitah, the Sabbatical year, is primarily defined as a Sabbath for the land (Lev. 25:1–2). As a consequence of the earth's Sabbath, privately owned land is legally deemed own-erless, and standard cultivation of crops is forbidden. A striking aspect of Shemitah observance—*biyur*—necessitates that once a given food is no longer available to wild animals in the fields, this same item must be removed from human domiciles and declared ownerless (M. Shevi'it 7:1). Thus observance of Shemitah serves to deflate the chasm between human and wild animal, between the natural world and human society. Significantly, this "Shemitah of land" is accompanied by a "Shemitah of money," in which all out-standing monetary debts among Jews are forgiven in an effort to eliminate poverty within the nation. Shemitah thus addresses both inequity in the social realm, and inequity between humans and the rest of Creation.[8]

Within Jewish tradition, this central tenet of divine ownership has found normative expression in specific religious practices. Prayer in particular bridges the gap between text and action, serving to embody the tenets of Jewish tradition in one's daily con-sciousness and behavioral norms. For instance, because the earth and all which fills it belong to God, Jewish tradition holds that one needs permission to take anything from it, and Jews acknowledge this by reciting a blessing. The Talmud states, "It is forbidden to enjoy anything from this world without a blessing. . . . Rav Chanina Bar Papa said: 'Anyone who enjoys something from this world without a blessing, it is as if he steals from the Holy One, Blessed be He' " (B. Berakhot 35a-b). Thus, blessings continually remind us, each of the many times a day that we take of its bounty, that the world is not ours to exploit at will and that our use of its richness must be responsible.

THE MIRACULOUSNESS OF THE EVERYDAY

> Mankind will not perish for want of information; but only for want of appreciation.[9]

The problems commonly referred to as the "environmental crisis" are actually only symptoms of what is essentially a crisis of values. Persuading Americans to alter ecologically unsound behavior will therefore require more than scientific information. We need a better way of seeing the world, an attitudinal shift. The educational task before us is therefore to raise a generation of people who are awake not only to the circumstances which threaten the planet, but also to the miracle which underlies its very existence. This, perhaps, is the most fundamental insight of a Jewish theology of Creation: life is a gift. The world's existence, and the undeserved opportunity we have each been given to witness and to participate in the drama of life, are incomprehensible expressions of God's mercy and love. I believe a large part of what we have to share is good news—a positive message of faith and love, of wonder and gratitude.

Judaism transmits a legacy of wonder through prayer. Several traditional Jewish prayers cite God acting in the everyday functioning of the natural world. For instance, in the daily morning service, Jews bless God "who shines upon the earth and those who dwell upon her in mercy, and renews each day, always, the act of creation," while the evening prayers bless God "who causes evening to fall and orders the stars in their heavenly constellations."[10] Seen in this light, the everyday functioning of the natural world appears as a source of wonder, and the prosaic as miraculous. Thus, thrice each day, Jews pause to thank God for "your miracles that are with us each day, and for your wonders and goodness that are with us at every moment: evening, morning, and noon."[11]

Judaism provides blessings for seeing rainbows and hearing thunder, for eating food and excreting waste, for smelling flowers and sighting the first buds of spring, and for witnessing sites of extreme ugliness and beauty. The opportunities for blessing are constant, and one must therefore be constantly alert. In fact, Rabbi Meir expected Jews to recite as many as one hundred blessings per day (B. Menahot 43b). Thus, not only can a Jew experience the world and respond with a blessing, but the habit of reciting blessings can cultivate sensory awareness and thus enable a Jew truly to experience the world. The daily regimen of blessings and prayers, which invite one to pause, reflect upon, and appreciate the gifts of God's world countless times throughout each day, is one of the greatest potential contributions of Jewish tradition to contemporary education, as it models how a sense of wonder can be cultivated and maintained in one's daily life.

GOD'S COMPASSION FOR ALL CREATURES

In the view of several biblical and rabbinic texts, God cares actively for nonhuman species, as well as for the integrity of Creation as a whole. "The Lord is good to all," summarizes the psalmist, "His mercy is over all His works" (Ps. 145:9). Biblical writings depict myriad species sharing in the bounty of Creation, and praise God for sustaining every living creature. "Sing praise upon the lyre to our God," exhorts the psalmist, "who covers the heaven with clouds, who prepares rain for the earth, who makes grass to grow upon the mountains. He gives to the beast its food, and to the young ravens which cry" (Ps. 147:7–9). "The eyes of all wait upon You, and You give them their food in due season. You open your hand and satisfy the desire of every living thing" (Ps. 145:15–16). Concerning plant life, "Rabbi Simon said: There is not a single blade of grass which does not have its star in heaven, which watches over it and tells it, 'Grow!' " (Gen. Rabbah 10:6) In recognition of this complex web of relationships, in the Grace After Meals, Jews bless God for nourishing and sustaining all creatures, not only human beings.[12]

Psalm 104 is a celebration of God's sustenance of other creatures alongside God's provision of resources for human cultivation. The import of these diverse texts is clear: divine care extends beyond human beings to the whole created world.[13]

THE PRESERVATION OF SPECIES

Already within the first Creation narrative, the Torah stresses God's concern for the continuation of each created "kind" (akin to what today we call species). Thus, Genesis 1 recounts not only the creation of grasses and fruit trees, but also the mechanisms by which each species is to be propagated indefinitely into the future.[14] Although the blessing to "be fruitful and multiply" is most commonly associated with the first human beings, in fact God blesses all animals created on the fifth day, saying, "be fruitful and multiply, and fill the waters in the seas, and let birds multiply in the earth" (Gen. 1:22). Not only the flourishing of human culture, but also the thriving of plants and animals across the earth in their natural habitats is a Divine command and blessing. In the Flood narrative (Gen. 6:19–20, 8:1), God's concern for every one of the world's animal species is dramatically demonstrated.

These narrative depictions of God's valuation of species are reinforced by Jewish laws which address the possibility of human-caused extinction. For instance, the Torah prohibits the slaughter of an animal and its offspring in one day.[15] A separate passage in Deuteronomy reads: "If a bird's nest chance to be before you in the way . . . you shall not take the mother bird together with the young. But you shall surely let the mother go, and take the young to you, that it may be well with you, and that you may prolong your days" (Deut. 22:6–7). Minimally, these laws constitute legal protection for individual animals from patterns of consumption which, if habitual, might eventually endanger the survival of their species.[16] Moreover, having interpreted the individual parent and offspring mentioned in each of these passages to represent their respective generations, a number of medieval commentators understood these laws actually to prohibit the extinction of any animal species. For instance, Nahmanides[17] writes, "The Torah will not permit an act of destruction, to eradicate the species, even though it permitted slaughter [of individuals] in the species. For one who kills the mother with the children in one day or takes them . . . it is as if he eradicates that species."[18]

MAINTAINING THE CREATED ORDER

Derived from the belief that the world is God's deliberate creation is also the notion that there is an essential order to Creation which expresses God's will and should therefore be respectfully maintained. Consequently, an ethic of restraining human creative activity pervades Jewish tradition. For instance, the weekly Sabbath, which is identified as a "remembrance of the work of Creation," is characterized by the prohibition of labor.[19] On the Sabbath, therefore, Jews bear witness to God as Creator by curtailing their own creative work and alteration of God's world.

Although contextualized in a society so unlike our own, the Torah directly addresses the proclivity of human beings to use our creativity to alter Creation in inappropriate ways. For instance, we read in Leviticus: "And my statutes you shall keep. You shall not let your cattle mate with a diverse kind; you shall not sow your field with mingled seed; a garment mingled of linen and wool shall not come upon you" (Lev. 19:19). Likewise in Deuteronomy: "You shall not sow your vineyard with diverse seeds, lest the fruit of the seed which you have sown, and the fruit of the vineyard, be forfeited. You shall not plow with an ox and an ass together. You shall not wear a garment of diverse kinds, of wool and linen together" (Deut. 22:9–11). Although the forbidden garment of wool and linen is harder to explain,[20] mainstream Jewish tradition understands these other laws to prohibit the hybridization of either plant or animal species. In this same vein, the Talmud further prohibits the grafting of different species of trees to one another (Qidushin 39a). In regard to the integrity of species, the order of Creation is to remain as God established it.

Furthermore, one reading of the Leviticus passage suggests that it explicitly advocates preserving natural processes as a general rule. Note that the set of specific laws just quoted from Leviticus is prefaced with the mandate "And my statutes you shall keep" (*ve-huqotai tishmoru*) (Lev. 19:19). The question immediately arises: what statutes? If this phrase were understood to refer only to the specific laws which follow, it would be redundant, in contradiction to traditional exegetical principles. Sifra[21] therefore explains that this phrase refers to a greater set of laws: "the statutes I have already imposed of old."[22] Similarly, the Jerusalem Talmud identifies the statutes we must keep as "*huqim she-hahaqti be-olami,* the laws that I engraved in my world" (Y. Kilayim 1:7). This biblical passage has therefore been understood to protect the integrity of inviolable categories and processes which exist within the created world, what we might call today "the laws of nature." Taken as a whole, then, these laws prohibit tampering with the very order of creation. Samson Raphael Hirsch[23] summarized Jewish law in this regard: "Respect the Divine order in God's creations. . . . You should not interfere with the natural order."[24]

This deferential stance is far from the norm in contemporary society. Each year, for instance, scores of synthetic chemical compounds are introduced into the biosphere. New technologies, including the growing field of "genetic engineering," advance with arguably insufficient controls, causing many concern over the possible future uses to which they may be applied. In addition, as an unforeseen consequence of our physically comfortable lifestyles (e.g., the use of automobiles and air conditioners), the global systems on which life depends are being altered in unpredictable and possibly irreversible ways.[25] As a result of these and other innovations, "tampering with the order of Creation" may well be the hallmark of our historical era when it is reviewed by future generations, whose lives will be shaped by our unrestrained experimentation with the planet.

GOD'S COVENANT WITH CREATION

In recent years, the theme of covenant has been developed by a variety of thinkers to characterize the relationship between God and Israel, as well as to provide a framework for Jewish ethics.[26] For example, the liberal theologian Eugene Borowitz contends that "the first and most formative experience in the development of Jewish spirituality was entering into the Covenant. . . . Judaism revolves around the Covenant experience of choice, promise, demand, redemption, and mission. . . . Believing Jews live in the reality of the Covenant."[27]

There is much in Israel's covenant with God and the notion of covenant itself which is essential to the formulation of a Jewish environmental ethic. For instance, Israel's covenant provides a conceptual framework that tempers the radical individualism which is a root cause of ecological destruction in contemporary society. For living within a covenantal community means that one must make the most private and personal of decisions in the knowledge that she is part of a community and a story larger than her own individual life to which she is responsible. According to Rabbi Joseph Soloveitchik, the notion of intergenerational responsibility is also central to the Jewish understanding of membership in a covenantal community.[28] Moreover, a specific corollary of Jewish covenantal responsibility has always been the bequeathal to future generations of a world blessed with the resources that make a full life possible.[29]

Even more important to our discussion, biblical sources reveal that God lives not only in covenantal relationship to Israel, nor even all humankind, but in covenant with the entire created world. Upon the abatement of the Great Flood, God declares to Noah: "Behold, I establish my covenant with you, and with your seed after you, and with every living creature that is with you; of the birds, of the cattle, and of every beast of the earth with you, from all that came out of the ark, to every beast of the earth" (Gen. 9:9–10). In fact, the participation of all creatures in this new covenant is stressed by the Torah, which uses every possible phraseology within the span of a few verses to assert its inclusiveness: "Every living being" (Gen. 9:12), "the earth" (9:13), "All living creatures of all flesh" (9:15), "All living creatures of all flesh on the earth" (9:16), and "all flesh which is on the earth" (9:17). The point comes across emphatically—God has forged a brit, a sacred covenant, with every living creature and in fact with the earth itself.

Later religious practices involving animals and land can be understood as practical expressions of this archetypal covenant.[30] For instance, as mentioned above, the land is given a Sabbath of its own: Shenat Shemitah, the Sabbatical Year (Lev. 25:1–5). Like the weekly Sabbath, which is identified as an eternal covenant between God and the children of Israel, the Sabbatical year can be understood to signify a covenant between God and the land.[31] Understood in this way, the laws of Shemitah establish honoring God's covenant with the land as an integral part of Israel's covenant. In deference to this earthly Sabbath, this covenant between God and land, Jews diminish the extent to which their lives are both distanced from natural seasons and cycles and privileged above other species.[32]

While the laws of Shemitah are only incumbent upon Jews residing in the Land of Israel, the covenants proclaimed within Jewish tradition embody teachings of universal, ecological significance. For they provide a conceptual vocabulary with which to acknowledge the relationship between God and nonhuman Creation, and model the restriction of human behavior in respectful deference to that sacred bond.

CONCLUSION

This essay is of course only a small part of a larger discussion. Thematic exploration of God's relationship with Creation does not suffice to resolve actual environmental ethical dilemmas, which most often entail choosing between more than one acknowledged and cherished value. The desires of particular human beings and the needs of other species, just like conflicting needs among people, must be adjudged on a case by case basis. Nonetheless, it is critical to consider these fundamental, nonhalakhic tenets and values when engaging in such deliberation.

In the final analysis, however, intellectual discussion regarding God's relationship with Creation and the application of Jewish law to actual environmental dilemmas are not sufficient to meet the challenges which confront us. Our personal relationships to God and to the rest of Creation matter, as well. For ultimately the factors which drive one to consume and to destroy are largely attitudinal, and reflect not only one's thinking, but also one's wealth in non-material sources of satisfaction. For instance, if we, as a society, are to wean ourselves from our unsatisfying addiction to material consumption, we will need, each in his or her own way, to develop inner resources and to achieve a sense of spiritual fulfillment and well-being. A person who seeks to satisfy her existential needs through financial security will never have enough. "Who is rich?" our sages asked. They answered, "He who is satisfied with his portion" (Pirqei Avot 4:1). And who is he, we must further ask today, who will be capable of being satisfied with his portion? I suggest it is someone whose spiritual needs are sufficiently met—one who has infused her life with a sense of purpose and belonging, of participation in a story larger than herself which is ennobling, and who has a solid and healthy connection to herself, to community, to Creation, and to God.

NOTES

1. Gen. Rabbah 10:7. See also Pirqei Avot 4:3: "Do not be scornful of any person and do not be disdainful of anything. For there is no person without his hour, and no thing which does not have its place."

2. In the second creation narrative, vegetation is described as being dependent on human cultivation, and animals are created expressly to meet human need. Interestingly, however, this need is an existential need for company, rather than a physical need for labor.

3. The sanctification of the Sabbath also generates a dynamic tension between holiness in time and holiness in space. For a fuller discussion of this tension, see Abraham Joshua Heschel, *The Sabbath* (New York: Farrar, Straus and Giroux, 1951).

4. See, for example, Deut. 30:19: "I call heaven and earth to witness against you this day: I have put before you life and death, blessing and curse."

5. For a fascinating discussion regarding the theocentric perspective of this text, see Robert Alter, *The Art of Biblical Poetry* (New York: Basic Books, 1985), pp. 85–110.

6. For example, consider the laws of kashrut which specify what foods can be eaten and in what combination, or the laws of Sabbath observance.

7. A careful reading of the creation narratives reveals the complex nature of the human being. On the one hand, Adam is a part of the created world and akin to other creatures. At the same time, Adam is also a unique creature, formed not only from the earth but from the breath of God, as well, and in God's image.

8. Particularly at a time when the vast majority of toxic dumps, landfills, trash incinerators, and the like are located in poor and often predominately minority neighborhoods, and we are confronted by a host of complex issues regarding population control and "third-world" development, the connection between these two realms of concern is profound.

9. Abraham Joshua Heschel, *Man is Not Alone* (New York: Farrar, Straus and Giroux, 1951), p. 37.

10. Siddur, blessings before the Shema in morning and evening services.

11. Siddur, Amidah prayer.

12. The text of Birkat Ha-Mazon, a traditional benediction recited after a full meal, predates the Talmud. Its first blessing thanks God "who nourishes and sustains all, and does good to all, and prepares food for all of His creatures that He has created."

13. It is challenging to reconcile the seeming amorality and even cruelty of the natural world with the traditional belief in a merciful and compassionate God. Such discussion entails distinguishing human society from the wild as distinct moral realms, exploring traditional responses to other instances of theodicy, and deliberating the precise nature of divine providence, topics beyond the scope of this paper.

14. Gen. 1:11: "And God said, Let the earth bring forth grass, herb

yielding seed, and fruit tree yielding fruit after its kind, whose seed is in itself, upon the earth: and it was so."

15. Lev. 22:28. "And whether it be cow or ewe, you shall not kill it and its young both in one day."

16. In fact, this biblical law may well be the first recorded legislation in history for protecting birds.

17. Rabbi Moses ben Nahman, also known as Nahmanides, or "the Ramban" (1194–1270), was a renowned Spanish scholar, philosopher, and kabbalist of the Middle Ages. All biographical citations in this paper are drawn from the *Encyclopedia Judaica.*

18. Nahmanides, commentary on Deut. 22:6–7. See also Bahya b. Asher on Deut. 22:7, *Sefer Ha-Hinukh Mizvah,* p. 294, and *Kol Bo,* chap. 3.

19. Siddur (traditional Jewish prayer book), Kiddush prayer for Sabbath evening. The connection between the prohibition of labor on Shabbat and the Creation of the world is expressed in Exod. 20:10–11: "And the seventh day is a Sabbath to the Lord your God. Do not do any labor . . . because in six days God made the heaven and the earth, the sea and all that is in them, and rested on the seventh day."

20. One possible insight into this prohibition might be that mixing of wool and linen in one garment entails the mixing of animal and vegetable material.

21. Sifra is an exegetical midrash that interprets the book of Leviticus.

22. Sifra, ad loc. See also B. Qidushin 39a.

23. Rabbi Samson Raphael Hirsch (1808–1888) was the leader and foremost exponent of Jewish Orthodoxy in nineteenth-century Germany.

24. Rabbi Samson Raphael Hirsch, *Horeb II* (London: Soncino Press, 1962).

25. See The Union of Concerned Scientists, ed., *World Scientists' Warning to Humanity Briefing Book* (Cambridge: Union of Concerned Scientists, 1993).

26. See, for example, Walter Wurzburger, *Ethics of Responsibility* (New York: Jewish Publication Society, 1994); David Hartman, *A Living Covenant,* and Eugene B. Borowitz, *Renewing the Covenant* (New York: Jewish Publication Society, 1991).

27. Eugene B. Borowitz, *Renewing the Covenant* (New York: Jewish Publication Society, 1991), p. 2.

28. See Joseph B. Soloveitchik, *The Lonely Man of Faith* (New York: Doubleday), p. 71.

29. For instance, see Midrash Tanhuma, parshat Qedoshim: "The

Holy One said to Israel: Even if you find the land filled with good things, you should not say, 'We will sit and not plant.' Rather, be diligent in planting! Just as you came and found trees planted by others, so you must plant for your children."

30. The laws of orlah may also be relevant here. Moses exhorted the generation of the wilderness: "And when you shall come into the land, and shall plant all kinds of trees for food, then you shall reckon their fruit as uncircumcised; three years . . . it shall not be eaten" (Lev. 19:23). While it is usually dismissed as an awkward choice of words, I find the use of the term "uncircumcized" in this biblical verse intriguing. Circumcision (of newborn or converting Jewish males) is the quintessential sign of entrance into a brit, or covenant. According to this biblical passage, the fruits of new trees are effectively circumcised by participating in natural cycles, free from consumption by the humans who planted them, for the tree's first three mature years. Might this prohibition against consuming a tree's first fruits, in fact referred to as the laws of orlah (lit. foreskin, or uncircumcized), therefore be understood to signify a covenant with the land?

31. See Exod. 31:16: "And the Children of Israel shall observe the Sabbath, to make of the Sabbath throughout their generations an eternal covenant."

32. Reinforcing the prohibition against cultivating crops and the laws of biyur discussed above, other Shemitah laws further restrict the "unnatural" use of natural substances, insisting for instance that what is primarily eaten raw should not be cooked, while what is used for food should not be adapted for medicinal or other purposes. See M. Shevi'it 8:1.

QUESTIONS FOR DISCUSSION

1. In this time of ecological crisis, what does it mean to honor God's covenants with each of us and with Creation as a whole? How might the apparent cruelty of the natural world be reconciled with the notion of a merciful God who cares for all creatures?

2. What is the tension between holiness in time and holiness in space? In what ways are each of these concepts helpful or challenging in the effort to foster ecologically sound values and practices?

3. What are other ways to cultivate self-restraint, mindfulness, appreciation, and wonder? Do you see this as a role for religion to play in your life? What does this material have to say, if anything, to people who are not Jewish and/or do not believe in God?

7

THE DANGERS OF MISINTERPRETATION
Earth Spirituality and Self-Deception
Roger S. Gottlieb

Humanity's responses to the perils and pains of existence give rise to many attempts to see the sources of our suffering, to escape or transcend our limits, and to form or recognize communities of solidarity—both with other people and with beings who are not people. The cry of the heart has gone out to gods and goddesses; to totem animals and sacred mountains; and to those with whom we would join on the barricades. In the desperate time of the present, as the cynics celebrate the end of alternatives to global capitalism, global industrialism, and global technoaddiction, who would not search for wisdom?

Yet every wisdom has its danger and every danger its wisdom.

MYSTICISM

This term is used to describe a variety of at times overwhelming, often life-defining experiences. For many those experiences are the living heart of the world's religion. Beyond details of dogma, institutional organization, or even ethical teachings, the direct encounter with the divine seems to make possible a temporary release from the boundaries of the social ego and the socially constructed understanding of the body. It is this encounter which promises an alternative to constricted forms of self-definition, and offers an answer to merely local claims about who we are, what we owe each other, and what we can be.

The examples of mystical experience are numerous, celebrated in every religious tradition. Consider, for example, the "Arhat," the type of the Sage in the original form of Buddhism which has come to be known as the Theravada. In his religious practices the Arhat seeks an end to the confinement imposed by an identification with a self bound to desires which inevitably cause pain. The question which arises for such a person is, of course, whether it is possible to be alive as a human being and *not* identify with such a self. Mystical wisdom arises when the student directly experiences a state of mind in which identification with self dissipates. As one early practitioner is reputed to have said, when questioned by a fellow seeker: "During my meditation I reached a point where I had no thought that `I am this; this is mine; this is my self.' "[1]

Or consider the prophet Elijah. Fleeing for his life from Jezebel's wrath after he put to death the prophets of Baal, he encounters God not in a mighty wind, an earthquake or a fire, but in a "still, small voice." (1 Kings 19:11–12).

Consider how the poet William Blake saw Christ suspended in air, dancing outside his window. Or the states of ecstatic no-self produced by Sufi dancing or tribal chanting; or the transformations of consciousness which come on a Native American Vision Quest, prepared for by days of fasting and isolation. Or consider the feminist image of a divine interconnection and sharing and mingling of mind, emotion, and body; an interconnection in which God does not speak from the Heavens or even within our hearts, but emerges in the sacred spaces which both separate and connect us.[2]

In all these and the legion more which could be discussed, we find the wisdom of mysticism. This wisdom provides an end, or at least a temporary alternative to, the ego's twisted identification with a psychic condition of permanent dissatisfaction, insecurity, and violence. From attachment to a particular social role, we move to an identification with a cosmic harmony for which possessions, status, and social group become merely relative, merely historical, essentially contingent. From attachment to our particular, personal, self-owned pains and pleasures, we move to a celebration of the infinite fields of energy which move through us.

Perhaps most important: while the intensity of the experience fades, and may be hard even to remember at times (it is said that Pascal, having had an experience of God, sewed an image of the sun into his clothes to remind himself), the wisdom of mysticism opens the receiver up to a clarity of understanding about what is of lasting importance in the realms of everyday, nontranscendent life. Variously known as love, grace, peace, or care, the wisdom of mysticism releases us from our bondage to patterns of emotion which ultimately serve neither ourselves nor others. The literal, temporary, contingent demands—that we earn a lot of money, that we be beautiful, that we make war on our "enemies," that we believe the government, that we manage to be successful at being "men" or "women"—these snarling dogs of desire ("fires," the Buddha called them) become the tame lap-cats of tamed desire. We escape—initially only for a moment but then for much longer if we are able to maintain the power of the memory of that moment—the demands, evaluations, and definitions of our social existence. Maintaining this memory requires stern but rewarding discipline, described in detail in the mystical traditions. If we follow it, the traditions promise, we will be ever more released from the bondage of false attachments.

And this is where the danger lies: the place where mysticism transcends itself into self-deception and folly and escapism. For mysticism can be and has been used simply to evade that which is frightening, confusing, or difficult *in* the social realm. Motivated, then, by an inability to face what is threatening in the world-as-it-is, we seek a mystical flight from the real.

For instance, we become entranced by, even addicted to, the *experience* of the mystical state. It is so lofty, or so pleasant, or such a relief from how awful we feel most of the time. And when we are under it or in it or up to it, we do not have to take seriously our suffering, anyone else's suffering, or the ways in which it is not only folly but also social evil which causes that suffering.

This danger of mysticism is that it becomes in Kierkegaard's sense merely "aesthetic": merely a series of experiences which do not contribute to the formation of an ethical and spiritual character. Merely something which, in the end, is another titillation, another object of desire, another way to pacify a self that has not been transformed, but merely thrilled or sedated.

Put another way, the danger of mysticism is that it can become an escape from concerns about other people. Entranced by the cosmic oneness of it all, we end up forgetting or ignoring the other people in the room, on our block, or on our globe. Feeling cared for by an infinite source of love, we forget (inadvertently? to some extent intentionally?) that we have the power and the obligation to manifest as well as receive that love, and that if we do not, our own access to the source will become more and more strained, desperate, and attenuated.

Many years ago a teacher of yoga and meditation instructed me: "Do not be distracted by sounds in your practice, but use them. For instance, if you are meditating and your hear a loud siren outside your window, instead of feeling interrupted you can simply take in that energy, move it up your spine to your crown chakra and use it to further your practice."

A useful tip I thought a first. But then I thought further, and asked him: "Sir, this sounds a fine idea if, for instance, the siren is simply from an ambulance on its way to a nearby hospital. But what if it is the siren of the police vans which, in Amsterdam, took Jews to be transported to the death camps? When is the sound a source of energy to be incorporated into the meditation? and when is it an indication that we need to end the meditation, look outside ourselves, and act in resistance to help innocent people who are being murdered? And what is the source of an ability to discern between the two?"

The dangers that mysticism may become merely aesthetic or serve as a spiritual bypass of the moral and the political are not unknown in religious traditions. In traditional Judaism, a person does not approach the mysticism of the Kabbalah until he is established in family and community relationships—and typically not until the age of forty. The entire history of Buddhism is marked by a split over precisely the nature of mystical enlightenment and the role of the enlightened person in the community. While Theravada Buddhism saw the Sage as ultimately no more than a person who provides an example to others that Enlightenment is possible, Mahayana Buddhism arose partly out of the critique of what it took to be the selfish and ultimately self-defeating character of that ideal. In its place, the Mahayana offered the image of the Bodhisattva, who refuses ultimate Enlightenment in order to help all other sentient beings to achieve it. Such a person is like a strong young man who, when his household is lost in a dangerous forest, stays with the group to help them all to safety rather than make his own way home.

Yet the awareness of these traditions is itself suspect in part because of the duality of all mystical encounters: at once a communion with energies which transcend society *and also* experiences processed, understood, and described in words by socially situated human beings. The pervasive sexism of even the most mystically founded traditions should remind us that while God or goddess may touch us directly, our response to that touch will necessarily bear some imprint of our contingent selves. The claim that we speak, as opposed to simply that we have experienced, a Truth Beyond Question has too often been a strategy for Power Over the Uninitiated.

And in our time the dangers of mysticism are especially real, because much of mysticism in the advanced industrial societies is disconnected from tradition, community, and personal responsibility. It was, after all, in great measure the widespread use of psychedelic drugs which brought an interest in ecstatic states back into a society defined by professionalism, technology, and television. The power of these drugs—for many people an instant revelation—was precisely their impotence. Since nothing had prepared us for what they offered—and we had not seriously prepared ourselves—the next day's psychic life was often no more holy than the day before. At best, the drug experience was a signal that there was more to life than was dreamed of at Harvard Business School or the

National Science Foundation. At best, it served only as a beginning to a long and difficult search.

Further, since the cavalier cultural raids on ancient and tribal traditions of the 1980s, one can learn the secrets of a South American shaman for the cost of a weekend's time and a few hundred dollars. (This will be a wonderful experience. And next month we can learn witchcraft. Or perhaps the mysteries of the Druids.) The consequence is that far from becoming an alternative to the limitations of social life, mystical experience becomes one more commodity—with no more ultimate spiritual meaning than anything else that can be bought or sold.

DEEP ECOLOGY

The crucial fact of our time is that we may be destroying the very life support systems which make human life possible. With less uncertainty we can say that we have *already* extinguished countless species, poured millions of tons of toxic wastes into the air, earth, and water, and altered the earth's atmosphere and climate.

A variety of conservation, preservation, and environmental movements and philosophies have arisen in response to this crisis. From the heart of the spiritual impulse and the memories of countless generations in which forest and grassland, bird and wolf and salmon were our home and family and intimate enemy, comes Deep Ecology.

The Deep Ecology of which I speak here is not the version presented in the technical language of philosophical ethics, where debates about varieties of intrinsic as opposed to instrumental value take place. Rather, I mean a passionate, spiritually oriented, mystical communion with the earth and its many beings, a recognition of kinship with those beings which no more requires philosophical justification than does the connection we feel with our parents, our pets, or our lovers. As such Deep Ecology is a spiritual philosophy; the deepest experiences which animate its adherents are profoundly mystical.[3]

This Deep Ecology is not, nor could it possibly be, a recent creation. As humans have evolved physically, cognitively, culturally, and spiritually in a setting bounded by beings who are not people, so a recognition of our delight in them and affinity with them has been present throughout all human cultures.

There is a Midrash (a Jewish spiritual story which aims to enlighten rather than legislate) which speaks of trees: "When a tree that bears fruit is cut down, its moan goes round the world. Yet no sound is heard." Or even more poignantly, in the words of the eighteenth-century Rebbe Nachman: "If a person kills a tree before its time, it is like having murdered a soul." Hildegaard of Bingen saw God in the physical world: "I, the fiery life of divine essence, am aflame beyond the beauty of the meadows, I gleam in the waters, and I burn in the sun, moon, and stars . . . I awaken everyting to life." The Koran was confident that "the creation of the heavens and the Earth is greater than the creation of humankind; Yet most people understand not." And the World Council of Indigenous Peoples stated in 1977 that in their past "the earth was our nurturing mother, the night sky formed our common roof, the Sun and the Moon were our parents."[4]

This recognition is also found in nondenominational, often explicitly nonreligious, nature writing which celebrates a luminous moment of seeing in which the natural world speaks to us. In her celebrated essay "Living Like Weasels" Annie Dillard describes a moment when, face-to-face with a weasel,

> our eyes locked, and someone threw away the key. Our look was as
> if two lovers, or deadly enemies, met unexpectedly on an over-
> grown path when each had been thinking of something else.[5]

Similarly, Aldo Leopold, one of the inspirations of modern environmental thought, speaks of seeing a "fierce green fire" in the eyes of a dying wolf he had himself shot, and of never again thinking of wolves, or mountains, or wilderness in the same way.[6]

Considered as a form of spirituality—as a way of moving beyond the conventional social understanding of the self or of the social construction of the body—Deep Ecology articulates a powerful and pervasive sensibility. It unifies and expands our childhood love for an animal, the times as adolescents when only the woods or fields seem to understand us, the moments of grace we feel watching a sunrise, or light glinting over ice-covered branches, or hearing birds sing on a surprisingly warm day in March. Knitting together these moments, a deep ecological perspective simply says: "You are more than your profession and race and religion and even gender. In your cells and sinews and even your atoms there is a tie to all this which surrounds you. Open yourself up to this source of grace and peace and love. More important, open yourself up to the love you feel for it."

Deep Ecology also, as Joanna Macy observes, signals something of our capacity to love and the reality of our connections to other beings across space and time.[7] Our sadness for the burning rainforests and casually eliminated species is a sign that despite everyting we can still love—and mourn. As Deep Ecology sings of the joy we feel in our delight of nature, so it must also have us join in the requiem for what we ourselves have helped to kill.

Deep Ecology, like all forms of mysticism, is also a form of knowledge. It reminds us of truths that industrial civilization and many forms of patriarchy have obscured: that we are physical beings, made of the same stuff as earth and stream and air; that we need wilderness because, as Edward Abbey observed, we ourselves are wild animals.[8]

Equally important, Deep Ecology highlights the limitations of a purely instrumental attitude toward nature, an attitude which cautions us to preserve the rainforest only for its potential cancer cures. As a philosophy based in powerful emotional experiences, Deep Ecology expresses simply and directly what many people feel: a love and concern for the natural world. As more familiar mystical experiences might alter our attitudes toward death, our fear of the unknown, or our petty insecurities, realization of our kinship with the earth confirms the need to question any unquestioned trashing of our dear relations.

Finally, an identification with nature can be the source of deep pleasure and deeper calm. Again as in revelations of the truth of God, an opening into sky or the call of the loon can soothe the anxieties and relieve the sense of overwhelming pressure to achieve or accomplish in the social realm. It might even, if we let it, help us learn not to be quite so (desperately, compulsively) busy. I can see the trees not only as the objects of my attempt to save the rainforest, but, in John Seed's words, I can also "see myself as *part* of the rainforest trying to save itself."[9] And I can then realize that even desperation to save nature has no real place. As the leaves on the trees that I love, I can only do my bit and then drift gently down to the forest floor and make way for more life.

And once again, here is where the dangers arise. For Deep Ecology (like other forms of mysticism) can slide too easily into the attempt to escape society, to see "nature" as a realm in which people are absent and in the celebration of which people can be ignored. If it is truly nature we love, we must not forget people, for they too are born of the earth.[10] If we would commune with plants, we must not (as Aldo Leopold himself suggested) forget the weeds in a city's vacant lot. And we must also show some concern for those kids playing in the city lot—at risk from broken glass and drug dealers, and for the most part lacking physical or cultural access to the wilderness we seek to preserve.

Just as we experience the mystical touch of God as socially situated existing individuals, so we come to "nature" through social life. We bring our historically defined expectations and needs. We have a concept of nature (as benign or threatening, comfortable or forbidding, infinitely powerful or dangerously at risk) which is very much the product of our own society's level of technological development. Especially in our own time we only *go* to the wilds with the very particular accomplishments of our society riding on our back— or on our feet or in our bloodstreams. E. O. Wilson observed: no matter how much the naturalist loves the jungle, he had better be very well equipped or before long a host of jungle dwellers will break him down into his constituent amino acids.[11] Every deep ecologist goes to the wilds with his vibram boots on his feet, his nylon back pack, and his swiss army knife.

Finally, there is the problem that at times the bland images of nature which emerge from Deep Ecology distort what "nature" really is like. For example, our mystically based love of life will not extend to the AIDS virus; and our wariness at tampering with the sacred character of nature may well be suspended when it comes to using genetic engineering to cure cystic fibrosis. Ghetto rats will probably escape the purview which holds all of life as sacred, as might the black flies which cause widespread blindness in Africa. Adopting a deep ecological perspective will not eliminate the hard choices we face—choices about how much to take for ourselves and how much to leave for others, how much to exercise the control we increase day by day and how much of it to surrender. And it will not turn the real world into a PBS special on butterflies or dolphins.

SOCIAL TRANSFORMATION

In human history, the long counterpoint to ecstasy which takes us out of our social setting is the longing for justice within it. Ethics and transcendence are the twin axes along which an authentic social life develops, and are the criteria for measuring the adequacy of a humane form of life. In contrast to the claims of mysticism, the pursuit of justice is very much an awareness of just how socially situated we are and how our concerns with making things better center on the alteration and improvement of this situation which defines us, grounds us, and sets our tasks. The longing for a more just social order can be found in the cautionary words of prophets, social reformers, and revolutionaries.

This longing exists, among other things, as a needed corrective to the ahistorical pretensions of mystical traditions—their claims to provide doctrines which originate outside of the social order. From a viewpoint that originated in politics, rather than spirituality, we are able, for instance, to critique the sexist teachings of early Buddhism. For all its self-understanding as a source of truth beyond the ego, it maintained the idea of women's social and spiritual inferiority. While the Buddha may have seen his way clear of the imposed caste system and the empty formalities of ritual sacrifices, he could not move beyond his own attachment to a patriarchy. What source could there be for even recognizing this failing except a socially based political critique? Such a source only rarely emerges from transcendent visions but rather typically stems from the cries of the oppressed themselves.

In our own time, Deep Ecology in particular and the conservation movement in general have by this time been the subject of extensive critiques: for ignoring the social basis of their own perspectives; for emphasizing wilderness and forgetting toxic waste dumps; for loving trees but lacking concern for children. These criticisms have helped move deep ecologists towards an understanding that environmentalism needs to embrace the concern of environmental justice: an awareness of and resistance to the unfair distribution of responsibility for and suffering from humanity's attacks on the environment. The radioactive dumps on native lands, the toxic wastes flowing into the poor neighborhoods, the outlawed chemicals exported to the Third World—can we really love nature if these things escape our vision?[12]

Finally, it must be stressed that for many the struggle for justice is *itself* a form of connection which can break the bonds of the ego. While social movements too often have devolved into the brutal tyrannies of a Stalin or the crass appeal to group hatred of a Farrakan, at their best they provide experiences where political solidarity blossoms into a kind of selfless love. At times people struggling for justice are freed from the usual petty isolations, jealousies, and fears. In the very struggle they find the joy of service and the spiritual clarity which comes from knowing the ultimate rightness of what they are doing.

AND YET. . . .

Too often confidence in one's ultimate rightness has led political movements into dogmatic violence. The history of too many revolutions is the history of the replacement of one autocracy by another. The history of too many left groups reveals secretarianism, verbal violence, and exclusion of others who deserve solidarity. We have seen the fundamental wisdom of the struggle for justice be obscured by rage, pompous posturing, or simple careerism.[13]

And thus as the political perspective is necessary for both a grounding and a critique of mysticism and Deep Ecology, so their spiritual insights and resources can be a corrective to the excesses of politics.

Mysticism in general can offer relief from identification with theories, rigidly held "positions," and the pursuit of institutional power. An emphasis on compassion, on empathy even for the guilty, on service rather than on the acquisition of personal status within the "movement"—these are values which can be forthcoming from a direct experience of the holy. For from that experience, once again, we may learn that the ego-bound concerns which motivate us toward arrogance and violence, even in the service of justice, are not the only reality. To make the point we need only compare Lenin's practice of threatening to expel any party leader who disagreed with him, with Gandhi's insistence that comrades vote against him if that was what their own inner wisdom dictated.

From Deep Ecology in particular, the world of conventional human-oriented politics also has much to learn. For one thing, Deep Ecology's emphasis on the value of the nonhuman offers a measure and a limit of what we are seeking when we pursue an improved "standard of living." The notion of a "sustainable" form of life begins to redefine what we are after: we begin to seek sustainability as much as "justice" and "freedom." And (as difficult as it is to find the right way of putting this) we have before us the prospect that the true subjects of political life are not just people, but also animals, plants, ecosystems, and perhaps the biosphere itself.

In the same vein, a mystical identification—or deep relationship—with the natural world allows us to orient political struggle away from entitlement and rage, in a direction not tied (or at least less tied) by a psychic addiction to the very social system which destroys us. As Marcuse observed, by rooting personal identity in the ownership of things, the consumer society binds its subjects to the principles of ever increasing production and consumption.[14] The recognition of spiritual values in general and the value(s) of nature in particular gives us a way out of the ecocidal cul-de-sac of the endless mall.

In more strategic political terms, concern for nature is a value which can provide the basis for a new kind of solidarity. We might remember that whatever else divides us as human beings, we all need to breathe. And virtually all of our hearts rejoice to the sounds of Spring. These commonalties may save us when the divisions of race, class, gender, ethnicity, or sexuality leave us deeply suspicious of each other.

While those getting very rich off of pollution are not likely to be convinced, as are many of those whose most immediate livelihood depends on exploitation of their surroundings, we have already seen cross-class, cross-race, and cross-nationality coalitions doing serious political work. An enormous dam project slated for India— supported by the World Bank and liable to destroy the habitat of endangered species and indigenous people alike—was stopped by a transcontinental alliance of local people, environmental activists, lawyers, and concerned citizens in India, Switzerland, and the United States.[15] In Wisconsin white activists have helped native peoples fend off multinational mining interests. These are but a few examples of arenas of cooperation based in the joint concern for the human and the nonhuman.

It may actually be that care for the environment will continue and flourish as one of the main motivating forces of politics in the twenty-first century. The abatement signaled in the United States by the Republican victories of the mid-1990s is, I believe, a temporary development. In any event, the "working class," as Andre Gorz observed many years ago, is not likely to mount a serious challenge to the established social order to get a 10 percent increase in pay.[16] Concern for the environment—a concern motivated both by "self-interest" and as interest for nature that we love and long for—*could* be a significant element in a major social transformation. If people can see what is truly at stake, they may yet rise to the challenge. And the spiritual understanding of this concern has been and will continue to be an essential element in the process. We have seen it already in the spiritual motivation of the radical ecology group Earth First!, in the convention challenging claims of the new, earth-oriented ecotheology coming out of mainstream religions, and in the politicized versions of spiritual ecofeminism.

Finally, and perhaps most surprisingly, there is in a general "deep ecological" orientation a cognitive corrective to the distortions of centralized, reductionist, commodified knowledge and social practice. In agriculture, for instance, the belief that modernized science and technology can replace the fertility of the earth or the expertise of local groups has led to a series of disasters. As Vandana Shiva has described it, the imposition of "advanced," commodity-oriented monocultures already erases a wide variety of crops, seeds, productive uses (for food, fodder, herbs, local consumption, and so forth, as well as sale), and—ultimately—peoples. The result has been polluted soils, drastically increased water consumption, less productive land use, and violent social dislocation.[17] In this approach there is respect neither for the earth nor for the people who have managed their fields and forests sustainably for centuries. A perspective which sees communion with nature as having spiritual as well as instrumental value might look very carefully at any attempt to supplant either natural processes or long-established local forms of culture and practice. Thus as a spiritual view of the ultimate value of people can provide an orientation for social life (though clearly not a simple way to resolve its conflicts and contradictions), so a spiritual view of nature can offer at least the beginning of an orientation toward production, consumption, and development.

And so, paradoxically, the wisdom of a mystical Deep Ecology can augment the powers and promises of the secular drive for just social transformation. Their mutual support is necessary, I suspect, if the environmental crisis is not to erode the conditions for human life on earth and simultaneously erode our very confidence in our right to exist on it. If we are to be truly touched by the Holy Spirit, our own spirit of holiness must reach out to the enormous family of life which surrounds us, shapes us, and gives us our own particular place in the vastness of time and space.

NOTES

1. For these and other accounts of Buddhism in this paper see, for example, Edward Conze, *Buddhism: Its Essence and Development* (New York: Harper, 1951) and Lucien Stryk, ed., *World of the Buddha* (New York: Anchor, 1969).

2. For example, Carter Heyward, *Touching Our Strength* (San Francisco: Harper, 1992).

3. There are many sources here. See, for example, Joanna Macy, *World as Lover, World as Self* (San Francisco: Parallax, 1994); Bill Devall and George Sessions, *Deep Ecology: Living as if Nature Mattered* (Salt Lake City, Utah: Peregrine Smith Books, n.d.)

4. For these quotations, as well as many sources on contemporary and traditional writings on religion and nature, see Roger S. Gottlieb, ed., *This Sacred Earth: Religion, Nature, Environment* (New York: Routledge, 1996).

5. Annie Dillard, *Teaching a Stone to Talk* (New York: HarperCollins, 1982), p. 14.

6. Aldo Leopold, *A Sand County Almanac* (New York: Oxford University Press, 1949).

7. Macy, *World as Lover*.

8. Edward Abbey, *The Journey Home* (New York: Penguin, 1977).

9. John Seed, Joanna Macy, and Pat Fleming, *Thinking Like a Mountain: Towards a Council of All Beings* (Philadelphia: New Society Publishers, 1991).

10. This critique is developed more extensively in Roger S. Gottlieb, "Spiritual Deep Ecology and the Left," *Capitalism, Nature, Socialism: A Journal of Socialist Ecology* 6, no. 4 (Fall 1995). Reprinted in *This Sacred Earth*.

11. E. O. Wilson, *Biophilia* (Cambridge: Harvard University Press, 1983).

12. See for example Al Gedicks, *The New Resource Wars: Native and Environmental Struggles Against Multinational Corporations* (Boston: South End Press, 1993); Robert D. Bullard, ed., *Unequal Protection: Environmental Justice and Communities of Color* (San Francisco: Sierra Club Books, 1994).

13. For an extensive critique of these defects in the history of U.S. left movements, see Roger S. Gottlieb, *History and Subjectivity: The Transformation of Marxist Theory* (Philadelphia: Temple University Press, 1987) and *Marxism 1844–1990: Origins, Betrayal, Rebirth* (New York: Routledge, 1992).

14. Herbert Marcuse, *One-Dimensional Man* (Boston: Beacon Press, 1967).

15. Bruce Rich, *Mortgaging the Earth: The World Bank, Environmental Impoverishment, and the Crisis of Development* (Boston: Beacon Press, 1994), pp. 44–47.

16. Andre Gorz, "Socialism and Revolution," in *An Anthology of Western Marxism: From Lukacs and Gramsci to Socialist-Feminism,* ed. Roger S. Gottlieb (New York: Oxford University Press, 1990), p. 218.

17. Vandana Shiva, *The Violence of the Green Revolution* (London: Zed Press, 1993) and *Monocultures of the Mind* (London: Zed Press, 1991).

QUESTIONS FOR DISCUSSION

1. What wisdom is held by mysticism and how has the intuitive mystical approach contributed to the rise of the environmental movement in such leaders as John Muir?

2. Is Deep Ecology a form of authentic mysticism as defined in the Jewish and Christian traditions—how does the mysticism of Hebrew Wisdom literature or the Franciscan movement differ?

3. What are the gifts—and dangers—of ecosocial transformation?

4. SUSTAINABLE COMMUNITY AND ENVIRONMENTAL JUSTICE

As we stand at the beginning of the twenty-first century it appears that a cycle is coming to an end, a cycle that might be defined by the term "development," implying that all peoples of the world are moving in a certain sociocultural linear direction. This term was given a particular valence by President Harry Truman (20 January 1949) in relation to the poorer, as "underdeveloped," and wealthier, as "developed," areas of the world. It has as a positive legacy the drawing together of the whole world into a self-conscious global village. However, it has come with the realization that we now confront two crises of dominant proportion, an earth at risk through ecological degradation and a growing disparity of wealth and levels of just development. Development, as it has been defined, has created an inverse relation between the crises of nature and justice. Attempts to alleviate the crisis of justice often aggravates the crisis of nature, a point often played out in the microeconomies of the rainforests in the Southern hemisphere or in the effort at global economic adjustment.[1]

Sustainable community and environmental justice truly require a holistic approach. This means bringing to the table a number of different resources as we work toward a redefinition and practice of community. It means first drawing upon the best of the sciences. The path to sustainable community with justice, in the context of an earth at risk, requires accurate knowledge.[2] This was the point of the second section in this volume. However, we have also seen that the concern for an accurate assessment of ecological devastation, for the science of ecology, has pulled into it a discussion about the theory or philosophy of science. This theoretical discussion, driven by practical concern, has been marked often by partisan debate since the formation of the Joint Appeal by Religion and Science for the Environment (1990).[3]

But finding a sustainable community with environmental justice also means defining an ethics that is worked out in relation to scientific knowledge (facts) and religious reflection (values).[4] In the fourth section of this volume, Susan Power Bratton begins this process by showing how environmental historians have related religion, or the lack of it, to the development of environmental ethics in the United States. She warns of the dangers that arise from proving cultural "myths" with an inaccurate selection of historical data and contrasts this with the clarifying work that can come when we accurately understand religion's role in shaping environmental ethics. After a series of self-critical questions, Bratton surveys seminal works in environmental, religious, and literary history.[5] The religious attitudes embedded in these themes are of interest to us. Whether consistently environmentally disruptive or as more nuanced by "nature-friendliness," Bratton finds ethical activity seldom developed consistently or guided by formal theology or philosophy. Fairness in reporting or historical accuracy has also made this a difficult issue to assess.

The relationship between environmental ethics and culture has not only received attention from mainstream religion throughout the last third of the twentieth century, deep interest has also turned around an understanding of indigenous worldviews.[6] The complexity of this relationship for North American Indian experience is reflected in George Tinker's work. He writes about the rich diversity of histories, spiritual traditions, and cosmologies that one finds[7] and is concerned about the failure to take Native experience seriously. To do so would require dealing with the relation of religious practice to sovereignty and land,[8] to individual and communal rights. The failure to see this relationship contributes to the genocide and ecocide which has been too often the Native experience in North America and elsewhere on the planet. Arguing thus, Tinker alerts us to some of the same mythic dangers alluded to by Bratton and to the ethical or ecojustice dimensions of our attitude to the environment. For many Native American peoples, environmental devastation is a manifestation of the colonialism and racism that has marked Indian-Euroamerican relations in post-Columbian times.[9]

Without mincing words Tinker turns to the terms of the study process which was shared at the beginning of this volume with the Boston Theological Institute. For Native Americans, each of the words "beloved," "God," and "creation" poses its own set of linguistic problems.[10] The confusion which Tinker highlights here recalls the importance placed upon our conceptual framework in articles by Clifford and Smart, a framework related to "mythic" ideas which, Bratton argues, require clarification and critical analysis. Tinker's concern about privileging human beings at the expense of the rest of creation needs to be considered in light of Clifford's contention about relative anthropomorphism (Section Three) and debate over the Anthropic principle (Section Two). However assessed, the concern that Euro-religion has little sense for balance and harmony with all life forms is critical not only to the theology of Native or First Peoples but to *global sustainability*. To follow Bratton's point, it matters little if in Judaism and Christianity one discerns a covenant with all creatures (Gen. 9:12–17) but fails to keep it. An American Indian theology attuned to the environment awakens us to this dissonance.

A greater regard for meaningful cultural diversity is a means for overcoming the West's own alienation from the natural world. The recovery of communal stories inherent in different cultures and the acknowledgment of meaningful ethnic political and territorial rights are both means toward the liberation that Tinker envisions.

Good science and the religious or wisdom traditions alone are not enough for framing an ethics for sustainable communities and environmental justice. A cross-disciplinary discussion is required, as seen in the article by Paula Gonzalez. As a biologist she frames her ethical concerns by drawing upon evolution, ecology, and the social sciences. She begins by giving us the long view, taking us on an imaginative journey through the major revolutions in earth history: photosynthesis, heterotrophy, and sexual reproduction. She brings us to the present evolutionary moment, characterized by what Thomas Berry has called the beginning of the Ecozoic Era. This era calls us to new holistic approaches as we become defined as a communion of subjects. How we live in this era in relation to the selection of technologies that we bring to bear upon the environmental crisis, Ian Barbour reminds us, depends upon value priorities and our definition of the good life. For Gonzalez this means learning from the earth's processes. Taking her lead from Paul Hawken and Amory and Hunter Lovins, this means learning to replicate nature's economy in human economy, the interdependence of producers, consumers, and decomposers. This thinking is required in order to transform the conceptions of development and technologies and practices that have flowed from such thinking if we are to develop just and sustainable communities.

Much work needs to be done to define the patterns of understanding and the methodologies that are needed in order to promote such an ethical vision. Gonzalez suggests the kind of paradigm shifts in mentality, defined by Thomas Kuhn and others,[11] with respect to ethics, cultural practice, and philosophical understanding. A comment about each is in order as we think about sustainable community and environmental justice.

To take Gonzalez seriously means that ethical reflection in the churches and faith communities of the twenty-first century must move more profoundly beyond the three tendencies in religious ethics identified by Paul Albrecht over the past seventy-five years: (1) an ethic of *agapé* going back to the origins of the Life and Work Movement (Stockholm, 1925), (2) a participatory and populist ethic with an overriding concern for those oppressed through racial, religious, or sexual identity, and (3) liberation theology, guided by a socialistic "science" in matters of praxis with a preference for the poor.[12] Since Albrecht's summary was made in 1988, the need for additional approaches to the environmental problem on the part of churches, government agencies, and society at large has become clearer, particularly in relation to global economic structural concerns.[13] The kind of increasing integration called for by Gonzalez, together with long-range thinking, is necessary to meet the environmental challenge.[14] Often, as with the Brundtland Commission's Report, the ethical concerns of a "secular humanism" are compatible with a Christian or other religious view of the situation.

Long-range ethical thinking about an earth at risk also requires a scope that is cross-cultural because the nature of the problem is global. The search for a global ethic for environmental security and economic sustainability also has implications for human rights.[15] Any transnational thinking requires the kind of interreligious dialogue implicit in Tinker's argument or as seen earlier in Section Three.[16] This is particularly true for reflection on an Earth Charter whose sponsors seek to identify the core values and principles that should guide global environmental conservation and sustainable development.[17] The debate entails derivative questions about human rights in the context of an emerging global politics which demands that we move beyond the patterns of national interest that have dominated political thought at least since the Peace of Westphalia (1648).[18] It draws in definitions of development that affect economic well-being and reflect indigenous and other religious worldviews,[19] something that is beginning to happen among the churches and other religious communities with respect to the question of global climate change.[20] The debate entails the value of all sentient life: Do such rights extend to rivers and forests? Does a captive dolphin have the right to sue for its freedom?[21] Are we obliged to protect our twenty-second century descendants from contamination by today's nuclear trash?[22] Such questions pick up the debate raised by "deep ecology" or "ecophilosophy" that were laid out in Section Three.[23] All of this is involved in Paula Gonzalez's proposal.

The cultural implications of her remarks ask us to think about the philosophical investment that we place in seeking to move beyond an earth at risk. While "ecology" deals with all living species, habitats, and ecosystems, and "environment" with the human social, economic, and material context for life, the terms are often used without discrimination, or are collapsed into each other, interfering with our understanding of culture and nature. Politics and disputes about the meaning of environmental degradation become directly involved in the implications of economic action and technical deployment as suggested by Gonzalez.[24] Our sense of the meaning and use of technology, raised earlier by Barbour and Weiskel,[25] is related to our understanding of the meaning of human activity.

Environmental issues indeed serve as a catalyst for debate about how we engage the world around us. For example, the struggle to avoid a depressive determinism, often detracting from political action, reaches into the soul of the environmental movement and can move in one of two directions. On the one hand, we might develop a neoliberal focus. Through market or central planning forces we might solve the environmental problem with the same tools that created it. We could expand the trading of pollution rights, allow for the development of wetlands, and sell off national lands to the highest bidder while maintaining some level of environmental law. On the other hand, we might focus on the problem of degradation itself and build into the prices of goods and services the full range of costs (from raw resource to recyclable waste). Still, our worldview might subordinate our sense of ourselves (culture) to a wider array of determining factors: Any human activity on behalf of the environment or the greater ecosystems of the earth is futile. The stronger interpretation of the *Gaia* Hypothesis would allow that in the end the system will correct itself—with the possible destruction of the human species. Certain end-time religious perspectives contribute to a similar "terminal generation" mentality. This variation of the nature/nurture controversy carries us back to the premodern period and debate over individuality and meaningful choice. How we think about ourselves is reflected in what action we deem appropriate as a culture.

How we think about ourselves is often defined in the metaphors that give poetic meaning to our lives. Gonzalez asks us to consider the movement in metaphorical self-understanding from kingship to stewardship and, finally, to kinship. Embedded in the Jewish Scriptures and developed with particular reference to Jesus Christ in the New Testament, the concept of stewardship has given a certain resonance to the relational context in which humanity stands with respect to the rest of nature.[26] Through its emphasis on respect for all forms of life, it acknowledges a variety of worldviews and allows for them to enter into conversation with one another.[27] Stewardship neither gives way to determinism nor becomes overoptimistic about the spheres of human freedom open to us. It demands full knowledge of the natural world and its proper use. Douglas John Hall writes about the potential latency of the metaphor of stewardship. He adds that as Martin Luther's vision of a justifying grace enabled people to overcome a sense of medieval guilt, thereby finding the courage to live, so, too, "the sense of being stewards of earth and of life itself could provide a generation of world-weary and apathetic survivors some feeling of purpose."[28] Stewardship defines our relational identity and draws us to our common task. "Kinship," the term preferred by Gonzalez, reminds us of God's covenant with all creatures and creation (Gen. 9:8–17) and of the natural world which is our context.

Rodney L. Petersen

NOTES

1. This is the point made by Wolfgang Sachs of the Wuppertal Institute for Climate, Energy, and the Environment (Wuppertal, Germany) in "Social Justice and Environmental Sustainability in the Post-Development Era," in Mohamed Suliman, *Ecology, Politics, and Violent Conflict* (London: ZED Books, 1999), pp. 59–75.

2. C. F. von Weizsäcker, *The Relevance of Science: Creation and Cosmogony*, Gifford Lectures, 1959–1960 (London: Collins, 1964). He writes, "Anyone neglecting to further his theoretical understanding of our complex world as much as he can, will in the long run do more harm than good in his practical efforts" (p. 9).

3. For further information, see The National Religious Partnership for the Environment (New York City, New York) and the Union of Concerned Scientists (Cambridge, Massahusetts).

4. The work of the Worldwatch Institute, with project director Lester R. Brown, continues to provide helpful yearly data in the *State of the World* reports. This material might be reflected upon through a number of different ethical matrices as provided by, e.g., Bernard Rosen, *Strategies of Ethics* (Boston: Houghton Mifflin Publishers, 1971). See James A. Nash, "Moral Values in Risk Decisions," in *Handbook for Environmental Risk Decisionmaking*, ed. C. Richard Cothern (Boca Raton, Fla.: Lewis Publishers, 1995), pp. 195–212.

5. The study of literature about the environment has spawned new academic disciplines, some of which work to draw together perspectives on the sciences and humanities and variously called ecocriticism, "green cultural studies," or some other appropriate name. See the journal *Interdisciplinary Studies in Literature and the Environment* and the *American Nature Writing Newsletter*. Related debates ask whether such interdisciplinary work will mute the concerns of eco-feminism or other rights-based ethical debate. See Lawrence Buell, *The Environmental Imagination. Thoreau, Nature Writing, and the Formation of American Culture* (Cambridge, Mass.: Harvard University Press, 1995). Several classic expressions of the role of nature in literature are collected by P. Anderson Graham, *Nature in Books: Some Studies in Biography* (Port Washington, N.Y.: Kennikat Press, reissued, 1970 [1891]). See recent collections of essays by Cheryll Glotfelty and Harold Fromm, Carl G. Herndl and Stuart C. Brown, and Daniel G. Payne.

6. Mary Evelyn Tucker and John Grim, eds., *Worldviews and Ecology: Religion, Philosophy, and the Environment* (Maryknoll: Orbis, 1994); Ninian Smart, *Worldviews* (New York: Charles Scribner's Sons, 1983); and Ian Barbour, *Myths, Models, and Paradigms* (New York: Harper & Row, 1974). The term "worldview" begins to be widely used in Wilhelm Dilthey in his historical studies at the end of the nineteenth century. Sigmund Freud offers some penetrating insight as revelatory about him as concerning the term in his article, "The Question of a Weltanschauung," in *New Introductory Lectures on Psycho-Analysis*, trans. and ed. James Strachey (New York: W. W. Norton, 1964), pp. 195–225.

7. See the following authors who make the point that there is not a monolithic Native American experience: Russell Thornton, *American Indian Holocaust and Survival* (Norman: University of Oklahoma Press, 1987); Ward Churchill, *Strategies for the Land: Indigenous Resistance to Geno-*

cide, Ecocide, and Expropriation in Contemporary North America (Monroe, Maine: Common Courage Press, 1993); and Robert Allen Warrior, *Tribal Secrets: Recovering American Indian Intellectual Traditions* (Minneapolis: University of Minnesota Press, 1995).

8. Walter Echo-Hawk, "Loopholes in Religious Liberty: The Need for a Federal Law to Protect Freedom of Worship for Native People," *American Indian Religions* 1.1 (Winter, 1994).

9. Donald A. Grinde Jr., and Bruce E. Johansen, *Ecocide of Native America: Environmental Destruction of Indian Lands and Peoples* (Santa Fe: Clear Light Publishers, 1995).

10. Important Native voices from those engaged in a range of ecological struggles are gathered together by Jace Weaver, ed., *Defending Mother Earth: Native American Perspectives on Environmental Justice* (Maryknoll: Orbis Books, 1996).

11. Thomas Kuhn, *The Structure of Scientific Revolutions*, 2d. ed. (Chicago: University of Chicago Press, 1970). See also Ian Barbour, *Myths, Models, and Paradigms;* cf. essays in Frank T. Birtel, ed., *Religion, Science, and Public Policy* (New York: Crossroad, 1987).

12. Paul Albrecht, "From Oxford to Nairobi: Lessons From Fifty Years of Ecumenical Work for Economic and Social Justice," *The Ecumenical Review* 40 (April 1988).

13. Ans van der Bent, *Commitment to God's World* (Geneva: WCC Publications, 1995); see David G. Hallman, *Ecotheology: Voices from South and North* (Maryknoll: Orbis, 1994).

14. World Commission on Environment and Development, Brundtland Report (1987), *Our Common Future* (New York: Oxford University Press, 1987). The Report notes the rapid deterioration of the global environment as threatening human life on earth. It seeks to delineate approximate and possible ways to deal with environmental issues. It stands for: (1) meeting the needs of the present without compromising the ability of future generations to meet their needs, (2) creating a sustainable situation for all countries, and (3) a concern for equality within and between generations, not just physical sustainability. This was the third in a series of UN reports, following the Brandt report *North-South* (1980) with its sequel *Common Crisis* (1983) and the Palme report *Common Security* (1985). It deals with major problems like the greenhouse effect, deforestation, soil loss, the debt crisis, the global commons, and the explosion of cities.

15. Hans Küng, *Global Responsibility: In Search of a New World Ethic* (New York: Continuum, 1993).

16. John Leslie insists that environmental issues are the national security issues of the twenty-first century, in *The End of the World: The Science and Ethics of Human Extinction* (New York: Routledge, 1996); cf. Samuel Huntington, *The Clash of Civilizations and the Remaking of World Order* (New York: Simon & Schuster, 1996), pp. 130–35.

17. "The Earth Charter: A Joint Initiative of the Earth Council and Green Cross International," report prepared by the Earth Council and Green Cross International in connection with the Earth Charter Workshop, The Peace Palace, The Hague, May 31, 1995; and see the document in progress, *Principles of Environmental Conservation and Sustainable Development: Summary and Survey*, prepared for the Earth Charter Project by Steven Rockefeller (Earth Charter Project, The Earth Council, San Jose, Costa Rica, April 1996).

18. Andrew Harrell and Benedict Kingsbury, eds., *The International Politics of the Environment* (Oxford, 1992); and Paul Wapner, *Environmental Activism and World Civic Politics* (Albany: State University of New York Press, 1996).

19. See the papers from the conference "A Religious and Moral Challenge: Environmental Justice," a briefing Sponsored by The National Religious Partnership for the Environment, January 9 and 10, 1995. See *Sustainable Growth—A Contradiction in Terms?* report of the Visser 't Hooft Memorial Consultation (Chateau de Bossey: The Ecumenical Institute, 1993).

20. *Overview of the World Council of Churches' Programme on Climate Change* (Geneva: WCC, 1995).

21. James A. Nash, *Loving Nature: Ecological Integrity and Christian Responsibility* (Nashville: Abingdon Press, 1991). Nash argues that Christianity can draw upon a rich theological and ethical tradition with which to confront the ecological crisis.

22. Christopher D. Stone, *Earth and Other Ethics: The Case for Moral Pluralism* (New York: Harper and Row, 1987).

23. Richard Sylvan and David Bennett, *The Greening of Ethics: From Anthropomorphism to Deep-Green Theory* (Tucson: The University of Arizona Press, 1994). Henryk Skolimowski develops an ecological humanism as an alternative to industrial society which sees: (1) stewardship as a prevailing metaphor for human activity in the future, (2) the world to be best conceived of as a sanctuary in a religious sense, and (3) knowledge to be defined as the intermediary between us and the creative forces of evolution. See *Eco-Philosophy: Designing New Tactics for Living* (London: Marion Boyars, 1981), p. 54.

24. We are following David Goldblatt here, *Social Theory and the Environment* (Oxford: Oxford University Press, 1996).

25. See also Jacques Ellul, *The Technological Society* (New York: Alfred A. Knopf, 1964).

26. In developing his ideas on stewardship, Douglas John Hall contends that a form of Christian Humanism that transcends the anthropocentric as well as the older Liberal perspective (faulted for its assumptions about humanity and history and failure to provide an acceptable theology of nature) must be pioneered. See his *The Steward: A Biblical Symbol Come of Age* (Grand Rapids: Eerdmans, 1994 ed.), pp. 103–21. In order to enlarge our vision of the full ramifications for stewardship, he cites the following five principles: globalization, communalization, ecologization, politicization, and futurization (pp. 122–54). See the modified or "weak" anthropocentrism of Holmes Rolston III, *Environmental Ethics: Duties to and Values in the Natural World* (Philadelphia: Temple University Press, 1988).

27. See the discussion in Section Three about "Living with Nature." On the problem of the disconnection between ecological belief and behaviour, see Walt Grazer, "The Vision that Heals," *Green Cross* 2, no. 4 (Fall 1996): 16–21.

28. Hall, *The Steward*, p. 7. See the author's comments about the history of the book, first published in 1982, with reference to the emergence of the "Justice, Peace, and the Integrity of Creation" process in the World Council of Churches (xii). A helpful study guide is available to Hall's understanding of stewardship by J. Phillips Williams, *A Study Guide for Douglas John Hall's* The Steward: A Biblical Symbol Come of Age (New York: Friendship Press, 1985). Other metaphors include those of "frugality " and "mercy." On the former, see James A. Nash, "Toward the Revival and Reform of the Subversive Virtue: Frugality," *The Annual of the Society of Christian Ethics* (1995): 137–60; and the latter, George H. Williams, "Mercy in the Grounding of a Non-Elitist Ecological Ethic," in *Festschrift in Honor of Charles Speel*, ed. Thomas J. Sienkewicz and James Betts (Monmouth, Ill.: Monmouth College, 1996).

8
THE UNDOING OF THE ENVIRONMENT
Assessing the European Religious Worldview
Susan Power Bratton

With the publication of Rachel Carson's *Silent Spring*[1] in 1962, not just concerned scientists, but Euro-American academics in general turned their attention to the "environmental crisis." *Silent Spring* was not a watershed work, however, because it discussed environmental abuses, but because it sounded the alarm against technology and even science. During the nineteenth and early twentieth century, Americans had become aware of land degradation, the health hazards posed by industrialization, and widespread wastage of natural resources. In 1864, for example, George Perkins Marsh published *Man and Nature; or Physical Geography as Modified by Human Action,*[2] and advanced the concept that the ruined monuments of glorious ancient civilizations of Europe and the Middle East now stood in deforested, degraded, and agriculturally depleted landscapes. In Marsh's view, human advancement could be destructive and needed to be curbed by a conservation ethic that kept humans in balance with nature.[3] The national attitude towards technology, however, remained largely positive and progressive, if not rabidly enthusiastic. Then World War II cast a dark shadow on Euro-American civilization's ability to make ethical decisions and to control the power of modern industry. Tracking the damages caused by such wartime advancements as commercial DDT distribution and nuclear testing, *Silent Spring* initiated a deep questioning of Western values concerning technological progress, our treatment of the natural world, and the proliferation of invisible and insidious environmental hazards.

In the soul-searching that followed *Silent Spring*, historians began to dig for the roots of the environmental crisis and hauled a number of potential culprits into the dock, including such diverse phenomena as patriarchy, capitalism, northern climates, coal reserves, and Christianity. The purpose of this chapter is to investigate the way environmental historians have related religion to the development or lack of environmental ethics and values in the United States. If the historians have started with cultural "myths" and selected data to prove them, their conclusions may be suspect. If, however, they have accurately identified what religion has or has not accomplished environmentally, historic work may encourage more refined religious (or cultural) response to environmental concerns.

SEMINAL WORKS IN ENVIRONMENTAL AND RELIGIOUS HISTORY

In 1967, two seminal, oft cited, and repeatedly contested works attempted to link religious and philosophical thought to environmental attitudes: "The Historical Roots of Our Ecological Crisis,"[4] by medieval historian Lynn White Jr., and *Wilderness and the American Mind*,[5] by American historian Roderick Nash. White proposed that Jewish and Christian religious traditions were an important source of western environmental disregard, because they desacralized the cosmos. Some authors, such as John Passmore in *Man's Responsibility for Nature*,[6] have accepted White's notion of Christian environmental despotism, arguing that the serious problems with "dominion" did not arise with the development of modern science. Christian environmental writers, as a matter of established ritual, attack White in the introductions of their articles, claiming that he misinterpreted the Hebrew scriptures.[7] Geographer Ti Fu Tuan broadened the cultural context of environmental disregard by suggesting that non-Western cultures with vastly different religious systems had also degraded landscapes and damaged their surrounding ecosystems.[8] Interestingly, Tikva Frymer-Kensky, a Sumeriologist, recently has suggested that Hebrew modification of divine gender served to make humans responsible to God for the management of the land (rather than make a female deity responsible for natural productivity). She writes: "In Genesis, humanity is given dominion over the world, but the rest of the [Hebrew] Bible shows that this power entails enormous responsibility in that human behavior can destroy land and world."[9] She credits the notion that nature is an "unruly female, the very antithesis of civilization," that therefore needs to be tamed and molded by man (specifically males), to the Greeks.[10]

Nash has found, in contrast, both Judaism and Christianity to be largely hostile to the idea of wilderness. He hypothesized that Classicism, Judaism, and Christianity, by separating the divine from nature, all encouraged hatred of the wild. Nash believed that the Puritans transported Christian distaste for the untamed to the thirteen colonies, and that Western religion became one of the major sources for the demise of the great American wilderness. In summarizing the development of American philosophies of wilderness, Nash, finding desacralization an improvement, minimized discussion of the mainstream of American religious thought (other than Transcendentalism). Nash proposed: "Wilderness could be sacred but in its own right and not as sign or symbol of some overarching divinity."[11]

I have already critiqued Nash for: (1) following the strategy, fashionable in the 1960s, of seeing Eastern religions as potentially correcting the deficiencies of Western ones; (2) utilizing secondary and higher order religious sources, which often delete environmental material, as less important than abstract theological proclamations; and (3) emphasizing individual cases, such as St. Francis of Assisi, without regard to their historic antecedents, and thereby underreporting Christian environmental interest.[12] Perry Miller's works, such as *The New England Mind: From Colony to Province* and *Errand into the Wilderness*,[13] encouraged Nash, correctly, to present the idea of wilderness as an issue in intellectual history. The historians of the 1950s and 1960s, however, had too limited a view of religious diversity in colonial culture and treated the Puritans as an archetype of supposedly Christian culture.

A more recent study by Jon Butler, however, portrays seventeenth- and eighteenth-century Europe as both declining in Christian practice and harboring a great diversity of religious expression.[14] Ted Ownby relates overexploitation of game resources (of the nineteenth century) not to Christianity but to masculine culture and values.[15] Grady McWhitney considers such environmentally questionable practices as free-range grazing and dog hunting to be the offspring of old Celtic cultural traditions which are pre-Christian in origin, and which came to the Americas with Scottish, Irish, and British peasants.[16] Jon Butler and Catherine Albanese both find that European settlers in the thirteen colonies were interested in the occult and folk religion, including astrology, and many avoided organized religion all together.[17] The writings of John Winthrop and Cotton Mather may, therefore, actually have been quite unrepresentative of colonial values, and Nash's conclusions about the Puritans may not represent typical frontier religious thought.

In addition, *Wilderness and the American Mind* does not adequately relate European religious belief to colonial environmental practice. Although there can be little doubt that the Europeans referred to Native Americans as savage and uncivilized and classified them with beasts, this may not be anything more than the three-millennia European habit of considering neighboring cultures less worthy than one's own. Following Jon Butler, one could easily argue that Euro-American wilderness consciousness grew as the United States became more Christian (especially if one includes Transcendentalism as a Christian sect) and as the nation developed a stronger, if very diverse, religious identity. Nash recognizes that Thoreau and John Muir associated God and spiritual experience with wilderness. He concludes, however, that this type of thinking temporarily reversed the old Puritan negativity, by assuming a more philosophical path, and was eventually displaced by the modern notion that "the association between God and wilderness as just as much a myth—as much an anthropomorphic fallacy—as the earlier tendency to link wilderness and evil."[18] The fact that important nineteenth- and twentieth-century environmentalists, such as Thoreau (an abolitionist) and Howard Zahnizer (framer of the Wilderness Act and a dedicated Free Methodist), might be Christian and heirs to the nineteenth-century Christian cause of social ethics is nowhere mentioned. David R. Williams, in contrast, in *Wilderness Lost: The Religious Origins of the American Mind*,[19] traces Puritan wilderness themes, not just into the work of Thoreau, but through the writings of Hawthorne, Dickinson, and Melville.

THE NEXT GENERATION—NATIVE AMERICAN RELIGIONS AND ENVIRONMENTAL PURITY

Through the 1970s and 1980s, a second, more diverse generation of historical studies appeared, most of which followed major environmental fashions such as ecofeminism. In a reversal of the trends prior to the 1960s, mainstream American Christianity received relatively little detailed (or objective) attention. Although the concept is rooted in Romanticism and the ideal of the noble savage, late twentieth-century diversity authors have repeatedly rejected "nonnative" Eurasian religions as environmentally destructive and touted Native American or "primitive" religious practices as environmentally sound. Nineteenth-century spiritualists claimed deceased Native American chiefs as spiritual guides. Today, college students turn to Sun Bear and his medicine wheel for religious insight, and the New Age movement encourages vision quests, sweat lodges, sun dances, and feathered fetishes.[20]

In the midst of reams of popular tripe, one must conclude that the best Native American studies have actually been among the few that convincingly tie religion to environmental attitudes and practice. Calvin Luther Martin in *Keepers of the Game: Indian-Animal Relationships and the Fur Trade*[21] traces the effects of Europeans such as fur traders and priests on the Micmac, and documents the impact of such cataclysmic influences as smallpox epidemics and Jesuit theology on native cosmology. Utilizing sources such as missionary diaries, fur trapping records, and early natural histories, Martin interprets the "despiritualization" of the natives as an underlying cause of the relaxation of long-term taboos on over-harvesting[22] and, therefore, of the ensuing environmental abuse. One might question whether the difficulties were actually due specifically to Christianity, or whether any invasion of a technologically more aggressive culture would have had a similar result. *Keepers of the Game* provides substantial evidence, in any case, that environmental change undermined the Micmac religious system, which in turn became ethically non-functional as colonization proceeded.

Make Prayers to the Raven: A Koyukon View of the Northern Forest,[23] by Richard Nelson, correlates beliefs to conservation practice, and relates nature to the Koyukon moral code. Nelson, who lived with the Koyukon, employs oral history to document their cosmology and then isolates elements originating in Christian influence. Not unexpectedly, Nelson concludes that the "traditional" elements in Koyukon religion are critical to their relationship with nature. Unlike Calvin Luther Martin's conclusions about the Micmac, Nelson has not found that Christianity has broken down Native American care for the environment, but rather that it functions as a largely benign intrusion into an older religious system still strongly tied to the natural landscape.

Comparison of the two works leads to the suspicion that both authors assume that Western religion cannot successfully provide an environmental ethic, nor can it syncretise with other religions in constructive ways. Although Nelson cites Martin, he does not discuss the differences in their results, or analyze the greater colonial pressure on the Micmac. Nor do these authors consider the fact that Christianity changes through time and, when selectively absorbed by practitioners of another religion, may no longer reflect the beliefs of the source of transmission. Although many readers of books such as these have concluded that native religions are environmentally "better" than Christianity or Judaism, one could just as easily conclude that environmental devastation is likely to follow cultural change and that invading cultures are likely to exploit rather than to conserve.

ECOFEMINISM REFLECTS ON THE
DEEP ENVIRONMENTAL PAST

A second "diversity" branch of environmental history, the ecofeminist school, has claimed that ancient goddess-oriented cultures were environmentally healthy societies that revered and cared for the earth as mother. Then, either economics and warfare took over, or Indo-European male sun-worshipers arrived from the east, and women and nature both became property to be exploited.[24] Merlin Stone, in *When God Was a Woman*,[25] makes the ancient Hebrews (assumed to be exceptionally sexually neurotic warrior Indo-Europeans bowing to a violent male deity) the major culprits in Euro-American environmental abuse. Stone, like many eighteenth- and nineteenth-century philosophers bent on debunking or "correcting" Christianity, takes a de facto anti-Semitic tact. Fortunately, for the good academic name of female scholars, Tikva Frymer-Kensky has gone to the trouble of thoroughly investigating ancient Sumerian and Hebrew myths and religious practices and has found that the loss of the goddess in various Semitic cultures was slow and required centuries, and was not due to a specific invasion. She hypothesizes that the suppression of the goddess accompanied social changes associated with the rise of the powerful and centralized city-state.[26]

In *The Death of Nature: Women, Ecology, and Scientific Revolution*, Carolyn Merchant, a competent and imaginative historian, has investigated the scientific revolution's mechanization and fragmentation of the natural world, and thus places the final masculine takeover of European mother-earth at much later date than the early bronze age.[27] In a second volume, *Ecological Revolutions: Nature, Gender, and Science in New England*,[28] she argues that in human cultures sources of production interact with reproduction, which in turn structure human relationships with the environment. In New England there were two major ecological revolutions when Puritan pre-industrial culture displaced Native Americans and then when the region industrialized. Originally, the native agricultural consciousness was dominated by the mythical corn mother, a reflection of the primarily female nature of agricultural activities, such as tillage. The exogenous land management system and cosmology of the European colonists then displaced those of the first nations. The Indian mimetic consciousness fell to objective reality, based primarily on vision, and transmitted by means such as the written word. Merchant recognizes that the European settlers were full of non-Christian ritual and mythology, including the use of almanacs as symbol systems that directed farming practices. She views the preindustrial production system as a combination of native and European practices, and as one that slowly shed the image of land as "howling wilderness," in moving towards "an organic cosmology and participatory consciousness that informed rural farming practices."[29]

Eventually "scientific" farming began to penetrate the consciousness of even backcountry farmers and displaced older European folk beliefs as well as Puritan ethics.[30] At the same time the growing market economy replaced subsistence farming, and the land was increasingly depleted of nutrients. Men moved into the public and political sphere, while women stayed home and performed domestic duties. Merchant presents two religious movements as reactions to the increasingly mechanized and male universe of the economy. Aside from establishing communal farms, which managed their lands well, Shakers had visions of natural landscapes and gardens and incorporated nature into their religious iconography. The Romantic movement helped to produce Transcendentalism, which in turn produced reactions to "market farming." For Merchant, Thoreau's bean patch was a social and ecological statement about what was wrong in New England culture.[31] Although Merchant is much more convincing than Nash in the way she relates "ideas" about nature to actual land management, she utilizes religion where convenient and then switches to other factors, such as industrialization. In presenting her ideas about the Shakers she does not set them in the overall context of nineteenth-century religious sectarianism. Nor, in the case of the religious ecological protesters, does she fully document their ethics or link them to their effects on other groups. She acknowledges the pagan underpinnings of much colonial thought about agriculture. Like Nash, however, her approach to Christianity is somewhat monolithic, and general English concepts about farming are not always separated from the particulars of the Puritan project.

ECONOMICS, TECHNOLOGY, AND THE ENVIRONMENT

A third major genre of the "second generation" is composed of the numerous published histories of environmental movements or of individual leaders such as John Muir. In general these works concentrate on Transcendentalism and its relatives and neglect other religious paths. This gives the impression that there is a strong dichotomy between the nature-conscious religious sects and other forms of Eestern religion. Part of the difficulty lies in the definition of what is or is not "orthodox" Christianity. Richard Cartwright Austin, for example, designated John Muir as a Christian prophet.[32] The major biographers of Muir, however, have identified him as someone who was greatly influenced by the Bible and by a stern, repressive Christian father, but who ultimately abandoned participation in organized Christian worship.[33] Clearly, Muir's thought is partially a product of Western religion and he is one of many nineteenth-century naturalists who used religious language. American myths and cultural ideology needs to be tracked more carefully. For example, Peter Schmidt, in *Back to Nature: The Arcadian Myth in Urban America*, suggests that "the church in the wildwood," with its nature-oriented hymns and encouragement to Christian outdoorsmen, is an adaptation of Arcadian myth,[34] but he fails to discuss the implications of this in terms of national attitudes.

If religion fades into the background in political histories, it disappears almost completely in a majority of the volumes chronicling the impacts of economic or technological change. In recent works by Albert Cowdrey, Timothy Silver, Michael Williams, and Gordon Whitney on environmental change in forested regions, technology and westward expansion take credit for major trends.[35] Williams, the only one of the four to include "Christianity" or "religion" in his index, does briefly discuss Christians relating forest clearing to redemption and also "promoting Christian values" through Arbor Day.[36] In general, however, religious references identify an individual or a cultural group, and little more.

An interesting deviation from the studies of New England that assume Puritan land management was somehow founded in religion is William's Cronon's *Changes in the Land: Indians, Colonists, and the Ecology of New England.*[37] Cronon looks at the European colonists as residents of tilled farms and villages who wished to establish their accustomed agricultural practices in their newly invaded territory. They, unlike the Native Americans, established long-term food storage for seasons of shortage, considered land individual or family property, and transposed permanent fencing onto fields once tilled by shifting cultivation. Game and timber became commodities. Following the example of their owners, settler livestock then dealt a death blow to the native subsistence system by trampling through unfenced gardens and destroying crops. If one accepts Cronon's major thesis, it would have made little difference what religion the new settlers favored as long as they thought of land as a form of capital or considered it important in family inheritance, divided it into stable fields, owned domestic grazing animals, and carried exotic diseases. The ancient Romans or Chinese, or even the Iron-age Celts, would have been just as disruptive of Native American culture had they managed to arrive in numbers bearing land grants. (And the Celts would not have needed anything on paper.) Although one could argue that capitalism arose with Calvinism, fenced fields, granaries, and counting one's wealth in cattle are far older than either.

Donald Worster is among the best of the range-and-river historians, yet his early studies barely mention religion, other than by developing almost unavoidable themes, such as Mormon theological motives for pursuing irrigation, and the more widespread notion that it was "God's wish that nature's desolation be turned into a garden."[38] Recently, in *Under Western Skies: Nature and History in the American West,*[39] Worster mentions religious elements in the agrarian myth, but does not develop or document the connections.[40] The volume does, however, dedicate an entire chapter to the question of whether the Black Hills are sacred or not. The essay includes some naive statements, such as: "All religion seems to spring from a feeling of profound nostalgia, a longing for a time when the daily world was more pure and orderly than it now appears. The religious person wants to escape the present and reenter that past existence."[41] The chapter nevertheless does catch some of the conflict between traditional Native American and Protestant world views. Worster suggests that "in Christianity such nostalgia has become paradoxically progressive."[42] and that Americans are "obsessed with abstractions."[43] The Native American community, in contrast, has a need for the "awakening of a new or revitalized religion"[44] as a matter of self-identity.

In *The Wealth of Nature: Environmental History and the Ecological Imagination*, published in 1993, Worster finally begins to capture the religious threads in environmental conservation and to tie them to economics. Worster presents Leonard J. Arrington's idea that the Mormons had adopted the economic values of the Puritans and produced a society that was both materialist and anticapitalist.[45] Worster then describes the irrigation programs of first the Mormon church and then the federal government as fulfillments of a myth that had religious origins,[46] and he proposes that "at the very heart of the irrigation myth is an affirmation of technology as a divinely ordained instrument of domination over the natural world."[47] Worster, however, leaves untouched the complex question of the Mormons' relationships to capitalism or to general nineteenth-century religious trends.

In a chapter centered on John Muir, Worster reviews the Lynn White Jr. debate and notes that it has had the healthy effect of making Protestants more conscious of biblical stewardship traditions. After a brief defense of the Puritans for passing the first North American laws protecting forests and game, Worster relates "the dissident tradition in American and northern European Protestantism"[48] to environmentalism, and then disappoints the reader by proceeding to prove that John Muir was "clearly a product of left-wing Protestantism,"[49] as also were John Wesley Powell (who explored the Colorado River), Stephen Mather (of the national parks), and Justice William O. Douglas.[50] Suggestively, he correlates four values found in northern European Protestantism with American environmentalism: moral activism, ascetic discipline, egalitarian individualism, and aesthetic spirituality.[51] Although Worster appears to be on the right track, he does not attempt to follow these themes through the Progressive movement, relate them to the Social Gospel, or work through the growing conflicts within Protestantism at the end of the nineteenth century.

If one accepts both the work of Cronon and Worster, a picture emerges that is far different from that presented by Nash. First, the most critical conflicts between Puritans and Native Americans were agricultural, technological, and economic. The settlers slowly recognized that they were damaging natural resources, but rather than handling this with religious taboos, they enacted laws to attempt to protect commodities. The Protestant religious response has been largely through "spiritual" values that actualize in lifestyles, including "green" responses, and that take social form in cooperative projects such as the dam-building of New Deal conservationists and the national park movement. Religious origins may, in fact, be clouded by legislative outcomes.

NATURE RELIGION AS AN AMERICAN PRODUCT

As the logical follow-up to the diversity movement, Catherine Albanese, in *Nature Religion in America: From the Algonkian Indians to the New Age*,[52] has corrected many of the faults of earlier volumes by recognizing that it is not just the cultural ideals that determine how we view nature, but also the natural surroundings that influence the construction of ideals. Albanese, however, is eclectic in what she considers "nature religion," and she chooses only those religious movements which show a strong affinity for the nonhuman. Disjunct in approach, the volume drifts from central figures in the New Republic, such as Jefferson, to the occult and then to New Age. Interestingly, in her textbook on American religion,[53] she fills in some of the gaps by dealing with questions of sacramentality, covering folk practice in the Appalachians and plotting the course of civil religion. While proving that "nature" is an important and continuing source of American religious thought and expression, Albanese leaves the reader with the impression that some forms of religion are "nature religion," while others are not. The reality is potentially much less dichotomous, but more of a gradient.

An irony of the available literature on the relationship between American religion and the environment is that volumes dedicated to topics in literature, art history, and landscape architecture and planning may have done a better job of documenting historic change in the relationship of Christianity and its offspring to the environment than the historians have. Criticism of religious themes is unavoidable in dealing with artists such as Thoreau, Hawthorne, Melville, or Thomas Cole. One of the most thorough treatments of this type is Cecelia Tichi's *New World, New Earth: Environmental Reform in American Literature from the Puritans through Whitman*,[54] which begins with Puritan eschatology and traces the subjects of the "New Jerusalem" and the millennium through writers of the Revolutionary period up to Walt Whitman. Tichi presents the early settlers as viewing their arrival in the Americas as initiating environmental reform. The idea of a "new earth" appears in a number of versions, from strictly premillennial to the beloved national landscape of *Leaves of Grass*. Barbara Novak's *Nature and Culture: American Landscape Painting 1825–1875*[55] incorporates religious expression as intrinsic to the development of the great outpouring of landscape painting in the nineteenth century, and documents an American infatuation with nature as God. Although a majority of aesthetic studies only deal with environmental management or politics indirectly, James Machor, in *Pastoral Cities: Urban Ideals and the Symbolic Landscape of America*,[56] manages to tie Puritan belief in a "New Jerusalem," and continuing Protestant interest in the millenium, to nineteenth-century urban reform. These studies may be successful in tracing religious themes through time or relating them to environmental reform movements because they concentrate on icons and myth in the broad sense, rather than on one specific notion of Christianity or nature religion. They thereby avoid some of the questionable categorizations of religion that appear in strictly historic studies.

Although Albanese's approach has not yet produced a third generation of environmental history that is both objective and adequately conscious of religious themes, there is presently an increasing interest in more traditional religious responses and in religion as a root of reform and as a purveyor of ecojustice. In 1995, Robert Fowler published *The Greening of Protestant Thought*,[57] which lacks any detailed analysis of Protestant environmental interests prior to Earthday 1970, but does a detailed job of tracking more recent theological dialog. Aside from recording the social reform activities of Protestant liberals, Fowler is open minded enough to give Evangelical organizations, such as Au Sable Institute and Evangelicals for Social Action, credit for articulating environmental issues in Christian terms. His discussion is heartening in that it documents a very broad base of support for Christian environmentalism in the American religious mainstream.

Fowler does not fully capture the political activism in the environmental realm, however, of either "ethnic" or extreme right-wing Christianity. Recent publications on environmental racism, for example, describe the leadership role of African American pastors and churches in fighting urban pollution and combating environmental abuse of minorities and the poor. Hispano organizers and Native American elders, similarly, wrestle with misuse of agricultural chemicals, industrial spills and pollution from mines.[58] Conversely, James Ridgeway in *Blood in the Face*[59] and Micheal Barkun in *Religion and the Racist Right: The Origins of the Christian Identity Movement*[60] describe fundamentalist Christian resistance to environmental legislation and the use of theological rationales to justify the creation of an "Aryan homeland." If Christianity ever presented a monolithic view of human relationship to nature, it certainly does not today. Although Carolyn Merchant includes a chapter on alternative spirituality in her recent review of radical environmentalism,[61] the historic literature still has not caught up with the outpouring of environmental religious thought, and the environmental roots of a majority of American religions, including Judaism, Islam, Buddhism, and the great diversity of Native American groups, remain underreported.

DISCUSSION

The early historic studies tended either to conceive of European religion as environmentally disruptive or to divide religions into two boxes—nature-friendly and nature-unfriendly. Merchant and Albanese appear to be on the right track when they present European religion as first colliding with the American landscape and then slowly beginning to adjust to it. Although the available literature still does not explain the variety of American religious perceptions, it is beginning to present an evolving complex of mythic and ritual response, with diverse means of incorporating the non-human. Environmental historians have often fallen to tautology. They reason that if new colonists disturbed the landscape or caused environmental devastation, it must somehow be rooted in their philosophy. This assumes that formal philosophy and theology are even understood or accepted among farmers, trappers, and lumbermen. Furthermore, many people say one thing and do another. Assuming that those who identify themselves as Christian practice ethics grounded in Christianity is risky.

Cronon's analysis, which almost completely ignores European religion, helps to clarify the difficulties with the religious historiography. Not just Nash, but a majority of the researchers working on these topics in the last three decades have made little effort to be certain that they are comparing the same types of social or cultural phenomena when contrasting Native American land management or ethics to European practices. Native American societies utilize religion and myth as rationales for interactions with the environment in cases where European culture utilizes philosophy, law, science, or economics. Although myths, such as the myth of progress or the agrarian myth, may also be important in Euro-American economic or even scientific communication, most authors switch cultural frameworks when comparing European religion to the belief systems of first peoples. Cronon reverses the inquiry and asks: "How did the two societies value, share, and manage the landscape?" This allows a more astute comparison between widely differing cultural approaches to the environment.

The historians themselves seem to have fallen into myth propagation, including the myth of Christian hegemony among the first European settlers, the myth of ancient religions as nature-friendly, the myth of women's religions as nature-friendly, and the myth of environmentalism as scientific progress. Nash, for example, often fails to distinguish the ideas of his historic sources from his own, and continues the nineteenth-century agenda of utilizing history as evidence for cultural progress in the United States. Although Nash's work appears too "liberal" to forward this bad habit, he writes of wilderness as a great American ideal in the same way his academic forefathers wrote of manifest destiny. The belief that the Puritans arrived all baptized and waving Bibles, that the United States was a "Christian nation" from its European colonial beginnings, appears to have encouraged Nash and many other authors, such as Fredrick Turner,[62] to assume that Christianity was an important culprit in the demise of "natural" America. Cronon, in contrast, does not need to invoke theological differences to explain why the New England landscape was so quickly covered with cows and stone fences after the Pilgrims hit the beach.

The lines of thought rooted in cultural and gender diversity often draw from the argument that ancient or first is better. This leads to historic confusion, not only due to lack of evidence for this idea if one incorporates technological change as a variable, but also because it tends to identify either a very early period (e.g., the rape of the goddess) or the period of colonization as the critical "fall from grace" from which contemporary America has never escaped. Aside from being a reversal of Puritan theology about the New Jerusalem, this type of thinking leaves the environmentally concerned person attempting to restore stone or bronze age culture in a machine age society. The historic literature itself is deeply conflicted over the legitimate role of religion. On one hand it argues that ancient Hebrew desacralization of nature was "bad." On the other, it sports a subtle cynicism about folk practices based on the lunar calendar or about Mormon desires to create a divinely ordained garden. This may be due to the increasing compartmentalization of religion in contemporary industro-technical culture, where it has become one of several viewpoints, rather than a central way of ordering human life.

One of the problems potentially caused by the intrusion of one religious system into another is that a new religion may not be adapted to the local landscape. The two great "missionary" religions originating in the Middle East, Christianity and Islam, have each spread from continent to continent, and through a great variety of social and economic classes and ethnic groups. Ethically, these religions emphasize general principles of social behavior and are neither site nor society specific in their approach. Both also originally spread in urban areas and along developed trade routes. The finding that cultures that are "in place" and that are relatively technologically stable conserve resources should be no surprise. A more productive question is: How do religious traditions adjust to landscape and technological change? There is a lack of studies on the relationship between religious systems of European origin and actual environmental management strategies. Ironically, when Cronon attempts to document European styles of environmental management prior to arrival in the colonies, he ends up ignoring religion as a major factor in agricultural organization in seventeenth-century England. This suggests that religious ethics were already far more compartmentalized in European than in Native American society, and had already been displaced, not just by science, but by European styles of government and economics. Albanese repeatedly notes in *Nature Religion in America* that the new natural environment would ultimately have an impact on religions of Old World origin. She does not, however, relate this to farming or fishing, or to the balance between religious ethics and other potential means of regulating human-environment interactions.

The literature has not effectively documented how the variety of religious thought in colonial America influenced the relation of the colonists to nature, if it did at all. No one has bothered to determine if Carolyn Merchant's results also apply to Georgia or Maryland, much less to New Mexico or California. Further, if current theory is correct and the United States became increasingly religious through the post-Revolutionary period and developed its own brands of Christianity, this would imply that the interaction between religion and nature should have changed mightily between the seventeenth and nineteenth centuries; and perhaps it did in the rise of Transcendentalism and numerous agrarian sects. Catherine Albanese has captured some of the impact of the natural environment on religion, while failing to discuss the religious bases for environmental ethics in detail. She also avoids the more complex questions, such as the relationship between democratic ideals, evangelicalism, and societal needs to constrain industrial and agricultural impacts on national natural resources. Not a single major historic work has attempted to tie the religious underpinnings of the major social reform movements of the nineteenth and twentieth centuries to the development of American environmentalism. Worster begins the task, but does not prove the general case. Exceptionally ironic is the lack of connection of the well-documented role of Christianity, as a social organizer, to "rights movements" and to the "rights" stream of American environmental thought.[63] Even Catherine Albanese views "nature religion" as somehow separate from the core of Christian and Jewish traditions. If this is the case, development of an environmental ethic has been primarily, as Merchant proposes, "reactionary" in American religious culture.

The present state of the literature suggests numerous constructive projects. First, the colonial situation needs further investigation. A careful analysis of the role of religion in European environmental management and ethics in the sixteenth and seventeenth centuries matched by careful tracing of "selection" and "evolution" in the process of colonization would help in evaluating religious response to new environmental settings. Second, there is a need for better documentation of the relationship of religion to the great American myths—including the "wilderness myth" and the "agrarian myth"—and their relationship to the proliferation of American religious sects and denominations, from the Shakers to contemporary Christian agrarian communities and even the right-wing Christian Identity movement. There is also a need for a better understanding of the "mainline" and the more orthodox traditions. Although Albanese covers the New Age, most people involved in natural resource harvest or land management in the United Sates are not followers of Sun Bear. What are ordinary Catholics and mainline Protestants up to? What are Latino traditions like? Are there differences among Native American communities in terms of the impact of Christianity on the relationship between Native American cultures and the environment? How does contemporary environmentalism relate to Christian and Jewish reform and social justice movements? Does the spread of Islam in the United States have environmental implications?

Lastly, there is the question of how quickly religion can adapt to and interpret changing natural environments. Protestant Christianity, for example, could be handicapped in developing specific environmental ethics for several reasons, including an emphasis on first order issues (e.g., "love thy neighbor"), a dependence on ancient texts written primarily in west Asia, and a concentration on eschatology. If we assume Judaism, Christianity, and Islam are inherently anti-environmental, we will, in turn, not expect them to make positive contributions to solving environmental problems. What makes the "great" religions and the peoples of the Book responsive to local and specific ethical issues? What underlies religious adaptation to technological, economic and environmental changes? What sort of religious evolution helps people to cope and to act responsibly, rather than to abuse and depreciate their fellow creatures and their own home and hearth?

ACKNOWLEDGMENT

I thank Julie Reuben, formerly of the Graduate Program in Arts and Humanities of the University of Texas at Dallas, and presently on the faculty of Harvard University, for her coaching in religious historiography and her criticism of early drafts of this essay.

NOTES

1. Rachel Carson, *Silent Spring* (Boston: Houghton Mifflin, 1962).

2. George Perkins Marsh, *Man and Nature; or Physical Geography as Modified by Human Action* (New York: Scribner. 1864).

3. Arthur Ekirch, *Man and Nature in America* (Lincoln, Nebr.: University of Nebraska Press, 1963), pp. 70–80. Early environmental history tended to focus on the landscape; see, for example, L. Dudley Stamp's *Man and the Land* (London: Collins, 1955), and H.J. Fleure, *A Natural History of Man in Britain* (London: Collins, 1951).

4. *Science* 155 (1967): 1203–07.

5. Roderick Nash, *Wilderness and the American Mind* (New Haven, Conn.: Yale University Press, 1967). Quotes here will be from the third edition published in 1982. A third historic volume published in 1967, Clarence Glaken's *Traces on the Rhodian Shore: Nature and Culture in Western Thought from Ancient Times to the End of the Eighteenth Century* (Berkeley: University of California Press, 1967), has also greatly influenced scholarship on Christianity. Although Glacken reviews Greek thought and early Christian traditions, and presents Western thought about nature as complex and variable, he provides little coverage of religion in the Americas, since he dwells on the impressions of European scientists and philosophers on the "New World."

6. John Passmore, *Man's Responsibility for Nature* (London: Duckworth, 1974). See the recent volume by Robin Attfield, *Environmental Philosophy: Principles and Prospects* (Brookfield, Mass.: Avebury, 1994), for an up-to-date-review of Lynn White's thesis.

7. See, for example, Susan P. Bratton, "Christian Eco-Thelogy and the Old Testament," *Environmental Ethics* 6 (1986):195–209.

8. Ti Fu Tuan, *Topophilia* (Engelwood Cliffs, N.J.: Prentice Hall, 1974).

9. Tikva Frymer-Kensky, *In the Wake of the Goddesses: Women, Culture, and the Biblical Transformation of Pagan Myth* (New York: Macmillan, The Free Press, 1992), p. 214.

10. Ibid., pp. 214–15.

11. Nash, *Wilderness and the American Mind*, p. 269.

12. "The Original Desert Solitaire," *Environmental Ethics* 10 (1988): 31–53.

13. Perry Miller, *The New England Mind: From Colony to Province* (Cam-

bridge: Harvard Univ. Press, 1939), and *Errand into the Wilderness* (Cambridge: Harvard University Press, 1956).

14. Jon Butler, *Awash in a Sea of Faith* (Cambridge: Harvard University Press, 1990).

15. Ted Ownby, *Subduing Satan: Religion, Recreation, and Manhood in the Rural South, 1865–1920* (Chapel Hill: University of North Carolina Press, 1990).

16. Grady McWhitney, *Cracker Culture: Celtic Ways in the Old South* (Tuscaloosa, Ala.: University of Alabama Press, 1988).

17. Butler, *Awash in a Sea of Faith*, and Catherine Albanese, *Nature Religion in America: From the Algonkin Indians to the New Age* (Chicago: University of Chicago Press, 1990).

18. Nash, *Wilderness and the American Mind*, p. 269.

19. David R. Williams, *Wilderness Lost: The Religious Origin of the American Mind* (Selinsgrove, Penn.: Susquehanna University Press, 1987).

20. Catherine Albanese, *America: Religion and Religions* (Belmont, Calif.: Wadsworth, 1992), pp. 359–69.

21. Calvin Luther Martin, *Keepers of the Game: Indian-Animal Relationships and the Fur Trade* (Berkeley: University of California Press, 1978).

22. Ibid., pp. 150–56.

23. Richard Nelson, *Make Prayers to the Raven: A Koyukon View of the Northern Forest* (Chicago: University of Chicago Press, 1983).

24. See Riane Eisler, *The Chalice and the Blade: Our History, Our Future* (San Francisco: Harper & Row, 1988); Elinor Gadon, *The Once and Future Goddess* (San Francisco: Harper & Row, 1989), or Elizabeth D. Gray, *Green Paradise Lost* (Wellesley, Mass.: Roundtable Press, 1979).

25. Merlin Stone, *When God Was a Woman* (New York: Dorset Press, 1976).

26. Frymer-Kensky, *In the Wake of the Goddess*.

27. Carolyn Merchant, *The Death of Nature: Women, Ecology, and Scientific Revolution* (San Francisco: Harper and Row, 1983).

28. Carolyn Merchant, *Ecological Revolutions: Nature, Gender, and Science in New England* (Chapel Hill: University of North Carolina Press, 1989).

29. Ibid., p. 144.

30. Ibid., pp. 196–97.

31. Ibid., pp. 248–60.

32. Richard Cartwright Austin, *Baptized into Wilderness: A Christian Perspective on John Muir* (Atlanta: John Knox, 1987).

33. See for example, Stephen Fox, *John Muir and His Legacy* (Boston: Little, Brown and Co., 1981).

34. Peter Schmidt, *Back to Nature: The Arcadian Myth in Urban America* (Baltimore: Johns Hopkins University Press, 1990).

35. Albert Cowdrey, *This Land, This South: An Environmental History* (The University Press of Kentucky, 1983). Timothy Silver, *A New Face on the Coutnryside: Indians, Colonists, and Slaves in South Atlantic Forests, 1500–1800* (New York: Cambridge University Press, 1990). Michael Williams, *Americans and their Forests: A Historical Geography* (New York: Cambridge, 1989). Gordon Whitney, *From Coastal Wilderness to Fruited Plain: A History of Environmental Change in Temperate North America, 1500 to the Present* (New York: Cambridge, 1994).

36. Williams, *Americans and their Forests*, pp. 10–11, 383.

37. Michael Williams, *Cronon's Changes in the Land: Indians, Colonists, and the Ecology of New England* (New York: Hill and Wang, 1983).

38. Donald Worster, *Rivers of the Emprie: Water Aridity and the Growth of the American West* (New York: Pantheon Books, 1985) p. 111. See other early works, for example, Donald Worster, *The Dust Bowl: The Southern Plains in the 1930s* (New York: Oxford University Press, 1982).

39. Donald Worster, *Under Western Skies: Nature and History in the American West* (New York: Oxford University Press, 1992).

40. Ibid., pp. 6–7.

41. Ibid., p. 141.

42. Ibid., p. 242.

43. Ibid., p. 143.

44. Ibid., p. 150.

45. Donald Worster, *The Wealth of Nature: Environmental History and the Ecological Imagination* (New York: Oxford University Press, 1993). Arrington published *The Great Basin Kingdom* in 1958.

46. Ibid., p. 117.

47. Ibid., p. 121.

48. Ibid., p. 189.

49. Ibid., p. 189.

50. Ibid., pp. 190–91.

51. Ibid., pp. 196–202.

52. Catherine Albanese, *Nature Religion in America: From the Algonkian Indians to the New Age* (Cambridge: Cambridge University Press, 1986).

53. Albanese, *America: Religion and Religions*. Albanese devotes an

entire chapter to the combination of folk religion and Christianity in the Appalachians, pp. 324–39.

54. Cecelia Tichi, *New World, New Earth: Environmental Reform in American Literature from the Puritans through Whitman* (New Haven: Yale University Press, 1979). See also Conrad Cherry, *Nature and Religious Imagination: From Edwards to Bushnell* (Philadelphia: Fortress Press, 1980), which documents the use of natural imagery in eighteenth- and nineteenth-century sermons, and the application of natural symbols to Christian moral teachings, including those concerning the New Republic and the social order. Another related work is by Alexander Karanikas, *Tillers of a Myth: Southern Agrarians as Social and Literary Critics* (Madison: University of Wisconsin Press, 1966). This volume relates antiurban, anti-industrial themes in southern writers, such as Robert Penn Warren, to a turning toward religion as something more enduring and meaningful than the social changes threatening post-Civil War southern culture.

55. Barbara Novak, *Nature and Culture: American Landscape Painting 1825–1875* (New York: Oxford University Press, 1980).

56. James Machor, *Pastoral Cities: Urban Ideals and the Symbolic Landscape of America* (Madison: University of Wisconsin Press, 1987).

57. Robert Fowler, *The Greening of Protestant Thought* (Chapel Hill: University of North Carolina Press, 1995).

58. See, for example, the work of Robert Bullard, including *Confronting Environmental Racism: Voices from the Grassroots* (Boston: South End Press, 1993), and *Dumping in Dixie: Race Class and Environmental Quality* (College Station: Texas A&M Press, 1987). Laura Westra and Peter Wenz have also produced an edited collection: *Faces of Environmental Racism: Confronting Issues of Global Justice* (Lanham, Md.: Rowman and Littlefield Publishers, 1995). For a theological perspective, see Dieter Hessel, *After Nature's Revolt: Eco-Justice and Theology* (Minneapolis: Fortress Press, 1992).

59. James Ridgeway, *Blood in the Face: The Ku Klux Klan, Aryan Nations, Nazi Skinheads, and the Rise of a New White Culture* (New York: Thunder's Mouth Press, 1995).

60. Michael Barkun, *Religion and the Racist Right: The Origins of the Christian Identity Movement* (Chapel Hill: University of North Carolina Press, 1994).

61. Carolyn Merchant, *Radical Ecology: The Search for a Livable World* (New York: Routledge, 1992).

62. Frederick Turner, *Beyond Geography: The Western Spirit Against the Wilderness* (Brunswick, N.J.: Rutgers University Press, 1983).

63. See, for example, Roderick Nash, *The Rights of Nature: A History of Environmental Ethics* (Madison: University of Wisconsin Press, 1989).

QUESTIONS FOR DISCUSSION

1. Do you think the most important works of the past three decades incorporate religion in any significant way?

2. How does the historiography influence the way religion is portrayed? Are there "environmentally friendly" and "environmentally unfriendly" religions?

3. Has religion had any impact on how humans have utilized or lived in the natural environment? Has religion produced or inhibited environmental ethics?

9

COMMUNITY AND ECOLOGICAL JUSTICE
A Native American Response
George E. Tinker

odern ecological devastation has put the lives and well-being of Native Americans at risk. Indeed, case studies from exemplary Indian communities are often used in order to demonstrate the range and intensity of ecological degradation and of ecojustice concerns among Indian people in general: land, water, mining, toxic waste deposit sites, and the like. It is ironic that those who have the deepest cultural connection to American soil would be among those most deeply affected by the modern, technological devastation of the land.[1] Yet it is the painful truth that ecological devastation, while it eventually effects the well-being of everyone, initially and most particularly affects Native Americans and people of color on this continent and Two-Thirds World people in general more directly and adversely than it affects White Americans, especially those of the middle and upper classes.[2] As Ward Churchill implies, genocide seems all too often to accompany ecocide.[3]

In the world today there are those who would regularly espouse an environmental consciousness predicated on Native American belief systems, summoning images of a simpler existence with a built-in concern for the whole of creation. This common notion that Native American peoples and other indigenous peoples have some spiritual and mystic insight on environmental issues confronting the world today is usually an instinctive if unstudied recognition of the differentness of those cultures. It thus tends to be a relatively intuitive claim based on little research and an overabundance of romanticizing. Even those who have had the opportunity to witness the poverty of our poorest reservations, evidenced by the rusting hulks of worn-out automobiles parked in various states of abandonment around reservation homes, continue to recite their own facile version of Native concern for the environment.

On the other hand, there are others who have a more openly racist concern for protecting the privilege of White power and discourse in North America. They find ways to use their position and prestige to deprecate Native American environmental consciousness. Sometimes this perspective is packaged in the clothing of modern academic research, typically by White scholars who use "Native American Studies," as Vizenor would again remind us, as a "trope to power."[4] Namely, some White scholars who specialize in Native American studies feel so threatened by the emergence of Native scholars that they have used their academic positions and their manipulation of the discourse more to empower themselves than in the quest for truth. Other commentators in the largely White liberal ecology movement seem to have their own racist power agenda. Namely, there seems to be a lingering self-defense (or defensiveness) among many in the more reactionary environmentalist set, like Earth First!, that other peoples have also abused the natural world—they just lacked the resources and technology to do it as exhaustively as Europeans and Americans have done.[5]

The truth of the native world is far more complex and sophisticated than either of these sides would allow. What follows is one Native American scholar's attempt to reflect theologically on the relationship between Native American peoples and what Western theologians would call "creation" and the contemporary ecological devastation of that creation. The occasion for this essay is the continuing program of the World Council of Churches' program unit called "Justice, Peace, and the Integrity of Creation" (JPIC) and the particular case study designed by the JPIC unit around the topic "Creation as Beloved of God." It was around this assigned topic that we assembled nearly two dozen Native American spokespeople from nearly as many tribes for conversation in May, 1995.

The modern "world system," driven by the economics and politics of domination, functions primarily on the basis of maximizing profits with only minimal regard for environmental concerns. In turn, this world system is sustained intellectually in no small part by the prevailing theologies of the powerful churches of Europe and North America and the philosophies taught in their universities. If the European and Amereuropean churches do not pay particular attention to these philosophical and theological foundations that underlie modern technology, economics, and international politics and their resulting contexts of ethno-ecojustice, then the political realities of interethnic and international injustice and ecological devastation have little chance of changing for the better.

"CREATION AS BELOVED OF GOD"

The first step in this theological reflection has to do with language and culture, and with the inappropriateness of typical Euro-Christian cultural language for referencing Native American cultural realities. As the heading of this section already implies, there are three words in the assigned program title that will pose problems for Native American peoples linguistically, culturally, and theologically—namely, the nouns and the adjective. If Christianity is to make any legitimate claim to universality, it must struggle to overcome the cultural limitations of its traditional categories of theological analysis in order to better accommodate peoples with radically different cultures and languages. Otherwise, the Christian enterprise is forever condemned to perpetrate imperialist acts of colonization and conquest.

"BELOVED"

Creation as beloved of God is actually very strange language for a Native American community to consider. Of course, it makes sense in the context of the World Council of Churches, especially given the scriptural tradition that understands God as typified by love in terms of the New Testament Greek word *agape*. But this is a relatively technical linguistic-cultural phenomenon that only works universally for Christianity with careful translation from the Greek and extensive ongoing education. In a cultural world that has been consistently abused by institutional Christianity[6] and one that has also struggled to maintain its own cultural and spiritual identity, the technicality of Greek language translation can be seen to be almost completely irrelevant or even antagonistic. This imposition of meaning is then heightened by the fact that no Native American community I know of refers to God's relationship with creation as characterized by "love." Of course, Native American peoples have nouns and verbs to describe emotive-bonding relationships between people, but we do not, as a rule, impute these same human emotive states, like love, to God. God and the spiritual realm can be happy or upset with things that humans do; they even have expectations for our continued participation in the maintaining of balance in the world. There is no sense, however, that God or the spiritual realm has any different regard for human beings than for the rest of creation, and there is certainly no notion of God's relationship with the whole of creation as marked by the human emotion of love.

This is in sharp contrast with Euro-Christianity and its consistent interpretation of its sacred text. For instance, most commentators on the Gospel of John insist that God's love for the world (John 3:16: "God so loved the world. . . .") must be understood as love for human beings. In this tradition of interpretation, the Greek word *cosmos*, translated as "world," must refer in this context only to the world of human beings. God's salvific act in Christ Jesus is here limited only to those who are most privileged in creation and are the proper object of God's affections. This privileging of humans runs the risk of generating and reinforcing human arrogance that too easily sees the world in terms of hierarchies of existence, all of which are ultimately subservient to the needs and whims of humans. This imposition of the word "beloved" functions necessarily to negate or at least falsify the traditional Indian understanding of God and God's relationship to creation. If we are to insist that *agape* actually refers to "acting in the best interests of another," rather than to the emotion of love, then we need to inquire seriously about the effectiveness of translating the Greek into a European language like English and then having to translate the translation before sense can be made of the original. Thus if one wants to affirm that God always "acts in the best interests" of human beings and of the whole of creation, why must we use the emotive word love as the only suitable language for articulating the concept, especially when that language usage proves to be foreign to specific cultural communities?

"GOD"

"God" is yet another problem for Native American people, except to the extent that we have already been colonized by past missionaries to assume that the word is an adequate gloss for our own naming of the Sacred Other. To begin with, the word God is a difficult word in modern theological and philosophical discourse. The givenness of its meaning for European and Amereuropeans has long since given way to a modernist and postmodernist angst that leaves the word without an immediately agreed-upon sense. Much more importantly in this context, there is a facile assumption that languages are merely codes for one another and that a simple translation settles all difficulties. Hence, the question too often asked of Native American peoples is: What is the word for God in your language?

Christianity and its sacred texts (the Hebrew and Greek Testaments) regularly impute to God attributes that are intrinsically humanlike, even if these attributes are seen as somehow more than human in God's case. Hence God is indeed identified not only as having emotions such as love and anger, but God is identified as the personification of love itself. The intense sophistication of Native American tribal spiritualities takes a different tack. Namely, what Christians would refer to as God is understood as a spiritual force that permeates the whole of the world and is manifest in countless ways in the world around us at any given moment and especially in any given place.[7] Wakonda, who is ultimately an unknowable mystery that is only knowable in particular manifestations, makes itself manifest first of all as Above and Below, Wakonda Monshita and Wakonda Udseta, symbolized as sky and earth, and called upon as Grandfather and Grandmother, he and she. Wakonda, which has no inherent or ultimate gender, is knowable only in the necessary reciprocal dualism of male and female. Thus, to assume that the simplistic gloss "God" somehow is adequate to translate and classify Wakonda (or Wakan Tanka, Gitchy Manitou, etc.) in English immediately falsifies the internal, cultural meaning of Waconda for Osage peoples (or Lakota or Ojibwe, in the case of the other examples). As a result of extensive colonization and missionization, Native Americans who would never do so in their own language have become perfectly comfortable in referring to God as "He" in English.

"CREATION"

Finally, the word "creation" presents problems insofar as it assumes either the Judeo-Christian creation story or something like it. While every tribe has several creation stories, they are simply not valorized the way the Judeo-Christian accounts are in Christianity. To begin with, the word is not a common usage in very many tribes, and when it is used it almost always represents a convenient English signifier that has no immediate referent in the speaker's own language. Moreover, when the word is used in a Christian context, it seems to Native Americans to connote a heavy dose of reification that is completely lacking in any Native American intellectual tradition. That is, in the Amereuropean context, creation is objectified as something that is quite apart from human beings and to which humans relate from the outside.

Another pronounced difference between Amereuropean and Native traditions is the usual assumption in the Native American tradition of the preexistence of the world in some form. Thus most Native American story-telling begins with the givenness of the world of which we are an integral part. Rather than conceiving of an initial creation that happened long ago and has little continuing relevance in a world in which only human redemption is in process, Native American intellectual traditions conceive of the world in constant creative process that requires our continual participation.

If the words "creation" and even "createds" have a distinctly borrowed flavor in an Native American context, there is no easy alternative for articulating "what is," or "that which we are a part of." Some sense of what is at stake is apparent in a Lakota phrase that may be illustrative. *Mitakouye oyasin* can be translated as a prayer "for all my relations." As such it is inclusive not only of immediate family or even extended family, but of the whole of a tribe or nation; of all the nations of two-leggeds in the world; and particularly of all the nations other than two-leggeds—the four-leggeds, the wingeds, and the living-moving-things. It is this interrelatedness that best captures what might symbolize for Native American peoples what Amereuropeans would call creation. More to the point, it is this understanding of interrelatedness, of balance and mutual respect of the different species in the world, that characterizes what we might call Native American peoples' greatest gift to Amereuropeans and to the Amereuropean understanding of creation at this time of such ecological crisis in the world.

HUMAN PRIVILEGE AND COMMUNITIES OF RESPECT

In the common Amereuropean interpretation of the biblical creation story (Gen. 1:28) human beings are significantly privileged over against the rest of creation. There is no similar privileging of human beings in the scheme of things in the world in Native American cultures. Neither is there any sense in which somehow humans are external to the rest of the world and its functions. To the contrary, humans are seen as part of the whole, rather than apart from it and free to use it up. Yet there are expectations of human beings. We do have particular responsibilities in the scheme of things, but, then, so do all our other relatives in the created realm: from bears and squirrels to eagles and sparrows, trees, ants, rocks, and mountains. In fact, many elders in Native American communities are quick to add that of all the createds, of all our relations, we two-leggeds alone seem to be confused as to our responsibility towards the whole.

I have long suspected that European Christianity has undergone a millennia-long transformation which has consistently shifted to put humans in opposition to the rest of creation. At the very least, this is signified in the theological, philosophical, scientific, and economic struggle for control over the world, its environment, and its "resources." This may have begun as early as the time of Aristotle, with the birth of so-called objective observation and description, an incipient scientific method. It continues its development during the European Renaissance with its neo-Aristotelian project of emerging taxonomic systems and the control over the world that seems to come from naming and categorizing. The philosophical and scientific basis for control of nature was initially rooted in the acts of naming. Perhaps the modern Amereuropean need for exerting control over the world was most explicitly founded by Descartes in a logical extension of both Aristotle and the Renaissance. Descartes most clearly announced the ultimate knowability of the world and the human responsibility to do the knowing (and hence, exerting control).

This philosophical movement toward greater and greater human control over their environment was paralleled by an ever increasing importance granted philosophically and theologically to the individual in European cultures. This shift toward the ascendency of the individual necessarily included a concomitant displacing of community values. I would argue that this shift meant not only the displacing of the importance of human communities, implicitly devaluing notions of the common good, but that it also meant displacing any lingering sense of the importance of a community inclusive of nonhuman entities in the created realm. In the Native American intellectual tradition and in cultural practice, human beings are not privileged over the rest of the world, nor are individuals privileged over the good of the whole community.

BALANCING THE WORLD FOR LIFE

If we allow for a full translation of the Euro-Christian, cultural-linguistic metaphor of "creation," we retain a substantial thought of extreme importance to Native American peoples. What is clear to all Native American peoples is that respect for Creation is vitally important to the well-being of our communities. While respect for all our relations in this world is critical for all Native American education, it is perhaps most readily apparent in the general philosophy of balance and harmony, a notion adhered to by all Native communities in one form or another, out of which emerges respect for "creation." Native American spirituality is characteristically oriented toward both the everyday and the ceremonial balancing of the world and our participation in it. When the balance of existence is disturbed, whole communities pay a price that is measured in some lack of communal well-being.

Once we have clarified the place of human beings in the ongoing processes of world balancing and world renewal, there are two aspects of what might be considered a general Native American theology that Christians and other Amereuropeans might do well to note. They can be initially categorized as reciprocity and spatiality. My contention will be that attention to these two important spiritual aspects of Native American cultures and what I am calling Native American theology can become radically transformative for the Amereuropean system of values and structures of social behavior.

RECIPROCITY

The notion of reciprocity is fundamental to human participation in world-balancing and harmony. Reciprocity involves first of all a spiritual understanding of the cosmos and the place of humans in the processes of the cosmic whole. It begins with an understanding that anything and everything that humans do has an effect on the rest of the world around us. Thus, Native Americans, in different places and in different cultural configurations, have always struggled to know how to act appropriately in the world. Knowing that every action has its unique effect has always meant that there had to be some sort of built-in compensation for human actions, some act of reciprocity.

The necessity for reciprocity becomes most apparent where violence is concerned, especially when such violence is an apparent necessity as in hunting or harvesting. Violence cannot be perpetrated, a life taken, in a Native American society, without some spiritual act of reciprocation. I am so much a part of the whole of creation and its balance, anything I do to perpetrate an act of violence, even when it is necessary for our own survival, must be accompanied by an act of spiritual reciprocation intended to restore the balance of existence. It must be remembered that violence as a technical category must extend to all one's "relatives." Thus, a ceremony of reciprocity must accompany the harvesting of vegetable foods such as corn or the harvesting of medicinals such as cedar, even when only part of a plant is taken. The ceremony may be relatively simple, involving a prayer or song and perhaps a reciprocal offering of tobacco.

Many tribes maintained very extensive and complex ceremonies of reciprocation to insure continuing balance and plentiful harvests. Even gathering rocks for a purification ceremony (sweat lodge ceremony) calls for care and respect, prayers and reciprocation. Ceremonies involving self-sacrifice (typically called "self-torture" or "self-mutilation" by the missionaries and early ethnographers) also come under this general category of reciprocation. In the Rite of Vigil (vision quest), which is very widespread among Native peoples of North America, as well as in the Sun Dance, the suffering the supplicant takes upon him or herself is usually thought of as vicarious and as some sort of reciprocation. Since all of one's so-called possessions are ultimately not possessions but relatives that live with someone, an individual is not giving away a possession when he or she gives a gift to someone else. In actuality the only thing a person really owns and can sacrifice is one's own flesh. These ceremonies are much more often thought of as vicarious sacrifices engaged in for the sake of the whole community's well-being. They came to the community as a gift from the Sacred Mystery in order to help the community take care of itself and its world. Thus, the Sun Dance is considered a ceremony in which two-leggeds participate with the Sacred in order to help maintain life, that is, to maintain the harmony and balance of the whole.

Hence hunting and war typically involved a complex ceremonial preparation before a contingent of warriors left their home to affirm the sacredness of life, to consecrate the lives that would be lost in war, and to offer prayers in reciprocation for those potentially lost lives.[8] In the hunt, most Native American nations report specific prayers of reciprocation, involving apologies and words of thanksgiving to the animal itself and the animal's spirit nation. Usually, this ceremonial act is in compliance with the request of the animals themselves as the people remember the primordial negotiations in mythological stories. Thus, formal and informal ceremonies of reciprocation are a day-to-day mythic activity which has its origin in mythological stories in which human beings were given permission by the animal nations to hunt them for food. The resulting covenant, however, calls on human beings to assume responsibilities over against the perpetration of violence among four-legged relatives. Even after the hunt or battle, those who participated must invariably go through a ceremonial cleansing before re-entering their own village. To not do this would bring the disruption of the sacred caused by the perpetration of violence right into the middle of national life and put all people at risk.[9]

Animals, birds, crops, and medicines are all living relatives and must be treated with respect if they are to be genuinely efficacious for the people. The ideal of harmony and balance requires that all share a respect for all other existent things, avoiding gratuitous or unthinking acts of violence. Maintaining harmony and balance requires that even necessary acts of violence be done "in a sacred way." Thus nothing is taken from the earth without prayer and offering. No model of "development," involving modern Western technologies, as far as I know, embodies or incorporates the indigenous ethic of reciprocity. It is not enough to replant a few trees or to add nutrients to the soil. These are superficial acts to treat the negative symptoms of development. The value of reciprocity, a hallmark of Native American ceremonies, comes from the heart of issues of sustainability, which is maintaining a balance and tempering the negative effects of basic human survival techniques.

SPATIALITY: PLACE VERSUS TIME

A fundamental difference between Amereuropean and Native American worldviews emerging from different priorities of space and time, has been long recognized. Native American observations were first codified by Vine Deloria Jr., the dean of Native American academics, in his 1972 milestone book *God Is Red*.[10] As I have also argued,[11] it is not a case of one culture being marked by temporality and the other by spatiality. Rather, it appears to be the case that space or time have become primary organizing categories of existence in one culture or the other. For Amereuropean peoples, temporality has been a primary category for many centuries, while space has been subordinate in all respects. The sacred is measured in temporality with a seven-day cycle requiring the repetition of a ceremonial event (mass or liturgies of worship) most typically on the first day of the cycle. Amereuropean philosophical and theological history is oriented to the meaning of time: progress, history, development, evolution, and process become key notions that invade all academic discours from science and economics to philosophy and theology. The Western worldview has an inherent blind spot which prevents any comprehensive or deep understanding of the scope of ecological devastation. To do no more than propose "solutions," such as reforestation projects, without acknowledging this blind spot, is only to address the superficial symptoms of maldevelopment.

In contrast, Native American communities are rooted in a

worldview shaped by reciprocity and spatiality. Indian ceremonial existence is inevitably spatially configured with the question of a ceremony's place taking precedence over that of its time. Even in the case of annual or periodic ceremonial cycles, spatial configurations involving spatial relationships between sun or moon and the earth are determinative. Hence the spatial relationship between the community and the sun at solstice or equinox, or the spatial appearance or nonappearance of the moon at full or new moon are more important than calendar dates and Julian months.

This foundational metaphor of spatiality in Native American cultures also begins to clarify the extent to which Native American spirituality and Native American existence are deeply rooted in our attachment to the land and to specific territories in particular. Each nation has some understanding that they were placed into a relationship with a particular territory by spiritual forces outside of themselves and thus have an enduring responsibility for that territory just as the earth in that particular place has a filial responsibility toward the people who live there. Likewise, the two-legged people in that place also have a spatially related responsibility toward all people who share that place with them, including animals, birds, plants, rocks, rivers, mountains, and the like. With such kinship ties, it should be less surprising that Native American peoples have always resisted colonial pressure to relocate them to different territories, to sell their territories to the invaders, or to allow the destruction of their lands for the sake of accessing natural resources. Conquest and removal from our lands, historically, and contemporary ecological destruction of our lands has been and continues to be culturally and genocidally destructive to Native American peoples as peoples.

A more subtle level to this sense of spatiality and land rootedness shows up in nearly all aspects of our existence, in our structures, symbols, architecture, and in the symbolic parameters of a tribe's universe. Hence, the land and spatiality are the basic metaphor for existence and determine much of a community's life. In my own tribe, for instance, every detail of social structure—even the geographic orientation of the old villages—reflected a reciprocal duality of all that is necessary for sustaining life. Thus the Hunka or earth moiety situated to the south of the village and the Tzi Sho or sky moiety situated to the north represented female and male, matter and spirit, war and peace, but they only functioned fully because they were together and together represented wholeness. Spirit without matter is motion without substance; matter without spirit is motionless and meaningless. Once again we see reciprocity in a symbiotic dualism, this time clearly configured spatially.

We should not think here of the oppositional dualism of good and evil that we have learned to identify as typical Western (i.e., ancient mid-Eastern) dualism. Native American duality is a necessary reciprocity, not oppositional. They are different manifestations of the same Wakonda, not of two Wakonda even though they carry personality specificity just as traditional Christian trinitarian doctrine would assert. While they are manifestations of the same Wakonda, they are different manifestations, both of which are necessary in order to have some balanced understanding of the Otherness that is the Sacred Mystery. Indeed, Wakonda has manifested itself in a great many other ways, all of which help our people to better understand the Mystery, our world, ourselves, and our place in the world. At this point, it may also be clearer why the European word "God" is inadequate to express the full complexity of what we have only begun to explore in the Osage word.

Even the architectural geography of our spirituality functioned politically to give the village group cohesion; it functions at a much more deeply spiritual level that still pertains for a great many Native Americans today. While an Osage person may be either Tzi Sho or Hunka, she or he is a child of parents who come from each of the divisions. Thus, each individual recognizes herself or himself as a combination of qualities that reflect both sky and earth, spirit and matter, peace and war, male and female, and we struggle individually and communally to hold those qualities in balance with each other. These value structures begin with spatial designs of existence and are rooted in those spatial metaphors as fundamental mores of communal behavior and social organization.

This is not the only spatial symbolic paradigm of existence that determines Native American individuality and community. The fundamental symbol of plains Indian existence is the circle, a polyvalent symbol signifying the family, the clan, the tribe, and ultimately all of creation. As a creation symbol, the importance of the circle is its genuine egalitarianness. There is no way to make the circle hierarchical. Because it has no beginning and no end, all on the circle are of equal value. No relative is valued more than any other. A chief is not valued above the people; nor are two-legged valued above the animal nations, the birds, or even trees and rocks. In its form as a medicine wheel, with two lines forming a cross inscribed vertically and horizontally across its whole, the circle can symbolize the four directions of the earth and, more importantly, the four manifestations of Wakonda that come to us from those directions. At the same time, those four directions symbolize the four cardinal virtues of a tribe, the four sacred colors of ceremonial life, the sacred powers of four animal nations, and the four nations of two-leggeds that walk the earth (Black, Red, Yellow, and White). That is, in our conception of the universe, all human beings walk ideally in egalitarian balance. Moreover, Native American egalitarian proclivities are worked out in this spatial symbol in ways that go far beyond the classless egalitarianness of socialism. In one of the polyvalent layers of meaning, those four directions hold together in the same egalitarian balance the four nations of Two-Leggeds, Four-Leggeds, Wingeds, and Living-Moving-Things. In this rendition human beings lose their status of primacy and "dominion." Implicitly and explicitly, Native Americans are driven by their culture and spirituality to recognize the "personhood" of all "things" in creation. If temporality and historicity lend themselves implicitly to hierarchical structures because someone with a greater investment of time may know more of the body of temporally codified knowledge, spatiality lends itself to the egalitarian.

ECOJUSTICE, SOVREIGNITY, AND A THEOLOGY OF LIBERATION

Given the fundamental differences between Native American cultural values and those of Amereuropean peoples, it should be no mystery that the relationship between the two has been consistently one of conquest, colonization, and finally the ecodevastation of our territories. Our theological reflection must now move toward a sharper assessment of the systemic causes of this ethno-ecodevastation from a Native American perspective and towards the development of possible solutions. We have already begun to argue that we must understand the connection between ecological and social injustice in the world if there is to be significant transformation from the current global crisis to a healthy and sustainable future. Hence, it becomes empty and quixotic to think of treating ecological devastation apart from treating issues of racism and ongoing colonialism, including especially those new forms of colonialism or neocolonialism. In particular, I am arguing that the two-fold problem of eco- and social justice is systemic in nature, and that the concerns of ethno-ecojustice must move beyond the mere naming of ecological devastations that are affecting Native Americans and other indigenous and poor peoples today. For example, many of us have been converted to the ecojustice vocation of recycling, a calling that has piqued our consciences as consumers to an extent that our kitchens and garages have become dangerous labyrinths of plastic, aluminum, and glass repositories. Yet our national situation with respect to garbage disposal and landfill capacity has gotten consistently worse. In spite of our new behavior as socially conscious individuals, the United States generated more landfill garbage during the decade of the 1980s (the decade we began actively and broadly recycling) than during its first two hundred years. Changing individual patterns of behavior has failed us as a strategy. We will need more holistic and systemic solutions. Systemic solutions call for theological and philosophical foundations.

It needs to be said here that by a theological response to the systemic I do not have in mind just another individualistic intellectual exercise but rather a theological reflection that is far more communal. Theology must become an exercise in expressing the self-identity of whole communities. For this sort of theology, we need stories rather than treatises, essentialist discourse, problem-resolution, or structuralist puzzle solving. Not even some poststructuralist deconstruction that never seems to emerge from the text will finally be able to touch the hearts and minds of whole communities. For theology of this magnitude, we must have stories. The Amereuropeans have stories, of course, but they tend to be stories of conquest: Columbus is the quintessential all-American culture hero, the perfect exemplar for the righteous empire, the "discoverer" and conqueror who knew no sin. Even Jesus, the most important culture hero of America, has become a conqueror in Western story telling. The sacrificial cross of Jesus has become a symbol of conquest that seems to encourage more conquest.[12] Thus the myth of Columbus and the stories of conquest continue to play themselves out with disastrous consequences in the lives of modern Native American peoples.

What Amereuropeans do not yet have is a story that accounts for their history of systemic violence in the world and their easy proclivity for rationalizing any act of military or economic colonization and conquest as somehow good. Instead, Amereuropeans and their politicians seem to engage in a behavior pattern wellknown in alcohol and drug addictions therapy as denial. Too many churches and too many politicians have lived out such a denial, like ostriches with their heads in the sand as if such ecodevastation and national injustice and immorality cannot possibly affect them, living in the protected comfort zones of American society. Easy answers are too often given that reflect some level of denial: It is too late to rectify injustices perpetrated against Native American nations; too much water has gone under the bridge. Or it is sometimes insisted that Native Americans are too small a percentage of the population to merit attention. We are forced, they claim, to concentrate on the vast majority of Americans, to maximize the good (and wealth) for the most people. Here the old Amereuropean philosophical tradition of utilitarianism (John Stuart Mill, etc.) continues to exert its powerful influence on the expediency of political practice to such an extent that abject racism can thrive with full rationalization "in the best interests of the state," and it becomes all too easy to think of Native American reservations as "national sacrifice areas."[13] Stories of conquest give way to stories of utilitarian rationalization.

In this analysis, I want to argue two correlative points addressing what I see as a key systemic aspect of the problematic, focusing on the rise of Western individualism and the systematic destruction of indigenous communities worldwide. I will insist that the dismantling of indigenous communities has happened at a philosophical as well as political level. To put it another way, I am arguing that modern ecological devastation is in no small part generated by the Western, European shift devaluing corporate interests in favor of the increasing prominence of the individual, and that this shift can be measured in the lack of political and economic respect and the lack of theoretical recognition given to the legitimacy of self-governing, autonomous, long-lived indigenous communities.

Let me state the argument as provocatively as possible. I would like to suggest a rather sweeping theological and political corrective to the modern ecological crisis, a corrective that may seem too sweeping, yet it is my conviction that only a fully systemic response can create wholeness out of such systemic destruction. I want to argue that a solution is called for that would ultimately put Indian peoples and other indigenous peoples in control of their own well-being, their lands and resources, and their political processes. Apart from such a solution the effects of modern resource development on the local ecosystems of too many Native American communities will remain a systemic problem that will continue to reoccur with repeated and escalating viciousness. Any effort that is satisfied with engaging a momentary struggle of resistance in a particular context of corporate or governmental environmental intrusion is bound ultimately to fail because of the systemic nature of the problem.[14]

NOTES

1. Donald A. Grinde and Bruce E. Johansen, *Ecocide of Native America: Environmental Destruction of Indian Lands and Peoples* (Santa Fe: Clear Light Publishers, 1995), p. 1.

2. Benjamin F. Chavis Jr., and Charles Lee, eds., *Toxic Wastes and Race in the United States: A National Report on the Racial and Socio-Economic Characteristics of Communities with Hazardous Waste Sites* (New York: Commission for Racial Justice, United Church of Christ, 1987); and Benjamin A. Goldman and Laura Fitton, *Toxic Wastes and Race Revisited: An Update of the 1987 Report on the Racial and Socioeconomic Characteristics of Communities with Hazardous Waste Sites* (Washington, D.C.: Center for Policy Alternatives, 1994). I find Gregg Easterbrook's popular news essay on Two-Thirds World pollution problematic, especially in what I see as his short-sighted proposal for resolving Two-Thirds World ecojustice concerns: Easterbrook, "Forget PCB's. Radon. Alar: The World's Greatest Environmental Dangers Are Dung Smoke and Dirty Water," The New York Times Magazine (September 11, 1995), pp. 60–63.

3. Ward Churchill, *Struggle for the Land: Indigenous Resistance to Genocide, Ecocide, and Expropriation in Contemporary North America* (Monroe, Maine: Common Courage Press, 1993); Mark Zannis, *The Genocide Machine in Canada: The Pacification of the North* (Montreal: Black Rose Books, 1973).

4. Gerald Vizenor, *Manifest Manners: Postindian Warriors of Survivance* (Hanover, N.H.: Wesleyan University Press, 1994).

5. This rather absurd and patently "Eurosupremicist" hypothesis is argued, for instance, by George Weurthner, who ultimately reduces pre-contact Native American peoples to environmental pillagers: "An Ecological View of the Indian," *Earth First!* 7 (1987). For a Native American critique of the position, see Ward Churchill, *Struggle for the Land*, pp. 420, 447ff; and M. Annette Jaimes, "The Stone Age Revisited: an Indigenist Examination of Labor," *New Studies on the Left* 14 (1991).

6. See George E. Tinker, *Missionary Conquest: The Gospel and Native American Cultural Genocide* (Minneapolis: Fortress Press, 1993).

7. This sense is much more than Paul Tillich's notion of pantheism.

8. See Francis La Flesche, "The War and Peace Ceremony of the Osage Indians," Bureau of American Ethnography, *Bulletin* 101 (1939).

9. Leslie Silko's famous novel, *Ceremony* (New York: Viking, 1977), is precisely about such a situation. The whole of the novel deals with the

healing and cleansing of a World War II veteran for whom a new ceremony had to be devised. The social and spiritual complexities of disintegration and alienation had made it much more difficult for the Laguna people and for himself. Thus, his healing has to do with the healing of the whole community and not just of himself.

10. Recently republished in a significantly revised issue: Vine Deloria Jr., *God Is Red: A Native View of Religion* (Golden, Colo.: North American Press, 1992).

11. George E. Tinker, "Spirituality and Native American Personhood; Sovereignty and Solidarity," *Spirituality of the Third World*, ed. K. C. Abraham and Bernadette Mbuy-Beya (Maryknoll: Orbis, 1994), pp. 119–32; "An American Indian Reading of the Bible," in *New Interpreter's Bible*, ed. Leander E. Keck et al. (Nashville: Abingdon, 1994), pp. 174–80; and "Native Americans and the Land: The End of Living and the Beginning of Survival," *Word and World*.

12. See George E. Tinker, "Columbus and Coyote: A Comparison of Culture Heroes in Paradox," *Apuntes* (1992): 78–88.

13. This term seems to have been coined in a study commissioned by the National Academy of Science on resource development on Native American lands. It was submitted to the Nixon administration in 1972 as input toward a national Native American policy. See Thadis Box, et al., *Rehabilitation Potential for Western Coal Lands* (Cambridge: Ballanger, 1974), for the published version of the study. Churchill, *Struggle for the Land*, pp. 54, 333, 367. Also, Russell Means, "The Same Old Song," in *Marxism and Native Americans*, ed. Ward Churchill (Boston: South End Press, 1983), p. 25; and Ward Churchill and Winona LaDuke, "Native America: The Political Economy of Radioactive Colonialism," in *State of Native America*, 241–66.

14. Al Gedick, *The New Resource Wars: Native and Environmental Struggles Against Multinational Corporations* (Boston: South End Press, 1993), pp. 57–82. Zoltan Grossman and Al Gedick, "Exxon Returns to Wisconsin: The Threat of the Crandon/Mole Lake Mine," *Dark Night Field Notes* 1 (summer 1994): 15–18.

QUESTIONS FOR DISCUSSION

1. Does this author's reticence to use the word "love" or "beloved" for creation apply to all native peoples or indigeneous tribal nations?

2. Does the Greek word *cosmos* apply to the "human world" only, or is it applicable to a wider interpretation which could indeed be "the ordered universe" that is all creation?

3. Does the originality of Divine Revelation through Jesus Christ send the message of Divine Compassion to the created world in a unique way that goes beyond "human justice" to the concept/message of "overwhelming love or compassion for all creation"?

10
DEVELOPING AN ETHIC FOR SUSTAINABLE COMMUNITY
An Action-Oriented Response
Paula Gonzalez

"**C**an you imagine a world that is just, compassionate and sustainable for all?" asked a large-print insert in the Institute of Noetic Sciences' *Review*.[1] Inside it stated: "So can we, and together we can help to create that future." This struck me for three reasons: (1) the question surely describes the deep desire of every human on this planet as we enter the new millennium, (2) the simplicity of both question and answer mask the enormity of the shift in human consciousness they proclaim, and (3) such a positive approach might kindle the imaginations of more people and attract them to develop a "let's-place-a-man-on-the-moon-in-ten-years" spirit! To address the reality of the unprecedented challenges facing *Homo sapiens* today three words are key: *imagine, together, and create.*

Before we can even begin to be imaginative and creative about solutions to the myriad of crises which face us, we have to analyze and evaluate our perception of reality. We must come to realize that often we late-twentieth-century humans do not live in the "real world." A majority of people in the industrial world live their day-to-day lives oblivious to or in denial of the profound transformation going on all around them. For many in the developing world the effort to survive often requires every bit of available human energy,

261

leaving little possibility of considering creative alternatives. Yet, the breakneck pace of "globalization," the ever-increasing ecological degradation, the exponential rate of population growth, and the inadequacy of social, political, and economic systems affect each of Earth's six billion humans every day—whether they realize it or not. Increasing rapidly the number of Earth's people who realize the scope and urgency of the challenges facing us and energizing ourselves to action must become the primary human agenda of the twenty-first century. This will require major redesign and restructuring of our presently dysfunctional human systems at all levels.

Consider the implications. *Catastrophic breakdown* can surely effect such paradigm shifts, but it is hoped that imagination and creativity—along with a "respiritualization" of the human endeavor—will forestall such a future. It is critically important that values-oriented groups and especially believers of every religious tradition become involved actively in this major transformation of human systems. Challenging their members to increased justice and compassion and to a new sense of concern for the created Universe should be on the agenda of every faith community.

This entails *a new understanding of the demands of faith* with regard to what usually have been thought of as "secular" issues. The *integral sacredness* of the natural world—understood by all faiths to be the handiwork of God—must be celebrated both in ritual and in everyday action. Destruction, exploitation, and pollution of the created universe—including our continuing to permit the desperate poverty of over half of our human sisters and brothers—must be seen as "sinful" and "immoral." For this transformed understanding to become widespread necessitates major changes in the education of clergy and others involved in "religious education."

IMAGINING A SUSTAINABLE TOMORROW

Even to imagine an optimistic scenario for the eight billion human inhabitants of planet Earth in 2025 requires a profound change of perspective. Instead of seeing "the environment" as something separate from people and their activities, we must relearn that humans are not just *connected* to "nature." We are an *integral part* of "it"— formed from the very air, water, and soil of our finite planet and energized by the sun. In our industrial frenzy we have forgotten that "nature" should be our primary teacher since it has been quite successful for so long! Sustaining "life" for nearly four billion years speaks well for the basic regenerative design of the many and varied ecosystems which comprise the biosphere.

The most important lesson to be learned is that the mechanistic, industrial model is basically flawed. *This linear model is not sustainable on a finite planet.* Eventually, all "resources" become exhausted and accumulations of "waste"—(the "used-one-time" materials of our throwaway society)—become life-threatening. This is exactly where the rapidly growing human population finds itself at this time. Already we are fighting over diminishing resources and experiencing ever-increasing "eco-illness," both individually and collectively. It is imperative that recognition of this become *widespread* very quickly across the globe—and we have the communication systems which make this possible! Lacking—at least on a broad enough scale—are the imagination and the political will. Denial of today's global realities is widespread among individuals of every nation and religious tradition, and at the boardroom level of the "corporations which rule the world."[2] It is as if people do not have the common sense to realize the consequences of killing the goose that lays the golden eggs!

Though not yet mainstream, there are hopeful signs that movement in the right direction has begun. In 1987, the report of the Brundtland Commission established a context within which many of our global problems can be addressed.[3] The 1992 Earth Summit in Rio de Janeiro has catalyzed an impressive list of international conferences—convened by the United Nations, nongovernmental organizations (NGOs) and private sector groups. Discussion and strategizing have begun to address seriously several of the major ideas in Agenda 21—the Rio Declaration on Environment and Development: Sustainability, accountability by nations of environmental impact of proposed activities, eradication of poverty and reduction of disparities in living standards, full participation of women, of youth and of indigenous peoples and the inherently damaging environmental effects of warfare.[4]

EARLY STEPS TOWARD SUSTAINABILITY

A hopeful sign of the emerging transformation is the movement that has given rise to an increasing number of volumes such as this one. The recognition is growing that the inevitable global changes—which *will* occur either through choice or catastrophe—require a values orientation. The millennial edition of *State of the World—1999* proclaims this clearly: "The trends of recent years suggest that we need a new moral compass to guide us into the twenty-first century—a compass that is grounded in the principles of meeting human needs sustainably. Such an ethic of sustainability would be based on a concept of respect for future generations."[5]

Yet active concern for humans alone will not be enough! We must relearn the *deep respect* for the *whole created universe* which characterizes many indigenous peoples even today. We must see ourselves as integral parts of what Thomas Berry calls "the sacred earth community"— challenged to modify our lifestyles so that we *participate* in the ever-regenerating cycles of life.[6]

It is interesting to learn that "respect" derives from the Latin, *respectus*—the art of looking back. We humans—especially the urban, industrial ones—need to "look back" to rediscover the relationships which are fundamental to the "web of life" which has evolved on our mysterious and wonderful planet. Used as a verb, respect means "to consider worthy of high regard; to esteem." Such an attitude results in acts of "reverence"—(honor or respect felt or shown). This attitudinal conversion to a profound ecological sensitivity is essential to the continuation of human life much beyond the end of the new millennium—and at the same time invites every person alive today to develop a refreshing, integrative spirituality which will enrich human life, individually and collectively. It is clear why the world's religious traditions have a major role to play in this endeavor.

MOVING BEYOND STEWARDSHIP

Perhaps the most important event of the twentieth century occurred in August 1969—humankind's first look at a photo of the whole earth taken by the Apollo astronauts! What a marvelous contribution to humanity's understanding of itself and its potential relationships. (I often refer to these photos of our tiny blue and green planet as "revelation according to NASA" and I continue to experience in audiences a deep sense of awe as I show these pictures of humanity's "common icon"). I believe these photos provide viewers with an intuitive awakening to a basic tenet of ecology—and thus of the "web of life" on our planet: "Everything is connected to everything else." We must explore diligently the scope of these interrelationships if *Homo sapiens* is to continue as part of the fifteen-billion-year *Universe Story.*[7] One of the clearest explanations of humans' possible relation to the earth is found in Elizabeth Johnson's models—absolute kingship, stewardship, and kinship.[8] Centuries of use of the kingship model—a patriarchical pyramid—are the reason for the current degraded state of the physical environment as well as of much of the social distress which plagues humanity today. "Stewardship" is a valuable concept which has inspired much generosity and concern for fellow humans, especially in the Christian churches. The problem with this view is that though humans are now "responsible caretakers," this model maintains the hierarchical dualism of the kingship model. This perpetuates the notion that we are "in charge"—even benevolently—when the reality is that we humans are *utterly dependent* on Earth's "resources," both living and nonliving. We are all *related*—the elephants, bacteria, oak trees, volcanoes, rivers, mosses, and we humans. The very molecules of which our bodies are composed have in other eras been part of countless other creatures! This is *kinship*, the essential mode of interrelationship since life emerged on this planet. What is called for, then, is an attitude of humility, reverence, and willingness to learn from our "elders"—(everything in the fifteen-billion-year history of the universe). *We humans are a very recent arrival.*

In the "real world" of twenty-first-century technologies, economic and political globalization, military conflicts and all the "business-as-usual" bustle of human activity, what can capture the attention of the large number of people it will take to bring the global ecological realities into mainstream consciousness? Will a proactive approach become widespread enough in time? Or will we wait until a string of ecocatastrophes provides the wake-up call needed to effect concerted action across the globe? Our choices—both individual and collective—over the next twenty years, will determine the answer. However, unless many more people have the ability to make "informed choices" the line of least resistance is highly probable. To help us realize that these are *moral choices* should be the role of the world's religious traditions and other values-oriented groups. Ecology 101 may seem like a strange addition to the "religious education" curriculum, but it is imperative that reeducation of both clergy and laity on these issues become a top priority.

Wackernagel and Rees make this a very understandable activity through their book, *Our Ecological Footprint: Reducing Human Impact on the Earth.*[9] They have calculated the amount of "ecoproductive" land which constitutes a "fair Earthshare" (in 1996) for each of the nearly six billion humans. Ecoproductive land includes the land required to provide for human consumption in food, housing, transportation, consumer goods, and services. It includes "energy land" (mines, oil fields, etc.), "consumed land" (buildings, bridges, railroads, etc.), agricultural land and forest land. Amazingly, an average person in the United States has an "ecological footprint" of 5.1 hectares—the area of about three city blocks! Yet, the present fair Earthshare is only 1.5 hectares—and the global population continues to grow exponentially, thus shrinking the fair Earthshare continually. It could be a real "wakeup" if a majority of Earth's peoples realized that at present the average world footprint is 1.8 hectares!

This means that humanity's consumption of Earth's "resources" is already 30 percent larger than nature can sustain in the long run— (and the "long run" approaches rapidly—while we continue adding eighty million people annually *and* promoting "the good life" which seems to be associated with ever-increasing accumulation of consumer goods). According to reports from the U.N. and many other sources, the 20 percent of people who live in the wealthy countries consume up to 80 percent of the world's resources. This means that the developed world alone *already* has an ecological footprint larger than the total carrying capacity of the planet. Indeed, if the average North American lifestyle were to be enjoyed by all six billion people who are entering the new millennium, *two additional planet Earths would be needed*—right now! Such statistics should invite us to serious meditation as we strive to explore the values which must underlie the enormous changes which have to be made. The involvement of religious people and groups in this exploration can be invaluable—not only in providing the deep motivation for change that is required but through the opportunity to invite their members to a life with a deeper meaning. There is a growing hunger for such a challenge.

BACKGROUND FOR UNDERSTANDING THE PHENOMENON OF "LIFE"

The "big picture" of what has occurred before in the drama of life on Earth can provide us with some of the lessons we must learn if we are to undertake the enormous redesign of human systems that is imperative. Nearly four billion years ago, the first living cells evolved—"simple" unicellular creatures (similar to today's bacteria) which could nourish themselves from the rich variety of chemicals characteristic of the Earth's early state. These prokaryotic organisms (organisms without a true nucleus) multiplied exponentially and as temperatures dropped and the planet stabilized chemically, they faced a serious environmental crisis. Either their numbers would be reduced to the carrying capacity of their surroundings or they would become extinct! Simultaneous with these large population increases another phenomenon had been at work—genetic mutation. Many different types of micro-organisms had developed, some of which could feast on dead organisms and others on compounds produced by the metabolism of other living forms in their environment. These new micro-organisms formed the first ecological "communities," and the growing web of interrelationships became the first aquatic ecosystem.

After about one hundred million years, a mutation appeared that enabled the "surrounding environment" to include solar energy directly. Some of the organisms developed chlorophyll-containing plastids which could convert radiant energy into glucose—*using only carbon dioxide from the air and water from the sea as raw materials.* Rising concentrations of oxygen, the major byproduct of this photosynthetic activity, initiated several dramatic events. As oxygen was released it reacted with the rocks, changing the chemical nature of the earth's crust. Also, the carbon monoxide, ammonia, hydrogen sulfide, and methane in the atmosphere were transformed as the concentration of oxygen increased rapidly. By two billion years ago, the transformation of lithosphere, hydrosphere, and atmosphere was significant; the prokaryotic communities began to be destroyed by the very oxygen they had produced—a major "ecological crisis" at that time.

This could have been the "end of life on Earth" but other mutations had produced cyanobacteria, the blue-green algae. These amazing organisms had learned to use oxygen in what is now the *near-universal process of respiration*—found in cells of every type of living creature from micro-organisms to mammals—and with a *tenfold increase in energy* for life functions! Atmospheric oxygen levels increased rapidly and the outer layer of atmospheric oxygen—the ozone layer—thickened to the point of no longer permitting passage of the most energetic photons. This protective blanket enabled many new forms to develop. When oxygen levels rose above 21 percent many of the cyanobacteria were threatened. But just below 21 percent (a marvelously maintained 20.74 percent) the "combustion" involved in respiration reached maximum efficiency and Earth's complex , interacting web of biosphere, hydrosphere, lithosphere, and atmosphere stabilized in the dynamic equilibrium we experience today.

The second great era of life began with the emergence of eukaryotic cells (cells having their genetic material enclosed in a nucleus) about two billion years ago. This new spurt of life has blossomed into a variety of forms which would have been unimaginable during the eons when micro-organisms were the dominant lifeforms. Colonial organisms began to evolve—some parasitic, some symbiotic. After about one billion years, heterotrophic organisms appeared on the evolutionary stage—creatures which could nourish themselves by engulfing other living creatures. Now predator and prey begun to coevolve into the patterned ecosystems of the Proterozoic seas.

But the greatest "surprise"—the mutation responsible for the enormous explosion of biological variety during the last billion years—was yet to come. The development of sexual reproduction opened the door to ever greater specialization of cell structure and function. About 700 million years ago, multicellular organisms appeared and developed for over 100 million years—until during the most severe Ice Age in Earth's history, *80 to 90 percent of species became extinct!* But many of the primal "biological inventions" weathered the cold 20 million years and blossomed again in the explosion of new forms which characterized the Paleozoic, Mesozoic and Cenozoic eras. Only during the last two million years of this long drama has the genus *Homo* been present—modern *Homo sapiens* only about 40,000 years. Recent human history has occurred in what will probably be known as the terminal phase of the Cenozoic era. During the past century especially, humans have developed industrial approaches which manipulate and control many of Earth's processes, plundering the soil, air, and water in a devastating manner.

NEW INSIGHTS, NEW PERSPECTIVES

It is becoming increasingly clear that the present mode of human existence is not sustainable. Thus, from the perspective of continued human existence, we live in an evolutionary moment perhaps as crucial as those which saw the emergence of early life, of photosynthesis, of heterotrophy and of sexual reproduction—the major milestones of life on Earth! According to Thomas Berry, we have entered the Ecozoic era and are called to view the universe as a *communion of subjects* rather than a collection of objects.[10] Perhaps, as James Lovelock suggests through the Gaia Theory, Earth may be a *single living system* in which the conditions for "life" have been produced and are maintained in a homeostatic state by the living creatures themselves as they have evolved.[11] Understanding such an Earth necessitates interdisciplinary approaches to its study, including not only the physical and biological sciences but also the social and political sciences, especially economics—(which must become transformed to "ecologics" if sustainability is to be achieved).

Many holistic approaches are beginning to suggest that we are in the midst of what Thomas Kuhn calls the growth of a new paradigm—a synthesis of scientific, technological, and cultural change to a planetary worldview.[12] In *The Global Brain*, Peter Russell focuses on the role that *human consciousness* plays in the movement toward a global civilization in a biosphere restored to health.[13] He envisions humanity as the "brain" or consciousness of Gaia—a view similar to that of Teilhard de Chardin's "noosphere."[14] Duane Elgin compares the development of the human species to that of an individual and suggests that industrial societies must turn away from today's rampant consumerism, with its accompanying ecological exploitation, as a primary value. They must move from adolescence into the maturity of a planetary "species-civilization" that can live harmoniously—and thus sustainably—within the web of life.[15] Elgin notes that a Gallup poll taken before the 1992 Earth Summit found that among a substantial majority of people, in eighteen of twenty-two very diverse nations and representing a wide range of income levels, the well-being of Earth was placed ahead of personal economic concerns. Many polls have shown similar responses, but the "business-as-usual" reality suggests that apparently many people consider the task so enormous that they may see their own intuitive response as "wishful thinking."

REDESIGNING FOR A SUSTAINABLE FUTURE

It is critical for more and more people to discover that there is a growing number of people throughout the planet who are undergoing the transformation of perspective and attitudinal change necessary to undertake seriously the redesign of the industrial model.

Actually, the "Second Industrial Revolution" is already underway, but this knowledge is far from "mainstream." To a great extent this is true because the media, which provide the vast majority of people with much of their information, are controlled by business and political leaders who refuse to accept the reports of large numbers of distinguished scientists about the state of the global environment. As soon as some of the real breakthroughs in moving toward a "greener" approach become better known, there will be a huge shift in what people are willing to buy and use.

Already today, increasing numbers of people are choosing to pay more for energy when they are assured that some percentage of their utility's power is generated from renewable sources. At the national level, Costa Rica has made a commitment to generate all its electric power from renewable sources by 2010 and Germany is planning to reduce income taxes and raise energy taxes. In the corporate world, British Petroleum has taken the threat of global warming seriously enough to include one billion dollars for solar and other renewable energy resources in their 1997 budget. BP Solar takes this concern seriously as it continues solar production. Royal Dutch Shell followed almost immediately with a five-hundred million dollar commitment.

Among auto manufacturers, Daimler-Benz, General Electric, Toyota, and Ford are investing in research on hydrogen fuel cells. Bill Ford, CEO of Ford Motor Company, predicts that the internal combustion engine invented by his great-grandfather will disappear. Declaring himself a "passionate environmentalist" he says, "There is a rising tide of environmental awareness. Smart companies will get ahead of the wave. Those that don't will be wiped out."[16] Being "smart" will also mean being wealthy as more and more corporations—and governments—realize that climate destabilization, resulting from burning fossil fuels, presents not only an enormous threat to human wellbeing but one of the greatest business opportunities in history! The many creative people who have begun to launch a "new industrial revolution" may become the Rockefellers and Carnegies of the early twenty-first century—though becoming wealthy is not the primary motivation of many of these committed pioneers. It is vital that people of all religious groups keep abreast of the many dramatic changes that will be occurring in the next decade as "earth-friendly" technologies become more readily available. Religious leaders should realize that incorporating *earth-regenerating changes* in churches, synagogues, and mosques can be invaluable in helping faith communities see "healing the Earth" as integral to their religious practice.

LEARNING FROM EARTH'S PROCESSES

In *Natural Capitalism: Creating the Next Industrial Revolution* Paul Hawken and Amory and Hunter Lovins present the principles that will guide twenty-first-century commerce (and thus twenty-first-century environmentalism): (1) Dramatic increase in the productivity of "natural resources," with "waste" minimized or eliminated; (2) Design based on biologically inspired models; (3) A business model that sells "services" rather than "goods"; and (4) reinvestment in "natural capital."[17] Some examples of how these principles are being introduced in various sectors of the industrial world indicate that an effort to "learn from nature" underlies these "earth-friendly" approaches. At last, the realization is growing that it is the ecosystem—not the individual organism—that is the fundamental unit of life on this planet. All the ecosystems which make up the biosphere—the "living layer" of Earth—are composed of interdependent *communities* of three types of living organisms: producers, consumers, and decomposers. These groups interact with one another in a series of regenerative cycles—powered by the sun— and always within the limits of the surrounding physical environment. The design error in the present linear industrial model becomes obvious when contrasted with the cyclic, interacting processes which characterize the natural world. In "industrial economics" raw materials are used by *producers* to make products which are marketed to *consumers*. The extraction, production and use of these materials, along with their disposal, result in huge amounts of "waste." Thus, on a finite planet, the supply of both raw materials and energy is diminishing constantly. Not only are the energy sources for these processes finite but the byproducts of their use are harmful to living organisms. Contrast this with a healthy ecosystem which has no "shortages" of raw materials nor accumulations of waste—and is powered by limitless and nonpolluting energy sources! Obviously, "nature" has much to teach us.

In natural ecosystems, the *producers*—green plants, the only true producers—make organic compounds through the process of photosynthesis. The only "raw materials" are atmospheric carbon dioxide and water, the latter containing minerals from the Earth's crust. (These primal elements—"air, earth, and water"—have been recognized by people throughout history as the source of life. It speaks well for the deep, integrative spirituality of humans throughout the ages that they have always associated with the Divine the sun's mysterious power to transform these simple elements into the "stuff of life.") The *consumers*—all the living organisms which cannot perform the amazing transformations of photosynthesis—depend on the green plants for our energy. (Frequent meditation on this reality could help greatly in moving people from the arrogant stance of the industrial paradigm to a reverent presence in the natural world. Religious leaders should introduce their members to this type of reflection as an integral part of their worship of the Creator.)

Perhaps the largest design error of the industrial model comes from ignoring the third living group in an ecosystem—the *decomposers*. For it is these little beings—bacteria, fungi, worms, and other tiny creatures—that disassemble all "dead" matter into the original "raw materials" from which the producers can again make "new" molecules. This cyclic activity can continue indefinitely—but only if we return to nature's regenerative capacity. This will require not only a complete redesign of all industrial processes but also a serious look at the lifestyle of the Western industrial world—for this is the dream of every person living today. Yet, it is clear that the planet cannot afford the wasteful, overconsuming lifestyle currently being enjoyed even by 20 percent of its human inhabitants. Thus, it is critical that people of faith take on the challenge of becoming actively involved in transforming this dream of "the good life" into something the planet can afford for all. To be "practicing one's faith" in the new millennium is to become engaged in *serious action* toward "Earth-healing."

CONSUMPTION AND WASTE IN THE "THROWAWAY SOCIETY"

This brief look at "nature's economics" illustrates where the designers of the "new industrial revolution" are getting their approaches. Clearly, designing industrial processes which are efficient and regenerative is increasingly being seen not only as "good planetary citizenship" but also as "good business." When the new approaches toward developing "greener" processes find enthusiastic support from people—both as buyers and as voters—significant changes can occur very rapidly, given today's information and communication systems. However, current suppliers of consumer goods are not likely to use their enormous advertising budgets to encourage reductions in purchasing or shifts to still expensive products emerging from economically risky processes. So, it will take a profound "conversion" of attitude and behavior on the part of "average citizens" to demand products and services which contribute to "Earth-healing." Here again is where churches, synagogues, and mosques—and other values-based groups—can make an enormous difference. Beginning with such simple—but difficult—actions as substituting "real" cups and plates for the after-service "coffee and donuts" can help people begin to question the level of waste we take for granted. Getting accurate information to people about the "sacrilege" of using Earth's resources so wastefully can help them to connect their religious beliefs to many of the everyday decisions about what they eat, use, and buy. But besides seeing these as moral issues, people must "know the facts," and this is where religious leaders can play an important role by incorporating these issues as part of conscience-formation for all age levels.

Paul Hawken has provided us with an astounding set of statistics about consumption and waste—especially in the United States. Noting that we humans are better at making waste than at making products, especially sustainable ones, Hawken says that for every 100 pounds of product manufactured, at least 3,200 pounds of waste is created in the process. People in the United States use more materials than anyone else in the world; their *per capita* consumption averages about 23 tons per year, which amounts to 125 pounds per day from all the resources and materials quarried, mined, harvested, and manufactured.

Because of the "throw-away" economy we have invented, "American alone wastes more than *1 million pounds* per person per year. This includes such commodities as 3.5 billion pounds of carpet sent to landfills, 25 billion pounds of carbon dioxide, and 6 billion pounds of polystyrene. In the United States, 28 billion pounds of food is wasted. Some 300 billion pounds of organic and inorganic chemicals are used in manufacturing and processing, while some 700 billion pounds of hazardous waste are generated by chemical production. By counting the waste developed in extracting gas, coal, oil, and minerals, another 34 *trillion* pounds per year are added to the waste stream. This does not include the waste generated elsewhere on our behalf. One example is the Freeport-McMoran gold mine in Irian Jaya. This mine annually dumps 66 pounds of tailings and toxic waste into Indonesian rivers for every man, woman, and child in America. A small fraction of the 125,000 tons of *daily* waste material is imported as gold. The remainder is left behind.[20]

TRANSFORMING THE INDUSTRIAL PARADIGM

It is virtually impossible for the average person even to imagine quantities such as those mentioned above, but three things should be clear from a careful reading of these facts: (1) On a finite planet, such waste cannot continue for long; (2) for all who believe that Earth belongs to the Eternal Creator it is a moral obligation to change to behaviors which honor this belief; and (3) the structural injustices of the present global reality—both ecologically and socially—challenge serious adherents to any religious tradition to profound reflection and action.

Psychologically it is critical that the positive, pioneering efforts that are already underway within the industrial societies become better known. Most people are not aware of these and—if they have heard of them at all—assume that they will call for "giving up" too much. Unless forced to it by catastrophic events, virtually no one will "give up" the comforts and conveniences to which we have become accustomed unless there are *realistic alternatives*. One of the major difficulties in conscienticizing people to the ecological realities is that they assume this means "freezing in the dark." Many "vote with their feet" away from informative sessions on these subjects, as any of us who have been involved in environmental consciousness-raising for thirty years can confirm. Only recently have faith communities begun to connect such programs with religious practice, and often attendance is limited to the rather small number of those already sensitive to "justice and peace" issues. It is imperative that these connections between faith and ecology be addressed regularly by religious leaders. Responsible decision-making about resource use must become part of the policy-making of each congregation. Assistance with environmental assessment is available from a growing number of sources. In *Eco-Church: An Action Manual*, Albert Fritsch has developed an important tool for groups who want to do some serious planning toward a sustainable future for their buildings.[21] What is exciting about some of the alternatives being developed is that they will enable congregations to *save money* while responsibly reducing consumption and pollution! An additional advantage is that people can "feel empowered" to make changes in their everyday lives at home and in the workplace. Doing the information-gathering associated with serious efforts to "green" places of worship and associated buildings and projects can promote strong bonds among those involved—real community-building!

HOPE THROUGH ALTERNATIVES

Even ten or fifteen years ago it would have been difficult for even the most avid proponent of "green technologies" to convince the majority of people that there were viable options which could provide an acceptable lifestyle without continuing to destroy Earth's life-support systems. However, each year more and more small pioneering groups are being joined by major corporations, cities, states, and federal programs in exploring sustainable alternatives, especially in reducing pollution and energy use in construction and transportation. The inefficiency of design which we have taken for granted is now being questioned actively. For example, the average car is only about 1 percent efficient—and hardly different from cars built fifty years ago. Only 1 of every 100 gallons of gasoline burned actually moves the driver; the rest is lost in air friction, accelerating and braking, and heating the road and tires. A hypercar being developed at the Rocky Mountain Institute has a scooter-sized engine, a gas turbine or fuel cell which provides a constant source of electricity and variable-speed electric motors which can recapture braking energy for reuse after temporary storage in a battery or flywheel. Nearly 95 percent less polluting than today's cars, it gets 100–200 miles per gallon.[22] It is not yet available at your local auto dealer, but it is amazing how rapidly such a car might become mainstream if an informed public demands it! Right now there is a rapidly increasing selection of vehicles being purchased by cities through the U.S. Department of Energy's Clean Cities Program. As of May, 1999, there are seventy Clean Cities coalitions currently working at acquiring alternatively fueled school buses and vans and installing refueling facilities for propane and compressed natural gas (CNG). The U.S. Postal Service has ordered 6,000 electric vehicles (EVs) to be delivered over four years, the first 500 in the very near future. This type of fleet order can have a great impact on the entire EV industry as increased volume decreases both production cost and purchase price. Surely people would be encouraged if they knew that all the American and Japanese auto manufacturers are introducing some mix of CNG, propane, bi-fuel, electric-gasoline hybrid vehicles at *current* auto shows. And they *will* know as manufacturers begin widespread advertising of the breakthroughs they are making toward a "greener" future.

An important initiative toward sustainability which began in Sweden is called The Natural Step (TNS). In 1989 Dr. Karl-Henrik

Robert, an oncologist, gathered fifty fellow scientists to develop a set of fundamental principles that could define a sustainable society. Four fundamental "system conditions" were agreed upon: (1) substances from the Earth's crust cannot systematically increase in the biosphere; (2) substances produced by society cannot systematically increase in the biosphere; (3) the physical basis for productivity and diversity of nature must not be systematically deteriorated; and (4) in order to meet the previous three conditions, there must be a *fair and efficient* use of resources to meet human needs. Several European companies have adopted TNS, along with about fifty city Swedish governments. In the United States,. a number of corporations such as Monsanto, Interface, and Mitsubishi Electric America have embraced the Natural Step principles. Training seminars are being conducted in every region of the country. The first Fortune 500 company to adopt TNS principles was the Interface Corporation, whose CEO Ray Anderson has introduced the first "products as service" to carpet users. Through an "Evergreen Lease" a company pays no installation charge—just a monthly fee for constantly fresh-looking carpet. Interface replaces tiles as needed and then *recycles the old ones*. Eventually all raw materials will come from old carpets and other petrochemical products and solar energy will be used in production. Their ultimate goal is "no emissions, no waste." This will be an industrial process operating exactly like an ecosystem! "We're committed to The Natural Step framework as our compass in our search for the path to sustainability," says Anderson. "But this is hard stuff. These are unrelenting principles."[23] It is quite exciting and a very hopeful sign when a major corporation is willing to "learn from nature." As more industries see these pioneers using "earth-friendly" practices they will become mainstream throughout the industrial world—especially when it is possible that these cyclic processes may actually turn out to cost less than today's approaches.

WASTING RESOURCES MEANS WASTING PEOPLE

It is clear that developing a new industrial paradigm will produce major changes in the labor field. Here there is enormous need for equally creative approaches or truly devastating situations will arise for workers. Because "natural capital" has not been included in the balance sheet, resource prices have fallen continually as our ability to extract, mine, and harvest Earth's natural resources has increased. When resources are cheap, business maximizes productivity by using more and more resources. This not only depletes the environment— it also *depletes labor*. Everyone knows that the assumption that greater productivity would increase leisure time has not worked out that way. Many find themselves working up to 200 hours a year more than 20 years ago—with no increase in "real" wages. Workers across the globe *sense that they have no real value* in the present economic model. This is a devastating realization for many young people today and a cause of much discouragement and even despair among today's labor force. This "social waste" is an important part of the "waste factor" which characterizes the industrial paradigm. Addressing the inequities and injustices suffered by workers has always been an imperative for communities of faith of all religious traditions.

However, the enormity of the shifts that are on the horizon should challenge religious leaders to become *actively involved* in the "invention" of humane labor arrangements during these major transitions. For example, with appropriate planning and retraining, it should be possible to prepare workers to shift from fossil fuel-related jobs to those in renewable energy fields—and usually within the same "energy companies." There is no need to repeat the dislocations that have resulted in lost jobs as manufacturing has become highly automated. However, to make this possible, corporate executives will have to undergo a major "conversion" to a more humane philosophy about their employees. Many of these business leaders belong to congregations, so it is probable that at least some may be challenged to realize their obligations to justice and compassion— but only if this prophetic message reaches them. Religious leaders must help these "captains of industry" connect their weekend worship with their weekday policy-making! Clergy-persons are called to be brave enough to preach this message—even at the risk of losing major contributions.

DESIGNING AND BUILDING A SUSTAINABLE FUTURE

For the "average person" in the industrial world to realize that the planet cannot continue to support today's lifestyle requires an *awareness* of the enormous *increase in consumption* that has characterized the post-World War II period. *Environmental Building News* provides statistics which illustrate how the "average American" has gone from enjoyment of modest comfort to expectation of virtual luxury. Average household size has changed from 3.67 members in 1940 to 2.64 in 1997. At the same time, the average new home has grown from 1,100 to 2,150 square feet. This is an increase in *per person area* from about 290 to 800 square feet! A high percentage of new houses have garages for at least two cars and more than two-and-a-half bathrooms. Central air conditioning, nearly unknown in 1940, has increased from 46 percent in 1975 to 82 percent in 1997! Larger houses tend to have higher ceilings and other "glamorous" features, with increased consumption of materials for each square foot of living space.[25]

Thus, the environmental impact is significantly higher. Because of increased surface area of those with sprawling floor plans—*energy use has grown proportionally.* The "cheap energy" we have been enjoying comes at extremely high "environmental cost." At workshops in various regions of the country many people are telling me that they are *experiencing* noticeable changes in climate. For over a decade, sobering statements about the effects of global warming have been issued by many distinguished scientists, along with data indicating that energy efficiency in buildings could be more than doubled through simple changes in construction practices and specifications for lighting, heating, and cooling. The realization that in the near future the industrial model must switch to renewable energy sources is only beginning to dawn on policy-makers in government and business.

"WALKING THE TALK"

One of the ways to hasten this inevitable shift is through "grass roots" efforts. As an educator and biologist it became clear to me in 1980 that the only solution to the "energy crisis" (and the increasing global pollution of air, water, and soil) would be to use the enormous amounts of energy available from sun, wind, and the depths of the earth—the "natural" energy sources of this planet. Also, though the term "sustainable development" was not yet in use, I realized that using natural energy sources was the only possible way in which poor people across the globe could achieve a decent standard of living without further destroying Earth's "natural capital." Many years of teaching had convinced me that "show and tell" was the most effective way to ensure *real* learning and I realized that *personal witness* is the most effective way to establish credibility. I began serious study about renewable energy—aided by joining a small local "solar energy association" which had begun in 1979.

Thanks to volunteers working on Saturdays for three years, an old chicken barn on the grounds of our Motherhouse was converted to a a passive-solar, super-insulated apartment, *La Casa del Sol,* now a residence for another sister and myself. The cost was ten dollars per square foot because we used mostly materials that had been discarded. The new materials we needed were purchased with funds derived from "giant yard sales"—(another way of modeling our regenerative design on the *decomposers* of healthy ecosystems). This experience resulted not only in a resource-efficient, all-electric dwelling—attractive and comfortable, with a monthly energy cost of fifty dollars—but in a *spirit of community and empowerment* among the forty-five volunteers involved off and on in the three-year project.[26]

Ten years later a second, more sophisticated project was completed—*EarthConnection, a Center for Learning and Reflection about "living lightly" on Earth.* This Earth-friendly, solar-heated, twenty-first-century structure incorporates as many resource-efficient features as we could afford—high insulation levels, state-of-the-art windows and lighting, increased thermal mass in floors to retain heat, low-flow faucets, and a unique modified geothermal heating system. An array of sixteen flat-plate solar collectors is mounted on the South-facing roof. A mixture of water and antifreeze—of a type which will not harm the ozone layer—is heated by the sun and passes through one mile of tubing. Half of this is embedded in the concrete floor and the solar-heated water is pumped through the floor providing for direct heating of the building in spring and fall and on sunny winter days. But most of our winter days here are quite gray, so (like squirrels) we store solar energy all summer by passing heated water from the collectors into an insulated bed deep in the earth around the building. When it is not sunny, the stored heat is circulated through a heat pump and released as heated air into the building's duct system. As soon as we can afford it we will generate much of our own electric power for the all-electric building using photo-voltaic (PV) panels in a grid-intertied system. Thus, we will use electricity generated by the local utility company when it is not sunny. However, with "net metering" (that is, payment by utilities for con-sumer-generated power) about to become a reality, if we design our PV system correctly our *net annual electric bill will be zero*—and we will have decreased significantly the amount of carbon dioxide for which we are responsible! This project is one of seventy grass-roots efforts described in the Union of Concerned Scientists' book, *Renewables Are Ready.*[27]

EarthConnection is a sponsored program of the Sisters of Charity of Cincinnati, a Roman Catholic congregation of Sisters—surely a "new ministry"! Having been involved as a consultant in a number of such efforts, I am delighted to report that this is a growing move-ment among religious communities. A recent ecumenical program, the *Solar Stewardship Initiative* has been launched recently by the North American Coalition on Religion and Ecology (NACRE) as part of the Million Solar Roofs program announced by President Clinton. The Solar Stewardship Initiative is "an environmental pro-gram initiative (viz., education and action project) developed by the NACRE and designed to involve the interfaith/religious commu-nity (and related nonprofit institutions). The Solar Stewardship Ini-tiative is designed to introduce energy efficiency and renewable energy technologies to local, state and regional communities within the United States, to promote these environmentally clean technologies, and to educate citizens in light of global climate change issues concerning the ecological, economic and ethical (stewardship) reasons for using these new technologies to generate electricity (PV) and to produce solar thermal hot water or heat (ST)."[28]

It would take pages to list the exciting, creative steps that are being taken by growing numbers of people around the globe to create a sustainable future. It is important that people of faith be among them! In preparation for the 1993 Parliament of the World's Religions, Gerald Barney, Founder of the Millennium Institute, prepared a report entitled *Global 2000 Revisited: What Shall We Do?*[29] In the opening letter to the assembled spiritual leaders, he invites them to become active participants, reminding them that " it is from our respective faiths that we derive our sense of origins, of self, of purpose, of possibility." He closes with a prayerful message which could be addressed to every person who has just stepped into the new millennium:

> Let us all listen to and allow ourselves to be guided by the creative energy that shaped and lighted the universe from the beginning.
> Let us all *awaken* to a new understanding of ourselves and the continuing revelation that takes place in and through Earth. Let us *take back our lives* from cynicism, optimism, addictions, and despair. Let us *act* with conviction and confidence.

NOTES

1. Institute of Noetic Sciences, *Noetic Sciences Review* 48 (April-July, 1999).

2. David Korten, *When Corporations Rule the World* (San Francisco: Berrett-Koehler, 1995).

3. Gro Harlem Brundtland, *Our Common Future* (Oxford University Press, 1987).

4. Michael Keating, *The Earth Summit's Agenda for Change: A Plain Language Version of Agenda 21 and the other Rio Agreements* (Geneva: Centre for Our Common Future, 1993).

5. Lester Brown and Christopher Flavin, "A New Economy for a New Century," in *State of the World, 1999*, ed. Linda Starke (New York: Norton, 1999), p. 21.

6. Thomas Berry, *The Dream of the Earth* (San Francisco: Sierra Club Books, 1988).

7. Brian Swimme and Thomas Berry, *The Universe Story* (San Francisco: Harper, 1992).

8. Elizabeth A. Johnson, *Women, Earth, and Creator Spirit* (Mahwah, N.J.: Paulist Press, 1993).

9. Mathis Wackernagel and William Rees, *Our Ecological Footprint* (Gabriola Island, B.C.: New Society Publishers, 1996).

10. Berry, *The Dream of the Earth.*

11. James Lovelock, *Gaia: A New Look at Life on Earth* (Oxford University Press, 1979).

12. Thomas S. Kuhn, *The Structure of Scientific Revolutions* (Chicago: University of Chicago Press, 1970).

13. Peter Russell, *The Global Brain: Speculations on the Evolutionary Leap to Planetary Consciousness* (Los Angeles: J.P. Tarcher, 1983).

14. Pierre Teilhard de Chardin, *The Phenomenon of Man* (New York: Harper & Row, 1959).

15. Duane Elgin, *Awakening Earth* (New York: Morrow, 1994).

16. Brown and Flavin, "A New Economy for a New Century," p. 18.

17. Paul Hawken, with Amory and Hunter Lovins, *Natural Capitalism: The Coming Efficiency Revolution*, New York: Hyperion Press, 1998.

18. Paul Hawken, *The Ecology of Commerce: A Declaration of Sustainability* (New York: HarperCollins, 1993).

19. U.S. Department of Energy, *Alternative Fuel News* 3, no. 1 (May 1999).

20. Paul Hawken, "Natural Capitalism," in *Mother Jones* 22, no. 2, (March-April 1997): 44.

21. Albert Fritsch with Angela Ladavaia-Cox, *Eco-Church: An Action Manual* (San Jose, Calif.: Resource Publications, 1992).

22. Paul Hawken, "Natural Capitalism," p. 52.

23. Paul Hawken, *Natural Capitalism*, 1998.

24. Center for A New American Dream, "Sustainability in the Market," in *Enough!* 1, no. 4 (spring, 1998).

25. Alex Wilson, "Small Is Beautiful: House Size, Resource Use, and the Environment," *Environmental Building News* 8, no. 1 (January, 1999).

26. Mother Earth News Staff, "La Casa del Sol," in *Mother Earth News* 99 (May-June 1986).

27. Nancy Cole and P. J. Skerrett, *eds.*, *Renewables Are Ready: People Creating Renewable Energy Solutions* (White River Junction, Vt.: Chelsea Green, 1995).

28. North American Coalition on Religion and Ecology, *Solar Stewardship Initiative Brochure* (Washington, D.C., 1999).

29. Gerald Barney et al., *Global 2000 Revisited* (Arlington, Va.: Millennium Institute, 1993).

QUESTIONS FOR DISCUSSION

1. What are the underlying reasons for our human sense of disconnectedness from nature and the rest of God's creation? How can we humans learn to see ourselves as an integral part of nature and connected to the whole of creation?

2. How does the sense of oneness or connectedness with our natural habitat related to our sense of the sacredness of the created world of nature? How does the cosmic or universe story of our origins help us to regain this? What function do ritual and prayer have in this process of renewing our sense of the unity of creation and how is this compatible with science and technology?

3. What specifically can be done to help our highly industrialized, global society change its perspective and transform its consumerist attitudes in order to redesign the industrial model and examine values we have come to accept?

5. STRATEGIES FOR EDUCATION, MINISTRY, AND BUILDING SUSTAINABLE COMMUNITIES

We have moved over the course of this volume from confronting knowledge about Earth's ecosystems under stress, through reflections on a dialogue between science and religion concerning ecology and environmental concern, to our ethical response to an earth at risk. We are now confronted with the questions of strategies for education, ministry, and the building of sustainable communities. Educational establishments have for too long embraced a culture of denial. Rather than providing leadership for social change, they have often shared in consumerist globalization.[1] To educate, that is, to bring up or lead forth, implies a shared or accepted conception of fullness or maturation and the vision and skills needed to advance such a conception. In this sense education happens in the context of communities that profess shared values and believe that such values need to be passed on to others in the same generation or intergenerationally.[2]

On the eve of the 1992 Earth Summit in Rio de Janeiro, Fernando J. R. da Rocha envisioned such values and challenged the environmental movement to develop effective patterns of education.[3] He focused on the ways in which universities might foster ecological literacy and environmental ethics.[4] A similar challenge has been brought to churches and other voluntary organizations in society.[5] Each of the authors in this section works with university divinity schools, graduate schools of theology, seminaries, and other communities of faith in which environmental education takes place.

The first paper in this section, by Donald B. Conroy, moves us to the area of education, but still within the context of the dialogue undertaken in the preceding sections. This discussion situates ecological education, public proclamation and public policy strategies within this historic dialogue and affirms the importance of interdisciplinary reflection on knowledge and values for successfully carrying out this next stage of engagement in the process.[6]

Conroy traces the roots of the interest in ecological ethics, especially in North America, within the environmental and scientific communities while noting ethical concerns of several scientific organizations. He then goes on to point out that international diplomats, scientists, and religious authorities have been calling for a new global eco-ethic, which embodies values leading to social and ecological sustainability. Finally, before presenting an analysis of several current congregationally and community-based educational and ministry programs, he presents a cultural justification for these curricular approaches that call for ecojustice and caring for creation.

Conroy's emphasis upon community-based education is followed by Richard Clugston's concerns with higher education.[7] Citing Thomas Berry's call to rework institutions and public policy so as to pursue mutually enhancing human-earth relationships, Clugston seeks to delineate a paradigm shift in the ways in which university divinity schools, schools of theology, and seminaries do their work. The Center for Respect of Life and Environment, of which Clugston serves as director, and Theological Education to Meet the Environmental Challenge (TEMEC), the program of which he and Dieter Hessel are working to direct, are seeking to do innovative work in schools which prepare the religious leadership of society. Their work is situated in a radical attempt to reshape institutional life.[8] It raises the question of the degree to which educational institutions as such should take a proactive role in reshaping civil society.[9] The nature of the instruction that is envisioned might be evaluated helpfully in the light of various types of university environmental curricula.[10] Such programs have been categorized in a fourfold schema as shaped by faculty expertise and administrative arrangements: (1) programs that sensitize students to ecosystems and environmental concerns, (2) those that focus on particular issues, (3) action-oriented programs, and (4) courses designed for environmental professionals.[11] Given the unique nature of schools of theology, with the possible exception of the last category each of these kinds of programs has a valuable place in the curriculum.[12]

Where it is occurring, this shift in academic priorities responds to an emerging worldview that is more conscious of the place of values in education. Nowhere in society is the struggle over worldviews and their implementation more intense than in contemporary academe.[13]

In the third chapter of this section, Larry Rasmussen takes up a theme of central importance for our deepening global awareness, and of particular interest to the World Council of Churches, that of community, or in its deeper theological sense, *koinonia*.[14] He begins with the illustration of an industrial ecological cycle, parallel to a food web in nature, and concludes that if we are to achieve communal or global sustainability, it will only happen as we mimic the design strategies of nature. Through this example Rasmussen encourages us to think of nature as community. By this he means "all that exists, coexists," i.e., creation is a community in which the parts and the whole are integrally related, an insight increasingly held by both scientific and religious modes of understanding. Rasmussen illustrates his point with helpful examples of learning to think in terms of cyclical rather than linear processes of industrial systems. This is the satellite picture of our planet, a planet that is not only blue/green with the fecundity of life, but also scared by widespread deforestation and spreading drought under an ozone canopy of diminishing protection. It is an earth with communities at risk.[15]

A community orientation requires a greater sense of identity with the earth and with future generations Wendell Berry's "seventh generation test" and movement down the ladder of abstraction to immediate criteria for making decisions about our use of the material things. This requires a change in our inner world, as Rasmussen puts it, a setting of our "moral gyroscope" such that "moral, spiritual and cultural dimensions are as crucial as technical ones," defining sustainability in such a way as to foster eco- and environmental equity.[16] Definitions range from sustaining "growth" (neoclassical economists) to ideas fostered by Deep Ecology showing that human economy is embedded in nature's economy. J. Baird Callicott reminds us of assertions from Aldo Leopold's day to our own which state that people, as a part of nature, should not by definition be seen as threatening to the health and sustaining power of an ecosystem. In fact, it is a degraded environment that is increasingly deepening regional social conflict.[17] Callicott's concern, and the definition of sustainability which John Lemons offers, parallels that of the Brundtland Report, which affirms "the continued satisfaction of basic physical human needs . . . and of higher level social and cultural needs."[18] If these needs can no longer be met in a given environment, then ecological devastation becomes one more element in a complex web of politics, economics, history, and psychology in the complex struggle for security.[19] Holmes Rolston III's concern that an "earth ethic" be embraced is especially apt: if we are Earth's primary species, how conceited and narrow of us to ignore the sustainability of the biotic community in which we share![20]

Perhaps we are beginning to learn at the onset of the twenty-first century that since we cannot break nature's laws, which are the foundation of creation, we must design a society that acknowledges them.[21] It is within this context that a humane technology is beginning to be explored, at least in theory.[22] This is the end toward which the Earth Charter movement tends. The vision and energy of churches, synagogues, mosques, and other centers of worship and of human encounter as well as other voluntary organizations, nongovernmental agencies, and institutions must temper human proclivities with deeper cultural and spiritual values.[23] In addition to such sodalities and modalities, this is also a vision that must be taken up by colleges and universities, institutions often begun by churches as institutions or by people concerned with the relation of values with knowledge against a social and political horizon.[24] For some missionary groups "earthkeeping" has become an important dimension of the call to discipleship.[25]

Rasmussen draws us to the intersection of science (facts) and religion (values) as adjudicated through history among people of all living faiths.[26] The decisive point here is whether an inclusive ethical vocabulary which permits different ontologies or worldviews to coexist can be developed, one that can occur in civil society under participatory democracy. This point is particularly pertinent in light of growing debate over whether a value-free education is possible.[27] Indeed, schools probably have never functioned in a fully value-free environment.[28] This is not to say that we should not try to devise an ethical vocabulary in as wide a way as possible. Rather, such a vocabulary recognizes that there is always an array of ontologies embedded beneath the surface of language. Catherine Larrère makes this point as she discerns overtones of the irrational in rhetoric that gives primacy to cultural issues over those of nature.[29]

If all education is developed in terms of a certain normativity of values, the environmental crisis calls us to develop patterns of training within a holistic epistemology and metaphysics. Each author in this book in one way or another reminds us that the environmental crisis is less amenable to a technological solution than to a pervasive philosophical approach,[30] and that the assumptions we bear about ourselves will be translated into those we have about our world. If this is the case, then religion, in addition to all indigenous knowledge, is a necessary player in the debate over life in earth's ecosystem, not simply an ancillary *kibitzer*.[31] When religion is taken seriously, then theology will be considered as necessary a discipline as physics. Theology is the science of religion.

Religious communities work out values in practice. Like many universities they transcend the ecosystem in their membership and commitment.[32] Universities themselves can be viewed as a subset of religious communities, as questions unresolved in worship are wrestled through in rhetoric and dialectic in schools birthed for such purposes. This argument rejects that of Habermas, who sees religious communities as cultural backwaters.[33] It also rejects those views of religion as ministering only to the needs of its adherents.[34] Rather, it follows Charles A. Taylor's idea that individuals work out their identities in communities of discourse.[35] Just as our ecosystem cannot be nurtured apart from its biotic diversity, so society needs its communities of faith for nurturing the larger civil society.[36] The hope grounded in transcendence brought to bear upon the environmental crisis begins to turn Lynn White's argument on its head. Only a hope which is stronger than the earth can save the earth. The wellness of the land in the Semitic religious traditions, in particular in Judaism, Christianity, and Islam, functions as a barometer for the moral and spiritual life of the people. Might we then also say that life in nature gives us the context for a salvation that transcends nature but is reflected in it?[37]

> In the temple he found people selling cattle, sheep, and doves, and the money changers seated at their tables. Making a whip of cords, he drove all of them out of the temple. . . . He told those who were selling the doves, "Take these things out of here! Stop making my Father's house a marketplace!" (John 2:14–16)

Rodney L. Petersen

NOTES

1. Chet A. Bowers, *The Culture of Denial: Why the Environmental Movement Needs a Strategy for Reforming Universities and Public Schools* (Albany: State University of New York Press, 1997). The work of innovative educators is celebrated in Gregory A. Smith and Dilafruz R. Williams, eds., *Ecological Education in Action: On Weaving Education, Culture, and the Environment* (Albany: State University of New York Press, 1999).

2. The assumption that education happens in community and in relation to general or communal ideas of maturation or fullness can be traced from Cicero's book, *De Legibus*, written first as a letter to his son Marcus, to present educational theorists. See the discussion in Derek Bok, *Universities and the Future of America* (Durham, N.C.: Duke University Press, 1990); and see work pursued by the Derek Bok Center, Harvard University, Cambridge, Massachusetts.

3. The result was a conference in Porto Alegre, Brazil, in which international environmental philosophers and educators inaugurated a dialogue on how to chart a new course linking environment and ethics through education. See J. Baird Callicott and Fernando J. R. da Rocha, eds., *Earth Summit Ethics: Toward a Reconstructive Postmodern Philosophy of Environmental Education* (Albany: State University of New York Press, 1996). Ongoing work toward environmental literacy is being pursued by University Leaders for a Sustainable Future, Tufts University (Medford, Massachusetts),

4. J. Baird Callicott and Fernando J. R. da Rocha contend that educational direction must be shaped in light of a multifaceted philosophical approach which not only draws on past-present and North-South axes, but recognizes Pacific and Atlantic Rim concerns as well. In additional to conventional economic thinking and the failure of nations in the North and South to deal with their own short-sighted economic proclivities, our authors cite the influential cognitive foundations of current economic reality in the Pacific Rim as grounded in instrumentalism and mannerism. Without influential global environmental ethics drawing upon all of the axial relations which they outline, the carrying capacity of the earth will be seriously threatened. See introduction to *Earth Summit Ethics*, pp. 1–21. See Walter Leal Filho, ed., *Sustainability and University Life*, vol. 5 of the *Environmental Education, Communication and Sustainability Series* (New York: Peter Lang Scientific Publishers, 1999).

5. See *A Call to Engagement for People of Faith Concerning the 1994 United Nations International Conference on Population and Development* by Leaders and Representatives of U.S. Religious Communities, Washington, D.C., July 26, 1994, convened by The Centre for Development and Population Activities (Washington, D.C.). Credit belongs to The Pew Charitable Trust's Global Stewardship Initiative for supporting such work to encourage communities of faith to become engaged with global environmental concerns.

6. The need for interdisciplinary discussion can be accredited to the Harvard University Environmental Seminar, headed by Dr. Timothy Weiskel, which has done significant pioneering work in this area.

7. Richard M. Clugston serves as Director of the Association of University Leaders for a Sustainable Future (ULSF), an affiliate of the Center for Respect of Life and Environment (CRLE). ULSF promotes academic leadership for the advancement of global environmental literacy and publishes *The Declaration*, a publication to promote the work of the association, three times annually.

8. In light of the Porto Alegre Conference and its Declaration on University, Ethics, and Environment (29 May 1992), John Lemons offers: (1) perspectives on environmental literacy, (2) traditional approaches to fostering environmental literacy, (3) the university reforms necessary to achieve environmental literacy, and (4) recent recommendations to develop accreditation and certification standards for environmental education programs and professions, and the implications of these recommendations. The work of TEMEC should be situated and evaluated in light of Lemons's work.

9. Since the inception of seminaries and schools of theology in this country, beginning with Andover Theological Seminary (1807), such schools have been on the leading edge of shaping the civil order in such voluntaristic movements as antislavery, child labor laws, women's rights and other concerns as they have grown out of various revival and theological concern. On Andover and schools in The Boston Theological Institute, see Petersen, *Christianity and Civil Society: Theological Education for Public Life* (Maryknoll: Orbis Books, 1995), pp. vii–xii. Current concern for more proactive work on the part of educational institutions, such as that expressed by Derek Bok or D. Langenberg, must be seen in this light. See Bok, *Universities and the Future of America* (Durham, N.C.: Duke University Press, 1990); and Langenberg, "Science, Slogans, and Civic Duty," *Science* 252 (1991): 361–63.

10. See selected issues of *The Environmental Professional*, esp. J. Disinger and C. Schoenfeld, eds., "Special Issue: Focus on Environmental Studies," *The Environmental Professional* 9 (1987): 185–274.

11. G. Francis, "Environmental Education in Academia: Escaping the Institutional Impass," *The Environmental Professional* 14 (1992): 278–83.

12. This is not to underestimate the significance of education for the environmental professional. In fact, the nature of modern technology with the requirement that some people become environmental professionals offers a special challenge to theological education. Here, as elsewhere, making even basic ethical decisions as they pertain to certain segments of society requires ever more sophistication. José Lutzenberger writes that education theory must take into account the difference of an earlier "transparent" technology from that of more sophisticated "opaque" technologies upon various population groups, the latter technologies requiring an educated elite to operate and control. See "Science, Technology, Economics, Ethics, and Environment," in Callicott and da Rocha, *Earth Summit Ethics*, pp. 23–45.

13. Reaction to modernity, frequently defined as the worldview shaped by seventeenth-century science interpreted in an increasingly dualist and positivist fashion, is marked in academia by schools of postmodernism (new age, literary/artistic, and philosophical) that offer greater attention to other sources of wisdom and understanding. Philosophical postmodernism (shaped by Ludwig Wittgenstein, Martin Heidegger, and Jacques Derrida) is divided by David Ray Griffin into deconstructive or eliminative postmodernism, frequently nihilistic and relativistic, or ultramodernism, and constructive or revisionary postmodernism involving a unity of scientific, ethical, aesthetic, and religious intuitions. See series introduction to *Earth Summit Ethics*, pp. x–xi. Also see Griffin's comments on contemporary postmodernism in distinction from earlier forms of antimodernism in Romantic and Luddite movements, pp. xii–xiii.

14. *Koinonia* was the topic of focused consideration at the Fifth World Conference on Faith and Order of the World Council of Churches, Santiago de Compostela, Spain, 3–14 August 1993. See the booklet, *Costly Commitment: Ecclesiology and Ethics*, ed. Thomas F. Best and Martin Robra (Geneva: World Council of Churches, 1995); and paper by Lewis S. Mudge, "Ecclesiology and Ethics in Current Ecumenical Debate," prepared for the World Council of Churches, Geneva, Switzerland.

15. Nicholas Hildyard, "Blood, Babies, and the Social Roots of Conflict," in Mohamed Suliman, ed., *Ecology, Politics, and Violent Conflict* (London: ZED Books, 1999), pp. 33–34.

16. Debate over definitions of "sustainability" and "sustainable development" begin with *Our Common Future*; see *Sustainable Development: A Guide to Our Common Future*. The Report of the World Commission on Environment and Development, prepared by Gregory G. Lebel and Hal Kane (Oxford: Oxford University Press, 1990).

17. Hildyard, "Blood, Babies, and the Social Roots of Conflict." For specific examples, see J. J. Otim, *The Taproot of Environmental and Development Crisis in Africa* (Nairobi: ACLA Publications, 1992). Additional literature is available from publishers in many Southern hemisphere countries.

18. John Lemons, "University Education in Sustainable Development and Environmental Protection," in Callicott and da Rocha, *Earth Summit Ethics*, p. 198. He draws attention to the Brundtland Report and offers additional definitions for the terms "sustainability" and "sustainable development."

19. As adversarial goals develop in the context of social conflict, to the extent that basic differences are linked to questions of survival or safety, one

can expect a social conflict to become protracted or even intractable. See Abraham Maslow, *Motivation and Personality* (New York: Harper and Brothers, 1954); cf. Louis Kriesberg, *Constructive Conflicts: From Escalation to Resolution* (New York: Rowman & Littlefield Publishers, Inc., 1998), pp. 58–99.

20. Holmes Rolston III, "Earth Ethics: A Challenge to Liberal Education," in Callicott and da Rocha, *Earth Summit Ethics*, pp. 161–92. See Rolston, *Environmental Ethics: Duties to and Values in the Natural World* (Philadelphia: Temple University Press, 1988). Often the meaning we give to words like "conservation," "wilderness," "natural resources," and their relationship with ourselves that is thereby implied, are embedded in a Cartesian dualism which betrays a narrow view of nature and a misconstrued understanding of creation.

21. Paul Hawken, *The Ecology of Commerce: A Declaration of Sustainability* (San Francisco: HarperCollins, 1993).

22. Robert M. Adams, *Paths of Fire: An Anthropologist's Inquiry into Western Technology* (Princeton, N.J.: Princeton University Press, 1996); see the comments by Weiskel earlier in Section One of this volume.

23. The work of Hans Küng raises up the importance of such reflection in relation to interreligious dialogue. See Küng, ed., *Yes to a Global Ethic* (London: SCM, 1996); and as exemplified in Steven C. Rockefeller, *Principles of Environmental Conservation and Sustainable Development: Summary and Survey*, prepared for the Earth Charter Project (revised April 1996).

24. Celia Deane-Drummond, *A Handbook in Theology and Ecology* (London: SCM, 1996).

25. See, for example, Katie Smith and Tetsunao Yamamori, eds., *Growing Our Future: Food Secutiry and the Environment* (West Hartford, Conn.: Kumarian Press, 1992); and Calvin B. DeWitt and Ghillean T. Prance, eds., *Missionary Earthkeeping* (Macon, Ga.: Mercer University Press, 1992); and J. Ronald Engel and Joan Gibb Engel, eds., *Ethics of Environment and Development: Global Challenge, International Response* (Tucson: University of Arizona Press, 1993). Work on the part of Mennonite reflief agencies should be cited as important illustrations of this.

26. The various understandings of nature by practitioners of different religions need to be carefully considered. See the brief prospectus by Paulos Mar Gergorios, "Nature," in *The Dictionary of the Ecumenical Movement* (Geneva: WCC Publications, 1991), pp. 715–18.

27. Peter Madsen argues that such is not possible and never has been the case. Furthermore, in light of the environmental crisis universities should function with environmental responsibilities in the social space

between social atomism and the social whole, in "What Can Universities and Professional Schools Do to Save the Environment?" in Callicott and da Rocha, *Earth Summit Ethics*, pp. 71–91.

28. For example, George H. Williams summaries five themes inherent in the foundation of Harvard College, drawn forth from its past: (1) the autonomy of the University with respect to Church and State, but an autonomy grounded in a certain religious epistemology; (2) a Christological theme as definitive of the relative autonomy of the University and the professor (of particular interest in the light of contemporary debate over issues of tenure); (3) the transferential theme from Old to New World and implied religious motifs; (4) the paradisaic theme with its romantic implications in University life; and (5) the idea that the University is the scene of a special kind of "spiritual warfare." See *Paradise and Wilderness in Christian Thought: The Biblical Experience of the Desert in the History of Christianity and the Paradise Theme in the Theological Idea of the University* (New York: Harper & Brothers, 1962), pp. 156–57; see also George Marsden, *The Soul of the American University: From Protestant Establishment to Established Nonbelief* (New York: Oxford University Press, 1994).

29. Catherinie Larrère, "Ethics, Politics, Science, and the Environment: Concerning the Natural Contract," in Callicott and da Rocha, *Earth Summit Ethics*, pp. 115–38.

30. Nicholás M. Sosa, "The Ethics of Dialogue and the Environment: Solidarity as a Foundation for Environmental Ethics," in Callicott and da Rocha, *Earth Summit Ethics*, pp. 47–70. See also John Young, *Sustaining the Earth* (Cambridge, Mass.: Harvard University Press, 1990); and note the eliminative implications of work in artificial intelligence as a reflection on another dimension of mechanism in the natural world, in Robert Wright, "Can Machines Think?" *Time* (March 25, 1996): 50–58.

31. Mary Evelyn Tucker, "Educating Eco-logically," *Journal of Curriculum Theory* 10, no. 4 (1996): 67–82.

32. Ninan Koshy, *Churches in the World of Nations: International Politics and the Mission and Ministry of the Church* (Geneva: WCC Publications, 1994); also see Paul Wapner, *Environmental Activism and World Civic Politics* (Albany: State of New York Press, 1996). Wapner gives detailed attention to the role of transnational environmental activist groups such as Greenpeace, the World Wildlife Fund, and Friends of the Earth.

33. Don S. Browning and Francis Schüssler Fiorenza, eds., *Habermas, Modernity, and Public Theology* (New York: Crossroad, 1992).

34. See this position as variously represented in the theologies of

George Lindbeck, Stanley Hauerwas, and John Millbank. See in Robert N. Bellah, "How to Understand the Church in an Individualistic Society," in R. L. Petersen, ed., *Christianity and Civil Society: Theological Education for Public Life* (Maryknoll: Orbis Books, 1995), pp. 1–14.

35. Charles Taylor, *Sources of the Self: The Making of the Modern Identity* (Cambridge, Mass.: Harvard University Press, 1989); and idem, *The Ethics of Authenticity* (Cambridge, Mass.: Harvard University Press, 1992).

36. See the Report by Leslie Lang, *Religion's Role in Preserving the Environment: A Nationwide Leadership Conference for Catholic, Jewish, and Protestant Seminaries,* April 1994 (The American Jewish Committee, Skirball Institute on American Values); and cf. Al Gore, *Earth in the Balance: Ecology and the Human Spirit* (Boston: Houghton Mifflin, 1992).

37. See in the Hebrew Scriptures, or Old Testament, Jer. 3:2–3 *et passim*; and Chris Wright, "Biblical Reflections on Land," in J. Mark Thomas, *Evangelical Review of Theology* 17, no. 2 (April 1993): 153–75.

11

CARING FOR CREATION
Community-Based Eco-Education and Public Policy Strategies

Donald B. Conroy

INTRODUCTION

The moral urgency of environmental responsibility within the religious community through preaching, education, and promotion of a new global ethic is gaining clarity. However, this also challenges the religious community regarding its own understanding of the significance of the doctrine of creation as well as its openness to respond to the implied ecological mission. Because of the speed of environmental devastation, according to the scientific community, in many regions and globally, this issue demands a new interdisciplinary dialogue resulting in a commitment to a timely ethical and pastoral response. The intent of this chapter is to situate this ethical education effort within an historical context not only of the science-religion dialogue but of several related discussions of ecosocial change which are now taking place. From within this context we intend to explore three emerging strategies for influencing the public in general as well as educating those in the faith community.

EXPLORING THE CONTEXT FOR
COMMUNITY-BASED ECO-EDUCATION

The turbulence of the late twentieth century can be viewed from several perspectives. One of these is to view it as a time of preparation for an era in which a new ethic of earth stewardship and a public policy of sustainable community development are being introduced. To discover what such a hopeful approach requires of the religious educator, the environmental reformer, or the public policy advocate, we need to look at the wider picture before choosing a precise strategy for influencing the public. The dialogue between religion and science plays an important and crucial role in this process. Still, on the other hand, it is not science alone that must give witness, for humans are beginning to realize that scientific knowledge by itself, even if it can be attained with great clarity, is insufficient for mounting a global educational effort and for moving the public will to change from unsustainability to earth stewardship values in politics, business, and community affairs.

This dialogue, as interpreted narrowly by those in the geo-biophysical sciences, is not sufficient to lay the new foundations; it must involve a wider range of the social, historical, and economic sciences along with ethics, theology, and religious studies in the discussion. Arising out of a wider spiritual and global consciousness is the call for a new earth ethic, a set of moral imperatives to be expressed within a commonly held ecological understanding. This vision is rooted in deeply perceived values in the new world community.[1]

In November 1992, the Union of Concerned Scientists entered the dialogue and raised the issue of collaborative ethical action. This statement broke new ground within the socially concerned scientific community when it said, "A new ethic is required—a new attitude towards discharging our responsibility for caring for ourselves and for the earth. . . . This ethic must motivate a great movement, convincing reluctant leaders and reluctant governments and reluctant peoples themselves to effect the needed changes."[2] In fact, by framing ecological issues in terms of the "human prospect," that is, possible futures and the choices they involve for humans, leading scientists now speak of a new dialogue between values and science.[3]

Science and technology alone cannot do the job of defining and clarifying the complex ethical issues needed to undergird the decisions which will affect our lifestyles, business procedures, governmental actions, and global policies, all of which must now take into consideration the earth's ecosystems upon which we depend for sustenance. Scientist William C. Clark, of Harvard University's Kennedy School of Government, has called for what was a generation ago unspeakable to scientists of the old school who held to so-called value-free science and only "technologically objective" solutions to be made by social engineers: "What kind of planet we want is ultimately a question of values. How much species diversity. . . ? the growth rate of the human population. . . ? climatic change. . . ? poverty?"[4]

Though science can tell us the "what" of ecological matters and technology the "how" as they pertain to sustainable development, it cannot *ultimately* resolve the value-laden "why" implicit in our complex choices. Science and technology must therefore engage in a deeper dialogue with other disciplines.

While these difficult choices facing all of us must be made with the help of science, they also call for enlightenment arising from philosophical reflection and faith. These choices point to the complex terrain of moral philosophy, ethics, and theology, and to sociocultural values analyzed in cultural anthropology, scriptural studies, and religious history from the dawn of civilization to the present. In the late 1980s, Gro Harlem Brundtland's plea for a global ethic, as chairperson of the World Commission on Environment and Development, was the exception. Now we find other internationally renown political leaders and parliamentarians entering into the discussion of values and ethics, as they respond to the compelling logic of *Our Common Future*, the report of the Brundtland Commission.[5]

An outstanding example of this thinking was at the United Nations Conference on Environment and Development (UNCED or the Earth Summit). In his opening address, UNCED Secretary-General Maurice Strong called for new ethical and spiritual awareness. He emphasized to the assembled diplomats and world leaders:

"The changes in behavior and direction called for here must be rooted in our deepest spiritual, moral, and ethical values."[6]

In the wake of the 1992 Earth Summit, sustainability has become a central focus for applying *Agenda 21* and the post-UNCED agreements of the 1995 Social Summit and the 1996 Habitat II Conference. All these events have infused the dialogue with a deeper quest for probing the interaction of *all sectors and disciplines* as we try to define the global ethical principles for sustainable community, environmental stewardship, and economic equity. In this same vein economist James Weaver of American University has astutely raised the relevance of the "value issues" in development thinking. He has shown that we cannot make headway in any of these development policy issues without honestly facing the implicit ethical dimensions implied by present day economic thought now considering social and ecological concerns.[7]

A well-known innovator, Herman Daly, formerly an economic advisor at the World Bank and now a fellow of the Center for Philosophy and Policy Studies at the University of Maryland, has pointed out ethical implications in the field of economics: "Economists have taught us to think that checks on self-interest are both unnecessary and harmful. . . . But with each passing year, the positive accomplishments of the economy have become less evident and the destructive consequences larger. There is a growing sense that it is time for a change. The change may well take the form of a paradigm shift."[8]

This need for a major shift in socioeconomic thinking and dialogue is reaffirmed by ecocultural thinker Thomas Berry in his assessment of the impoverished state of contemporary classic economic thought. While discussing the deficit in the U.S. national budget and the impending environmental disaster, Berry points to the difficulties that have arisen when the industrial economy disrupts the natural processes with unsustainable technological choices, thus upsetting the earth process. In *Dream of the Earth* Berry writes, "When nature goes into deficit, then we go into deficit. When this occurs to a limited extent on a regional basis, it can often be remedied. The difficulty is when the entire planetary system is affected."[9]

It soon becomes clear, as we carry on this dialogue, that, in addition to the "hard" or physical sciences, the socioeconomic sciences are also not "value-free." Scientific treatises on economics and society are often based on models with implicit value systems which are far from life-enhancing and sustainable. Because economics is such an intrinsic part of our current problem, many think the entire discipline must be reworked to become part of a sustainable solution by explicating the underlying values and implicit choices, before putting any economic solution forth as an objective system of thought, giving us a definitive and valid framework for sustainable development.

In the fall of 1996 the World Bank issued its significant report on ecovalues as part of its series promoting environmentally sustainable development, entitled *Ethics and Spiritual Values.* Ismail Serageldin, vice president of the World Bank for Environmentally Sustainable Development, noted that he has a two-step approach to work out a truly practical or "operational" definition of sustainability. He has, first of all, set up a systematic method of analyzing every project proposal from three aspects of sustainability—economic, environmental, and social. Using "capital" in an analogous, but real sense, of identifiable wealth, opportunity, or value, Dr. Serageldin notes: "We [at the World Bank] can measure opportunity in terms of at least four kinds of capital: man-made, natural, human, and social."[10] He approaches the dialogue on sustainability by defining it "in terms of capital per capita that we leave to future generations." By means of this construct he has created balance sheets for national accounts not only in terms of material wealth and fiscal accountability, but also for a nation's social and cultural wealth.

He stretches traditional World Bank thinking by publishing this new accounting method for 192 countries in *Monitoring Environmental Progress* (World Bank, 1995) and *Sustainability and the Wealth of Nations: First Steps in an Ongoing Journey.*[11] According to this system, man-made capital is "less than 20 percent of the total wealth" and "most wealth is in human and social capital."[12] Thus the importance of primarily investing in people is self-evident. This new dialogue is well beyond the traditional questions of the geo-biophysical sciences. It legitimizes and expands the values discussion within the ecology-economics-ethics "trialogue," and gives greater hope for this new direction in the public conversation leading to better sustainable development policy.[13]

THE AMERICAN ROOTS OF A GLOBAL ECO-ETHIC: TRACING EMERGING ENVIRONMENTAL CONSCIOUSNESS AND ETHICAL VALUES

One of the first questions that appeared when the environmental crisis was identified as an ethical issue in the 1960s at the World Council of Churches New Delhi Conference was the following: Is there an environmental ethics tradition within the religious community, in particular, within the Judaeo-Christian heritage? If so, how has it impacted the present situation? Can it be drawn on to influence future policy? Lynn White Jr. weighed in negatively, accusing the Judaeo-Christian tradition of being antienvironmental.[14] White declared that the "domination" theory of the Bible (Genesis) led to the Western World's rape of nature. A number of theologians and ethicists refuted White's central thesis; they examined the Judaeo-Christian tradition in much greater detail and found significant themes which support a strong environmental ethic. This led to a clearer refutation of White's accusation in the 1980s, a period which witnessed growing Christian involvement in the environmental question.

From the early sixties the Christian community has expressed its concern ecumenically at a number of international and regional conferences beginning with Lutheran theologian Joseph Sittler's famous "Call to Unity" speech in 1961 in India at the World Council of Churches (WCC) Assembly. In Seoul, Korea, at the WCC 1990 World Convocation on Justice, Peace and the Integrity of Creation, the theme of environmental ethics came into the global spotlight. Out of this came the theme of "Creation as Beloved of God."[15] This convocation was followed in February, 1991, by the WCC Seventh World Assembly in Australia whose theme "Come Holy Spirit—

Renew the Whole Creation!" affirmed the severity of the environmental crisis and the ecological responsibility of the churches. Within the Catholic Church during the late 1980s, Pope John Paul II began to make significant comments on environmental development concerns in his encyclical letter *On Social Concerns* and in his 1990 World Day of Peace statement entitled "Peace with God the Creator, Peace with All Creation."[16]

Following the 1986 Assisi gathering of representatives from five major world religions making declarations on "Man and Nature," a number of inter-religious conferences have been held.[17] These include the May 1990 Intercontinental Conference on Caring for Creation in Washington, D.C., and the September 1990 Symposium on Spirit and Nature at Middlebury College in Vermont. In 1995 the "Ethics and Spiritual Values" Symposium was an associated event of the Third Annual World Bank Conference on Environmentally Sustainable Development.[18]

The rise of eco-ethical consciousness and the attempts to educate the public and form public policy should be cited. To detect this tradition of ethical concern, we must go back a century. Wallace Stegner traces the early North American interest in earth ethics to its beginnings as a reaction to the encroaching industrialized civilization. These early critiques were offered by "nineteenth century travelers, philosophers, artists, writers, divines, natural historians . . . whose purpose was to know [the earth], celebrate it, and *savor its beauty and rightness.*"[19] This is evident also in the parade of historic witnesses from Emerson and Thoreau to the important contribution of George Perkins Marsh, an environmental pioneer, best known for his publication *Man and Nature* (1864). This work was revised and brought out again in 1874 under the title of *The Earth as Modified by Human Action.*[20] Marsh challenged the industrial captains of America's late nineteenth century for their fixation on the "endless resources" of the frontier that they ruthlessly plundered.

Along with other trailblazers, Marsh founded the American Forestry Association in hopes of influencing the public. By the 1870s Americans were beginning to revere pristine natural settings and to recognize a special value in wilderness areas. Public concern inspired a rider to the General Revision Act authorizing the President of the United States to set aside "forest reserves on the Public Domain." With the help of his chief forester Gifford Pinchot, President Theodore Roosevelt took advantage of this law and designated twenty-one new forests, or national preserves, totaling sixteen million acres.[21]

This outlines a recurring strategy in secular environmental thought and action. First, an influential and charismatic figure discerns a problem. Then, a group forms around this prophetic individual or his ideas with considerable press attention. As awareness rises among the public, Congress begins to feel political pressure and enacts needed legislation so that a new body of regulatory law protecting some aspect of nature grows up. This pattern was seen in such environmental pioneers as George Bird Grinnell and F. V. Hayden. After Hayden came the renowned public environmental educator and activist John Muir, who single-handedly organized the Sierra Club and inspired the creation of Yosemite, Sequoia, and Grant National Parks. By 1916 thirteen national parks had been established, and in that same year the National Parks Act put in writing the purpose of such park reserves: public use and enjoyment without impairment. These public parks greatly helped to make Americans and others around the world more aware of environmental values; they embody a powerful form of public education concerning the value of the natural world.

Three additional moments in this developing moral awareness are important to understand our present approach to environmental ethical education and formation of public policy in North America.

First, in 1949 Aldo Leopold's *A Sand County Almanac* was published posthumously, explicating, at long last, ethical principles for the conservation movement. As Stegner points out in his article, "It All Began with Conservation," that in the time since its publication "*A Sand County Almanac* has become a kind of holy book in environmental circles."[22] Second, the contemporary environmental movement dates itself from the 1962 publication of Rachel Carson's *Silent Spring*. This shocking disclosure of DDT pollution reoriented environmental efforts away from predominant attention to preservation issues toward a wide-ranging concern for environmental pollution. It gave rise to an emerging environmental awareness that led to Earth Day 1970 and the creation of the Environmental Protection Agency. Finally, with the 1996 publication of *Our Stolen Future*, another very important stage of this same movement has appeared. This volume attempts to move the American public to a new stage of awareness and catalyze public policy, similar to that of the antitobacco movement, by noting the toxic effects of human technology. The recent findings of the impact of toxins on genes and immune systems underscore the need for a renewed effort for an eco-ethical dialogue and a new stage of public education.[23]

These scientific and environmental efforts have laid a foundation for undertaking a new ecological education initiative within the religious community and in the public arena.

A NEW CONTEXT FOR ECO-EDUCATION: EMERGING EVOLUTIONARY CONSCIOUSNESS AND SUSTAINABLE COMMUNITIES

Working from a holistic perspective, both the social crisis and the ecological crisis follow the late modern world's mechanistic world view and result from this antienvironmental perspective. According to cultural and social philosopher Joe Holland, the devastation of the poor is the human prototype of the wider devastation of the total biosphere. He thinks of this as a sort of "early warning system" for the entire human community.[24] Strategically the breakdown of the natural and human ecologies may be calling attention to the possible "breakthrough" into a postmodern, regenerative world view and a new global-local culture undergridding the sustainable communities of the future.

To get a true perspective, the educator, communicator, or preacher attempting to influence the public must look deeper than the public education strategies of the late modern industrial era. The reasons for this are multiple. First, ever since Marshall

McLuhan's insights of the 1960s, it has been clearer each decade that we stand at the beginning of a new communications revolution and its concomitant political reality. This electronic era has just begun to impact our daily life.

Second, cultural analysts such as Alvin Toffler have followed with insistence that the magnitude of the present transformation goes qualitatively beyond the two prior sociotechnological shifts of the agriculture revolution of the late neolithic era and the modern mechanized revolution of the industrial era. Finally many contend that the postmodern experience also leaves the past nine thousand years of patriarchal domination, which followed an earlier, more matriarchal era. Thomas Berry and Brian Swimme contend that we are rapidly leaving the Cenozoic Era and replacing it with a new era they name the "Ecozoic," when humans become the aware dimension of the planet's consciousness. I prefer the term "Ecosymbolic Era" as human conscious is being transformed by the cybernetic environment of multimedia computer networking that mimics natural ecosystems.

In this new era humans are seen to interrelate with the planet's ecosystems through sustainable values embodied in cultural symbols and ecofriendly technologies. Therefore, an ecosymbolic equilibrium must be struck within the total system, which is at present out of balance with serious species loss, climate change, and rapid consumption of vital resources. These transitions of the sociocultural context form a "Gestalt" or multidimensional configuration which radically changes the way we must approach public education and any significant earth stewardship ministry effort. Yet this must be done at a time which is often skeptical of even scientifically verified information regarding the condition of the planet and thus disregards the ethical responsibilities humans have for the state of the environment.

To grasp these symbolic changes the historical perspective of the present transformation must be noted. The primal society's "oral language" shift empowered small, familial bands to be formed into larger organic tribal communities which gave great value to the immanence of the Divine in nature or creation. This was followed by classical and medieval society's methods of communicating more and more through the handwriting delivered in patriarchal decrees (laws) and authoritative teachings (dogmas) which emphasize Divine Transcendence. By the 1700s, the classical cultures of the first axial age began to give way to the modern era's printed word, which has dominated through the middle of this century.

With radio, television, and now computerized internet access to information of confusing quality, postmodern humans of the electronic era are perplexed and paralyzed by instant news, genetic manipulation of life forms, and profound changes reflected in the social means of communication. This "media" shift is global and local simultaneously; it involves the rise of new mega-cities and the flight back to the electronic village away from the industrial centers of the city. The city or "civitas" has been the mainstay and basis of civilization up to now; the future is much more ambiguous.

IMPACTING THE COMMUNITY: ECO-EDUCATIONAL MODELS BASED ON A NEW DIALOGUE BETWEEN SCIENCE AND RELIGION

We now turn from foundations in science, economics, and history to education, ministry, and communications by looking at three approaches to eco-educational programs. The educational strategies considered here deal with congregational models, bioregional approaches, and community-centered programs. For theological and higher education models I refer to the following chapter and to the on-going work of the National Association for Science, Technology, and Society.

1. *First, the congregationally based ministry models*—from simple one-time Earth Day programs to sophisticated interdisciplinary ecoministry projects—all have in common the entry into ecoeducation through the local congregation, synagogue, or parish. These can take a variety of forms from convocations, seminars, and workshops to more extensive adult education and retreat programs. To give the

reader an idea of the range and possible approaches of this type of eco-educational pedagogy, the following review of introductory materials from five recent models or formats for congregational use is presented here. They are also commonly available and provide educators with the various types of introductory resources needed to enter this emerging area of environmentally oriented religious education.

The first is the *Introductory Packet for Environmental Mission and Ministry*, which has been produced by the North American Coalition on Religion and Ecology (NACRE). This packet is intended to give the local congregation resources to initiate ecoministry as an ongoing part of its mission and to make use of a five-step process it can employ to introduce a one- to three-year program. The five steps or stages of the NACRE "Caring for Creation" process are: (1) *discovery*, which engages the public (individual or group) to see anew the eco-ethical issues of earth stewardship and sustainability; (2) *exploration*, which introduces the connection of earth-values to wider stories (religious tradition and scientific context); (3) *integration*, which celebrates creation in terms of preaching and worship through which commitment to ecovalues and mission emerges; (4) *empowerment*, which forms and trains leaders within the congregation or community to carry out ecoministry or public mission; and (5) *eco-action*, which undertakes environmental activities through actual models of sustaining, restoring, and regenerating the earth.

With this packet of resources designed for the introductory year when the ecoministry team is formed and initiates a "Caring for Creation" program, the foundation is laid for two subsequent years of local community involvement. During the second year the ecoministry and education team involves the whole congregation as a creation-centered community. In the third year, when the congregation reaches out to the surrounding interfaith community and bioregion through eco-action projects, public policy formation becomes the crucial focus.[25]

The second resource, entitled *God's Earth Our Home*, is a mainstream Protestant packet, designed by the National Council of Churches' Unit on Economic and Environmental Justice. The packet is designed to be used in a twelve-session meeting process, but can be successfully adapted to about five sessions within an adult or youth education series. The material for the sessions falls under four main headings: "Theological Affirmations," "Our Economy and the Environment," "Renewal of Community Ministry," and "God's Call, Our Response," which shows how to become a model congregation.[26]

The third resource packet was introduced by the United States Catholic Conference following the USCC Bishops' pastoral letter *Renewing the Earth* (1993) and is titled *Renewing the Face of the Earth*. In addition to the pastoral letter as a study document, the packet includes materials for a whole range of pastoral activities within the local parish community: suggestions for initiating parish programs; liturgical, homiletic, and prayer aides; parish bulletin inserts; and an order form for a special video entitled "Hope for a Renewed Earth." In 1995 a follow-up packet and video were published by the USCC Office of Environmental Justice called *The Earth Is the Lord's*. This subsequent resource includes the message of Pope John Paul II, "Peace with God the Creator, Peace with All Creation," environmental justice materials, parish committee planning ideas, additional homily helps, and answers to difficult questions.[27]

The fourth resource, *Let the Earth Be Glad,* was assembled and published by the Evangelical Environmental Network. This biblically based packet helps the local community reflect on the ecological stewardship dimensions of the Scriptures and to respond to the environmental crises of our time. The packet contains four themes: Biblical Roots—Theological Foundations for Caring for God's Creation; Seeds of Worship—Tools for Worshipping the Creator through His Handiwork; Fruits of Creation—The Provisions and Abuses of God's Good Creation; and Supporting Branches: An Evangelical Declaration on Care of Creation.[28]

The fifth resource comes from the Jewish community. It is called *To Till and to Tend: A Guide to Jewish Environmental Study and Action*. This collection of articles from Conservative, Orthodox, Reform, and Reconstructionist viewpoints also contains guidelines for nineteen environmental projects and programs for different age groups and an annotated list of books, videos, and other informational aides. This is complemented by a very practical but well constructed handbook done by a Shomrei Adamah regional committee, called *The Green Shalom Guide*.[29]

These five models contain a range of scientific and theological materials. They offer resources adapted to the practical teaching, ministry, and outreach needs. They display considerable respect for the scientific data while making the necessary adaptations and applications for community learning.

2. A *second type of model or paradigm in eco-education* approaches the topic from a bioregional perspective that is deeply ecumenical or interfaith oriented. One example of this is the NACRE "Homes for Appalachia" project that builds on the bioregional ecocrises with a clear concern for ecojustice as well as ecostewardship. This is an approach based on pastoral teachings on Appalachia. Both Methodist and Catholic bishops have written excellent messages which include ecojustice. The need now is to form a pastoral approach that bridges the impoverished areas of Appalachia and the affluent suburbs of the East Coast. NACRE took the theme of sustainable housing as a necessary part of sustainable community development. Here a five-part adult eco-education program presents the bioregional issues and how to minister to the ecoregion.

The pastoral message *At Home in the Web of Life* actually provides the connections between Christian environmental and social teaching found in the Bible and tradition with the bioregional history as successive human groups have settled in this mountainous region of eastern North America.[30] This document has successfully dealt with complex integration of the various cultural, ecological, economic, ecojustice, and theological issues by using this interdisciplinary method. It sets forth the theme of "sustainable communities" by defining them as "communities where people and the rest of nature can live together in harmony and not rob future generations."[31] It explains that creating such communities is urgent because of recent social and ecological disasters. As the industrial age of Appalachia with its steel mills and coal mines is ending, a new era of economics influenced by the electronic revolution is approaching. The downside is marked with a series of disasters: large-scale unemployment; the demise of many small businesses; clear-cutting of forests; destructive strip-mining; dumping of out-of-state garbage, including toxic chemicals and radioactive materials; and warehousing of prisoners from the unsustainable cities of the East Coast. While acknowledging these problems, the document notes the creative voices of many people who yearn for an alternative and sustainable future. It outlines the choice, based on the Bible and church ecosocial teachings, between a culture of death and a culture of life in which the social and natural ecology is respected and cherished. The document is divided into three sections, namely, the land and its people, the Bible and the church's teaching, and the call of the Spirit to action. Each section demonstrates how to communicate the eco-ethical message based on sound scientific, economic, and cultural analysis.

3. A *third educational model* is the "Gateway City" model or strategy with an ecumenical approach for dealing with the ecoproblems of the city and its surrounding biocultural region. One example of this is the "Solar Energy for Sustainable Communities" (SESC) program as part of the NACRE Solar Stewardship Initiative (SSI). This is designed to introduce a bioregion to a stewardship ethic in three stages. First, the program begins with the formation of a local or bioregional steering committee consisting of business leaders, leaders from religious and educational institutions, and environmentally minded citizens. An introductory program is offered to promote the concept of renewable solar energy as a "breakthrough" sustainable technology now available. A college, seminary, or ecologically minded retreat center can be suitable for cosponsoring the seminar, which is designed to attract potential leaders to become educated in the new technologies. After one or two initial seminars introducing earth stewardship and sustainable community, a special workshop is planned to train those recruited from the first-session leaders in the skills of installing photovoltaics, solar thermal hot water panels, and other active and passive solar technologies. These

can be installed in churches or institutional settings as models for local demonstration to attract others to the second and subsequent stages of the project.

At the second stage the steering committee is expanded to form a regional (or gateway city) committee to advise, raise program funds, and promote the importance of the new solar technologies for ethical, economic and ecological reasons. At this stage a business or large institutional model is equipped with the new technology after a special evaluation and strategy process. With the completion of the second stage, preparation for the third stage is undertaken through a steering committee and a local coordinator. The goal of this stage is to integrate sustainable stewardship values into the regional planning effort with the wider introduction of solar energy and the subsequent introduction of new communication and planning technologies. This effort results in intersectoral planning for a sustainable community for five, ten, and twenty years ahead and introduces practical implementation of the sustainable ethics as essential (not peripheral) to the community development process, which has often involves unprincipled efforts by developers and financial institutions. Two examples of this process are the "Solar Energy for Sustainable Communities" projects in Grand Rapids, Michigan, at the Dominican Educational Center and in Greensboro, North Carolina, at the Beloved Community Center.[32] At the local community level the full process leads to making concrete the generalizations of *Agenda 21*, the *Sustainable America Report* of the President's Council on Sustainable Development, and the Earth Charter process.[33]

CONCLUSION

In the process of working through the complexities of earth stewardship and sustainable community development theory and principles to implement the practical stages of public education, leadership training, and regional planning, a much clearer ethical and ecological understanding is being achieved. Although many imperfect models and strategies exist, in the long run effective strategies are becoming evident through a more concrete and process-oriented way of continuing the dialogue among the different groups associated with environmental concern. These often unrelated groups within society must find ways to apply the ethics of earth stewardship and the principles of environmental sustainability or we face more social and ecological "breakdown" which is already threatening large regions of the earth.

NOTES

1. Cf. Hans Kung, *Global Responsibility: In Search of a New World Ethic* (Crossroads: New York, 1994) and Steven C. Rockefeller, *Principles of Environmental Conservation and Sustainable Development: Summary and Survey*, unpublished study for the Earth Charter project (April, 1996).

2. Union of Concerned Scientists, "World Scientists' Warning to Humanity" (1992).

3. Cf. The Human Dimensions of Global Change Conference, November 1991, Washington, D.C., cosponsored by several scientific organizations, including AAAS, wherein the "human prospect" terminology is being used.

4. William C. Clark, "Managing Planet Earth," *Scientific American* 261, no. 3. (September 1996), 47–54. This summary article introduces a special issue which is now reprinted as a book.

5. Cf. World Commission on Environment and Development, *Our Common Future* (New York: United Nations Publications, 1987).

6. Statement by Maurice F. Strong, Secretary General UNCED, Opening Session of UNCED, 3 June 1992, Rio de Janeiro, Brazil (Geneva: United Nations Press Office), p. 12.

7. Cf. James Weaver, "Economics, Development, and Environmental Issues" (prepared for the NACRE Chautauqua Symposium and UNCED Preparatory Meeting, April 1991).

8. Ibid.

9. Herman Daly and John Cobb Jr., *For the Common Good: Redirecting the Economy Toward Community, the Environment, and a Sustainable Future* (Boston: Beacon Press, 1989), p. 6.

10. Thomas Berry, "Economics as a Religious Issue," in *The Dream of the Earth* (San Francisco: Sierra Club Books, 1988), chap. 7, p. 71.

11. Cf. Ismail Serageldin and Richard Barrett, eds., *Ethics and Spiritual Values* (Washington, D.C.: World Bank Publications, 1996), p. 5.

12. See *World Bank Publications, ESD Studies and Monograph Series*, no. 5 (Washington, D.C., 1996).

13. Ibid.

14. Cf. D. B. Conroy, ed., *Eco-Ethics and Economics: A Report on the Chautauqua Symposium on Ecology, Ecumenics, and Economics* (Washington, D.C.: NACRE, 1991).

15. Cf. Lynn White, "The Historic Roots of Our Ecologic Crisis," *Science* 155 (1967): 1203–07.

16. Note that in 1979 at MIT the WCC Conference on Faith, Science, and the Future made mention of ecological concerns. See Paul Abrecht and Roger Shinn, eds., *Faith and Science in an Unjust World* (Geneva: WCC Publications, 1980).

17. See appendices of *And God Saw That It Was Good*, ed. Drew Christiansen and Walter Grazer (Washington, D.C.: USCC, 1996) for texts of John Paul II's and various documents issued by Catholic bishops conferences, including those of Australia, the Dominican Republic, Guatemala, Northern Italy, and the Philippines, pp. 211ff. Also cf. Stratford Caldecott, "Christian Ecology," *Catholic International Report* (August-September 1996), pp. 29–36, for an analysis of the Catholic papal teaching on ecology.

18. See *The Assisi Declarations* to which were later added Ba'hai and Sikh declarations (Geneva: WCC Publications, 1987).

19. Cf. Ismail Serageldin and Richard Barrett, eds., *Ethics and Spiritual Values, Environmentally Sustainable Development Series*, no. 12, (Washington, D.C.: The World Bank, 1996).

20. Emphasis mine. Cf. Wallace Stegner, "It All Began with Conservation," *Smithsonian* 21, no. 1 (1990): 35.

21. Cf. ibid., Stegner's marvelous description of this polymath from Vermont who first began in earnest to trace how primitive humans lived on the land.

22. Threatened by a congressional override of his prerogative, Roosevelt quickly completed his work with Pinchot and then signed into law the bill which would have stopped him. "It All Began With Conservation," p. 43.

23. Cf. Theo Colburn, Dianne Dumanoski, and John Peterson Myers, *Our Stolen Future* (New York: Dutton, 1996) which notes that toxins are affecting a wide range of human health problems from increased cancer to low sperm count.

24. From unpublished writings of Dr. Joe Holland, professor of ethics and philosophy, University of St. Thomas, Miami, Florida.

25. To obtain this, contact NACRE Resources, 5 Thomas Circle, NW, Washington, DC 20005, and request the NACRE "Introductory Packet for Environmental Mission and Ministry," or see www.caringforcreation.net

26. To obtain this, contact FaithQuest, 1451 Dundee Avenue, Elgin IL 60120.

27. To obtain this, contact USCC Publishing Services, 3211 Fourth Street, NE, Washington, DC 20017-1194.

28. To obtain this, contact The Evangelical Environmental Network, 10 East Lancaster Avenue, Wynnewood, PA 19096-3495.

29. To obtain *To Till and to Tend*, contact The Coalition on Environment and Jewish Life, 443 Park Avenue South, 11th Floor, New York, NY 10016. For *The Green Shalom Guide: A How-to Manual for Greening Local Jewish Synagogues, Schools, and Offices*, ed. Naomi Friedman and De Fischer Herman, contact Shomrei Adamah, 706 Erie Ave., Takoma Park, MD 20912.

30. Catholic Bishops of Appalachia, *At Home in the Web of Life* (Catholic Committee of Appalachia, 1995 [second printing, January 1996]). To obtain it, contact Cath. Com. of Appalachia, P.O. Box 662, Webester Springs, WV 26288.

31. Ibid., p. 3.

32. See *EcoLetter*, spring-summer 1996 (Washington, D.C.: NACRE): 8ff.

33. Cf. PCSD, *Sustainable America: A New Consensus* (Washington, D.C.: U.S. Government Printing Office, 1996).

QUESTIONS FOR DISCUSSION

1. How does the contemporary cultural transformation impacted by the electronic media affect the choices or strategies the eco-educator, preacher, or policy advocate makes when they deal with the global consumerist society of the twenty-first century?

2. Why must the science-religion dialogue be further extended to the social, historical, and economic disciplines? And how can this dialogue be approached within academic institutions and professional associations as well as congregations?

3. What types of generational and social groups within a community or congregation are more likely to respond to new ecologically sustainable approaches to earth stewardship and environmental regeneration?

4. What learning activities can be used on secular and religious days, which commemorate environmental themes or heroes, such as Earth Day (April 22), UN Environment Day (June 5), the Feast of St. Francis of Assisi (October 4), and similarly designated occasions, to deepen a public understanding of ecological issues and values?

12

GREENING THE CAMPUS
Transforming Higher Education to Care for the Environment

Richard M. Clugston

A new academic paradigm is beginning to take shape in theological education and in higher education generally. This paradigm emphasizes a deeply ecological understanding of human nature; an appreciation of spiritual as well as material reality; and a commitment to reorient the curriculum, operations, and outreach of academic disciplines and institutions in order to create just and sustainable communities. This chapter sketches the substance of this new paradigm and explores how it is taking root in a range of disciplines and institutions.[1]

A PARADIGM SHIFT IN ACADEMIC KNOWLEDGE

Thomas Kuhn in *The Structure of Scientific Revolutions* defined paradigms in two ways. In his broader definition, a paradigm is the set of fundamental assumptions concerning the nature of reality and the good life. The narrower sense of paradigm is a practical model for translating this broad world view into a particular knowledge-finding or problem-solving model.[2] For example, if we assume reality is only matter/energy forming complex structures through natural selection, then subjectivity is epiphenomenal and, in a sense, absurd. The good life is maximizing short-term gratification and minimizing immediate pain in a soulless universe. An hour of prime time television programming is paradigmatic, in the narrow sense, of this world view. It translates these basic assumptions into a formula for an hour of entertainment, catering effectively to short-term gratification, arousing us with sex and violence, and concentrating on the exploits of the "fittest" celebrities and action heroes. So, too, do our experimental research designs (or classroom designs) express practically the fundamental assumptions of the dominant world view.

Paradigms do shift, however. If we were highly educated Europeans at the end of the fifteenth century, we would have assumed our Terra Firma to be the center of the universe. Our own life as a microcosm would have been full of correspondences with the larger macrocosm—all of which was filled with divine presence and intention. The cosmos was an organic whole in which we should find our divinely appointed place. The world view that would later come to dominate the modern era—mechanistic, probabilistic, existentially absurd, utilitarian, and individualistic—would be unimaginable, as would the technologies and social enterprises spawned by this world view. The scientific and industrial revolutions radically transformed the guiding assumptions, as well as the technological expressions, of higher learning.

We are now undergoing a revolution in paradigms. The fundamental assumptions that have organized the modern project are being questioned, and alternative philosophical and practical positions are being developed as paradigmatic for the consolidation of a new relationship to nature.

PARADIGM SHIFTS

Kuhn describes the process by which fundamental "paradigm" shifts occur in basic assumptions about the nature of reality as well as the resulting research and technical applications. He describes the phases of such a shift:

1. Significant problems are discovered in the old paradigm. These are outcomes not predicted by the theoretical model, yet which become increasingly apparent and difficult to ignore.

2. A new theoretical frame is offered which accounts for the anomalies, is more elegant, rings true, and provides real solutions. It acquires a critical mass of advocates who organize politically to alter the assumptions and orientation of the field. The crisis is resolved through a paradigm shift.

3. The new orientation is developed into a highly articulated and applied system of what Kuhn calls normal science. The new assumptions, once seen as controversial, are accepted as given and fade into the background. The new paradigm is institutionalized.[3]

We are just beginning to glimpse the major features of a new, postmodern paradigm. Yet, its theoretical assumptions and practical experiments are coming into being and slowly being consolidated. Thomas Berry makes the case that our critical social task is to rework our policies, institutions, and professions to contribute to mutually enhancing human-earth relationships.[4] Al Gore argues that concern for the earth should become the central organizing principle of government deliberations and policy.[5]

While such voices have not been heeded in the popular arena of talk shows, sound bites, and short-term budget decisions, there are many individuals working to reshape their professional activities to promote a sustainable future. The work of academics is particularly important in articulating this new knowledge. Within academia there are many hopeful developments suggesting the emergence of a deeply ecological paradigm. Such developments are occurring in three major, interconnected areas: the basic work of academic disciplines; the transformation of teaching and learning, including a focus on the administration and operations of the campus; and new forms of general education. The following describes the scope and provides some examples of academics' efforts in these three areas.

1. Paradigm Changes in Academic Disciplines

Many academic disciplines as well as entire institutions are beginning to experience major paradigm shifts. Academic work—research, teaching and service—is organized by disciplines such as psychology, engineering, and theology. It is the responsibility of eminent scholars in each of the disciplines to define what is understood and appropriate to pursue within them. The department is the local, campus-based manifestation of the discipline. What is taught in these local places is largely determined by the current body of fact and theory accepted by the disciplines. Academics move from campus to campus but remain in their disciplinary field. Thus, "greening" higher education depends significantly on the active engagement of disciplinary leaders in promoting ecologically sensitive theory and sustainable practices as central to the scope and mission of their fields (e.g., in peer review criteria for journal articles and in the themes and organization of professional associations).

Many of the best and brightest in their fields are waking up to the nature of the ecocrisis and are engaged in transforming their disciplines at both the national and local (campus) levels. Members of various professional associations have started special interest groups, divisions, or sections focused on environment and sustainability. For example, the American Institute of Architects (AIA) made sustainability a central theme of its 1993 annual conference, and sponsored a sustainable design competition. The AIA also provides an environmental education program for teachers called "Learning by Design." The American Planning Association and the American Academy of Management both have formed special interest groups. The American Academy of Religion has an ecology and religion section.

Professional journals are emerging, such as the *Journal of Interdisciplinary Studies in Literature and Environment* (*ISLE*) provides a forum for critical studies of the literary and performing arts proceeding from or addressing environmental considerations, including ecological theory, conceptions of nature and their depictions, the human/nature dichotomy, and related concerns.[6]

The Tufts Environmental Literacy Institute (TELI) Faculty Development Program is an example of a national effort to green disciplines and teaching. TELI's program provides university faculty members in disciplines ranging from drama to engineering design with the opportunity to weave environmental issues into their courses. For example, in economics, students taking "Economics and Policy" are paired up with staff from the university's operations division to explore the potential costs and benefits of solar energy, energy efficiency measures, and alternative fuels for campus ecology and economy. In history, students in "Time, Nature, and Humanity: Historical Perspectives on Global Ecologies" explore the evolution and development of the environment and ecosystems over time, and how they have shaped and influenced human history (ULSF, 1996). Other institutions such as St. Mary's College of Maryland have developed similar initiatives to encourage faculty members to build environmental concerns into their courses at the local level.

In reflecting on the changes that need to take place in management theory as taught in business schools, Thomas Gladwin, in the October issue of *The Academy of Management Journal*, asserts that, "since the Enlightenment, we have progressively differentiated humanity from the rest of nature, and separated objective truth from subjective morality. The greatest challenge of postmodernity may reside in their reintegration. A similar challenge may exist for theories of management."[7]

In parallel ways, special interest groups in many fields are coalescing to change their core assumptions and practice models. The American Institute of Architecture, in one of the most comprehensive professional ethics efforts, adopted the Hannover Principles to govern the planning and design of the built environment. These principles lay out the following design imperatives:

- Insist on the right of humanity and nature to coexist in a healthy, supportive, diverse, and sustainable condition.
- Recognize interdependence. The elements of human design

interact with and depend on the natural world, with broad and diverse implications at every scale. Expand design considerations to recognizing even distant effects.

- Respect relationships between spirit and matter. Consider all aspects of human settlement including community, dwelling, industry, and trade in terms of existing and evolving connections between spiritual and material consciousness.

- Accept responsibility for the consequences of design decisions upon human well-being, the viability of natural systems, and their right to coexist.

- Create safe objects of long-term value. Do not burden future generations with requirements for maintenance or vigilant administration of potential danger due to the careless creations of products, processes, or standards.

- Eliminate the concept of waste. Evaluate and optimize the full life cycle of products and processes, to approach the state of natural systems in which there is no waste.

- Rely on natural energy flows. Human designs should, like the living world, derive their creative forces from their perpetual solar income. Incorporate this energy efficiently and safely for responsible use.

- Understand the limitations of design. No human creation lasts forever and design does not solve all problems. Those who create and plan should practice humility in the face of nature. Treat nature as a model and mentor, not an inconvenience to be evaded or controlled.

- Seek constant improvements by sharing knowledge. Encourage direct and open communication between colleagues, patrons, manufacturers, and users to link long-term sustainable considerations with ethical responsibility, and reestablish the integral relationship between natural processes and human activity.[8]

These principles formed the foundation of the "Declaration of Interdependence for a Sustainable Future," adopted by the World Congress of the International Union of Architects (UIA) and the

American Institute of Architects (AIA) in June 1993. This declaration committed its members to place environmental and social sustainability at the core of practices and professional responsibilities, to improve standards for sustainable design, and to ensure that the existing and future built environment be up to sustainable design standards.[9]

In the management and architecture examples above, and in many more, the focus is to shift the fundamental value assumptions and the practice models of these fields to recognize the embeddedness, interconnectedness, shared subjectivity of humans and nature, and to link spirit and matter. Guidance for the ecologically sensitive reform of any discipline is given by Jim Nash: (1) Revisiting the discipline's body of knowledge to draw forth its ecological potential, and to guide it towards its ecological horizons. (2) Reorienting the discipline toward an earth ethic so that its code of conduct includes respecting and assisting the whole community of life. This involves affirming the centrality of sustainability as defined by the norms of equity, bioreponsibility, and frugality. (3) Integrating spiritual, ethical, and scientific understandings into a coherent picture of a meaningful reality in which we actualize our vocation. While we should frame hypotheses humbly and seek empirical disconfirmation, we must also open our hearts and minds to the deeper mystery and meaning of existence. (4) Recognizing that knowledge is not value-neutral, but shaped and utilized by social systems with particular interests. Thus we are responsible to critically reflect on the ends our knowledge serves, and to ensure it contributes to desirable public ends, e.g., sustainability in personal lifestyles, communities (including the academy), and political systems.[10]

2. Pedagogy and Campus Design

Much of the recent criticism of higher education attacks it for failing to prepare students to perform in the information age. This critique asserts that decent jobs in the twenty-first century will require people who are extremely adaptable, possessing higher order, symbolic skills. Colleges and universities are faulted not so much for what they teach, since specific facts and skills soon become obsolete—but for how they teach. The lecture format and multiple choice test promote the passive absorption of material, thus imparting the wrong aptitudes.

Students need to be engaged and actively learning, working in teams to solve problems and create products (since that is what real work entails). Reform in this context emphasizes setting clear and high expectations for mastery of learning objectives, and then encouraging faculty and students, often in cooperation with real-world settings, to figure out the best way to accomplish these objectives. Active learning engages students constantly and consistently in discussing and processing information. Pursuing a range of learning paths (other than lecturing, reading, multiple choice testing) also allows people with different learning styles to thrive.

The impetus for such reform is not "preserving the planet," but preparing students to succeed in a global community where knowledge doubles each six years and technologies and jobs change rapidly. A variety of postsecondary institutions have implemented broad-based, active, and experimental learning programs—some, such as Prescott and Goddard Colleges, with environmental foci. Teaching and learning is being reshaped by the introduction of computers (with CD-ROM), interactive television, and other technologies.

David Orr describes the buildings, grounds, and daily operations of our colleges and universities as a "crystallized pedagogy," embodying the economics, psychology, sociology, aesthetics, and so on, of these institutions.[11] The central concern here is that institutional members are conscious of the extent to which their practices contribute to a sustainable future. Particularly important is the linkage of academic research and coursework to the functioning of the institution. Two examples of institutions which have made strong commitments to model sustainable ways of living are the Center for Regenerative Studies at California State Polytech and the Slippery Rock University Master of Science in Sustainable Systems.

According to the director of the Center for Regenerative Studies, the "idea is to create a community in which students and faculty members learn about and demonstrate sustainable and regenerative systems." The students are focused on energy efficiency, alternative sources of energy, sustainable food production, and, most importantly, changes in lifestyle habits which "don't destroy ourselves." All of the students living in the center must minor in regenerative studies and commit to doing the necessary chores.[12]

Slippery Rock's programs in agroecology, built environment, and energy and resource management utilize an on-campus site demonstrating responsible renewable energy use, building design, and landscaping and sustainable agriculture. These systems mimic the diversity, stability, and resilience of natural systems demonstrating the sustainable provision of food, energy, and shelter. Sustainable community development is the leading edge of planning and design. As Rees comments, "The postwar pattern of Western urban development is not only ecologically unconscionable but economically inefficient and socially inequitable. In contrast, sustainable development implies that the use of energy and materials be in balance with such 'natural capital' processes as photosynthesis and waste assimilation."[13]

These—and many other schools—are putting in place sustainable food, shelter, and transportation systems. This involves using community gardens and/or community-supported agriculture, and other local products, as much as possible. It also encourages building (or remodeling) the campus to create "ecovillages" incorporating more solar design, cluster housing, wildlife areas, and less automobile-based transportation; socially and environmentally responsible investments; recycling; reducing disposables; carpooling; and participatory, inclusive decision making. Universities such as Tufts, Brown, Bucknell, and many others have extensive greening initiatives.[14]

Campus Ecology: A Guide to Assessing Environmental Quality and Creating Strategies for Change and *Green Guide: A User's Guide to Sustainable Development for Canadian Colleges* offer students, faculty members, and administrators tools to transform their campuses into more sustainable environments. *Campus Ecology* was written by a group of former students at UCLA who undertook an extensive audit of campus practices and developed a set of strategies to reduce energy and water use as well as the amount of solid waste. This book provides a comprehensive audit guide for assessing current campus practices in paper recycling, investments, waste disposal, pesticide use, and so forth. It gives background information on each of these areas and provides case studies of institutions that have developed innovative ways of becoming more environmentally friendly. Currently this book is being distributed by the Campus Ecology Program of the National Wildlife Federation (NWF), which also offers consultation and support to campuses seeking to become green. NWF's Campus Ecology Program has also published a more detailed guide to encourage administrators and faculty to green their campuses, titled *Ecodemia: Campus Environmental Stewardship at the Turn of the Twenty-first Century.*[15]

The *Green Guide* is the product of a joint effort of the Canadian National Roundtable on the Environment and the Economy and the Association of Canadian Community Colleges. It provides a framework for understanding the nature and urgency of creating environmentally sustainable colleges. Its case studies illustrate the diversity of initiatives taken by community colleges to respond to the environmental challenge, including those in renewable resources, environmental management, and sustainable development. The guide also provides a range of tools and resources that can be used to green any institution.

These guides provide complementary perspectives for understanding the scope and process of greening a college or university. The *Green Guide* emphasizes sustainable development and illustrates how community colleges can develop both campus operations and training programs to promote it. *Campus Ecology* encourages students to understand and improve campus operations. Neither delves far into restructuring the curricula of postsecondary institutions to provide the philosophical understanding for changing our relationships to the planet. But both provide many practical steps institutions can take to improve those relationships.

3. *"Post-modern" General and Professional Education*

Constructive, postmodern general education affirms a deeply eco-logical world view. It reintegrates spirit and matter as well as the disparate disciplines in a coherent, cosmological framework. This education emphasizes core ecological concepts, such as energy flow, interdependence, carrying capacity and cycles, grounded in a deeper sense of an unfolding, uncompleted universe. Here ecology is understood not only as the study of the relationships between organisms and their environment, but as the ultimate grounding of all beings in life-giving mystery and an unfolding universe. This general education core emphasizes sustainable technologies that can be developed that are more coherent with the processes of the natural world. Professional education builds on this core. In business, law, health services, tourism, education, and other fields, sustainability becomes the bottom line, with a special commitment to the skills and technologies needed to create local, self-reliant communities.

One example of such integration is Seattle University's efforts to develop an interdisciplinary, college-wide initiative. This ecologi-cally oriented, field-based, integrative program emphasizes:

- A focus on ecology and its central concept of ecosystems.
- Linkage of the human with the natural, so that we shall study both natural ecology and human ecology and how they intertwine.
- An integrative understanding interweaving the natural sciences, social sciences, and humanities.
- Community involvement with citizens-based groups as well as mainline environmental groups, government agencies on the local, state, and federal levels, businesses, schools, the state environmental education community, and so forth.
- Service-based internships.
- The inclusion of a spiritual dimension. The recognition that our planetary ecological crisis is also, at root, a spiritual crisis, means that we shall draw deeply upon our Christian, Catholic,

Jesuit traditions, as well as other values, to fashion a new vision and cultural approach to the epochal questions that face us.

- Finally, this program shall hold sustainability as a key value and goal. In this program we shall seek innovative ways to help sustain ecosystems and communities.[16]

LIBERAL ARTS FOR AN ECOLOGICAL AGE

Many factors are converging or cumulating to produce a paradigm shift in higher education. Various models, emerging from the new physics, ecology, and biology, are informing a post-modern sensibility. Most importantly, there is a general "values" revolution taking place which effects higher education. While people do not agree what values should inform education and the culture, they do agree that both should be emphasizing more than materialism and hedonism. Central to this emerging "postmodern" general education core is a revision of basic assumptions about the nature of reality and the good life that dominate higher education.

Modern American life is dominated by an incessant stream of messages (particularly in advertising) aimed to convince the public that the good life can only be had by owning and consuming more. To be normal and acceptable in contemporary culture is to value status and material acquisitions. As Robert Bellah observed in *Habits of the Heart*, "That happiness is to be attained through limitless material acquisition is denied by every religion and philosophy known to man, but is preached incessantly by every American television set." In modern culture things are manipulated and exploited for gain, and individual egos compete with one another for the highest paying jobs, in order to demonstrate their importance and to be able to purchase everything they want.

The aims of life have been reduced to egotistical, material goals because universities and their disciplines (especially psychology, sociology, economics, and natural sciences) represent reality as insensible, lifeless matter, congealed through chance combinations that confer adaptive advantage. These produced individuals—atom-istic egos who seek to gratify a range of physiological needs (mostly oral and genital, according to Freud). Society is thus structured to refine the array of gratifications available and to increase wealth so that the successful can partake of the great feast available at the regional megamall.

From a deeply ecological perspective, the good life lies in waking up to deep interconnections with all that is, and living a lifestyle which is sufficient materially, but which focuses on enhancing spiritual development as well as the life possibilities for all members of the earth community. The following assumptions can guide a reformed liberal education in reworking basic under-standings of space, time, and self:[17]

1. Ecological interconnectedness, in which the universe is con-ceived as a web of interrelated systems. There are no isolated, dis-crete "selves" or "atoms." In this systems-view, each level of organi-zation (e.g., atoms, molecules, cells, individual plants and animals, social communities, ecosystems, and biosphere) is governed by principles or field characteristics that regulate structure and process at each level and that cannot be reduced to "the sum of its parts." Each entity is best regarded as a "holon"—functioning both as a whole composed of parts and as a part of other wholes.[18] This is a deeply ecological understanding in which the cycles and flows of nature and the subtle influences of all upon all are factored into our models of reality.

2. Evolutionary, developmental direction, in which the universe is an unfolding, purposive process—one that is not merely driven by random chance, mutation, competition, and survival of the fittest. Rather, in the words of Carl Rogers, it exhibits a "formative direc-tional tendency" (a telos), in which individuals and ecosystems develop toward greater order, greater interrelatedness, and greater complexity (Rogers). This unfolding process is psychic and spiritual as well as material.

3. Psychic-spiritual as well as material-physical reality character-izes all natural phenomena and all living beings. Within the dy-namic activity of natural process—the whirling of subatomic

mass/energy, the metabolism of cells, individual development, and the course of evolution—there is a deep flow of life and feeling, a mysterious presence which breathes and pulses within the energies and forms of the universe, creating and sustaining them and giving them the impetus to develop. Mystics, philosophers, prophets, and poets have called this ground of being by many names—the living God, Christ, Allah, Brahman, the Tao, the Fertile Void—and they have described their revelatory experiences of this great radiant presence and creative impulse animating all things. In reality, the spiritual, psychic, and material are mixed together as variable aspects of social and natural processes. An adequate account of events must reference and integrate the perspectives of all three.

A major task of education is to enable us to resonate to the life and feeling that exists in everything. The universe is, according to Thomas Berry, a "communion of subjects, not a collection of objects" (Berry, 1988). Those qualities most central to the human experience—self-consciousness, insight, desire, creativity—have resonances throughout the universe. Everything is full of life and feeling. There is a sentience, as Teihard said, at the heart of every atom, and as Lovelock and others describe, at the level of Gaia—the planet as a whole. Albert Schweitzer termed such sensibilities "reverence for life." What Schweitzer experienced as he passed through the herd of hippos on the Ogowe river was the crystallization of such a relationship to the life around him. The German word for reverence, *erfurcht,* carries the connotation of awed humility in the face of a vast and mysterious power. Schweitzer experienced the universe as alive with the divine. Each person, each creature, became "sacred," possessed of a "will to live" and deserving of deep moral consideration (Schweitzer). Sensing this "will to live" means awakening to the "thou," the soul of things. There are no longer any "things," no brute, senseless objects—no world of it, in Martin Buber's terms. Everything is living, unfolding, awakening with presence, destiny, and integrity.

4. Personal task or vocation in life to awaken to this spiritual/ecological reality and to live in accordance with its principles or laws. Research in developmental psychology and anthro-

pology indicates that people awaken through embracing and consciously refining the natural process of transformation. This formative process operates in each individual's cells and systems, pushing the maturing individual toward a more encompassing identity. Successful passage through the stages of human development requires the continual "transcendence" of more limited forms of being to higher levels of cognitive and moral reasoning and generative relatedness to others. The mechanism that prompts this repeated transcendence throughout the life cycle is the disintegration of limited, time-bound identities—a natural process of crisis and transformation in which the individual dies to an old, no longer viable identity and is reborn into a new, broader and deeper, perspective.

As a person comes to understand and embrace this transformative process, he or she awakens to this spiritual and ecological reality. Each person has a destiny or vocation—a configuration of tasks, roles, and relationships which awaken him or her to a deep sense of meaning and vitality. The purpose of life is to realize this destiny. Following this call draws the individual into the trials and ordeals of a heroic journey (ultimately to a confrontation with death). But by following it a person exchanges "neurotic" suffering—the suffering that comes from living within a false sense of self and reality—for the legitimate, productive suffering and the authentic joy of following the voice of conscience—or in Roszak's terms, the voice of the earth.

Whether a person moves toward this sense of deep interconnection with life or away from it into a more bitter, alienated, and dead existence depends significantly on how that person exercises his or her will. The desires one encourages and indulges, what one believes and attends to, and one's courage in acting morally and compassionately—all are consequential in bringing one closer (or pushing one farther) from this sense of radiant presence and vital connection to all that is. Yet it depends on much outside the individual's control, e.g., on grace or fate.

5. The necessity of humble, compassionate, and sustainable practices. A preoccupation with economic growth and consumption is fundamentally contrary to awakening the ecospiritual sensibility

which we are striving to cultivate. A person—or a society—possessed by the craving to have more money and more things, to get ahead and be important, can no more appreciate the "oneness" of being than a clump of cancerous tissue can participate in the rhythms of a healthy body. Both have grown out of accord with the needs of the whole, seeking their own advancement without regard for others. Nor should we expect that to sense the deeper sentience of the natural world, when in our everyday life we are cut off from it, and constantly manipulating its elements for our advantage. To approach the world as a thing to be exploited—to be bought, manipulated, and sold for profit—is to close the channels of experience to the sacred.

In his *Encyclical on Social Concern* (1989), Pope John Paul II observes, "There are some people—the few who possess much—who do not really succeed in 'being' because they have . . . no other horizon than the multiplication or continual replacement of the things already owned with others still better. . . . They are hindered by the cult of 'having.' And there are others—the many who have little or nothing—who do not succeed in realizing their basic human vocation because they are deprived of essential goods."

Living harmoniously requires creating modes of human sustenance, shelter, transportation, entertainment that do not exploit, pollute, or deplete the indigenous life systems, but enhance their natural unfolding.

Psychological health requires that we—in our personal lifestyle choices, political advocacy, and neighborly behavior—reduce our dependence on capital and energy intensive (high input) consumption, as well as refuse to use products and services which cause harm to others. Without embodying this sustainable way of living, we cannot escape deep complicity in an exploitative system. Even if we profit materially from this system, we shall suffer psychologically from its evils. Making a difference for life is primarily a matter of producing and consuming in ways that revitalize the soil, preserve biodiversity, treat animals well, enhance local self-reliance, and create genuine options for the poor.

Our psychological well being (the good life) cannot be gained at the expense of others: that which we do to others—people, animals, the earth—we do to ourselves. Our flourishing depends on the flourishing of all, for we are, in fact, all interconnected. Beyond obtaining a certain minimum of material necessities common to us all, and those particular things necessary for the development and expression of our talents, life is impoverished by acquiring more things. There is an ecology of the human psyche very much in tune with the ecology of our biosphere in which frugality and sacrifice are essential to happiness.

THE LEAD INSTITUTION INITIATIVE

Various academic institutions, disciplines, and educational reform initiatives are becoming cognizant of the environmental challenge, and are taking steps to transform their theories, practices, and constituencies in the direction of ecojustice.

The lead institution initiative, a project of "Theological Education to Meet the Environmental Challenge" (TEMEC),[19] identifies and supports schools that take the sustainability challenge seriously and are seeking to reform their curricula and practices in the postmodern direction described above. TEMEC assists seminaries, schools of theology, and universities in developing course work, community life, and institutional practices which respond effectively to the environmental challenge. This project seeks to make "ecojustice" a central focus of scholarly work and teaching in higher education, and of action at the personal, institutional, an social policy level. The basic norms of ecojustice ethics include: ecological sustainability, fair participation in social policy decisions, sufficiency of production-consumption, and community life that is celebrative, cares for otherkind and uses appropriate technology.

To realize this goal, TEMEC is engaged in the (1) development of conferences in different regions of North America to broaden the TEMEC network and deepen efforts to focus theological education on eco-justice; (2) development of "lead institutions" as demonstration sites for the kind of education envisioned; (3) establishment of an annual institute focused on ecology, justice, and faith; and (4) preparation and publication of resources that provide orientation and resources for students focused on renewing creation and seeking ecojustice.[20]

Lead institutions are academic institutions that have made a real commitment to respond to the environmental challenge by undertaking particular programs of religious studies and beginning new patterns of institutional life featuring environmental stewardship. These institutions have a sufficient number of faculty, administrators, and students deeply concerned about the "environmental challenge" and wrestling with its implications for theological education. They are also currently engaged in significant efforts to deal with ecological foundations/sustainable practice issues in teaching, scholarship, service, and practice.

Most important, these lead institutions are accomplishing three critical and interrelated tasks. They are: (1) bringing faculty members from usually isolated disciplines into effective interdisciplinary collaboration on ecological issues, (2) embodying a just and sustainable community on campus, and (3) addressing global and regional issues of sustainability—focusing on effective understanding of and responses to the interconnected problems of overpopulation, consumption, poverty, and environmental degradation.[21]

Included in our initiative are Seattle University, The School of Theology at Claremont, St. Thomas University of Miami, and Appalachian Ministry Resource Center in Berea, Kentucky. These schools offer concrete examples of efforts to transform curriculum, practices, and outreach for a sustainable future.[22] These are all just beginnings in an institutional and cultural context which offers very little support for practical greening initiatives, let alone the reintegration of spiritual and material understandings in interdisciplinary, praxis-oriented programs.

NOTES

1. Much of the material included in this chapter has been published in short articles in CRLE's quarterly *Earth Ethics.*

2. Thomas Kuhn, *The Structure of Scientific Revolutions* (Chicago: University of Chicago Press, 1962).

3. Ibid.

4. Thomas Berry, *Dream of the Earth* (Sierra Club Books, 1989).

5. Albert Gore, *Earth in the Balance* (New York: Houghton Mifflin Company, 1992).

6. *Journal of Interdisciplinary Studies in Literature and Environment,* unpublished announcement, 1995.

7. Thomas Gladwin, James Kennelly, and Tara Shelomith-Kraus, "Shifting Paradigms for Sustainable Development: Implications for Management Theory and Research," *The Academy of Management Journal* (October 1995).

8. William McDonough, "Declaration of Interdependence for a Sustainable Future," American Institute of Architecture (June 1993).

9. Ibid.

10. James A. Nash, *Loving Nature: Ecological Integrity and Christian Responsibility* (Nashville: Abingdon Press, 1991).

11. David Orr, *Ecological Literacy* (n.p., 1992); *Earth in Mind* (Washington, D.C.: Island Press, 1994).

12. Lyle, 1995.

13. William Rees and Mark Roseland, "Sustainable Communities: Planning for the Twenty-first Century," *Plan Canada* (May 1991).

14. *Ecodemia: Campus Environmental Stewardship at the Turn of the Twenty-First Century* (as well as *Campus Ecology*), available from the National Wildlife Federation's Campus Outreach Division, 1400 16th St., NW, Washington DC 20036.

15. Ibid.

16. Seattle University Grant Proposal, Seattle University, 1995.

17. While no general or professional education curriculum is organized around precisely these five assumptions, they represent my summary of these five essential components, which I believe will become increasingly central to postmodern higher education.

18. Arthur Koestler, *Ghost in the Machine* (London: Arkana, 1970); Fritjof Capra, *The Turning Point* (n.p., 1982).

19. "Theological Education to Meet the Environmental Challenge," (TEMEC) brochure, 1995; Cosponsored by the Center for Respect of Life and Environment and the Project on Ecology, Justice, and Faith, and funded by The Pew Charitable Trusts' Global Stewardship Initiative.

20. Ibid.

21. *After Nature's Revolt: Eco-Justice and Theology,* ed. Dieter Hessel (Minneapolis: Fortress Press, 1992).

22. Due to space constraints, the program descriptions and development steps cannot be included here. Please contact the Center for Respect of Life and Environment (CRLE), 2100 L St., NW, Washington, DC 20036 or the respective institutions mentioned here for these details.

QUESTIONS FOR DISCUSSION

1. What is a paradigm shift? Is a paradigm shift occuring or might such be described as a paradigm "conversion"?

2. Five assumptions are offered concerning the nature of reality and the good life. How would you evaluate these? Do they define reality and a good life as you understand these terms?

3. Do the institutions of which you are a part see the environmental challenge as an aspect of their operational life or mission? If either is the case, how would you evalute the institution? If neither is the case, why do you think this is so?

13

EARTH COMMUNITY
Redesigning Our Industrial Models for Global Sustainability

Larry Rasmussen

What on earth is to be done? What is to be done if community on various levels—from the biophysical world as a whole to the local neighborhood—is the organizing theme of earth ethics and sustainability itself? Where are the guideposts and examples? What stakes out the account of responsibility we seek?

Ask the Danes. In 1990 three schoolchildren in Kalundborg, Denmark, received an assignment. They were to produce a model in environmental studies showing how industrial wastes were being exchanged among several local companies.

Kalundborg, Denmark, is a small city on the shore of a deep fjord on the Great Belt, a body of cold saltwater running through Denmark and connecting the Baltic and North Seas. A medieval cathedral marks the center of town, and its streets are lined with the one-, two-, and three-story buildings of solid colors, cleanliness, and subdued, practical affluence that typify Scandinavia. Kalundborg is perhaps only more industrial than most, despite its rural surroundings and character.

What the students found was this. A coal-fired power plant, an oil refinery, a pharmaceutical company specializing in biotechnology, a sheetrock plant, concrete producers, a producer of sulfic acid, the municipal heating authority, a fish farm, some greenhouses, local farms, and other enterprises had all discovered mutually beneficial ways to trade waste. The Asnaes Power Plant started the process in the 1980s by recycling its waste heat in the form of steam. It had formerly condensed the steam and returned it to the fjord that emptied into the Great Belt. Now the steam goes directly to the Statoil refinery and the Novo Nordisk pharmaceutical company. It also provides surplus heat to greenhouses, a fish farm owned by the utility, and town residents (3,500 oil-burning heating systems in town were shut off as a result).

The Statoil refinery is connected to the Asnaes power plant in another way. After the water the refinery pulls into its system is used as a coolant, it is sent along to Asnaes where it serves as a coolant a second time. Statoil itself produces surplus gas as a consequence of the refining process. The gas was not used prior to 1991 because it contained excessive amounts of sulfur. The refinery has since installed a process to remove the sulfur and the cleaner-burning gas is sold to Gyproc, the sheetrock factory, as well as to the coal-fired utility plant (saving 30,000 tons of coal). The retrieved sulfur itself is sold to Kemira, a chemical company. At the Asnaes Power Plant the process that removes the sulfur in the smokestacks also yields calcium sulfate, which in turn is sold to Gyproc as a substitute for mined gypsum. Fly ash from coal generation is used for road construction and concrete production. Waste heat from the refinery is used to warm the waters of a fish farm that now produces 250 tons of turbot and trout annually. (The fish grow more rapidly in warmer water.) Fish sludge goes to local farmers as a natural fertilizer.

Meanwhile, Novo Nordisk, creator of insulin and enzymes, has developed a process to use the 700,000 tons of a thin, nitrogen-rich slurry it previously dumped into the fjord and thus into the Great Belt. The slurry is now pumped free to local farmers who, after the addition of chalk-lime and processing at 90 degrees Centigrade for an hour (to kill any remaining microorganisms), use it as a fertilizer. The farmers in turn grow biomass for Novo Nordisk's fermentation vats. Yeast cake from the vats is used to feed the farmers' pigs.[1]

The students' report detailed all this and then drew an analogy wiser than the students knew. They likened Kalundborg's industrial ecology to food webs in nature. They were correct. Kalundborg had unwittingly heeded the basic earth principle that "waste equals food." *By being a closed system,* nature recycles everything in such a way as to contribute to further cycles. Robert Frenay, who with Paul Hawken reports the case of Kalundborg, quotes the poet George Meredith at this juncture: "Earth knows no desolation. She smells regeneration in the moist breath of decay."[2] Nature's own blueprints go beyond linear thinking and "cradle-to-grave" designs.[3] Nature uses "cradle-to-cradle" designs instead.[4] The "moist breath of desolation" smells of "regeneration." The students didn't state it that way, but describing nature's food webs is much the same.

Sustainability, if it happens, *will only issue from careful listening to nature and mimicking its basic design strategies.* Learning from nature to mimic its design strategies is the first answer to the question of what is to be done.

Yet this begs the real question. *Which* nature, and how is it *to be understood?*

Ask the Danes. The industries of Kalundborg did not set out to mimic nature. Differently said, Kalundborg half-stumbled onto the basic requisite for sustainability: understanding creation, or nature, as a genuine community and aligning human configurations to the rest of it. More precisely, the Danes *acted* as though nature *is* a community, whether they understood its detail or not.

On one level this first requisite for sustainability is simple. "Comm-unity" is nature's way. All that exists, coexists. Yet the West's deadly combination of recent centuries, now globalized, has not understood it at all. Its confidence in humans as a species apart (some humans far more than others!); its confidence in docetic, "ungrounded," denatured reason; and its confidence in earth-oblivious economic messianism as a transforming power for good have ripped open the seams of earth and left it panting for breath and exhausted.

COMMUNITY

The basic premise for both actions and outlook is the simple sentence above: All that exists, coexists. Community rests at the heart of things. The dance of reality is "a permanent dance of energy and elements"[5] in a "vast communitarian chain"[6] that embraces the entire cosmos.

On one level this is only to acknowledge the shift in science from the mechanistic to the relational as the lead understanding of natural systems. On another level it is to reaffirm the more daring conviction of the doctrine of creation in numerous religious communions. Namely, that creation is a community in which the whole and its parts bear an integral dynamism and spirit, itself an expression of divine creativity. An interiority inhabits living materiality.

A sacramental reservation about messing with natural systems is one response to this. Such reservation is also a clue for the "new sort of science and technology governed by a new sort of economics and politics" that Charles Birch called for at the Nairobi Assembly of the World Council of Churches in 1975.[7] A profound conservatism toward all that makes for life is another way to say it. A fearsome respect for creation's integrity, and for earth as a slow womb, is still another.

Essential to this is the understanding that no clear line between life and not-life exists. Not when the galactic story, the solar system story, the earth story, the life story, and the human story weave and bind as one integral story.

Try breathing, for example. It only works because of the one-time furnaces of now dead stars. They were the sources of gases and processes crucial to the eventual formation of oxygen. For that matter, *all* the atoms in our bodies, with the exception of primordial hydrogen itself, were produced in supernova explosions. The atoms of the first generation of stars were thrown into space and cycled and recycled into new stars, planets, and eventually living creatures. All of us, all creatures past, present, and future, originated in stardust and the transformations of the universe in its long pilgrimage to date.

Even now, as you read this, the inticate togetherness of things doesn't allow an easy line between life and not-life. If, for example, you were to watch the night side of earth from a satellite's orbit you would see better than 100 flashes of lightning per second. They are part of the grand nutrient cycles of nature. Lightning annually converts more than three million metric tons of atmospheric nitrogen to nitrogen dioxide. Forest fires set by the lightning release additional nitrogen. Decomposing plant and animal matter contribute more. Rain carries the nitrogen back to water and soil where, after passing through microbial stages, it is taken up again by plants and then animals. On this elaborate journey, nitrogen separates and recombines with hydrogen, oxygen, and carbon, as virtually all life forms absorb and use it and pass it along in altered form. There are innumerable smaller cycles within larger cycles here, but there is no separating life and not-life in the being of it all. All is a part of the other. You, I, and other creatures live because that lightning is part of nature's nutrient cycle.[8] If lightning were not "alive," we wouldn't be either.

Turning again to religion, its traditions and the perennial wisdom of most philosophies have typically affirmed that creation is the great community, just as they have professed this integral, comprehensive community as the basic referent for our lives and all others. We are kin to all else because we share a common origin in divine creativity. And we share an ongoing journey as *creatio continua*. Not least we share a common destiny in the destiny of the universe itself.[9]

This religious and scientific understanding of nature as both the aboriginal and comprehensive community has meaning for our basic disposition and for Birch's new science and technology governed by a new economics and politics. For starters, it means that if the galaxies are subsystems of the universe, our solar system a subsystem of our galaxy, Earth a subsystem of our solar system, life a subsystem of Earth, and we a subsystem of Earth's life, then we belong here. We are at home here. Our lives, their excitement and their fulfillment, are here. We are most ourselves when we are most intimate with the rivers, mountains, forests, meadows, sun, moon, stars, air, soil, rocks, otherkind, and humankind.[10] This and no other is our own primordial community. And this primordial community is a home without an exit.

How "efficient" and "realistic" is it, for example, to cut down a slow-growing century-old tree in the Tongass forest of Alaska, sell it for the price of a pizza, ship it off to Japan, with the help of fossil fuels render it there as little bags for snacks, ship these to the United States for sale, then dispose of the bags in the landfill by way of an elaborate and expensive, fossil-fuel-burning garbage collection system or, at best, an elaborate, expensive recycling program? If nothing goes away, how realistic and efficient is it to use 26,000 pounds of PVC annually (polyvinyl chloride, a plastic) in Germany for plastic soles and sneakers alone, and then add lead as a stabilizer for the PVC? The lead dust from the shoes is carried by rain into the sewers where, with additions from elsewhere, it makes it difficult to recycle sewage sludge for agriculture. The linear, industrial solution is to add a treatment plant to remove the lead. Another kind of solution avoids all this with a shoe design that doesn't use PVC and lead, isn't more expensive, and is environmentally benign. But that requires learning how the complex cycles of nature work.[11]

Why not find out, to make the point from another tack, what property allows a fly's wing to beat hundreds of times per second without breaking? Tom Eisner and others discovered that fly and dragonfly wing hinges are made of the most perfect rubber known. Or what gives the dragline silk of the golden-silk spider a tensile strength twenty times that of steel and a capacity at the same time to stretch and rebound from 20 percent of its original strength? Biophysicist Lynn Jelinski thinks genetically altered plants might mass produce a spiderlike silk of this kind for any number of uses, from sails to bridges. But it requires understanding spidersilk as well as plants. Michael Braungart notes that the colors of many birds, from green to purple, are produced without blue pigment. The blue of a jay, for example, is created by refractions of light resulting from prismatic structures in the feathers. Since blue fabric dyes are generally highly toxic and toxins are by definition that which nature can only recycle for ill and never good, why not develop fabrics and finishes by using optical properties rather than toxic pigments?[12] Or why not design farming as Braungart and the Hamburg Environmental Institute did on the basis of natural cycles around a series of ponds? "The ponds process local sewage and waste by growing aquatic plants and algae. The plants draw off excess nutrients and leave the water a nutritious and safe habitat for fish. The plants are harvested as livestock food or are used with waste from the livestock as fertilizer for nearby fields. Pigs feed on vegetables and snails that grow at the site. Ducks and geese consume algae and provide nutrients for the fish. Water purified by the process flows back into the local watershed. All this arises from knowing local ecosystems and earth as a closed sphere."[13]

As we have seen, industrial ecology can do the same kind of listening to earth as a closed community system. That is the point of Kalundborg. The revolutionary trick is to convert the ingrained linear processes of industrial systems into cyclical ones that mimic nature as a community.

PATHS NOT TAKEN

Being explicit about actions, structures and paths *not* taken can also clarify *which* nature is to be mimicked and how it is to be understood. When the number and cumulative impact of human beings is what it now is, what we do *not* do, or refrain from doing any longer, is as important to sustainability as what we do. The deceptively simple first law of ethics, "do no harm," is still good advice.

Sustainable development as green globalism is rejected. It is rejected despite its standing as a sincere attempt at good stewardship of ecumenical earth. Green globalism is rejected because its starting point, framework, and means are fatally askew. Wrapping the environment around a globalizing economy as the centerpiece of sustainability is the extension of a course with deep roots in earth-destructive modernity, rather than the needed path not yet taken. The roots are both institutional (corporations and nation-states) and social-psychological (humans as a manager-engineer-entrepreneur-consumer species).

Differently put, spaceship economics and planetary management violate the pluralism of place and the integrity of ecosystems integral to nature's own complex functioning as a community. "Singular man" stands erect *vis-à-vis* "singular nature" (Raymond Williams), perpetuating the abstractions of nature/humanity apartheid even when the language mimics that of community empowerment. Thus sustainable development's correct realization that we genuinely belong to the cosmos and that nature is a closed, curved system is arrogantly twisted into a scheme where, finally, some know what is in the interest of the rest. Soon the tilt is toward yet another master theory, a transcendent technology and a comprehensive set of global practices. Things are no longer soulsize, with multiple voices attuned to the complexity of things on the ground in places very different from one another. Chains of responsibility and accountability are too long and too distant in these global management schemes. High levels of participation on the part of all effected are not the structures of the basic decisions, and cannot be. Nor is there much recognition that the size of governing forces, whether political, economic, or cultural, needs to be trimmed back to match the limited talent available in the ordinary flawed human beings of whom even the most impressive social orders are composed. Sustainable development as green globalism on the model of spaceship earth is, then, wittingly or not, just the latest version of imperial hubris. It may be well-intended but it is very wrong, for both *homo sapiens* and the rest of nature.

Granted, green globalism is better than some other hues, and sustainable development in this scheme is not an unmitigated disaster. It is preferable to the brown globalism of cowboy economics in its updated version of The World Trade Organization (WTO). The political economy of present dominion theology is even further from effective community than is sustainable development, with its newfound themes of participation, empowerment, and social justice. From the point of view of earth, brown globalism *is* an unmitigated disaster. Green globalism is a mitigated one.[14]

In brief, what is rejected here as the framework for policy is the spectrum usually identified as *the* range of choices: namely, globalizing capitalism as more eco-qualified or less eco-qualified. What is affirmed is quite another institutional, cultural, and social-psychological orientation. It turns on community economics, politics, science, and technology, with community understood at various levels from local to regional to transregional and global, but *all* of them within the orbit of nature as *the* primordial, comprehensive, and closed community. This means "day-care" political economy with its margins of safety and room for maneuverability, as well as space for both freedom and surprise. Elasticity and adaptability are prized, within the clear limits of nature's offerings. And community scale runs to smaller rather than larger, even when there are lots of kids and the overall population is high.

A SKETCH, MORE EXAMPLES, AND A GUIDE

But what is "community scale" and the proper political economy?

Gregory Bateson enjoyed telling of an exchange at New College, Oxford. The main hall at New College was built in the 1600s and used oak beams forty feet long and two feet thick. They eventually suffered from dry rot and oaks large enough to replace them were not known to the college administrator. It was suggested that the administrator inquire with the college forester whether some of the lands given to Oxford might have trees adequate for the renovation. The forester replied, "We've been wondering when you would ask the question. When the present building was constructed three hundred fifty years ago, the architects specified that a grove of trees be planted and maintained to replace the beams in the ceiling when they suffered from dry rot." Bateson's comment: "That's the way to run a culture."[15]

Many peoples and societies *have* had this sense of responsibility for future generations and a way of life that takes such actions as these. The fabled "seventh generation" test for actions, policies, buildings, and institutions themselves *is* "the way to run a culture," even if those of the seventh generation should decide that beams in the main hall might not be the best use of the replacement oaks. In passing, let it be noted that there is nothing humanly unconstitutional about such future-oriented action.

Beyond the seventh generation test, what else enables a community to last? Wendell Berry once offered "Seventeen Sensible Steps." The question, what on earth ought to be done, has answers here.

1. Ask of any proposed change or innovation: What will this do to our community? How will this effect our common wealth?
2. Include local nature—the land, the water, the air, the native creatures—within the membership of the community.
3. Ask how local needs might be supplied from local sources, including the mutual help of neighbors.
4. Supply local needs *first* (and only then think of exporting . . . products, first to nearby cities, and then to others).
5. Understand the ultimate unsoundness of the industrial doctrine of "labor saving" if that implies poor work, unemployment, or any kind of pollution or contamination.
6. Develop properly scaled value-adding industries for local products in order not to become merely a colony of the national or the global economy.
7. Develop small-scale industries and businesses to support the local farm or forest economy.
8. Strive to produce as much of [your] own energy as possible.
9. Strive to increase earnings (in whatever form) within the community, and decrease expenditures outside the community.
10. Circulate money within the local economy for as long as possible before paying it out.
11. Invest in the community to maintain its properties, keep it clean (without dirtying some other place), care for its old people, and teach its children.
12. Arrange for the old and the young to take care of one another, eliminating institutionalized "child care" and "homes for the aged." The young must learn from the old,

not necessarily and not always in school; the community knows and remembers itself by the association of the old and the young.

13. Account for the costs that are now conventionally hidden or "externalized." Whenever possible they must be debited against monetary income.

14. Look into the possible uses of local currency, community-funded loan programs, systems of barter, and the like.

15. Be aware of the economic value of neighborliness—as help, insurance, and so on. They must realize that in our time the costs of living are greatly increased by the loss of neighborhood, leaving people to face their calamities alone.

16. Be acquainted with, and complexly connected with, community-minded people in nearby towns and cities.

17. Cultivate urban consumers loyal to local products to build a sustainable rural economy, which will always be more cooperative than competitive.[16]

Berry's own community is rural. The seventeen steps reflect his participation in furthering sustainability at home in Kentucky. Nonetheless, much here is also the gathering wisdom of neighborhood-oriented community organizing groups in large cities. The Danes of Kalundborg, both rural and urban, would understand Berry's provincialism, at least in part (their strong dependence on international trade would bend it somewhat). Certainly Common Bread does.

Common Bread is part of the "Community Supported Agriculture and Subscription Farming" movement. It works at rural/urban intersections. The scheme is cooperation between a grower and a community of citizens in a nearby city who purchase shares in a community farm. The shareholders hire the farmer/gardener (and sometimes the land) and may themselves assist with planting, cultivating, and harvesting. A core group also provides administration and helps with distribution of the produce. Each share entitles the holder to a given volume of fresh, organically grown produce during the growing season and for winter storage.

Community Supported Agriculture, presently a conscious network in the United States, Japan, and Europe, is a response to many things at once: a growing concern for the safety and nutritional value of food purchased supermarket-style (we often don't know where our food comes from, how it was grown, how it has been altered, or the human and environmental costs in producing it); the waste and other costs entailed in obtaining food that has often traveled thousands of miles to get from farm to table; the difficulty of farmers, especially small farmers, to make a living without a support system; the ability of the land to meet the needs of future generations (thus the need for conscientious citizen interest and participation in its present welfare on the part of people who hold a stake other than market profit); the need of urban dwellers to be people of the land and responsible toward soils and farmers upon which and whom they are dependent for life.[17]

This approach has spinoffs and makes connections. It tends to think sideways and cyclically. Common Bread Restaurant and Bakery in south Minneapolis purchases from a community-supported subscription farm thirty miles away. It shares this philosophy on its menu jacket:

> At Common Bread we are trying to reduce the distance that food has to travel to reach your plate. We have a commitment to seeking out and purchasing directly from local growers whenever possible. We use foods in season to the extent possible, even going so far as to visit local farms to learn first hand the challenges of growing vegetables, fruits, and poultry in our northern climate.
>
> We live in one of the most abundant agricultural states in this country, yet, the average food we eat travels more than 1300 miles to reach our table. For the most part we do not know where our food comes from, how it is grown, and how it has been altered if it has been processed.[18]

Common Bread is located in one of the poorest, most physically degraded sections of south Minneapolis. It chose that location as part of its commitment. The commitment was not only to wholesome food but to employment and training of locally unemployed people and provision of a community-making place for neighbor-hood groups to meet. (The restaurant's program, which is more than its menu, designed this from the start. Breaking bread together is evidently more than just eating together.)

Does Common Bread suffice as an example of sustainability and the meaning of earth community? Does Kalundborg?

No. If we multiplied them *ad infinitum*, we would still cause earth's distress, though considerably less of it. Kalundborg has impressively walked down the Business Council for Sustainable Development's path of eco-efficiency as the second industrial revolution. But like the rest of Denmark, it has not yet dislodged the high levels of consumption of rich nations, or weaned itself from fossil fuels and their contributions to global warming, or disengaged from a system of global trade and finance that promotes affluence in some sectors and poverty in others. Until those moves are made, and appropriated carrying capacity altered, sustainability will not be Denmark's, Europe's, Latin America's, or the rest of Earth's.

For its part, Common Bread does most all the right things. But it will likely not "make it." The support base is small, the enterprise is vulnerable, and most precarious of all, it daily bucks the system, receiving little support from it. (It has a single farm, a modest number of somewhat transient subscribers, a restaurant in a blighted area with little money and unlikely to draw clientele from "outside," a program that runs on largely volunteer labor, and a lack of systemic supports within an economy that favors agriculture as industry and restaurants, even restaurant chains, in well-traveled corridors.)

Yet both Kalundborg and Common Bread, like Berry, know where sustainable community begins: with a cultivated sense of community responsibility as part of an ecological mode of thinking. Continuing this sense of community responsiblity and ecological thinking, what more needs be said?

There is a guide for sustainable community scale. It is one of the moral norms of sustainability itself—namely, subsidiarity. Subsidiarity is the means of participation and accountability best tuned to the pluralism of place and the scale most likely to be responsible. We consider it in some detail.

Subsidiarity has a long tradition in Christian ethics. One of the more recent formulations is a papal one: "Just as it is gravely wrong to take from individuals what they can accomplish by their own initiative and industry and give it to the community, so also it is an injustice and at the same time a grave evil and disturbance of right order to assign to a greater and higher association what lesser and subordinate organizations can do."[19] This means that what can be accomplished on a smaller scale at close range by high participation with available resources should not be given over to, or allowed to be taken over by, larger and more distant organizations.

The key is *appropriate* scale and action. For sustainable community, that may in fact mean actions, policies, and institutions that are *more global*. Subsidiarity also means massively deconstructing what is now globalized. Food, shelter, livelihood, and other needs which can be met on a community and regional basis, with indigenous resources, talent and wisdom, should be met here, with firm commitments to Berry's "pluralism of place." Even large cities can better relate to the bioregions in which they and surrounding areas are embedded.

Most of the other explicit norms for sustainable community—participation, solidarity, sufficiency, material simplicity and spiritual richness, and responsibility and accountability—are also better served when the principle of subsidiarity is heeded. If converting linear processes (the industrial paradigm) to cyclical ones (nature's economy) is one key to sustainability, making "feedback" visible and close to home is another. Local and regional initiative and self-reliance tend to promote these, just as they tend to promote higher degrees of cooperation, mutual support and collaborative problem-solving. Not least, subsidiarity tends to preserve resources in the community as the "commons"[20] people depend upon, know best, and care most about.

Stephen Viederman gives particular emphasis to the role of human imagination and collaboration in arriving at sustainable community. This requires "the space and time for people to begin to envision the future they desire for their [own] communities, and to ensure access to power that will make it happen."[21] That "first task" is more likely accomplished on the scale for which subsidiarity is the guide.

Yet this is not slavish "localism," since subsidiarity asks not for the most local, but the most appropriate level of organization and response. "Most appropriate" includes the *morally* most appropriate level. Small *as* beautiful, and the local as the *basic* unit of the global, may locate the starting blocks. But in a world of maldistributed resources and power, the local cannot be the only locus of responsible action, just as it is not the only place we meet and live together. Trade and other exchanges of resources, for example, are as necessary in their own way as is transnational cooperation to address global warming and regions suffering "overshoot." The necessary guideline is not "no trade" or "no markets," or even "minimal trade" and "minimal markets." The guideline is to minimize the *appropriation* of carrying capacity *from elsewhere*, thus risking other people's and otherkind's lives in the present and for the future. The guideline is also *restoration* of diminished carrying capacity and the empowerment of peoples whose resources have been diminished as a systemic feature of globalizing dynamics. *Oikos* economics, of an ecumenical earth, uses subsidiarity as a key guide.

Sustainability guided by subsidiarity betters its chances by incorporating resiliency into social systems. The practices of economy and society ought to be ordered in such a way as to be able to shift and adapt, like nature, to changing conditions. In nature, biodiversity is the mechanism by which adaptation to demanding changes occurs, the means by which nature is resilient in the face of often traumatic change. As such, it is the basic source of all future wealth and well-being.[22]

Paul Hawken's two principles of good social design, drawn from nature, would improve the odds in favor of greater resiliency. They express "day-care" thinking. Good design "changes the least number of elements to achieve the greatest result" And good design "removes stress from a system rather than adding it."[23] In short, easier and simpler is better. Easier and simpler, with room for error, favors sustainability. The return to how nature works is an apt reminder that sustainability, and thus subsidiarity, necessarily involves the total earth-human process. *Creation* as a community remains the first stipulation, just as the integrity of ecosystems remains the first value.

THE MORAL GYROSCOPE

From a different angle, the requirements of sustainable community include rejecting a certain moral-spiritual universe and offering another. This is vital to the question of what is to be done, since an inner world to match the outer one is a requirement of sustainability itself. Sustainability will not happen, nor itself be sustained, if no living inner world accords with the outer world we seek. Moral, spiritual, and cultural dimensions are as crucial as technical ones.

Broadly speaking, what is untenable for sustainability is a moral universe that circles human creatures only and does not regard other creatures and Earth as a whole as imposing moral claims we need worry over. An anthropocentric moral universe perpetuates dualistic humanity/nature apartheid thinking and moral and spiritual autism. Imperviousness and unresponsiveness then reign, an incapacity to be touched in ways we truly feel.

Mary Wollstonecraft's words of two hundred years ago, from *Vindication of the Rights of Women*, pertain here: "Those who are able to see pain, unmoved, will soon learn to inflict it."[24] Mary Pellauer, using Wollstonecraft, says that something like this happens to our morality and spirit when our emotional nerve system becomes calloused.[25] The point is that, like race and gender in some quarters, the standing of nature in modernity is overgrown with such moral callousness. Nature's suffering and pain leave us unmoved. So we soon inflict pain, with little understanding. Or, seeing it, we are unmoved. Socialization renders nature a matter of utilitarian interest only, or, on our better days, of esthetic and recreational interest. But the life of otherkind is not a realm of binding moral obligation. If nature beyond us is not scenic, edible, or otherwise useful, it does not stir us.

Sustainable community offers a moral system with more sensitive skin. It does so by according inherent moral value to the full sweep of nature. All creatures great and small, and inorganic matter as well, have worth that rests proximately in their membership in the Community of Life. "All that participates in being" (H. R. Niebuhr) has standing. For the religiously inclined, the value ultimately resides in creation as the expression of divine creativity and goodness. Compassion and justice and the mending of community thus envelop more than human members. Suffering and pain is felt and acknowledged, even when they are unavoidable.

Within this expanding moral universe, the broadest moral guideline is one suggested by James Gustafson. Human beings, given their power and place in earth's present reality and their nature as self-conscious moral creatures, may inevitably be the measurers of all things. But the measure itself is that we "relate to all things in a manner appropriate to their relations to God."[26] The "good" which all things are is more than their good for us, and our own interests are relative to larger wholes than those of immediate human welfare. Human interests are thus relativized in the interest of the more inclusive life communities of which we are part and upon which we utterly depend.

For those whose moral universe does not finally rest in the presence and power of the divine, the orientation and socialization suggested here still argues for inherent value and the Community of Life as the human reference point. "The integrity of creation" and biotic rights, or Aldo Leopold's categorical imperative—"A thing is right when it tends to preserve the integrity, stability, and beauty of the biotic community. It is wrong when it tends otherwise"[27]—offers the framework for contemplated actions and policies. So do "justice" and "neighbor" in most religious traditions, even when shorn of explicitly religious ties.

Not all human communities have lost the emotional sense of a comprehensive moral universe. Many nonanthropocentric ethical systems have been lived. Some still are. Systems far less desacralizing of nature than modernity's have guided many past human communities. But the issue now is how we "reenchant the world" (Weber) and conduct human life in a manner appropriate to larger wholes and at the same time address earth's distress, billions of human beings' distress included. That is a daunting challenge on a new scale for earthethics. (Incidentally, Leopold himself argued that his purpose in "The Land Ethic" was no more than to enlarge the boundaries of the community "to include soils, waters, plants, and animals, or collectively: the land" for those whose lives had taken such an odd turn as to forget these.)[28]

Sustainability's comprehensive communitarian ethic, itself a *decisive concrete earth action,* is not nature romanticism or the simple imitation of nature. It necessarily goes beyond the earlier plea to listen to nature and mimic natural designs. Much of nature *is simply too casual about suffering.* For human morality this is unacceptable, even after acknowledging mortality, unavoidable suffering, and "death's limited rights" (Bonhoeffer). A moral framework inclusive of nature as a subject of high moral standing is *not,* then, simply a transfer of the rest of nature's behavior to human conduct. In important, even unavoidable ways, we remain the measurers.

Predation, for example, is an essential part of nature's cycles. It is not a pattern of morality we praise and advocate, however, at least not on our better days. To be sure, "red of tooth and claw" has been justified as conduct redounding to society's good, notably in some versions of fascism, Social Darwinism,[29] and certain phases of revolutions. But it is a course that, like nature in some forms, devours its own children. It is rejected here as a moral paradigm.

In short, while we necessarily draw lines, make distinctions, and intervene in ways that, *like* nature, take life for the sake of life, *unlike* the rest of nature, we also draw lines, make distinctions, and intervene so as to prevent and relieve suffering in ways the rest of nature often does not. Inherent value is real. But it does not mean equal value. That said, one of the most difficult and ongoing tasks of earthethics is to decide where what lines are drawn and where what distinctions are made as humans intervene in the larger panorama of a nature too casual about suffering. Human beings, a part of nature, cannot escape their distinctive work as moral creatures.

The stakes are so high because morality is as crucial to sustainability as knowing nature's basic designs. The proper disposition of both humility and responsibility is nicely captured by the centuries-old suggestion of the rabbis that we keep a piece of paper in one pocket reminding us that we are dust and ashes, and in the other a reminder that the world is here for us and its fate in our hands.[30] A new account of responsibility, well beyond modernity's own, is required.

CLOSING

Earthcommunity and ethics is humanity's next journey in a world that has become game and booty and landfill. Compared with the many we are, far too few will have a place worthy of Earth creatures. The globalization affecting all things, not least Earth's life sources themselves, is not, in fact, truly global.[31] The economic drive pushing the forward stampede is concentrated in the industrialized world and its extensions in the "developing" world. It is a globalization that includes most people as measured by impact, but excludes most as measured by benefit. The ranks "of the window-shoppers and the jobless are growing faster than the ranks of the global army of the employed."[32] This "surplus of gifted, skilled, undervalued, and unwanted human beings is the Achilles heel"[33] of this globalizing new world order.

At the same time that such globalization proceeds, the structures of collective accountability weaken. The sum of individual corporate decisions determine far more of what happens to people's lives and the environment than any public policies arrived at through democratic means and carried out by governments. There is no polite way to say it: the forces of stampeding economic globalization without global community and responsibility are destroying a beloved world. Theirs is a brown globalism tinged with green at rich world edges. It is virile, comprehensive, and alluring as a materialist way of life but it is deaf to earth's requirements for comprehensive sustainability. And unfortunately, what distress affluent materialist forces do not inflict is inflicted by the misery of those who remain, precious children of God whose lives and livelihoods are omitted from the essential power equations.

There is another way. Millions yearn to walk it and strain to do so. The choice, in Berry and Swimme's somewhat awkward terms, is between "the Technozoic era" of a commercial-industrial-information order with "an even more ordered control of things," and "the Ecozoic era"[34] of mutually enhancing earth-human relationships framed and instructed by creation's integrity. The choice is between an extension of the cumulative human revolutions in agriculture, industry, and information, all reconfiguring nature for the sake of society (some social strata more than others), and a fourth revolution that understands nature's economy as basic to the social reconfiguration needed for the sake of both human and otherkind.

In these pages that choice turns on community, and on earth-faiths and ethics appropriate to it. All citizens, bar none, are invited to love Earth fiercely and vow fidelity to it.

Hope is real and there are grounds for it. Something is clearly afoot, though it is "mostly offcamera."[35] Local citizens' movements and alternative institutions are emerging, trying to create greater economic self-sufficiency, internalize costs to Earth in the price of goods, sustain livelihoods, work out agriculture appropriate to regions, preserve traditions and cultures, revive religious life, maintain human dignity, repair the moral fiber, resist the commodification of all things, be technologically innovative with renewable and nonrenewable resources, revise urban designs and architecture, preserve biological species and protect ecosystems, and cultivate a sense of Earth as a sacred good held in trust and in common.

This inspiring melange has no one configuration. By definition it probably ought not to, given the pluralism of place and peoples and their insistent, varied participation. Barnet and Cavanagh, who judge this disparate movement as presently "the only force we see that can break the global gridlock,"[36] close their study with a judgment about the stakes: "The great question of our age is whether people, acting with the spirit, energy, and urgency our collective crisis requires, can develop a democratic global consciousness rooted in authentic local communities."[37] Such authentic communities are not *only* local, we have argued. But community from the local to the cosmic *is* the focus and frame for meeting the great adventure upon us.[38]

The issue is not whether rooted and realistic changes can be made, radical ones among them. They can. The issue, rather, is whether we acknowledge the ascendancy of ethics. Do we realize that the key to sustainability of inclusive nature rests in the character of the social order that is ours? Has it hit us with full force that sustainability is less a matter of our wits than our collective morality, that it turns on "justice, peace and the integrity of creation"?

Faith is the name of the strong power behind the renewal of moral-spiritual energy. It squarely faces the fact there will never be decisive proof beforehand that life will triumph; yet it still acts with confidence that the stronger powers in the universe arch in the direction of sustaining life, as they also insist upon justice. World-weariness is combatted by a surprising force found *amidst* Earth and its distress. Creation carries its own hidden powers.

Said differently, the religious consciousness—and dream—which generates hope and a zest and energy *for* life is tapped *in* life itself. The finite bears the infinite, and the transcendent as "the beyond in the midst of life" (Bonhoeffer) is as close as the neighbor, soil, air, and sunshine itself. Life defending itself against the death of life is in fact one of the works of nature itself, in us. God, like the devil and life itself, is in the details. The turn to Earth, then, is also a turn to those sources that enable what has not yet come to pass to do so.

Or has it already come to pass, time and again? Dorothee Soelle says she believes in resurrection "because it has already happened." And so it has, and does. That, not the endless list of woes that tally as Earth's distress, is the reason for Joe Wood's line:

> The heart, after all, is raised on a mess of stories.
> Then it writes its own.[39]

Those stories will be genuine Earthstories. They will reveal Dag Hammerskjold's truth: "God does not die on the day we cease to believe in a personal deity, but we die on the day when our lives cease to be illuminated by the steady radiance, renewed daily, of a wonder, the source of which is beyond all reason."[40] Then we will understand Alice Walker's salutation of *The Color Purple*'s last letter: "Dear God. Dear stars, dear trees, dear sky, dear peoples. Dear Everything. Dear God."[41]

And we will understand Maya Angelou's closing in her Inauguration Day (1993) poem. Then,

> . . . on the pulse of this new day
> [We will] have the grace to look up and out
> And into [our] sister's eyes, and into
> [our] brother's face, [our] country, [the planet],
> And say simply
> Very simply
> With hope—
> Good morning.

NOTES

1. This example is a composite of information provided by Paul Hawken, *The Ecology of Commerce: A Declaration of Sustainability* (San Francisco: Harper Business, 1993), pp. 62–63, and Robert Frenay, "Biorealism: Reading Nature's Blueprints," *Audubon* 97, no. 5 (May 1995): 75–76.

2. Frenay, "Biorealism," *Audubon*, p. 74.

3. "Cradle-to-grave" analysis is increasingly popular in ecosensitive and cost-conscious production circles. By carefully tracking the environmental consequences of production processes from initial acquisition of resources to end use, it results in cleaner production and often lower costs. McDonough's point is that "end use" isn't "end use" at all for nature, and product design needs to mimic nature in such a way that this use in turn is part of, not a "grave," but another "cradle."

4. Frenay, "Biorealism," *Audubon*, p. 74.

5. Leonardo Boff, *Ecology and Liberation* (Maryknoll: Orbis Books, 1995), p. 40.

6. Ibid., p. 36.

7. This excerpt from Birch's address is cited by Dieter T. Hessel, "Where Were/Are the Churches in the Environmental Movement?" in *Theology and Public Policy* 7, no. 1 (summer 1995): 21–22.

8. Example taken from Frenay, "Biorealism," p. 74.

9. See Denis Edwards, *Jesus the Wisdom of God: An Ecological Theology* (Maryknoll: Orbis Books, 1995), p. 143.

10. Berry, *The Meadow Beyond the Creek*, p. 75. Unpublished manuscript, used with permission.

11. Examples from Frenay, "Biorealism," pp. 70–71, 78.

12. Ibid., p. 72.

13. Ibid., p. 74.

14. The tenor of brown globalism echoes in the series of advertisements run by Mobil oil in major newspapers in 1995. In language that matches Schumacher's "forward stampede people," and has no place for "home-comers," the first of the series titled "A Global Vision" begins this way:

> As one of the world's largest international oil companies, our vision is simple: To be a *great* global company. And that means seizing opportunities with good economics wherever they occur.

The advertisement goes on to say that "with the current world surplus in energy," the difficulty is culling "great" projects from "the basket-load of 'good' projects." Mobil seeks to do this culling. In the process it brings "the synergies of long experience and worldwide operations" to "some areas of the world that are opening up." A series of "partnerships" designed "to assist governments with their economic development plans" is the scheme. Examples are then offered, some "colossal in scale," like the new twenty billion-dollar-plus partnership with Qatar for liquefied natural gas. Others have been "enjoyed for years" "because of a shared vision that host governments have supported with attractive commercial terms."

The only identification of people in this "global vision" is in the words "we" (Mobil), "governments" and "consumers and producers." There is no reference whatsoever to the environment. All the language is cowboy global economics: getting the hydrocarbons of "resource-rich nations" to "energy-hungry markets elsewhere," "expanding a Mobil presence that dates back in some countries more than a century" or, as noted, newly moving into "some areas of the world that are opening up." Even the complaint is the cowboy complaint of tied hands, too little freedom to venture and "open up the world," and unnecessary imposed limitations: "The pursuit of energy opportunities overseas is . . . needed because potentially rich domestic resources [in the United States]—onshore and offshore—remain off limits to the industry."

The foregoing is taken from "A Global Vision," the op-ed page of the *New York Times*, 10 August 1995, emphasis in the original.

15. As passed along by Frenay, "Biorealism," p. 106.

16. Wendell Berry, "Community in Senenteen Sensible Steps," *Utne Reader* 68 (March-April 1995): 71.

17. This description and rationale is taken from a flyer entitled "Community Supported Agriculture and Subscription Farming," as provided by Daniel Guenther, a farmer/gardener working near Minneapolis, Minnesota.

18. From the menu, Common Bread Restaurant and Bakery, Minneapolis, Minnesota.

19. Pope Pius XI, *Quadragesimo Anno* (1931), as cited in *The Westminster Dictionary of Christian Ethics,* ed. James F. Childress and John Macquarrie (Philadelphia: Westminster Press, 1986), p. 608. "Subsidiarity" is from the Latin *subsidium,* meaning "help."

20. A comment to the famous essay of Garret Hardin, "The Tragedy of the Commons." Hardin's treatment is deceptive. Commons in preindustrial societies were generally well-regulated by the communities to which they belonged and which depended upon them. Hardin's portrayal of the destruction of the commons goes like this. Each farmer discovers that it is in his/her self-interest to add a cow to his/her herd in the pasture (the commons) because he/she accrues all the economic benefits from the additional cow while sharing the costs (the common pasture). When many farmers act on this, the burden on the commons degrades it and may even destroy it as productive pasture. But this logic and practice is not that of the commons at all. It is that of free-standing individuals treating the commons, not as a commons, but an open-access system from which each might take as much as he/she can. A calculation of self-interest, with "nature" as essentially free goods, and the market as the nexus, is the picture here. This is industrial system logic, not commons logic. Commons logic means community regulation of shared resources.

21. Stephen Viederman, "The Economics of Sustainability: Challenges," p. 17 of unpublished manuscript. Used with permission.

22. Hawken, *The Economy of Commerce,* p. 190.

23. Ibid., p. 166.

24. Pellauer's citation of Wollstonecraft is from the latter's *A Vindication of the Rights of Women* (1792; reprint, New York: W.W. Norton, 1967), p. 256.

25. Mary Pellauer, "Moral Callousness and Moral Sensitivity," in *Women's Consciousness, Women's Conscience: A Reader in Feminist Ethics,* ed. Barbara Hilkert Andolsen, Christine E. Gudorf, and Mary D. Pellauer (San Francisco: Harper and Row, 1985), p. 49.

26. James M. Gustafson, *Ethics from a Theocentric Perspective*, vol. 1 (Chicago: University of Chicago Press, 1981), p. 113.

27. Aldo Leopold, *Sand County Almanac* (New York: Ballantine Books, 1989), p. 262.

28. Ibid., p. 239.

29. Social Darwinism's earthfaith conveniently forgot that the "survival of the fittest" principle was supplemented by another which said that creatures who learned to cooperate stood a better chance of survival.

30. Michael Lerner, *Jewish Renewal; A Path to Healing and Transformation* (New York: Gross/Putnam, 1994), p. 107–108.

31. Richard J. Barnet and John Cavanagh, *Global Dreams: Imperial Corporations and the New World Order* (New York: Simon & Schuster, 1994), p. 427.

32. Ibid.

33. Ibid., p. 425.

34. Brian Swimme and Thomas Berry, *The Universe Story* (San Francisco: HarperCollins, 1992), pp. 249–50.

35. Barnet and Cavanagh, *Global Dreams*, p. 430.

36. Ibid.

37. Ibid.

38. For an account of what has happened to community in the modern world and what constructive responses need to be made, especially to provide basic moral formation of human character and conscience to address the fraying of social fiber, see Larry L. Rasmussen, *Moral Fragments and Moral Community* (Minneapolis: Fortress Press, 1993).

39. Joe Wood, "What I Learned About Jews," *The New York Times Magazine*, 10 April 1994, p. 45.

40. Dag Hammerskjold, as cited in a review of Oscar Hijuelos' *Mr. Ives' Christmas* by Michiko Kakutani, "A Test of Faith for a Father Who Longs for Grace," *New York Times*, 28 November 1995, sec. C17.

41. Alice Walker, *The Color Purple* (New York: Washington Square Press, 1982), p. 249.

QUESTIONS FOR DISCUSSION

1. Define community as the term is understood in this article. What elements of our religious traditions are most challenged by this definition of community? How are religious traditions themselves used to define community?

2. A set of industrial processes are described that mimic nature. Summarize this description and think if such might exist in your own community. How can you work with the businesses or other institutions in your area so as to develop a more integrated pattern of sustainability? How would you define sustainability?

3. Consider Wendell Berry's "Seventeen Sensible Steps" or the "Natural Step" program. How do they apply to your own workplace or to an institution or corporation with which you are familiar?

APPENDIX:
GLOBAL WARMING GRAPHS

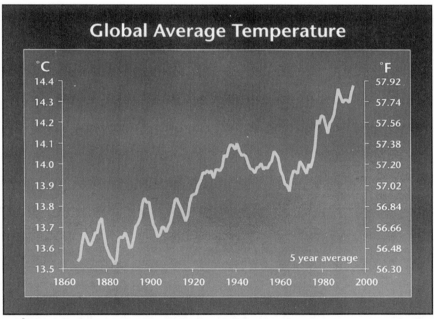

Figure 1. The global average temperature has risen by approximately 1°F over the last century. (Data from J. Hansen et al, GISS).

Source: Office of Science and Technology (OSTP), *Climate Change: State of Knowledge* (Washington, D.C.)

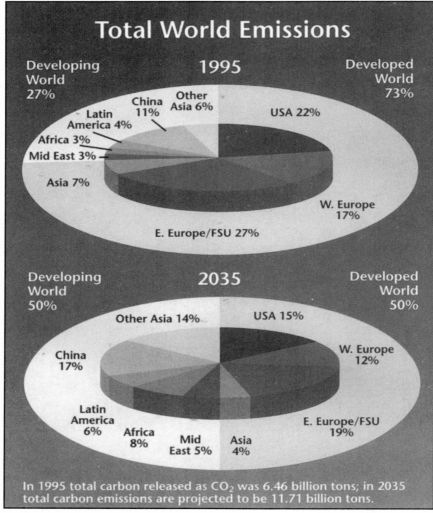

Total World Emissions

1995

Developing World 27%

Developed World 73%

China 11% Other Asia 6%

Latin America 4%

Africa 3%

Mid East 3%

Asia 7%

USA 22%

W. Europe 17%

E. Europe/FSU 27%

2035

Developing World 50%

Developed World 50%

Other Asia 14%

China 17%

Latin America 6%

Africa 8%

Mid East 5%

Asia 4%

USA 15%

W. Europe 12%

E. Europe/FSU 19%

In 1995 total carbon released as CO_2 was 6.46 billion tons; in 2035 total carbon emissions are projected to be 11.71 billion tons.

Figure 2. In 1995, the industrialized nations of the world contributed nearly three-quarters of the global emissions of carbon dioxide, with the U.S. being the largest single emitter. By 2035, developing nations will catch up and contribute half of the global emissions, with China becoming the largest single emitting country. Rapid population growth, industrialization, and increasing consumption per person in the developing world will contribute to this shift. (IPCC, IS92A Emission Scenario.)

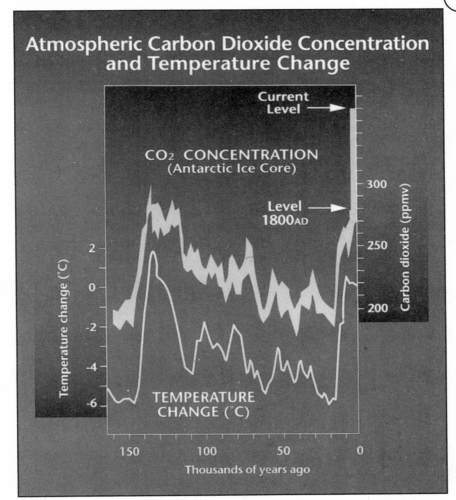

Figure 3. Data from tiny air bubbles trapped in an Antarctic ice core show that atmospheric CO_2 concentrations and temperatures from 160,000 years ago to preindustrial times are closely correlated. CO_2 values since 1800 are shown for reference only. (Data from Barnola et al, Vostok Ice Core; data available from the Carbon Dioxide Information Analysis Center, Oak Ridge, TN.)

Figure 4. The CO₂ level has increased sharply since the beginning of the Industrial Era and is already outside the bounds of natural variability seen in the climate record of the last 160,000 years. Continuation of current levels of emissions will raise concentrations to over 770 ppm by 2100, a level not experienced since about 50 million years ago. (Data from Barnola et al, and IPCC IS92A Emission Scenario.)

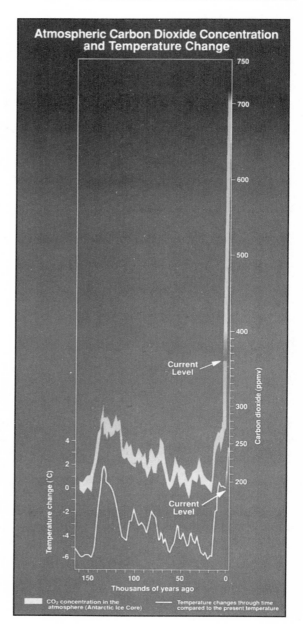

ANNOTATED BIBLIOGRAPHY

The following select bibliography is a distillation of a much larger resource. This listing constitutes a starting point for the exploration and integration of environmental and religious thought and action as related to the dialogue between religion and science. The complete bibliography is available at the ICORE/NACRE website <www.caringforcreation.net>. The reader is also encouraged to use the listing posted on the Harvard Divinity School website <http://divweb.harvard.edu/csvpl/ee/hsev> by Timothy Weiskel. For those without internet access, please contact the International Consortium on Religion and Ecology at 5 Thomas Circle, N.W., Washington, DC, 20005, or by phone at (202) 462-2591.

Austin, Richard Cartwright. *Baptized into Wilderness: A Christian Perspective on John Muir.* Atlanta: John Knox Press, 1987. Muir's religious ecstasy has inspired Austin's. In this book, Austin hopes to inspire others. He reasons further that protection of nature must be rooted in love and delight—in religious experience.

Barbour, Ian. *Ethics in an Age of Technology.* San Francisco, Calif.: Harper, 1993. Published after the distinguished Gifford Lectures series by the author, this book deals with conflicting ethical issues arising from technology, and explores the relationship of human and environmental

371

values to science, philosophy, and religion. The author shows how these values are relevant to technological policy decisions.

Barney, Gerald O. *Global 2000 Revisited: What Shall We Do?* Arlington, Va.: Public Interest Publications, 1993. A report on the critical issues of the Twenty-first Century, prepared for the 1993 Parliament of World's Religions from a social scientist to a religious audience. See also Barney's more recent *Threshold 2000* (CoNexus Press, 1999), which deals with critical concerns and values for the new global age.

Berry, Thomas, and Brian Swimme. *The Universe Story.* San Francisco, Calif.: Harper San Francisco, 1992. From the big bang to the present and into the next millennium, this book celebrates the total community of existence as it unites science and the humanities through a profound and poetic modern myth.

Birch, Charles, William Eakin, and Jay B. McDaniel, eds. *Liberating Life : Contemporary Approaches to Ecological Theory.* Maryknoll, N.Y.: Orbis Books, 1990. Responding to the urgency of the ecological crisis, prominent academics and activists articulate the foundations for an ethic of life, all of life. Resources in scripture, in theologies of liberation, and considerations of science, spirituality, and cosmology are incorporated to define their theology of nature.

Boff, Leonardo. *Ecology and Liberation: A New Paradigm.* Maryknoll, N.Y.: Orbis Books, 1995. The author critiques common approaches to ecology—conservationism and environmentalism among them—as failing to look closely at the systematic causes of ecological degradation, and particularly, their impact on the world's poor. A thought-provoking introduction to a holistic and integrated theology for the new millennium.

Brown, Lester, Christopher Flavin, and Hilary French et al. *State of the World 1999.* New York: W. W. Norton and Company, 1999. After sixteen years of excellent reporting on the state of the world's ecosystems and progress toward a sustainable society, *State of the World* is now accorded semiofficial status by national governments, UN agencies, and the international development community. Easy to read and understand, it has been translated into over 27 languages, and used in more than 500 college and university courses. Check out the Worldwatch Institute's website www.worldwatch.org.

Brown, Noel J., ed. *Ethics and Agenda 21.* United Nations Publications, 1994. Includes various perspectives on the United Nations Environment Programme, including those of the science and technology community, as well as religious and spiritual insights. Includes a summary of Agenda 21, agreed upon at the Earth Summit held in Rio in 1992.

Bruggeman, Walter. *Using God's Resources Wisely*. Louisville, Ky.: Westminster/John Knox Press, 1993. In this unique book, the author explores readings from Isaiah and how they related to the environment and urban crisis. He focusses on Jerusalem, its failure, demise, and prospect, and sees alarming parallels in today's urban crises. Excellent tool for Bible Study groups.

Carson, Rachel. *Silent Spring*. Cambridge, Mass.: Riverside Press, 1962. Thomas Berry claims the publication of this book ushered in the Ecological Age. Ms. Carson writes about the unity of nature and the devastating effects of pesticides on biosystems.

Clinebell, Howard. *Ecotherapy: Healing Ourselves, Healing the Earth*. Minneapolis, Minn.: Fortress Press, 1996. Dr. Clinebell presents a practical synthesis to guide pastors and other ecoleaders in understanding the vital relationship of personality theory, therapy, education, and spiritual development of the person and the earth.

Daly, Herman, and John B. Cobb Jr. *For the Common Good: Redirecting the Economy Toward Community, the Environment, and a Sustainable Future*. Boston: Beacon Press, 1989. Dr. Daly is an economist with the World Bank and makes an important contribution on the thought of an ecologically sound economy. The economics of ecology is an area that Daly and theologian Cobb develop here.

Durning, Allen. *How Much is Enough?* New York: Norton & Company, 1992. Challenges the idea pervading the First World that more is better, and that a fulfilling, satisfying life can be bought with consumer goods. Durning urges a "culture of permanence"—a society that lives within its means, and that seeks fulfillment in friendship, family, and meaningful work.

Elder, John C., and Steven C. Rockefeller, eds. *Spirit and Nature*. Boston, Mass.: Beacon Press, 1992. Leaders from major religious traditions from around the world speak out about what spiritual resources we may turn to in our age of unprecedented danger to the planet.

Elgin, Duane. *Awakening Earth*. New York: William Morrow and Company, Inc. 1993. Vitally important perspectives on humanity's evolutionary journey, with remarkable breadth and depth. The author presents a hope-filled view that humanity is roughly halfway through seven major transformations in culture and consciousness required to build a sustainable, compassionate and creative future.

Engel, J. Ronald, and Joan Gibb Engel. *Ethics of Environment and Development.* Tucson, Ariz.: University of Arizona Press. 1990. The authors look at the ethical aspects of sustainable development from the points of view of science, society, and religion. Careless technology, greed, political indifference, and the needs of the poor make imperative a new global ethic to include a "nonaggression pact" with nature and the human family.

Fox, Matthew. *Creation Spirituality.* San Francisco: Harper San Francisco, 1991. Fox uncovers the ancient tradition of a creation-centered spirituality that melds Christian mysticism with the contemporary struggle for social justice, feminism, and environmentalism.

Gelbspan, Ross. *The Heat Is On.* Reading, Mass.: Addison-Wesley, 1997. An accomplished journalist explores the science and politics behind the issue of global climate change.

Gore, Albert. *Earth in the Balance.* New York: Houghton Mifflin, 1992. Passionate defender of the environment for more than twenty years, Al Gore is now convinced that the engines of human civilization have brought us to the brink of catastrophe. He argues that only a radical rethinking of our relationship with nature can save the earth's ecology for future generations. Chapter 13 deals with the spiritual and religious aspects of the crisis.

Gottlieb, Roger S., ed. *This Sacred Earth.* New York and London: Routledge, 1996. An extensive survey of the interrelated fields of ecology, religion, and environmental values. Also, contains key religious documents on the environment, suggestions for further reading, and organizational contacts with addresses.

Granberg-Michaelson, Wesley. *Redeeming the Creation.* Geneva: WCC Publications, 1992. This book sets out the implications of the United Nations Conference on Environment and Development (the Earth Summit) for the churches and the ecumenical movement.

Hallman, David G., ed. *Ecotheology: Voices from South and North.* Maryknoll, N.Y.: Orbis Books, 1994. Theological and ethical dimensions of the ecological crisis are addressed by voices of both North and South. Perspectives include insights from ecofeminism, and indigenous peoples.

Hawken, Paul. *The Ecology of Commerce.* New York: Harper Collins, 1993. A successful businessman asks the question: "Can we create profitable, expandable companies that do not destroy, directly or indirectly, the world around them?" Hawken claims that business is the only mechanism powerful enough to reverse global environmental and social degradation, and outlines a series of economic strategies that will over-throw the conventional wisdom among both economists and environmentalists.

Hill, Brennan R. *Christian Faith and the Environment.* Maryknoll, N.Y.: Orbis Books, 1998. This volume is an excellent summary of the Christian attempt to face the environmental crisis and to reconcile the diverse traditions especially within the Western churches. Recommended as a survey of the scriptural, theological, and ecclesial themes emerging in the late 1990s as the Christian community strives to connect ecological realities and pastoral applications.

Korsmeyer, Jerry D. *Evolution and Eden: Balancing Original Sin and Contemporary Science.* Mahwah, N.J.: Paulist Press, 1998. The author, who was a senior physicist at the U.S. Department of Energy Bettis Laboratory before studying Catholic theology, examines how evolutionary theory impacts a traditional understanding of original sin and vice-versa.

Korten, David C. *When Corporations Rule the World.* New York: Kumarian Press, 1995. A serious look at global economics and its impact on social and environmental realities of the planet done by a Harvard MBA professor who also had years in the field working on development projects. He spells out the activities of the international financial community and transnational corporations which show little concern for basic ecological and social values. His 1998 sequel, *The Post-Corporate World,* explores the untenability of the promise of unregulated, run-away capitalism and its effect on society and the environment, and what this means for the future liveability of our global society.

Makower, Joel. *The Green Consumer.* New York: Penguin Books, 1993. Shows how your everyday purchases can affect the earth's resources and offers a comprehensive guide to what products to buy, and to avoid. Information about a broad spectrum of environmental issues, including names and addresses of environmental organizations.

Maynard, Jr., Herman B. and Susan E. Mehrtens. *The Fourth Wave: Business in the Twenty-First Century.* San Francisco: Berrett-Koehler Pubs., 1993. Going beyond present third wave thinking into an ecosensitive worldview of business and global economics, the authors chart out the characteristics needed for business leadership in the coming century.

McCarthy, Scott. *Creation Liturgy.* San Jose, Calif.: Resources Publications, Inc., 1987. Here is a theological work that connects Christian liturgy to its twin roots in the Hebrew religion and the rhythms of the natural world.

McDonagh, Sean. *The Greening of the Church.* Maryknoll, N.Y.: Orbis Books, 1990. Focuses on the moral and religious necessity of caring for the Earth, and what is required if the Catholic church is to be a credible agent for promoting a sound ecological vision. Elaborates a "pro-life" theology that goes beyond questions of human fertility to embrace the entirety of life on earth.

Naar, Jon. *Design for a Liveable Planet.* New York: Harper and Row, 1990. Explains in straightforward language the causes and effects of environmental pollution and offers solutions—practical steps you can take to begin cleaning up and prevent further damage.

Nash, James A. *Loving Nature: Ecological Integrity and Christian Responsibility.* Nashville, Tenn.: Abington Press, 1991. The former Executive Director of the Churches' Center for Theology and Public Policy in Washington, D.C., and a theologian, Nash explores the setrious challenge of the ecological crisis and our flawed understanding of the rights and powers of humans in respect to the natural world. He shows a deep understanding of the Christian Protestant tradition.

Oelschlaeger, Max. *Caring for Creation: An Ecumenical Approach to the Environmental Crisis.* New Haven: Yale University Press, 1994. An exceptional ethical analysis by a journalist and scholar who was previously opposed to religious involvement in the environmental movement and is now a strong advocate for the essential importance of the involvement of the religious community if the movement is to be successful.

Pointing, Clive. *A Green History of the World: The Environment and the Collapse of Great Civilizations.* New York: St. Martin's Press, 1991. The major rewriting of history as seen through an ecological lens raises issues about how humans have treated the natural world from earliest times to the present. Truly enlightening for ethicist and scientist.

Rolston, Holmes. *Environmental Ethics: Duties to and Values in the Natural World.* Philadelphia: Temple University Press, 1988. Although not well known, Holmes is an environmental ethicist whose clarity of thought is helpful to all who search out new Ecological Age standards to inform their thinking.

Sachs, Wolfgang, ed. *Global Ecology: A New Arena of Political Conflict.* London and New Jersey: Zed Books, 1993. This book examines the contradictions in much of the sustainable development jargon at the international level and the dangers it involves in terms of "managing nature."

Tucker, Mary Evelyn, and John A. Grim, eds. *Worldviews and Ecology.* Maryknoll, N.Y., Orbis Press, 1994. Important collection of essays, including insights from traditions as diverse as Jain, Jewish, ecofeminism, deep ecology, Christian, Hindu, and Bahai, as to how humans can live more sustainably on our fragile planet.

Waskow, Arthur. *Seasons of Our Joy.* New York: Bantam Books, 1982. This book gives an overview of Jewish holidays, including the "Tu B'Shvat," or holiday of the trees, which Waskow uses to give a good overview of Jewish thought on environmentalism.

Wackernagel, Mathis, and William Rees. *Our Ecological Footprint.* Philadelphia: New Society Press, 1996. This concise work makes a very bold attempt to answer the major questions on sustainability of the earth and its ecosystems in view of present human impact on the planet. Good resource for teachers, planners, and bioregional activists.

CONTRIBUTORS

IAN G. BARBOUR, PH.D., is Bean Professor of Science, Technology, and Society, emeritus, at Carleton College, Northfield, Minnesota. A winner of the 1999 Templeton Prize in religion and science, he is also the author of several books on theology, science, and technology, including *Myths, Models, and Paradigms: A Comparative Study of Science and Religion* (Harper & Row, 1974); *Religion and Science: Historical and Contemporary Issues* (HarperCollins, 1997); and *Religion in an Age of Science* and *Ethics in an Age of Technology* (HarperCollins, 1991 and 1993), which are the Gifford Lectures he delivered in 1989–1991.

SUSAN POWER BRATTON, PH.D., holds the Lindaman Chair of Science, Technology and Society, at Whitworth College, Spokane, Washington. She is the author of *Six Billion and More: Human Population Regulation and Christian Ethics* (Westminster Press, 1992) and *Christianity, Wilderness, and Wildlife* (University of Scranton Press, 1993). She is a frequent contributor to Christian environmental literature.

RICHARD J. CLIFFORD, PH.D., is a member of the Society of Jesus (Jesuits) and professor of Old Testament at Weston Jesuit School of

Theology, Cambridge, Massachusetts, and is known for his scholarship on the concept of creation in antiquity. He has done research and published in the field of ecology and biblical sources. His works include "Creation Accounts in the Ancient Near East and in the Bible" (*Catholic Biblical Quarterly*, monograph series no. 26, Washington, D.C., 1994).

RICHARD M. CLUGSTON, PH.D., is executive director of the Center for Respect of Life and Environment (CRLE), in Washington, D.C. Dr. Clugston is also publisher and editor of *Earth Ethics* and director of the Association of University Leaders for a Sustainable Future and the Secretariat for the Earth Charter USA Campaign. Prior to Going to Washington, D.C., he worked for the University of Minnesota for eleven years, first on the faculty in the College of Human Ecology, and later as a strategic planner in Academic Affairs. Among his publications in sustainability and ethics are "Higher Education's Ecological Mission," in *Education for the Earth: The College Guide for Careers in the Environment* (Princeton: Peterson's Guides, 1995) and "The Praxis of Institutional Greening," in *Theology for the Earth Community: A Field Guide* (Orbis Press, 1996).

DONALD B. CONROY, S.T.L., PH.D., is president of the North American Coalition on Religion and Ecology (NACRE) and executive director of the International Consortium on Religion and Ecology (ICORE). After teaching at Duquesne University and working in the U.S.C.C. Department of Education, he founded the NIF Research Institute in 1980 and NACRE in 1989. In addition to being publisher and editor of *EcoLetter*, he has written in the fields of religious education and ecology; his writings include "Awakening the Sleeping Giant: The Church and the Environmental Crisis" (*America*, 1990), an ecological education video resource *Race to Save the Planet* for National Public Television (1991) and *Leadership Guide for Climate Change Education* (SEREF Publications, 1999).

PAULA GONZALEZ, S.C., PH.D., is a member of the Sisters of Charity of Cincinnati. She is a futurist and environmental activist and a former professor of biology at Mount St. Joseph College, where she founded the EarthConnection Center for environmental learning. Since 1970 she has done some 1,300 seminars, workshops, and retreats on environmental, lifestyle, and planetary issues. She has authored several works in the field of environmental concerns, including works on renewable energy and a cassette course on environmental literacy and spirituality entitled *Healing the Earth* (St. Anthony Messenger Press, 1991).

ROGER S. GOTTLIEB, PH.D., is the Paris Fletcher Distinguished Professor of the Humanities at the Worcester Polytechnic Institute, Worcester, Massachusetts. Professor Gottlieb's scholarship has focused on the intersection of politics, nature, and spirituality; his works include *A Spirituality of Resistance: Finding a Peaceful Heart and Protecting the Earth* (Crossroads Press, 1999) and *This Sacred Earth: Religion, Nature, Environment* (Rutledge Press, 1996). He writes a regular column, entitled "Reading Spirit," for the magazine *Tikkun.*

IAN H. HUTCHINSON, PH.D., is professor of Nuclear Engineering at the Massachusetts Institute of Technology and Head of the Alcator C-Mod Tohamak research project at the MIT Plasma Science and Fusion Center. His research in plasma physics is directed toward practical development of fusion, the energy source of the stars. He is author of *Principles of Plasma Diagnostics* (Cambridge University Press, 1993), the standard text on how to make measurements on plasmas, the fourth state of matter. He has also been active in the Veritas Forum at Harvard University, where he has explored the relationship between faith and science.

RODNEY L. PETERSEN, PH.D., is executive director of the Boston Theological Institute (Newton Centre, Massachusetts) and adjunct professor in the BTI Member Schools. Dr. Petersen has spearheaded many projects on theology and science. He has authored and coedited several publications, including *Preaching in the Last Days* (Oxford University Press, 1991), *Christianity and Civil Society* (Orbis, 1995) and *Consumption, Population, and Sustainability* (Island Press, 2000).

CHARLES J. PUCCIA, PH.D., is the former Science Director for the combined project on ecology and religion with the National Religious Partnership on the Environment at the Union of Concerned Scientists, Cambridge, Massachusetts. Dr. Puccia is primarily known for his work in the field of theoretical ecology and ecological modeling. His works include *Qualitative Modeling Complex Systems: An Introduction to Loop Analysis and Time Averaging* (Harvard University Press, 1986).

LARRY RASMUSSEN, PH.D., is the Reinhold Niebuhr professor of Social Ethics at Union Theological Seminary, New York City, and is known worldwide in the field of social ethics and theology. Professor Rasmussen has written numerous books and articles, including *Earth Community, Earth Ethics* (WCC Press, 1996), and has contributed to *Ethics for a Small Planet: New Horizons on Population, Consumption, and Ecology* (SUNY Press, 1998).

MICHAL FOX SMART, M.S., is former director of education for the Coalition on the Environment and Jewish Life (COEJL), where she worked on ecological education; she has her degrees from Cornell University (natural resources) and Princeton (religion). Michal Smart has traveled and lectured widely around the United States on ecology and religion; she has also developed Jewish environmental and outdoor study programs for synagogue schools and youth camps. Her writings include "Foundations for a Jewish Ethic Regarding Consumption," in *Consumption, Population, and Sustainability* (Island Press, 2000).

GEORGE TINKER, PH.D., associate professor of Cross-Cultural Ministry at the Iliff School of Theology (Denver, Colorado), is widely traveled and is active in Native American issues as well as ecological concerns. Dr. Tinker is an ordained Lutheran minister in the Evangelical Lutheran Church in America (ELCA). He has written the scholarly study *Missionary Conquest: The Gospel and Native American Cultural Genocide* (Fortress Press, 1993).

TIMOTHY C. WEISKEL, PH.D., is director of the Harvard Seminar on Environmental Values at the Center for the Study of Values in Public Life, which he directs at Harvard Divinity School. Dr. Weiskel is known for his work in interdisciplinary studies in paleopathology and other sciences related to ecology. He has also taught at Harvard University's John F. Kennedy School of Government dealing with issues on the environment and public policy. Among his works are *Environmental Decline and Public Policy: Pattern, Trend, and Prospect* (Pierian Press, 1992).